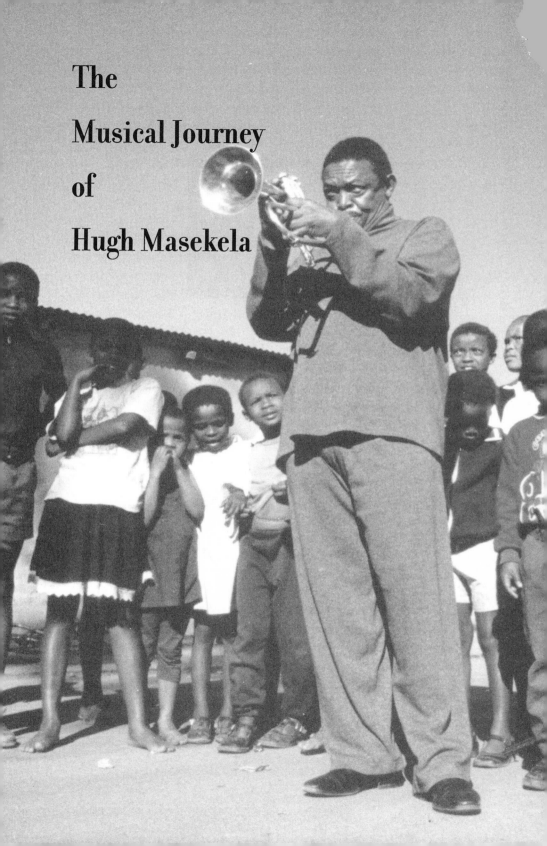

The
Musical Journey
of
Hugh Masekela

STILL GRAZING

Hugh Masekela
and
D. Michael Cheers

Crown Publishers / New York

Published by Crown Publishers, New York, New York.
Member of the Crown Publishing Group, a division of Random House, Inc.
www.randomhouse.com

CROWN is a trademark and the Crown colophon is a registered trademark of Random House, Inc.

Printed in the United States of America

Design by Leonard W. Henderson

Library of Congress Cataloging-in-Publication Data
Masekela, Hugh, 1939–
Still Grazing : the musical journey of Hugh Masekela / Hugh Masekela and D. Michael Cheers.—1st ed.
1. Masekela, Hugh, 1939– 2. Jazz musicians—Biography. I. Cheers, D. Michael. II. Title.
ML419.M325A3   2004
781.65'092—dc22   2003022698

ISBN 0-609-60957-2

10 9 8 7 6 5 4 3 2 1

First Edition

H.M.

In loving memory of my beloved mother, Polina Bowers,
my dear father, Thomas Selema Masekela, my maternal
grandmother, Johanna Mthise Mabena-Bowers, and
my paternal grandparents, Mamoshaba and Hopane Masekela.
This book is dedicated to all their children, grandchildren, and
great-grandchildren and the glorious clans of the Ma-Ndebele,
Ba-Tlokwa, and Bakaranga from which they come.

D.M.C.

In loving memory of Milton, Marie, and Karen—my mother,
father, and sister—who never had the opportunity to experience
the beauty of Africa!

PART I

Home

1

I GREW UP IN A SMALL town in South Africa named Witbank, a one-street, redneck, right-wing Afrikaner town, surrounded by coal mines and coal trains with endless carriages and coal-packed containers crisscrossing the horizon, pulled by steam engines we called "Mankalanyana," churning smoke up into the air. I remember seeing women in the mornings and at sunset running alongside the coal trains with large tin cups collecting the coal nuggets that fell from the cars. It was a tough town where African miners drank themselves stuporous to blot out memory of the blackness of the mines and the families and lands they'd left behind, often never to see again. But even when the burning coal and dust blackened out the sun, we still had music to sing our sorrow and illuminate our ecstasy.

When I was four, I was a pageboy in my Auntie Lily's wedding to Nico Sikwane. For the reception that night, the Jazz Maniacs, South Africa's top township orchestra, played selections from their swing and mbhaqanga repertoire (mbhaqanga was the dominant music of the townships in South Africa—a sound as joyous and sad as anything in the world, but I'll get to that later). The band members were all dressed in black tuxedoes, bow ties, and starched, white shirts. The featured soloists were the young saxophonists Zakes Nkosi, Mackay Davashe, Kippie Moeketsi, and Ellison Themba. Kippie's brother was the dapper pianist, who dressed as flamboyantly as the great American Jelly Roll Morton, smiling all the time, showing off his shining gold-capped tooth. I stood wide-eyed next to the lead trumpeter, Drakes Mbau, fascinated by all the gleaming silver instruments, the drums, guitar, and double bass. The band was tight and played all night, swinging and smiling and sweating and creating a widening circle of bliss that enthralled and hypnotized the wedding guests and left me thrilled and wrung out, dazzled and slack. The band played and danced as if possessed by some uncontrollable magic. I fell asleep on the stage while the party raged on, and dreamed of big bands into the early morning. It was in those days in Witbank that music first captured my soul, forced me to recognize its power of possession. It hasn't let go yet. But I'm getting ahead of myself.

On April 4, 1939, against a historical backdrop of white domination and black rebellion, Pauline Bowers Masekela, who everyone called Polina, gave birth to me inside my grandmother's house at 76 Tolman Street, on a dusty, tree-lined avenue in Kwa-Guqa Township, Witbank, about one hundred miles east of Johannesburg. The *Star*—the widely circulated, white-owned daily newspaper, did not publish my arrival—or, for that matter, any news about black people. There were only a few African-language newspapers—not that African editors would have trumpeted the arrival of Ramapolo Hugh Masekela.

Giving birth was a new experience for my mother; I was her firstborn, delivered by my grandmother, Johanna Bowers, with the help of a midwife. My sister Barbara was born two years later in 1941, Elaine in 1947, and Sybil in 1953. Pauline was half-white, and therefore officially classified as colored (African of mixed heritage), a mixed birthright that meant a lot to the government—but more about that later. In the early 1900s, Pauline's mother, my grandmother Johanna, had married Walter, a Scottish mining engineer turned high-fashion shoemaker. They waited three years for a marriage certificate before finally getting one from the government; this was long before the passage of the Mixed Marriages Act of 1949, which declared all future marriages between whites and others illegal. Walter and Johanna had two children, Solomon and my mother, Pauline. Walter Bowers, I learned later in life, was a philanderer who left Johanna to live with Mary, a colored "shebeen queen" in the industrial, central Johannesburg suburb of Doornfontein (shebeens were illegal bars where millions of nonwhite South Africans—who were, until 1961, forbidden to drink alcohol—drank themselves blind).

Walter Bowers went on to father four children with Mary before leaving her to go to a rural town in Natal, where he started another family. This was followed by another move, to Kimberley, the diamond-mining capital of South Africa, where he started yet another family. His sexual meandering left a trail of "colored" families all over South Africa. Before his death in 1938, Walter was also involved in gold and diamond smuggling, an activity in which he involved all of his women. Once Johanna and her sister Martha were arrested and imprisoned for their involvement in one of Walter's smuggling schemes. Already suffering with swollen legs, Martha was assaulted by the police, causing permanent damage to her legs.

Johanna Mthise WaMandebele a Kwa Nnzunza, Mahlangu, Mabena, Mdungwa, Mganu-Ganu ka Maghobhoria Bowers, my grandmother, came from akwaNdzundza, the royal clan of the Ndzundzas, an aristocratic house of the Mahlangu Ndebele royal family. The Ndebele kingdom stretched over most of the northeastern part of the country, a mineral-rich territory that British and Dutch settlers fiercely contested during the Boer War (1899–1902). Out of pure goodwill and honest charity, the Ndebele granted Dutch settlers land in which to carve out a settlement. But when English troops gained the upper hand and overran Dutch strongholds, the Dutch confiscated the remaining Ndebele territories, murdering any resisters, and leaving my young grandmother and most of her people landless, destitute, and on the run. When the British and Dutch finally made peace, together they expropriated almost all the ethnic lands of this region to establish new mining towns such as Witbank, Middelburg, and Oogies. Here the "conquered natives" were settled into townships from which were drawn pools of unskilled laborers to work as domestics, cleaners, gardeners, sanitation workers, construction gangs, and so forth. Many of the prouder people who spurned white employment went into business for themselves as traders, carpenters, hawkers, tailors, or criminals. Johanna and her siblings, Martha and Jacob, established shebeens to serve the demands of the township's homegrown drinkers and the thousands of migrant laborers who were conscripted from the hinterlands to work the mines. Shebeens became a core township industry and in Witbank, Johanna was one of its most highly respected proprietors.

Johanna was a short, stocky woman just past fifty when I became aware of the fact that she was my mother's mother and I was living on a semipermanent basis in her house in Witbank. Grandparents raised just about all young children because moms and dads, needing to find steady, full-time employment, had little time to raise their offspring properly. The decent-paying jobs were in the cities of the Witwatersrand, starting from Springs, thirty miles east of Johannesburg, the cradle of gold.

Johanna's sister, Elizabeth Motsoene, whom we called Ouma Sussie, lived up the street at number 80. Not too far away from our street were grazing fields, green rolling hills and valleys, and seemingly endless fertile plains. The soil of these valleys was rich black alluvial clay, cool and crunchy. It tasted sweet in your mouth. Later in life, when I would get caught in the rain on the twisted, rolling fields of the Mississippi Delta, Georgia, South Carolina, or Alabama, the steaming aroma of the soil always reminded me of the taste of Witbank's red and black earth.

My grandmother's two-bedroom house had plastered concrete walls outside, a shiny red porch, and a small gate at the entrance arch. The kitchen was the main room of the house, its centerpiece an old iron coal-stove surrounded by pots and pans hanging on the wall. The stove vented through a long metal chimney that burrowed through the white plywood ceiling and past the tin corrugated roof to spew out sulfurous coal smoke, competing with the rest of the township fires to pollute Witbank's blue skies in the mornings and evenings. This was an era of black-painted windows—the days of World War II—when, as children, we were told that Hitler's warplanes were parked on South West Africa's airport tarmacs, waiting for an order from Berlin to come and bomb us to smithereens.

This was but a small portion of our worries. Through the center of Witbank ran a creek that bisected the town by race: one half for the Afrikaans-speaking Boers (whites) and the English and the other for the "kaffirs, "koolies," and "boesmans"—all vulgar names invented by whites for blacks, Indians, and coloreds. The Boers, whose political beliefs bordered on fascism, were farmers, traders, mining engineers, construction foremen, city council employees, truck and train drivers, and primarily Nazi sympathizers. Even the English-speaking whites in Witbank were right-wing conservatives. Being black in Witbank meant being called a kaffir, bowing and smiling, cap in hand, for the white folks, knowing your place and never looking forward to getting anywhere in the world. You were a "bloody fucking kaffir," and if you didn't like it, it was your ass.

Every weekend the mines disgorged thousands of men who came to drink in the township's shebeens, to let off steam, bloat their bellies with sqo or mbamba (homemade brews), and later vomit it all out as they staggered back to their barracks, often carrying their less experienced drinking brothers over their shoulders. The drinking helped them forget the train that brought them to Witbank to come and work on contract in the mines for sixteen-hour shifts for slave wages that totaled a measly five shillings a day if they were lucky. The liquor helped them forget their parents, children, friends, wives, lands, and herds, which they would not see for another nine months while they lived celibate in filthy, sardine-can barracks. The miners came from all over southern Africa, from Mozambique and Angola and most of southern Africa's hinterlands, where the mining companies recruited them. The contracting officers promised them what seemed like a wonderful life. It was only when they reached the mines that they realized what they had signed up for, but by then it was too late to turn back. Nine months later, some of them returned home only to find their wives had married someone else, their lands had been taken by Boer farmers, their cattle sold, and their whole clan moved off the land by the government. Arriving home with little or no money and a ruined home life, the miners had little recourse but to sign up for another nine months with the mining companies.

Many miners died young from black-lung disease or tuberculosis, or had serious accidents that led to amputations if not death. With no disability benefits, most of these men usually found themselves working in the mines until old age. When they died, little effort was made to contact their relatives so their loved ones could have a proper funeral and burial. Their bodies were usually given away to scientific researchers or disposed of as cadavers for use in some white medical school. It was a bloody tragedy.

I learned to accept that booze—nips (¼ pints), half-jacks, half-pints, and straights (full bottles)—was a part of life. I grew up impressed by good drinkers. I watched my uncles and aunts and other people in and around my home drink constantly. Most middle-aged women in the township wore black, mourning a deceased husband, son, or brother who had died from violence, black lung, TB, or booze. Most of my family, on my mother's side, drank. Moneyed and educated people sat and drank in the living room or dining room. Johanna's unskilled laborer friends and women drank in the kitchen. The coal miners drank in the backyard. I started drinking when I was fourteen. Years later, while in therapy, the counselors asked my fellow junkies and me to chart our family histories and circle the drinkers in red. My diagram was covered with red circles.

We were surrounded by music, everywhere we went. I spent those years playing with cousins, including Boikie and Dexter Tolman and Gigigi, the grandson of Johanna's brother, Jacob Mabena. In the afternoons we played soccer with worn tennis balls on the gravel streets, where one of us occasionally kicked a concealed rock and lost a big toenail, stepped on a rusty nail or a piece of corrugated iron or thorns, or broke a leg or arm while falling from a tree or fighting off mangy dogs. We'd swim in dirty rivers and dams, and slide down grassy hills in sleds made from old car fenders, all the while singing our children's street songs, like "Picky, Picky Mabelani, Sal-Sala Gentlemani, Ah! Billy Bof, Ah Kaka Billy Boff." These songs didn't make sense and we didn't care; we were bonding, playing our bloody games, singing our foolish songs.

When there was a wedding, the townships came alive. Up to a month before the ceremony, a white flag was hoisted at the front gate of the intended's home. Every night leading up to the wedding, a street choir of relatives, neighbors, and family friends paraded up and down the avenues practicing wedding songs in Zulu, Sotho, and Tswana. The wedding itself was a near-riotous celebration with the choirs of the bride and groom challenging each other in a competition of poetic songs and harmonies in praises to the couple. The songs were filled with advisory lyrics, sympathetic wishes, and taunts, and were accompanied by ululations from the old women, admonitions from the male elders, feasting, dancing, and debates. The bridal couple would march in front of one of the choirs composed of the bride or the groom's family and friends. The two choirs would challenge each other all afternoon up and down the street, singing, "They have taken her away from us, she's gone, our little baby"; "Sweep, sweep away the dirt, girl, never feed your family surrounded by filth"; "Your aunt is a tart, they sleeep with her behind the garbage cans"; "She too young to be wed"; "While her head was spinning from the joy of being in love, they whisked her away"; and countless other songs with the strangest and funniest lyrics and dances—composers and choreographers unknown. And of course a band usually was hired to play at the reception.

There was music in the air, but Johanna did not allow records to be played in the house. A zealous, God-fearing, Lutheran prayer woman, my grandmother considered playing records blasphemous in those early days. However, her widowed sister, Martha Motsoene, had three children—Aunt Lilly; Lincoln Putugwana, who was studying to be a teacher at the renowned Kilnerton Training Institute outside Pretoria; and Aunt Tinnie, a high school dropout who helped run the shebeen. Uncle Putu and Aunt Tinnie were crazy about music, and they played Putu's treasured 78-rpm records on his wind-up gramophone whenever he came home for the holidays. They would dance the jitter-bug and sing full-throated with the records, especially the ones by the Glenn Miller Orchestra, featuring the Modernaires. Putu's favorite song was "Chattanooga Choo-Choo"; he would play it over and over. Uncle Putu played these records so often that at the age of three I started to sing along with them, even though I had no idea what the words meant (I'm still not sure). I was fascinated by the gramophone and would carefully wind it up while Uncle Putu held it steady for me. Putu had the most beautiful baritone voice, and although I am more of a screamer, my uncle remains the greatest influence on my singing style. I still imitate his phrasing, breathing, and pronunciation.

This was my first obsession with music. From then on, my heart and soul opened to every kind of music. Living in a country that is so pregnant with every kind of ethnic and traditional music and people obsessed with buying records, I became a music addict. To this day, I consume music with exactly the same disposition I had toward it when I was a child.

Many homes back then had gramophones. More well-to-do ones had plug-in or battery-driven "radiograms." They all blasted their music at high volume—especially on weekends, when folks would leave their doors wide open so that the music would waft out over their yards and into the streets. I spent many an hour leaning against the fence of someone's home, listening to their records, when I should have been running an errand for Johanna. I would often reach my appointed destination having forgotten the message I was supposed to deliver, which would of course lead to a whipping. But it was worth it.

The music of Louis Armstrong, Louis Jordan and his Tympany Five, Count Basie, Duke Ellington, Cab Calloway, Glenn Miller, Benny Goodman, and Tommy Dorsey, who were all the kings of the swing era, had a very heavy influence on South Africa's big bands of that time. Bands like the Jazz Maniacs, the Harlem Swingsters, the Merry Makers, and the Merry Blackbirds played many of the songs made popular by the American orchestras, like "Take the A Train," "In the Mood," "One O'clock Jump," "Tuxedo Junction," "I'm Getting Sentimental Over You," "The Continental," and scores of others. These African bands sported the same fashions as the Americans and read music from orchestral arrangements published by Chappell Music, which were available at music shops in the main cities and towns. The African bands also composed township versions of American swing music, styles that came to be known as *marabi*, *mbhaqanga*, *jit*, and *kwela*, hybrids that have stood the test of time, many of which are still popular today.

Singing male quartets like the Manhattan Brothers and the African Ink Spots were heavily influenced by American groups like the Mills Brothers and the Ink Spots. The Andrews Sisters, Ella Fitzgerald, Ma Rainey, Bessie Smith, Lena Horne, Billie Holiday, Dinah Washington, and Sarah Vaughan inspired home-grown singers like Dolly Rathebe, Thandie Klaasen, Snowy Radebe, Dorothy Masuka, and Miriam Makeba. Sepia film shorts and movies like *Stormy Weather* and *Cabin in the Sky* had a major influence on South Africa's urban African fashion and hip lifestyle—the zoot suits with gold chains, two-toned shoes, and wide-brimmed hats, the women's flared dresses and white, ankle-length socks, the bump-and-grind dances, wild jitterbug, gold-capped teeth, switchblades, dark glasses, and "hip" walks were all adopted in the streets and townships of South Africa. The urban African-American lifestyle has never ceased to influence African urban life. African-American music has always played a major role in the lives of Africans all over the continent, especially in South Africa.

But back at Johanna's shebeen, where no records played, life went on. My grandmother may have been a devout Christian, but her real obsession was with business—trading, dealing, and hustling. She ran a strict, organized shebeen, which sold a brew called Barberton—a very potent sorghum beer—that distorted people's faces and often caused swellings of the legs, lips, cheeks, hands, feet, eyes, and liver. This debilitating concoction anesthetized those of her clients who drank it. It quenched the thirst of the hard-working miners who just wanted to forget, for a while at least, the suffocating woes of their world. She also sold healthy, unspiked sorghum beer, brandy, gin, and whisky, which were consumed in the dining room and living room of her house by her educated friends—teachers, ministers, businessmen, nurses, lawyers, doctors, preachers, burglars, thieves, and con men—the elite of the booze world.

But even without records, music surrounded us, especially on the weekends. The drinkers and miners would arrive at the shebeen and sing sad folk and traditional songs like "Ngeke ngiye Kwa Zulu Kwa Fel' u Baba" (I'll never go back to Zululand. That's where my father was killed); "Languta Tsotsi, u ta ku tekela mali Tsotsi" (Watch out for the city slicker, the pickpocket and the mugger. They're all out to take your money); "Matsidiso, ngwana Rakgadi, ha e sale, u tsamaya, ua re siya re le bodutu, Wa re u ya Gauteng" (Matsidiso, my aunt's child, ever since you left us lonely and sad, saying you are off to Johannesburg, you promised to write to us but we never heard from you); and

"Ndemka Kudala ekhaya, Ndi Khumbul' iKhaya Lam" (I've been gone so long from home, my heart cries out with longing for the home where I was born).

Come Sunday, migrant laborers would dance in their knee-high rubber boots to the accompaniment of feverish rhythm guitars, war chants, and hollered commands. They'd mesmerize onlookers with their complex dance routines, slapping the outsides of their boots, smashing their heels together to produce rhythm patterns and choreography that left their audiences astonished. The boots had been issued to them for use in street-sweeping, hosing, ditch-digging, and mining, but these workers transformed them into percussion instruments capable of producing the most complex and beautiful rhythms.

The township was ringed by a carnival of ethnic dances put on by thousands of Zulu, Swazi, Venda, Chopi, Baca, Fingo, Hlubi, Tsonga, Tswana, Sotho, Ndebele, Pedi, Zingili, Lobedu, and Karanga warrior ensembles. They'd stomp the grounds of empty velds and parks, grassy knolls and vacant lots, chanting, drumming, hand-clapping, singing; in their colorful traditional costumes made of beads, feathers, and leather, they'd supplicate at the spiritual feet of their ancestral gods. Kicking up clouds of dust with their bare feet, they caused the grass and the earth under them to tremble and give way to a past that they had come to glorify in rhythm and song, while also sending a salvo of terrifying curses to remind their oppressors and colonizers of their impending doom for leaving Europe to come and enslave the Africans. The warlike dances fascinated the urban throngs who watched them. Gigigi and I and our friends would seek out their venues, gape in pleasant wonder, and later try to imitate their every graceful move.

Bible-thumping "born again" men and women of the Holy Sanctified Donkey Church, a palm-leaf-crowned baby donkey in the lead, would sing soulful African gospel at the gates and tall fences of the houses in the township, pleading with us all to repent, to accept God. "Guquka," they'd yell, wiping drenched foreheads with their white handkerchiefs. Their prayer women paraded in purple blouses and leopard-skin-patterned velvet hats, black skirts, stockings, and shoes, singing louder than any tabernacle choir could, punctuating their songs with an occasional "Hallelujah!!! Aaamen!!!"

Prayer women and church wardens from all other religious sects— (Presbyterian, Methodist, Anglican, Lutheran, Dutch Reformed, Swiss Mission, Assembly of God, Catholic, African Methodist Espiscopal) sang from their citadels and processed through the township's streets, competing with blaring radiograms, vocal groups, wedding choirs, traditional healers' ensembles, gramophones, and children's troupes playing in the streets, an ear-filling commotion that made the weekends resound with festivity. My friends and I rushed from one street to another, from squares to open fields, following Lekganyane's Zion Christian Church brass bands as they marched in their military khaki uniforms, white boots, black caps, with sheriff stars pinned to their lapels, singing, "Our God is with us here on earth, clearly visible, generous and infallible." We marched behind these battalions for God, lifting our knees high, following the ethnic pipers as though bewitched. We drank in the noises and reveled in the hilarious chaos of the weekend's African sorcery and madness—oblivious of cold, rain, wind, dust, or curfew.

As the weekend came to a close, we would hang outside in Johanna's backyard, under the apricot and apple trees, where the miners on makeshift benches droned like bees as they downed gallon after gallon of homemade hooch next to the chicken coop, singing heartbreaking chants about their homelands and the squalor of their hostels. *We are crying over the filthy, funky, stinking, flea-ridden barracks and hostels we live in where they feed us that mishmash mush food that they dish into our iron plates, with an iron shovel. We think about our loved ones back home who we may never see again, because they might already have been forcibly removed from where we left them or wantonly murdered in the dead of night by marauding gangs or racist white farmers. We cry for our lands and herds that were taken away from us with the gun and the cannon, the dog, the tear gas, and the poison, with the bomb and the gatling, and when we hear that choo-choo train, a-steamin' and a-smokin' and a-chuggin' and a-wailin' in the far distance, then we cuss the choo-choo train, the choo-choo train that brought us to this godforsaken Witbank—Whooo! Whooooo!* As the evening wore on, the miners' loud arguing always signaled Johanna, who had to throw the rowdy ones out on the street and point them back to their barracks. Some would fight all the way to their bunks at the mines, bloodying each other and sometimes killing each other. The weekend always came to a regretted end with the Sunday-night church bells clanging in a new week.

Nobody cared too much about the mineworkers' lives. No one in Witbank, not even Johanna, knew their real names or cared too much when they died. To Johanna they were just customers, faces in the crowd who drifted into her shebeen to drive their blues away and to put coins in her money apron. Some of her earnings ended up in the pockets of the municipal police and superintendent Lynn, the king of Kwa-Guqa, an English bastard.

After the weekend ended, the township dust settled on blades of grass, windowsills, corrugated iron roofs, porches, and tree leaves until the next weekend's revelry once more raised it into the air. A child could not ask for a more spectacular fantasy.

In the mid-1940s, after World War II ended, affluence struck South Africa and money started showing up everywhere, even in the townships. The shebeens did brisk business; Johanna's apron sagged with silver coins. Her brassiere burst at the seams to accommodate the countless pound and ten-shilling notes she kept shoving into her bosom. Shebeen queens like Johanna had no cash registers. She just threw the coins in her apron and stuffed the notes into the deep canyon between her bountiful breasts. Sometimes she did not count the money for days, especially when business was exploding over the weekends. Yes, times were good. Old General Smuts, what a pretentiously kind and clever bastard he turned out to be after the war. Still, the Boers remained red and mean and poor. The English? They had these little twitches at the corners of their mouths that made it difficult to determine whether they were smiling or just plain nervous. Those British, they were sly sons of bitches. Yes sir! Both seemed redder in the summer. The Boer women in their bonnets and long floral dresses accompanied by straw-hatted, ruddy men, seemed to turn even redder at the sight of black people. Their scowls were mean enough to drive a little black boy into a hole. They looked as if something smelled foul whenever black folks were in their midst. As kids, we figured they were just jealous. They had no rhythm, they couldn't sing or dance, couldn't play the drums, and didn't know how to laugh. Johanna said Boers and the English were still trying to learn how to smile and that God had made their teeth dark yellow and rusty so they would be ashamed to show them. This was punishment, she said, for being so mean to us.

On Saturday mornings the Indian market in Witbank's town square was always overflowing with hundreds of Boers from the surrounding farms selling their summer harvests of every imaginable vegetable, legume, fruit, and livestock to the Indian traders. Around seven o'clock, the merchants opened their stalls and started shouting, "Chickens, velly, velly cheap. Bananas, mangoes, paw-paw, chickens—come buy, velly cheeeeep. Small one, two-and-six, beeg one, five-and-six! Come on, velly cheeeeep."

Barbara and I became aware, from infancy, that being black meant that we were going to be harassed by white folks all our lives. Whenever we went to town on Saturday morning with Johanna to the Indian market or to buy at the white-owned shops, one thing was very obvious: Johanna did not command the same respect she had at home. Instead, white and Indian store owners called her "girl" or "nanny." Oddly, in town, Johanna was humble and soft-spoken. When Barbara and I complained to Johanna that whites were calling us little baboons, she scolded us. If we questioned her reasoning, we were disciplined once we got back across the creek to our side of town. Johanna, as fierce as she was in the townships, was shit-scared of white folks.

Not surprisingly, there were many fights at 76 Tolman Street. The coal miners who came to drink in the backyard often started fights that they never finished because Johanna would intervene and beat the shit out of them—thrashings that sent the powerfully built Mozambicans, Malawians, Ndebeles, and Swazis staggering out of her yard. Johanna had three tenants who rented a couple of rooms in her backyard. One tenant was Uncle Bassie, a young colored man in his late twenties, who was a presser at the dry-cleaning store in town. Bassie was like a long-lost son to my grandmother, chopping firewood and breaking the huge nuggets of coal, helping with the painting around the property, putting up fences, and doing a little plumbing here, a little carpentry there—generally being the man of the house. Unlike Bassie, Johanna's actual son, Uncle Khalu, lived in Brakpan and came to Witbank during certain weekends and holidays only to romance his girlfriend, Tilly Miga, and fight with her brother, called Boy, or, even worse, with his own mother. Bassie was an ideal substitute for Khalu. The two men hung out in Kwa-Guqa's hot spots together, chatting up women and coming home late at night singing bawdy songs, happily drunk with their arms around each other's shoulders. George rented the other room. A red-lipped man who was always drunk, he was a quiet and dignified office clerk from Malawi. His girlfriend, Molly, was born and raised in Witbank. She ran away from home in her early teens to come and shack up with George. They were madly in love with each other, drank heavily together, and fought a great deal.

One Sunday morning, George and Molly were arguing in their back room when Molly suddenly ran to the coal shed next to the chicken coop, grabbed an ax, ran back into the room, and continued the fight with George. A few seconds later, George emerged with the ax embedded in his forehead. Bassie, Johanna, and the other early drinkers tried in vain to dislodge it from his skull as the thick blood oozed from the wound, trickling down his face and clotting on his white shirt. Everybody was scolding Molly, who was trembling and weeping like a little baby. Johanna screamed louder than anyone: "You evil little satanic bitch, jezebel whore piece of shit! I hope the poor boy dies so that the white people can hang your little stinking black ass straight into hell where you belong—with the devil. That way I can be rid of both of you for good!" George, protesting through the river of blood flowing from in and around his mouth, gurgled weakly, "No, Auntie Johanna, don't let me die!" Johanna shot back, "Shut up, you bloody *makwerekwere* shit. I'm tired of both of you bloody nincompoops!" I was terrified, whimpering and trembling at this horrible sight.

Uncle Khalu finally rushed George to the clinic on his motorcycle, where the doctors were able to remove the ax and stitch him up. Sitting in Johanna's kitchen later that morning, George was still shaking from the shock of the axing and his hangover from the previous night's booze-up. He was unable to steady his glass of brandy, and spilled its contents every time he tried to take a sip. Molly was unfazed as Johanna and the others continued to berate her. She kept sucking in her breath and sighing irritably. I was in awe of her.

As Barbara and I grew older, we'd help Johanna brew, sift, and ferment her intoxicating potions. We also kept watch out for the police, and threw stones on the tin rooftops to warn the shebeeners of raids. When the police approached the neighborhood, our signaling caused a din that rang through the township like a hailstorm. After all, Witbank was a drinking town, and most of Kwa-Guqa's men lived to drink. Every street had a few shebeens, evidenced by the ashen faces of most people over eighteen who bore the dazed and confused look associated with too much bad booze.

Every Saturday morning, Johanna fed Barbara and me a laxative or inserted an enema that was usually administered with the help of Aunt Tinnie, Ouma Sussie, and Aunt Dolly holding our legs, arms, heads, and shoulders down while my grandmother stuck the pump up our asses, dispensing the liquid formula into our intestines. Despite these weekly internal cleansings, both Barbara and I strangely had sickly childhoods. We were especially bedeviled by bouts of bronchitis, influenza, and pneumonia. We were sometimes near death. I can remember several periods when Barbara would sit beside my sickbed, crying. One time my grandmother really did think I was dying. Her prayer women friends from the Lutheran church, in their mustard yellow and black uniforms, all sang hymns throughout the night between prayers administered by church ministers who were there to impress upon God the seriousness of my condition and to beg Him for my life to be spared until a much later date if possible. The Lutheran hymns were all sung in the Pedi language of my father.

> *Morena re ho Khunametsi, dipelo di go inametshi, Monghadi yo re Shokelang, Re kwe ba re go tsomang.*
> (God, we are on our knees, our hearts are bending over. O Master who sympathizes with us, heed us who seek thee.)

> *Ke lla ke le bothateng, ke le mo mahlomoleng, Jesu yo o mpakoletseng, A ko u Nkhomotse hle.*
> (I weep from the trials and tribulations, from sadness and heartbreak. Jesus, who died on the cross for me, I pray that you quiet my soul.)

> *Jesu o letsatsi, o monate jwang. Nthlomogele pelo, ke mo bohlokong. O mphe le bophelo joalo le lefung.*
> (Jesus you are the sun, you are so nourishing. Rain down your sympathy on me. I am in pain. Give me life now and even in death.)

> *Tlishang tebego le lobeng modimo a ya phelang. Yo le barongoa seetsheng e le ba mo retang.*
> (Bring on your thanks and pray to the living God, of whom even His messengers in the light sing praises.)

To this day, their melancholy but beautiful melodies and haunting harmonies still evoke for me my state of ignorance and innocence as I lay on my supposed deathbed.

The songs were deeply soothing and almost surreal, with a childish charm and sweet melancholy that rang in my ears long after they ended, echoing through my dreams and blending with the crowing of the roosters, the cackling of the chickens, and the singing of the birds in the early winter dawn. That's when sleep was most delicious, when I prayed not to awaken to face the morning's biting cold and the howling winds that blew the township dust into my eyes and sand into my ears and between my teeth.

Sometime later, when Barbara lay in that very same bed, near death, it was the exact same group of people who were again assembled by Johanna to conduct a similar prayer meeting during the nights, while I wept endlessly in the next room. But I was filled with unshakable confidence that the music would come through for my sister as it had for me, and miraculously my belief was confirmed. These were the moments when the power of music firmly impressed itself into our lives. When the prayer women sang, they seemed to put their deepest emotions into the appeals contained in the hymns. With tears running down their cheeks, their eyes crimson from weeping, they gave the impression of being in direct, personal communication with God. Even though we were very young children, the power of their commitment made a very deep impression. The strength of those songs still clings to us, the proof is in our continued presence in this world.

Strong as was her love for us, beatings were still a regular thing with Johanna. I always seemed to get into trouble with her, which always led to the strap, a twig from the old apricot tree, or the most excruciating, painful pinches in the armpits—all of which left my body black and blue.

There's one instance that I've always remembered. Johanna discovered I had been stealing money from the pouch she wore that served as a cash register while she sold booze. When business was slow, Johanna would disappear into the bedroom adjoining the kitchen, or into the toilet outside in the yard, or behind the coal shed, and lift her dress and hide the cash in her money apron. (She did not know that Gigigi and I were spying on her.) At night she hung her apron from her iron bedpost. Gigigi persuaded me to steal a few pennies, then three pence, then sixpence, then shillings, and finally half-crowns. Because Johanna snored like a hibernating bear, I found it easy to sneak into her apron and lift coins. She would have never discovered my scheme had it not been for the grocer who mentioned to Johanna that I was spending a lot of money on fatcakes and fish and chips for my friends. My grandmother beat me for several days and a few nights as well. Some nights she would wrestle me from a sound sleep and throw me outside. I didn't mind the beatings so much. It was sleeping outside that terrified me, as it would any four-year-old brought up on ghost and witchcraft stories. We were told that ghosts of people who had died were roaming the township at night and ready to carry people away to the graveyard where they would feed on their victims or torture them until they were left witless for life. I would bang on the front door of Johanna's house, crying and begging her to please let me in. "I will never do it again, Ouma Johanna. I will be a good boy. Please let me in."

I wasn't the only family member to feel Johanna's wrath. Uncle Khalu and Johanna frequently fought. Khalu was a mean street fighter, but his mother often got the better of him. One afternoon, Gogo Kappie-Kappie, Johanna's mother, sent me to call my grandmother because she had something very important to discuss with her. I ran down Tolman Street to Johanna's house, and when I walked through the gate, I heard her cussing Khalu in the coal shed behind Molly and George's room, next to the chicken coop. When I rushed to the scene I saw Khalu's face and clothes covered in blood. Johanna's right thumb was dangling at the joint where he had bitten his mother. Johanna was hitting Khalu across the backyard, all the while cussing him as he tried to fight back. Although he had an athlete's physique and stamina, Johanna sent her son staggering like a punch-drunk boxer just before a TKO. I ran back to Ouma Sussie's to tell everyone at her house what had happened. Uncle Putu, Aunt Lily, Aunt Tinnie, and Ouma Sussie ran back down the street to stop the fight at Johanna's house. Although Johanna and her son argued and fought often, there was a tenderness and deep affection between the two of them. When Khalu came home he always brought his mother beautiful gifts such as dresses, handbags, and shoes, crockery and other housewares. They attended church together and always walked hand-in-hand after worship service.

Three years later, two jealous Dutch co-workers murdered Khalu because he was a light-skinned black manager of a cinema where they all worked. At Khalu's funeral, I saw Johanna sadder and more heartbroken than at any other time I lived with her. Losing her son in such a violent way took its toll on her. She never bothered to attend the court trial, because deep in her heart she knew the white boys who murdered her son would get away with a slap on the wrist. Indeed, the Dutchmen got off with a one-hundred-pound fine each and a warning from the judge not to go around killing natives anymore.

Johanna's rough exterior aside, she showered me with much love—more than I received from anybody except my mother. During my sick days, she spent sleepless nights and days at my bedside wiping my brow, feeding me medicine and her traditional elixirs, rubbing my chest with Vicks and wrapping me in hot towels. I remember her praises and rewards when she thought I was a good boy, her sadness whenever I would go and visit my parents in City Deep Gold Mines, her joy on my return, the prayers she recited for my health, good fortune, and protection. She carried me on her back wrapped in a blanket while she scrubbed, cooked, swept, and brewed her intoxicating potions. She carried me even while she was in the middle of a fight, while I hung on to her for dear life. She called me "Minkie Mouse" because I was so small, and when she was really happy, she called me "Mousie." When I left Witbank in 1945 to live with my parents in Springs, Johanna and I cried at the Witbank station. "Don't forget to come and visit your grandmother, Minkie Mousie. I don't know how I will live without my little Mousie." Barbara and I visited Johanna every holiday, even if it was just for a few days, until she later came to live with us in Alexandra Township.

I never could reconcile in my mind the cruelty she could demonstrate alongside the kindness, love, and generosity she would pour out. Throughout my whole life, until she died in 1994, at the age of 104, she loved me dearly, always inquired after me, and stood up for me when anybody would try to put me down. Johanna was deeply proud of my achievements, but always encouraged me to pray for humility. Her memory will always remain with me.

2

IN 1945 MY PARENTS SUMMONED Barbara and me to live with them. They had moved from City Deep to Springs, a mining town thirty miles east of Johannesburg. We were to live in Payneville, a model African township two miles east of the center of town, where my father opened the first milk depot and fruit and vegetable market for the municipality. The town had a colored section on the south side and a large Indian merchant community on the northern end; a rail fence surrounded the entire settlement. The houses were some of the first built for Africans to have flush toilets. The place had electricity, street lamps, a modern clinic, a nursery school, modern schools for the older children, a shopping center, parks, and a cinema. I was very excited about going to live there, not to mention finally being able to live with my parents. It never entered my mind that Payneville would be a passing dream, to be destroyed a few years later by apartheid. Every city and town in South Africa had an African township or two like Payneville, until the forced removals of the 1950s. After that, mega-townships like Soweto, with its population of five million, constructed specifically for Africans, became the rule. Colored and Indians were removed to their own townships.

A self-made man in every sense of the word, my father taught himself architecture, carpentry, landscape design, horticulture, and sculpting. His personal library contained books by Sri Aurubindo, Aldous Huxley, Lin Yutang, Albert Einstein, Winston Churchill, George Bernard Shaw, William Shakespeare, and Evelyn Waugh, as well as Byron, Keats, Dumas, and Booker T. Washington. He was also a self-taught and noted sculptor, and a friend of the famed painter

Gerard Sekoto. My father and Sekoto refused to be called native woodcarvers and sketchers, the terms used for African artists. They demanded to be called sculptors and artists just like their white counterparts, who often copied their styles and made huge profits by doing so. My father, Sekoto, and other African artists of their caliber were prevented from gaining recognition for their work. Sekoto, who became known as the father of South African art, went to Paris in 1947, where his works were exhibited in many solo and group shows. My father's pioneering works were later commissioned by many rich whites in South Africa and exhibited in top galleries around the country. Today a few fortunate African collectors own some of his works.

My mother was a great cook and teacher, and a skilled organizer (she later became president of the National Council of African Women). Although she was a descendant of a Scottish father and a Ndebele mother, and could have opted for the semi-privileged life of a colored, Pauline chose to be an African community leader. She was fluent in a number of indigenous languages.

Their marriage was a difficult union for their awkwardly juxtaposed backgrounds, given the pressures from their relatives and friends and the absurd racial restrictions of South Africa's social and legislative environment. Some of my father's relatives openly voiced their disapproval of his choice to marry a colored woman when so many women from his tribe, church, profession, and social environment were available. Similarly, some of my mother's relatives never understood why she'd married a black Karanga from the north, when so many eligible light-skinned gentlemen had wanted to marry her. It was a sick state of affairs, which haunted Barbara, Elaine, Sybil, and me throughout our lives. It never mattered how much most of my father's family grew to respect and love her; there were always those in my father's family who despised my mother. My sisters and I were never considered *black* enough to be seen as African, nor were we light enough to be totally accepted by our colored relatives and their friends. Throughout my childhood, adolescence, and early adulthood, many times I've been asked the same question: "Hugh, tell me really, what are you people, Africans or colored or in between?" Angered by the question, I usually tempered my response: "We're just human beings." Our parents taught us to be proud of what we were; it has always been easy to explain our origins, those of my grandparents and parents. We learned to trace our family roots as far back as possible. It always amazes people when I tell them that my maternal grandfather was a mining engineer from Scotland.

• • •

In 1946, after attending preschool across the street from our house, I was accepted into St. Andrew's Anglican Primary School, where, because of my high marks, I was immediately promoted to Sub A, the third-year class. One day on my way home from a school trip to gather clay, I was kicking a tennis ball back and forth with my friends as we ran alongside the tar road back to Payneville when a runaway car hit my best friend, Washa, while he was running to get the ball away from the middle of the road. He must have flown over fifty feet through the air before he landed on the grassy side. He never breathed again. Washa was only eight years old. The white man who hit him never stopped, and there was never an arrest. Mr. Buitendacht, the township superintendent, under whom my mother worked as a social worker, came to the school and gave a speech warning us not to play in the roads because we were in the way of white peoples' cars. Even though Payneville was a model township, Springs was very racist and surrounded by other Afrikaner right-wing communities such as Brakpan, Nigel, Benoni, Welgedacht, and Delmas. In 1945 a mining strike was stopped when the army, summoned to shoot black miners, killed scores of them and forced the survivors back to work at gunpoint. This was three years before the apartheid administration took over the government.

Sandwiched between a few minor skirmishes with my playmates and trying to stay out of white folks' way, we usually rode wild donkeys on Saturdays in the blue gum forest on the southern fringe of Payneville, before going to catch a Gene Autry or another cowboy movie. There was always a weekly serial featuring Dr. Fu Manchu, Tarzan, Captain Marvel, or Superman. It was hard to hear from all the cheering, whooping, and laughter. Also, we only spoke Afrikaans, Zulu, and Sotho, and understood very little English. But we still memorized the dialogue and recited along as the film unwound.

It was popular culture that really expanded my English vocabulary. As in the films we saw, most of the words to the songs on the 78-rpm records I played on the gramophone were not easy to make sense of, but it didn't stop me from singing along with the vocalists and scatting along with the instrumentals. My friends and I wore the gramophone out with songs like Louis Armstrong's "I'll Be Glad When You're Dead, You Rascal You," "Blueberry Hill," "Rockin' Chair," and "When It's Sleepy Time Down South"; Louis Jordan's "Caledonia, Ain't Nobody Here But Us Chickens," and "Ain't That Just Like a Woman"; Nat "King" Cole's "Mona Lisa" and "Route 66"; Ella Fitzgerald's "A-Tisket, A-Tasket,"; the Andrews Sisters' "You Call Everybody Darling," "Rum and Coca-Cola," and "Boogie-Woogie Bugle Boy"; Jim Reeves's "Oh My Darling

Clementine"; Cab Calloway's "Hi-dee, Hi-dee Ho!"; and Red Foley's "Chattanooga Shoeshine Boy."

My parents soon realized that I had become inseparable from the gramophone and sang along perfectly with all the American records, as well as those of South African performers, like the Manhattan Brothers' "Jikel' Emaweni," "Madibina," and "Makanese"; the love ballads of the African Ink Spots, like "Ndi, Nje" and "Carolina Wam"; and modernized Xhosa folk songs.

They decided to seek a piano teacher for me, hoping that music lessons would enhance my talents and wean me off the gramophone. During the 1940s there were many piano teachers in the townships, men and women who'd been been taught by missionaries so that they could accompany school choirs and play the organ in church. Many more had been self-taught in the 1920s, when they accompanied vaudeville groups like Emily and Griffiths Motsieloa's troupe and Wilfred Sentso's Synco Fans, and learned to read music and write arrangements for small combos and big bands. Township music teachers imparted what little knowledge they had picked up from such groups and from the Salvation Army, police, and military bands, to whatever students they could find. "Madevu" (his nickname referred to his massive beard) was such a pianist, and he was already teaching a couple of girls from the senior grade at St. Andrew's. I became his third and favorite student. After a few months of afternoon lessons, I began to excel.

In a few months' time I was playing excerpts from Bach, Mozart, Handel, Haydn, Beethoven, and Lizst, along with piano arrangements of nursery rhymes. My teacher's favorite nursery rhyme was "Lavender Blue Dilly-Dilly." At the year-end recital, I performed "Lavender Blue" with the school choir to applause from the parents and teachers and endless guffaws from my friends, who all thought it was square white music. It was really embarrassing, but my parents insisted that I continue with the lessons and not pay any attention to my detractors. My mother would say, "Don't mind them, Boy-Boy, they're just jealous because they can't play an instrument or sing." Wanting to try something new, I yearned to play some boogie-woogie jazz on the piano. Once in a while I would sneak in a snatch of boogie-woogie while I practiced my sonata excerpts. One afternoon my teacher caught me and was so furious that he reported me to my parents—he told them this was music for drunkards and harlots, sinners and gangsters, and that it would get in the way of my classical talents. He warned my parents that if he caught me playing boogie-woogie again, he would stop teaching me. Surprisingly, my parents didn't seem too concerned. They just asked me to try to do my best not to infuriate my teacher and to stay with the program.

In mid-1947 my father graduated from the Johannesburg Technical College, to become one of the first Africans to obtain a diploma as a health inspector and was offered a better-paying job in Alexandra Township, a post that would require him to spend many months in the field vaccinating people against smallpox, malaria, and other infectious diseases. My mother was unwilling to leave Payneville. This enraged my father. She argued that we were a comfortable family, living in an electrified, semi-luxurious home. She felt that my father had a good job. He had actually pioneered a municipal-subsidized fruit and vegetable market and milk depot where you could buy a pint for two pennies, and the market produce was dirt-cheap, endearing him to the large impoverished section of the community. She explained to my father how abandoned they would be if he left. I was doing extremely well in school and needed to continue my piano lessons, and there were no piano teachers in Alexandra Township. My mother had a good job as a social worker; the community had embraced her, and Superintendent Buitendacht had just appointed her chief social worker. "I really don't understand why we have to move, Tom," she shouted.

I heard the loud argument from my adjoining bedroom. My father was incensed. He was the husband, and my mother had to obey him, period! She disagreed and all hell broke loose.

My mother was a petite woman, only four feet nine inches tall. My father, on the other hand, was six feet three inches tall and built like an ox. He beat my mother all around the house. He kicked her over and over again while she lay coiled on the dining room floor. Eventually she passed out. I came running out of my bedroom, horrified at the sight of my mother's blood all over the floor. I was certain my father intended to kill her. I was only eight and small for my age, but I tried to measure up to my dad. I begged him to stop. He slapped me across the kitchen floor, and when I landed at the bathroom door, I saw stars and heard birds tweeting in my ears. Dazed, I couldn't believe what was happening.

My dad left the house in a fury and swore that if he found us in the house when he returned, he would kill us. He was totally psychotic as he slammed the front door and kicked everything in his way, including Bonzo, our new dog, who ran away whimpering out of the backyard, toward Third Avenue.

My mother, semiconscious, was lying in a pool of blood. Her whole face was swollen, one of her eyes was closed, her skin had turned dark purple and bloody blue. It was around eleven o'clock at night. My father had locked their bedroom door and left with the key so that my mother could not even change clothes after she washed the blood from her face and hands. There was no transportation around at that time of night, so we walked to the clinic near the entrance to the township. My mother's dear friend Mrs. Zondi lived in an apartment behind the municipal clinic, where she was head nursing sister. She treated my mother's wounds as best she could, and insisted that we spend the night with her. My mother refused her offer. We left and walked, cold and barefoot, about two miles to the Springs train station. It was May, with winter coming. The nights were really cold. Mrs. Zondi loaned my mother the train fare for the two of us. At the time, Barbara was in Witbank with Johanna. At around midnight we caught the last train to Johannesburg. Shivering and still stunned, my mother and I sat holding each other in a dazed silence as the train made its way to the City of Gold.

My mother and I arrived at the Doonfontein train station, outside of Johannesburg, which was just a stone's throw away from the shebeen owned by Ouma Mary, Walter Bowers's second wife. It was after midnight, but the joint was still jumping. When we walked through the back door, Ouma Mary and her daughter Aunt Meisie burst into tears, and were quickly joined by her sons, Uncles Boetie and Victor and their siblings Sidney, Basil, and Ollie. My mother, with her swollen face and half-closed eye—and the other one blood-shot from crying—tried to recount to them what had happened hours earlier. Everyone cried uncontrollably. Ouma Mary immediately closed the shebeen for the night, giving the boot to her puzzled customers. Seeing how exhausted we were, she prepared a place for my mother and me to sleep in her train-carriage-shaped house with its long corridor that ran along at least ten rooms from the kitchen to the front lounge.

Early the following morning, before the sun came up, Uncles Putu, Nico, Bigvai, Nakeni, and Kwakwa and my father arrived. They were all wearing overcoats and Italian fedoras. My father was carrying a small suitcase of clothes he had brought for my mother and me. I noticed that his eyes were also red from crying. With his sniffling and endless nose-blowing, he could hardly speak. Though he had come to make peace and apologize, Ouma Mary was livid. I was hoping she would speak up and not allow my mother and me to return to Payneville with my father. I was terrified of what he would do to us once we got back home. My aunts Lily, Tinnie, and Clara came to Doornfontein around lunchtime. I had no idea what they were discussing. A few hours earlier I had seen my mother for the first time since the previous night. Her face and head were covered with a large, black, chador-like scarf. We began crying, but my mother assured me she was fine. "Go and play, Boy-Boy, Mama's okay." Uncle Victor and Uncle Boetie were furious to see their "Ous Panie"—which is what they called their stepsister—in such a sorry state, and were bent on revenge. But Ouma Mary was against any physical retaliation.

"You boys should just stay put," she shouted. "This is none of your business. We have settled this business peacefully. Yours is just to remember your manners and hold your bloody tongues. Tom will beat you to death if you want to take your chances fighting with him. That man will fuck you up! He'll beat the shit out of you two, so you better stay put."

I had heard stories of how my father once nearly beat five men to death one night when he was returning from George Goch with my mother. These guys tried to rob them and rape her. They all ended up in the hospital. The Masekelas had been raised as farm boys in the Northern Province, where Tsongas, Pedis, Ndebeles, and Vendas grew up perfecting boxing, head-butting, knee-banging, and kicking—all from a young age. But this made things even more puzzling to me. Why would my father, knowing his strength, want to beat my mother? It still baffles me more than fifty years later. That evening, Aunt Elizabeth arrived with Uncle Junius in his new Chrysler. They took my mother back to Springs. I was allowed to stay and spend the weekend until Sunday afternoon, when I took the train alone back to Springs and boarded a bus to Payneville, where I found our home bubbling with relatives. While my uncles sat in the backyard picnicking, my mother and aunts were inside cooking and baking. We enjoyed a good meal. Afterward I went to play soccer with my friends, while my father worked quietly on a wood sculpture in the backyard.

My father eventually moved to Alexandra Township to begin his new job. Uncle Kenneth took over the running of the milk depot and vegetable market for the Springs Town Council. He soon struck a deal with the town council and bought the dairy and turned it into a successful business venture, at a time when few Africans had such an opportunity. We moved into a house across the street from the milk depot on Second Street, and Uncle Kenneth took over the house on Central Avenue, and married Bellie, who gave birth to their first son,

Billy. Kenneth became even more popular in his new job than my father had been. My father visited us on some weekends, and during this time my mother gave birth to Elaine.

After reconciling their differences and with my father promising to control his temper, Pauline finally gave in and we joined Thomas in Alexandra Township in the winter of 1947. "Come on, my dear," Thomas pleaded. "Come to your house in Toneship, instead of this little box here in Springs. Superintendent Buitendacht, who is now manager of Native Affairs in Germiston, has a job for you there, which you can have at the snap of your fingers. It is only a thirty-minute bus ride from Alex. Come and start a new life there. I have a school ready for Minkie and Barbara. You have many friends and relatives in Alexandra. And you will love it."

One of the reasons my mother didn't want to move to Alexandra was that the township did not have flush toilets or electricity. The other was its reputation as the most crime-ridden township in all of South Africa. Everybody was shit-scared of Alex—"Dark City" as they used to call it. Many of its residents lived one day at a time, because there was no guarantee they would live to see the next. Life was unpredictable in "Toneship," teeming with preadolescent knife-wielding thugs and adult gangs armed with all kinds of guns. There were Zulu gangs, who were lethal with their sticks, and Basotho gangs, called Ma-Russia, who always wore their traditional blankets and were even more deadly than the Zulus with the sticks they hid under their colorful blankets. There were the Baca, Fingo, and Hlubi clans, who worked as garbage collectors. When they were pissed off, the whole township would smell of rotten garbage. In the evening, Alexandra Township's streets were buzzing with tens of thousands of workers returning from their menial jobs in downtown Johannesburg or the suburbs, where they were employed in every occupation that was considered too lowly for white folks. Among them were shoplifters, pickpockets, burglars, prostitutes, pimps, small-time gangsters, and hustlers of every kind. The streets also teemed with hawkers of fruits and vegetables, fatcakes and mielies (corn), and roadside ethnic fast foods and washerwomen carrying large bundles of white people's laundry balanced on their heads for the weekend's ironing, with little babies tied to their backs with moth-eaten blankets.

Dust, mixed with the foul sulfur smoke of red-hot braziers and coal stoves, was visible in the glare of the headlights of buses, occasional automobiles, and trucks. Horse and donkey carts delivering firewood and coal helped to raise even more dust than was already caused by thousands of pedestrian feet shuffling through Dark City's unlit streets. They all hoped that they wouldn't fall victim to the Friday-night *bulvangers* ("bull catchers," slang for muggers) who were anxiously targeting their week's pay packets. Terrified screams periodically pierced the trudging rhythm of weary feet above the blaring horns of vehicles, the tinkling bells of hundreds of bicycles, and the yells of milkmen, meat sellers, and drivers of junk carts. Dogs ran in and out of the multitudes, chasing after bitches in shameless heat. Gramophones blared out the music of township Kwela bands, pennywhistle combos, male and female trios and quartets, famous singers from home and abroad, gospel choirs and American swing bands. The streets were lined with buckets of feces mixed with urine in front of every home (whose backyards sported countless rented rooms and shacks), waiting for the migrant night-soil collectors who were infamously known as *sampunganes*. This was a name they detested enough to empty the contents of urine-filled buckets on the front porches of the homes of mischievous children who dared to shout *"Sampungane!"* at them. Mothers screamed out in shrill tones the names of their children, calling on them to end their street games and come home into the yards, out of the menacing darkness of Toneship's dangerous streets. This was Alexandra Township, a far cry from Payneville.

But Alexandra wasn't all bad for me—it wasn't bad at all. In a few days' time I met a huge cast of colorful characters on our block who taught me a lot about life, for better or for worse. First there was Steve, who lived in our yard. His uncle, Mabaso, was the chief water-meter reader for the Alexandra Health Committee's Maintenance Department. The property we were living on belonged to the Health Committee. We lived in the main house. Adjacent to our house across the driveway was a row of adjoining two-room apartments. In the first flat lived a fat, motorcycle-riding, pitch-black, mean-tempered man named Malatsi. Supposedly he was an investigating detective for the health committee. His job was to find out who lived in Alex illegally, who was smuggling stolen goods, who was not paying their water and sanitation rates, and all other infringements against the committee. But residents despised him because he was an informer for the nearby Wynberg South African police force. When the police raided the township, they were merciless and destructive in their search for fugitives, contraband, or illicit liquor. Mostly the police were corrupt and the community's hatred for them was venomous. Malatsi didn't speak to anyone, and, knowing his role as a spy for the police force, no one in the community spoke to him, but only behind his back in whispers of disgust. Rumor had it that Malatsi was indirectly responsible for the deaths of many people in the community, and was one of South Africa's worst sell-outs.

Mabaso lived with his wife, Bessie, a beautiful, light-skinned colored woman, who spoke fluent Shangaan. She was tall and dimpled, with flowing long hair, which she wore braided under a headscarf. She had pearly white teeth, a gorgeous figure with a narrow waist, a perfectly shaped pair of large, sculpted legs, and a friendly disposition. These physical attributes were spoiled by the fact that Bessie must have weighed over three hundred pounds. She usually wore just-below-the-knee German-print frocks and an apron. Whenever she would sweep around her apartment's courtyard, Bessie exposed her gargantuan, porcelain thighs right up to her drawers. I could never figure out whether she did this on purpose or was simply oblivious of the disturbance she caused among the women, or the excitement she provided the men, whenever she bent over.

My friends and I took pleasure in ogling Bessie, even though we often got caught by a woman neighbor behind the back of the outhouse lavatories, where we would raise the back cover and peep past the shit pail to watch her pee. This curtailed our behavior for a while, but the urge to catch a peek at Bessie's drawers and thunder thighs was irresistible. Playing marbles was actually the best game for ogling, because we played mostly on our knees, our heads to the ground and our eyes on Bessie's prized thighs. Spinning tops was another low-to-the-ground game that allowed us to bend down and see those drawers. We were already dirty-minded little motherfuckers who couldn't wait to feel those knobs in our short pants, our little dicks painfully hard as we jostled for a better position to eyeball Bessie's elephantine thighs.

My new playmates and I weren't the only ones given a free peep show; the men from the neighborhood were always conveniently on hand, coincidentally shaving or brushing their teeth at the communal tap, helping around the yard with the flowers or the vegetable patch, playing with the dog or feeding it, repairing a bicycle, doing a little carpentry, gossiping over the fence, having a haircut, crushing coal nuggets, chopping wood, or simply standing around contemplating the weather—whatever excuse was handy for an opportunity to catch a glimpse of Bessie's thighs. I always suspected that Bessie enjoyed the attention, but never let on that she was aware of our behavior.

Mabaso's mother also lived with them. She only spoke Shangaan and was a quiet, peaceful soul with a wad of snuff always deftly packed between her bottom lip and teeth that had turned brown from the tobacco. Between chews, she spat far into the distance, her ebony face encased in swarthy, wrinkled skin with a small nose and maroon eyes always staring into space. Her brain was probably numb from the ever-present nicotine juice oozing from the snuff, and she always wore an expression that seemed to cry out, "What the hell am I doing in this godforsaken and cursed place?"

Kokwana (grandmother, in Shangaan) was what we called her. It was always entertaining to watch Grandmother and Bessie argue about where she splattered the spent tobacco that she dug from under her bottom lip. Kokwana would flick it into the air and slowly replenish her desire for nicotine with a toot of the fine brown powder from her round tin. She'd inhale two big sniffs in each nostril before hiding the tin under her multilayered, beaded Shangaan *mutsheka*, a traditional skirt.

Cocky Tlhotlhalemajoe and his brother Mangi lived across the street from our house. To the left of their house was Ntate Montsho, who had an old 1930 Ford Prefect that he was always fixing and hand-painting with cheap glossy black paint. Montsho had a beautiful daughter, Sarikie, a little scorcher whom Cocky was banging. To the right of Cocky's house lived Ped, Cocky's cousin, who was about six years older than us, and already scarred by knife wounds on many parts of his body. He was good-looking, but mean like the devil. Ped was fearless and ready to pick a fight at any time with anybody. Ped's family was just as rough, from his parents to his dog, Ginger, who never barked but sired just about all the puppies on the block. His sister Dikeledi wore micro-mini gym tunics that showed her thunder thighs. We all had a crush on her, but never mentioned it around Ped for fear of being murdered on the spot. Dikeledi was attending school at Alexandra High, where my uncle, "Rams" Ramatswi, was the principal. Ramatswi was as black as they came, but passed for colored and refused to speak any of the ethnic languages, pretending not to understand a word. If he had been an actor, Rams would definitely have won an Oscar. He especially liked to visit my home so that he could act out his colored role, a habit that my mother found rather amusing, since she hardly ever thought of herself as being colored. She humored Rams nonetheless.

Across from Ped's house, next to us, lived an even rougher character, Ndevu, Ped's best friend. Ndevu was mean with a knife, had been to reformatory a few times, and had already put a few boys in their graves. He usually walked away from the crime and the courts with an airtight self-defense plea. Up the street from Ped's house lived his other cousins, Bomber, Mothlabane, and little Johnson Moloto. Bomber was built like a battle tank, his face and head riddled with stab marks. His taut, muscular body rippled with power. Nobody wanted to be in a fight with Bomber. Mothlabane, on the other hand, was a tall, lanky, weed-smoking golf caddy with a gift of the gab, sharp clothes, and mean township dance steps. He was always high, always telling stories, and always laughing. When he heard my name was Minkie, he christened me Mickey Janks, after the great golfer. Whenever he saw me walking down the street, he'd holler, *"Mickey Janks Seghobhadzela, Mosimane o sa jeng Kolobe."* (Mickey Janks, the one who always asks for road directions; the boy who never eats a pig.) Only Mothlabane really understood the deeper meaning of these praises. We all just accepted them and never asked him to break it all down. Next to Ped's house lived a tall, stringy, gap-toothed brother named Rex. He worked as a chef at a top Rosebank hotel. He was a sharp dresser, always carried a walking stick, and was never without a smile on his face. Rex, I soon discovered, was Alexandra Township's toughest street fighter. He was not an instigator, but many brothers who fancied themselves to be ass-kickers would often—unsuccessfully—challenge Rex.

One Sunday afternoon I saw Rex walking down Twelfth Avenue with a beautiful young woman who was wearing a black and white polka-dot dress with matching black and white shoes. I had not seen her around Alexandra, and imagined she was someone he had picked up from Rosebank. They had just gotten off the bus from town when Juba, a tall, muscular, light-skinned man, started taunting Rex and his lady friend. Rex was cool. He flashed his customary smile. With his arm around his woman's tiny waist, Rex tried to ignore any confrontation. He was wearing a white pinstriped suit, a black shirt, a white tie with black polka dots, black and white two-toned brogue shoes, a silver belt and a matching walking stick, with a white rose in his lapel. The couple wore wide-brimmed straw hats, also adorned with polka-dotted bands, hers with a ribbon in the back that hung down almost to her shoulders. Rex ignored Juba and slowly walked into his yard, where, after taking off his jacket and their hats, the couple sat on his front porch and tried to enjoy a raspberry drink on that September afternoon, all while Juba continued his ranting and raving.

My friend Steve picked up his top and string and, with a knowing smile, suggested that we walk over to Ped's house and join him and Dikeledi, who were looking on from their front yard. The commotion was beginning to stir the neighborhood. Most of the neighbors and the kids were now leaning over their front-yard fences or peering from the front porches in the direction of

Juba, watching his loud and boisterous shenanigans in the street. Uncle Rams was visiting with my parents. None of them were aware of what was going on, because they were inside enjoying tea and Marie biscuits.

Juba wore a short-sleeved khaki shirt, a size too small, to show off his biceps, triceps, and pectorals, with his muscular abs rippling through his unbuttoned shirt. Veins were sticking out over his glistening muscles as he paced up and down in front of Rex's yard, all the time screaming how he was going to rub Rex's face in the stagnant water on the side of the street and kick his ass right down to the bus stop at the corner of Selborne Road, the only tarred street in Alexandra, where the buses made their last stop before depositing the rest of the passengers at the bus terminal. Rex sat there smiling, drinking raspberry soda with his woman, while the two of them listened to Louis Jordan records on his battery-driven phonograph. It was at full volume, blasting "Pinetop's Boogie-Woogie," "Ain't Nobody Here But Us Chickens," "Caledonia," and "Ain't That Just Like a Woman."

Juba kept shouting: "Come out, Rex, don't be hiding like a little Boy Scout behind that woman. I'm gonna teach you a lesson, Rex. You've been having it too easy, boy, beating up on all those mama's babies and making people think you are the strongest man in Alex. Today everybody's gonna find out that Juba is the real crocodile in this township. I'm gonna make you shit in your pants and piss all over this street, bubba. Come on out here Rex, you sissy. Come on out and fight."

Rex continued to ignore the taunts, and calmly replaced Jordan with Louis Armstrong. Juba's shouts were now competing with "When It's Sleepy Time Down South," "Basin Street Blues," "Ain't Misbehavin'," "When You're Smiling," and "I'll Be Glad When You're Dead, You Rascal You."

More onlookers were now filling the street. Some were on their way back to their domestic jobs in the suburbs, and others were heading home from the bus terminal. The human traffic seemed to fuel Juba even more. "Come on, Rex, you are wasting all these people's time. They are dying to see me kick your ass up and down this fucking street." Still unmoved by Juba's bravado, Rex continued smiling and nodding his head. My friends and I could see that Rex and his girlfriend were now laughing hysterically. Just when it seemed as if Juba's antics were losing their appeal and the crowd was beginning to thin, Juba blurted out some bile that crossed the line. He started an assault on Rex's mother, how she was a witch and had slept with every man in Alex, and how the police had all lined up at the barracks to have their turns with her.

The music stopped. Rex's smile vanished. He went inside his house, but quickly returned, barefoot and shirtless, wearing just black training shorts. His lanky body appeared dangerously slight in comparison to Juba's rippling physique. At first I was worried for Rex. Steve quieted my apprehension. "I think you better be praying for Juba. He's really gonna need it."

In a matter of seconds they were going at each other. Juba threw the first hard punches at Rex, who stood there as if he were being brushed with a feather. Juba continued pummeling Rex's face and body, but Rex withstood the assault. Perspiration was flowing from the two of them as if water had been doused onto their glistening bodies. Finally, Rex got tired and said, "I've got to get back to my girl."

Steve anticipated Rex's onslaught: "Watch this, it's all over now." And with that, it was Rex's turn. Juba had punched himself out, but had done little to hurt his opponent. Rex pulled Juba's head from the back of the neck and butted his own against it. There was a thunderous, cracking thud. Dazed, Juba staggered back. Rex grabbed his head again and this time banged it against his left knee, then the right knee. Then Rex held Juba by his shoulders and kneed him in his rib cage with his left knee. There was a loud snapping sound, as if a large branch had been broken off a tree trunk. Juba slumped to the ground. Blood oozed from his mouth and nostrils. He never moved again.

Ped broke the silence. "It's all over."

I was mesmerized. I had never seen someone get killed. "Are all of Rex's fights this short?" I asked. "This one was too long," said Bomber.

The people quickly dispersed at the sound of the ambulance and the police cars in the distance. When the police arrived, two white officers took statements from a few curious onlookers. Juba's body was bundled and then loaded into an ambulance. In ten minutes the police were finished with their business. Rex was not arrested. And a few minutes later, life was back to normal on Twelfth Avenue, with Rex's phonograph blaring Ella Fitzgerald's "Sentimental Journey."

Gonna take a sentimental journey, gonna set my heart at ease . . . All the while Ped's dog, Ginger, went about his business with a juicy meatbone under a peach tree.

3

Throughout the 1940s our family frequently made arduous trips to see my father's parents, Hopane and Mamoshaba, on their farm in Walmaanstal, north of Pretoria. Getting to my grandparents' farm was always a nightmarish experience. We would take the bus from Alexandra Township to Germiston, and change there for the train to Pretoria. South Africa was, of course, very much a segregated country. There were signs that read EUROPEANS ONLY and NON-EUROPEANS ONLY all over the country. The train stations had white sections and black sections on the platforms. The trains were arranged so that the white and black carriages came to stop at their designated places on the station platforms. That way the different colored folk could easily board and depart from their parts of the station and never mingle with the whites. The train drivers, stationmasters, ticket sales clerks, train conductors, and railway police were all white. If you were caught in the wrong compartment, you were thrown off the train at the next station—if you were lucky enough not to go to prison and get the shit beaten out of you. Lord have mercy on your black soul if you entered through the white entrance or sat in their waiting rooms. A white person, on the other hand, had no problems if he or she invaded a black space. They were either assumed to be there in an official capacity or quickly made aware that they had erred. They were only jailed if regarded to be communists or troublemakers who insisted on hanging out with black people.

The police machinery was put in place to ensure that apartheid functioned smoothly and that anyone who broke the law was brought immediately to justice. Even Hitler's Nazi machinery never equaled the timely responses of the police forces to disruption, or the swiftness with which black "lawlessness" was defused. The apartheid system was evil and perverted, but ran like a clean machine. If you were over the age of sixteen and not white, your every moment and movement had to be accounted for. To travel from one township to another, to the local town center, to another province, to work, to church, or wherever, you had to have permission, and you only had seventy-two hours to stay in an area where you were not a resident. If you were in the wrong place at the wrong time, it was your ass, and there was no telling where you would end up or what your fate would be. It could be jail. You could be farmed out for cheap labor, or just disappear forever—probably ending up dead in some police station. Your corpse would end up in an unknown grave in some concealed area known only to your executioners.

Women traveling with children and elders were not harassed as much as adult males. We therefore never went to Walmaanstal with my father by train, only if he was driving. Somehow the police always showed respect for an African who drove a car. It was only when we used public transport that we traveled with "Polina," as the Batlokwa fondly called my mother. Pretoria was a city whose Afrikaner men could be compared to America's Ku Klux Klan. It was the sacred meeting and plotting area for Afrikaners. It was not uncommon to see an African male assaulted by a gang of Boers, as these racists were commonly referred to, for walking on the sidewalk with whites or daring to talk back or for just being black.

From Pretoria Station, we would take the Pietersburg train deep into redneck Afrikaner territory. Disembarking from the black section of the train, we would take the black-operated bus to a remote village stop, from where we would walk through arid, hilly country to Hopane's farm.

Seeing us approaching his farm from the distant horizon, Hopane would stand on a mound of earth and sing our praises for the next half hour. Trudging toward our grandfather from inside a cloud of dust, we marched with parched lips and sweat pouring from our bodies, our clothes and brows dripping in the baking heat of the northern Transvaal. We couldn't make out what Hopane said from his mound, praising us profusely while we trudged toward him. With the breeze blowing in our direction from where he stood, we were only able to catch a few of his praises. I never knew what he was saying. We could hear only the last phrases of the praises as we came to within earshot.

Hopane and Mamoshaba scratched out a decent living in those days on their farm, growing maize and raising chickens for eggs and cows for beef and milk. Hopane painstakingly constructed a wall of stone around his farm with his own hands. This intense labor gave him severe arthritis in his back, making it difficult for my grandfather to raise his legs when he walked. He sort of shuffled around. You could hear his feet dragging as he walked about his house—*shush-shush-shush-shush-shush*. My grandfather was a dignified man who prided himself on his work on the farm—but cussing under his breath and endlessly spitting as he went about his work. On many nights he would sleep with the chickens in order to catch the snakes that slithered into the chicken coop to feed on the baby chicks and eggs. With the sunrise and the rooster crowing, Hopane would emerge victorious, with several dead reptiles hanging from his shoulders. But Hopane was most proud that he had educated his six children, including my father, Thomas Selema.

Mamoshaba was the talkative one. She did a lot of cooking in the kitchen's outdoor courtyard, where she held my sister and me as her captive audience while she prepared food. She asked endless questions about the people she knew in Alexandra, Springs, and Witbank; all her relatives and those of my mother's clan. Impatient as I probably was with my grandmother's never-ending banter, our visits were nonetheless wonderful. The country air, helping with the milking and herding of the cows, feeding the animals, collecting the eggs with Hopane, and following my grandfather around as he shuffled about the farm, listening to his endless retelling of our family history, how we were related to one Batlokwa, Venda, Tsonga, and Ndebele family after another, were the lessons that helped me define who I was and where my roots lay.

In 1948 the conservative-dominated National Party won parliamentary elections and gained control of the South African government. Apartheid—a word that literally meant separateness in Afrikaans—became national policy. Two years later the Group Areas Act was enacted. It was designed to segregate communities and relegate the black population to a small allotment of the nation's land. In 1951, Hopane and Mamoshaba were among the first victims of the Group Areas Act when their farm was proclaimed a "black spot" in an area designated "for whites only." Unable to fight the repressive government, my grandparents came to live with us in Alexandra Township. Although Mamoshaba seemed to enjoy the change—making friends with just about everybody she met—Hopane became bitter and sad. The new laws had yanked his life's work right from under him. His precious farm had been taken away with only a pittance for compensation. Hopane hardly ever spoke after that. He just sat on our Alexandra porch from early in the morning, morosely shaking his head in amazement as he watched the daily activities of our neighbors and the people walking back and forth to the bus terminals. The passing cars and the weekend's carnival, with all the fights and neighborhood commotion, drove him up the wall—he would just sit on the porch, grunting and spitting in disgust. At sunset he would shuffle into the house and keep to himself the rest of the evening.

One night my father's temper got the best of him—again. Hopane had spilled some soup that he was carrying to his room, and my mother asked me to go outside and get a rag. It seemed innocent, but somehow my father felt my mother was accusing her father-in-law of being a slob. My father struck my mother several times, until she was left cowering and dazed against the kitchen wall. I jumped between them. "Papa, please!" I cried. He was about to hit me, but quickly changed his mind when my grandfather turned around and screamed at him to stop. "Selema, don't you dare lay another finger on that poor girl. Don't you remember the savage thing you did to her in Springs? I've been with your mother for more than sixty years and have never once laid a hand on her. Don't you dare!" My father stormed out of the house. After midnight I heard him return without saying a word. Things were never the same between my parents after that. My father became withdrawn, almost a stranger in our home.

City life became too much for my grandfather. He felt trapped in a situation far beyond his control. All the crazy happenings in our home and around the township made him so irritable that he often quarreled with Mamoshaba. My parents decided that she should go and live with my uncle Kenneth in Springs, but the move didn't help. Hopane became angrier, more difficult and withdrawn. He began to eat less and less, and six months later he fell very ill. Hopane practically willed himself to die. His daily routine was reduced to shuffling back and forth between his bedroom and the front porch. He died in 1952—from a broken heart, I believe. I was only thirteen, but I remember my grandfather's passing with a deep bitterness. His funeral was especially sad for me because he did not deserve to be in Alexandra Township when he passed away. His dream had been to live his last days on his farm in Walmaanstal and to be buried there. His death and burial in Alex was not only painful for our family, but soon afterwards his widow lost what little zest she had for life as well. Hardly a year went by before Mamoshaba fell deathly ill. The cause of her death was definitely the shock of her husband's passing and the impact of losing their farm. We buried my grandmother in Kwa-Thema Township cemetery. Thema was the new settlement for Africans who were forcibly moved from Payneville, Springs, after it too was proclaimed a "black spot" located in an area designated "for whites only."

Aside from witnessing the destruction of my grandfather's legacy and life, life in Alexandra during the late 1940s began taking a form that would shape my political and racial ideology. The legacy of dispossession, and racial social engineering, ensured that blacks would not—for the foreseeable future—enjoy the benefits of our continent's wealth. The government had made it plain that Africans were less than second-class citizens. Their attitude was clear: Let them fight, kill each other, drink themselves to death, infect each other with venereal diseases, and work for little or no wages. Twelfth Avenue, where we lived, was the main artery through the township, leading to the main bus terminal at Number Two Square. People off for work would start for the terminal as early as 4:00 a.m. By the time I was up an hour and a half later, I could hear their feet shuffle on the gravel road in unison like an army of soldiers marching to the beat of a silent drum. Alexandra, like Kliptown and Sophiatown Townships, were black freehold communities where Africans could own property. It was also a political haven for radical activist leaders like Dr. A. B. Xuma, Walter Sisulu, Ida Mtwana, Lillian Ngoyi, Oliver Tambo, Albert Luthuli, and Nelson Mandela—all African National Congress stalwarts—who honed their organizational and oratorical skills at Number Three Square in Alexandra.

With the growing anger toward the apartheid government, resistance rallies led by the ANC began to attract large numbers of protesters throughout the country's townships, D. F. Malan's white minority government retaliated by imposing even more stringent laws.

At times our modest home resembled a guesthouse, with the large number of relatives or stray kids living with us. Getting up in age, Johanna sold her home in Witbank and also moved in with us. In the mornings I would hurry to St. Michael's Primary School with my friend Mohale Mpiti, and by 8:00 a.m. we were at our assembly places listening to our principal, Mr. Phahle, make the daily announcements before leading us in prayer. Assembly always ended with us singing the Lord's Prayer. As with the American records I sang along with, I didn't understand the words. I loved it when we came to the part that went *hellow whered been darn nay, dye kin no come, bye wee bee darn, own ess ess east ease een hervey.*

I had been at St. Michael's Primary School for two months when my mother transferred from her job in Germiston to become head social worker at Alexandra's Entokozweni Family Welfare Center, where many of the community women came to learn about cooking, sewing, life skills, health education, child therapy, and family planning. The center's head administrator, Helen Navid, was a militant political activist, a fiery Communist who did not have one drop of prejudice flowing in her body. Helen and my mother became close friends. She was also friends with Father Trevor Huddleston, an antiapartheid activist she worshiped, and worked closely with her other white socialist colleagues, such as Joe Slovo, Ruth First, and the leadership of the ANC. The center also ran a night school for adult education, and Theo Mthembu, the legendary boxing manager and trainer, operated the Entokozweni Boxing Club. Theo, who worked with my mother as a social worker, became renowned worldwide for producing many international champions, including our national hero, Baby Jake Matlala. My mother said to me, "This is a rough township, Boy-Boy. Kids who play tennis or the piano get bullied. What you have to learn is how to defend yourself, because, believe me, you are not going to be able to avoid fights. The greatest soccer players come from Alex, and because you are so good at football, it's going to win you many friends. Still, you're going to need to be fast with your hands and nimble on your feet. I am not encouraging you to fight, Boy-Boy, but this is the way it is in Alex."

Three times a week, after dinner, I'd walk up Twelfth Avenue to the Center for evening sparring, skipping, and other boxing rudiments. By eight o'clock, Theo would let us go so he could work with the budding professionals. Hanging around the fighters was a tonic. We were all given boxing nicknames. I was the "swimming crocodile" because I tried to emulate the great Jersey Joe Walcott by running backwards and sideways all over the ring, feinting, bobbing, and weaving while throwing punches. Everybody's hero was Joe Louis. We had scrapbooks filled with photographs of the "Brown Bomber" and his wife, Marva, from his army photos to boxing posters. It was really a heartbreaker for the club members when Rocky Marciano put Louis away. But retelling the story of Louis's victory over Max Schmeling (with our own embellishing tidbits) soothed our sorrows. It felt good to hear about how a black man put away a Nazi cracker—especially since we were under the foot of apartheid. We also were crazy about Sugar Ray Robinson, Sandy Saddler, Ezzard Charles, Jack Johnson, Battling Siki, Rocky Graziano, and many others we'd read about. *Ring Magazine* was our bible.

In my Standard Two class at St. Michael's, one of my classmates, Dan

Rafapa, played the role of the typical township bully, always messing with the girls, trying to get his hands up their thighs or fondling their breasts. Some of them humored him because he was always laughing, but my deskmate, Shirley, a newcomer like me, didn't like Dan's advances. Pretending to be infuriated, he climbed on top of our desk and made as if to kick her in the face. He put his left sneaker on my open history book, smudging it. That was it. I flipped and told him to cut it out. There was immediate silence in the classroom. He said, "What did you say?" I answered, "I said cut it out, man!" He got down from the desk in disbelief, put his face to mine, and said, "After school it's you and me, sonny." Little did I know that Dan was Alex's junior mosquito-weight boxing champion. After school one of the boys brought two pairs of boxing gloves from the principal's office and we went toe-to-toe. Dan beat the shit out of me, but he couldn't drop me, so I got in a few good ones. It seemed like hours later when they stopped the fight, but I was still standing. My face was on fire from his leather, and I didn't know it, but I was crying. Cheers went up for me. No one had ever stood up to Dan before. From that day on, I got respect from everybody in the school, and Dan became one of my best friends. The boxing lessons had come in handy. Polina was right again!

Alexandra Township was also the soccer capital of South Africa, and the majority of the black national team were home-grown heroes. We spent most of our Sunday afternoons at the Number Two Square football grounds, especially if teams like the Young Fighters and the Moroka Lions were playing. When the top teams weren't playing in the township, we attended ANC rallies for the fiery oratory and to cruise the crowds for girls. When my friend Mohale spoke to the girls, they seemed to melt from his every word. But every time I tried my hand at it, I would go cottonmouthed and say something stupid like "Do you think it's going to rain?" The girls would look at me with puzzled expressions. Mohale would just shake his head, but he remained a loyal friend. Women did not care too much for soccer, but were staunch supporters of the ANC. At times my mind wandered from the speeches to the parading beauty pageant. It really pissed me off that I couldn't get my rap together.

In 1947, King George came to South Africa with his Royal Family, Queen Mary, Princess Elizabeth, and Princess Margaret. Our parents bought us new black and white uniforms and we were handed Union Jack flags to go and stand on the side of the Old Pretoria Road and wave the British flag and sing "God Save the King" as the Royal Family approached. We expected the king and his family to stop and at least say hello, because some of the schoolgirls had bouquets of flowers to give to them. Instead, they just passed by in their long convertible Rolls-Royce limousine, waving their white-gloved hands with dry smiles on their pink faces as their motorcade drove past to Pretoria. Our respect for England was deflated from then on. Our folks were pissed off because they'd bought us new uniforms they could not really afford. As children, we were hurt because we had worked so hard to learn the words to the British anthem.

In January 1948, all of my classmates were promoted to Standard Three, and we were excited about the new school year. Five months later, on May 26, the white electorate voted the Afrikaner National Party into government, and the shit immediately hit the fan. At the helm were the chief architects of apartheid, Prime Minister D. F. Malan, his coalition government, its lieutenants, and their think tank, the Broederbond. These men were directly responsible for setting South Africa centuries behind the rest of the developed world at a time when the country was almost on par with the standards of many Western countries. The Nats came to power with the clear intention of reducing Africans to a national cheap labor pool, and to all intents and purposes they legislated slavery. For us children, the first blow was the abolishment of the African Children's Feeding Scheme. Depriving already disenfranchised people of this simple, humane subsidy immediately politicized us. Before this, children in South Africa were never directly affected by politics. But now even people who had never cared for politics were singing "Malan's Laws Have Got Us Under the Yoke" and other protest songs. It was the first protest song I ever sang in unison with thousands of other voices.

All over the country, the ANC's rallies and demonstrations grew larger, leading to industrial strikes and stay-at-home protests that had a crippling effect on the nation's white economy. The government didn't like this. Suspected sell-outs like Malatsi went into hiding. Rumor had it that he had been reassigned to Pretoria to work as a consultant with the new government to help train collaborators in ways to further infiltrate the township and gain information on those opposed to apartheid.

The National Party's ongoing destabilization campaign was having a devastating effect on Africans, coloreds, and Indians. The Afrikaner intelligentsia believed segregation was essential for national survival, and thus there could be no common South African society. In the shadow of this calculated social and political deprivation, an embryonic defiance campaign was taking shape in the form of an upsurge in national consciousness among Africans, coloreds, and Indians who were not intimidated by the new laws. As if that were not bad enough, during my final year at St. Michael's in 1951, certain members of Alexandra's youth gangs would often raid our school after hours and try to abduct some of the more attractive older girls. A few of the braver boys who tried to stand up to them ended up brutally slashed and stabbed. One notorious dagga-smoking and benzine-sniffing trio, Stoffies, Bree, and Nako, chose to make our school their personal turf. Reputed to have raped and murdered many young women, they terrorized St. Michael's and had knife duels with some of our boys who chose to challenge them. One of our classmates, Miriam Nkomo, a top student in my class, was abducted from her home by these thugs and held captive for two weeks. Following her ordeal, she returned to class, but Stoffies waited for her every day after school without fail, and continued to force her to be his girl. In cases like this, the police never helped, and Miriam's family was too terrified to come to her defense. These hooligans were finally arrested for brutally murdering and mutilating several young women. They were sentenced to hang. The rest of Alexandra Township breathed a sigh of relief.

Some of my schoolmates became lifelong friends, fellow exiles, and activist colleagues. I had met our principal's two sons, Rose-Innes and George Phahle, long before I came to Alexandra Township. Their mother, Hilda, and Polina were childhood friends, and our families had visited each other since our infancy, and it was then that our friendship began. Zanele Dlamini's family was also very close to my parents because her brother worked as a health inspector under my father at the Alexandra Health Committee. And her social-worker sisters had similarly worked with my mother during their apprentice years. At St. Michael's, Zanele and George, along with Jiji and Aggrey Mbere, were a class behind me, and Zanele's sister, Kushu, was my classmate. When I came to St. Michael's, Rose-Innes was doing his final year in preparation for high school at St. Peter's Secondary School in Rosettenville, twenty miles from Alexandra. Today, Rose-Innes is a professor at Vista University in Soweto. Jiji is one of Africa's leading gynecologists. His late brother, Aggrey, was South Africa's ambassador to Rwanda. Sadly, George and his wife, Lindi, along with other exiled South African activists and a few Botswana neighbors, were assassinated in 1985 during the apartheid government's "death squad" incursion into Botswana. In all, fourteen people were killed. Zanele Mbeki is currently South Africa's First Lady.

4

AFTER I GRADUATED FROM ST. MICHAEL'S, my parents insisted on my going to St. Peter's, a boarding school run by missionaries. My uncle Putu was studying at their seminary and my friend Rose-Innes was already attending, but I wasn't so keen on it.

I only had a few months during my summer vacation to process my impending transformation. I was going to miss Polina's daily bouts of affection, laughter, and good cooking. My mother loved to squeeze me against her bosom and kiss me on the forehead. "Boy-Boy," she would say, "you're gonna grow up to be a very strong man, and look after your mother when she gets old. You're gonna be just fine. You're such a good boy." My father showed his affection in a different way, and even though he was a man of few words, I could tell my absence was going to be tough on him as well.

As my departure date grew nearer, the whole family got in on the act of helping me pack for school. My father bought me an iron trunk at the Indian supply store, large enough for my clothes, sheets, pillowcases, and blankets. After squinting and cussing while adjusting her wire-framed eyeglasses, my grandmother tried to settle her nerves and thread the sewing cotton through the needle. She soon gave up and let me do it for her. A few hours' later, home-made labels with my name written in indelible ink had been stitched on all my belongings. Barbara, Elaine, and I enjoyed Johanna's antics. Her fidgeting with the needle and thread was a hilarious comedy routine for us. It made us laugh uncontrollably. Johanna would try to be straight-faced, but after a while, she joined in the family revelry. To keep the good times rolling, I would let go an occasional fart. Straining to keep from laughing, Johanna reacted: "You little shit! Where's the castor oil?" Elaine went into hysterics, begging me to stop farting.

Over the December holidays, Rose-Innes came by to brief me about St. Peter's. He told me what to watch out for, who the troublemakers were, how to deal with the bullies, which teachers to be careful with, and especially about the boys' hostel warden, Father Rakale, whose nickname, he told me, was "Bankbroke"; Rose-Innes said this was because every time the boarders requested some upgrading of the hostel's conditions, Father Rakale would dismiss the idea and bark effeminately, "The school is bank-broke." The warden sounded like a crude bastard. Rose-Innes then described all the funny characters, nuns, monks, and beautiful girls at the St. Agnes hostel. All this made St. Peter's sound like an exciting place to be. From Rose-Innes's account, St. Peter's produced some of South Africa's greatest African scholars and leaders, such as writers Es'kia Mphahlele and Peter Abrahams, and African National Congress leaders Oliver Tambo and Duma Nokwe.

One Saturday morning in February, the time came for me to leave our family's cocoon. It was a solemn morning. No speeches. No tears. My father slipped me one pound for pocket money. We all embraced, and I was off for school. I was pretty composed leaving the house. When Rose-Innes and I walked to the bus terminal, many of our neighbors, including my boyhood friends, came out to see me off. Ped, Cocky, Steve, Bomber, and Mothlabane waved from our gate. I was going to miss these narrow, dusty roads, the street tennis-ball soccer, the weekend street festivals, the fights, the flashy cars, the fast women and their sharply dressed boyfriends. No more peering at Bessie's prized thighs; no more lazy Saturday afternoons at the movies.

After a bus ride to downtown Johannesburg, we walked to Park Train Station to see some friends of Rose-Innes. The platforms were bustling with students, couples holding hands, kissing, or just looking into each other's eyes before boarding the trains that would carry them back to their schools all around the country. There was so much chatter on the "Non-Europeans Only" side of the platform I could barely make out what people were saying. Every time a train pulled out of the station, students were screaming good-byes, laughing or crying, leaning out of the windows trying to get one last embrace with those running alongside the cars. I looked over to the whites on their side of the platform. The women, with their wide-eyed children in tow, sneered at us with disgust written across their creamy pink faces. Their tension eased when a white policeman strolled by to ensure that no kaffirs crossed the line to the whites-only side of the platform. They despised the black college students who were returning to Fort Hare University in the Eastern Cape, Rhodes University in Grahamstown, the University of Cape Town, and Wentworth Medical College in Durban. One of the white cops shouted, "Get back, you blerry black kaffirs. I don't care how much book you know, to me you're just a bunch of blerry kaffirs. You better know your place, you blerry black monkeys." The following year, 1953, the Reservation of Separate Amenities Act imposed the systematic segregation of train stations, buses, movie theaters, hotels, and virtually all other public facilities.

Rose-Innes and I hurried across town to the Faraday Train Station, from which the Rosettenville buses left. Walking briskly up Eloff Street, we passed all of the landmark clothing and department stores, as well as the Bantu Men's Social Center, the main hangout for Johannesburg's top African musicians, sportsmen, actors, poets, writers, and socialites. The center also had a dormitory for students attending the Jan Hofmeyer School of Social Work at the Jubilee Center next door, where the Johannesburg Municipal Native Brass Band also rehearsed alongside leading African theater groups. It was the headquarters for Khabi Mngoma's pioneering workshops for opera and classical music. Next door was the Wemmer Men's hostel for migrant laborers, which was across the street from the Harlem Cinema and Faraday Station.

As we made our way through downtown Johannesburg's labyrinth, the sidewalk cafés were open, and white big shots with their fat cigars stepped out of their fancy cars to sit with their women at these bistros. Some were strutting in and out of the plush Carlton Hotel, which housed some of the most expensive specialty shops and haberdasheries in all of Johannesburg. These folks were spending, in one afternoon, more money than a lot of black folks made in months, if not a whole year. I felt sorry for the African doormen and porters at the hotel, with their pretentious smiles and "yessirs," hoping their bowing and cheesing would at least earn them an extra tip from these pale-faced bastards.

With the afternoon summer sun still high in the sky, Rose-Innes and I boarded the bus for St. Peter's. Rose-Innes told me a lot of the students arrived just before curfew at six, just in time for dinner. "It's good that we're early, so you can meet some of the people I told you about, familiarize yourself with the surroundings, and get settled in your dormitory." We got off the bus at a

shopping area of Rosettenville called "the Hill," and walked down Third
Avenue toward St. Peter's, a cloistered campus, comprised mostly of African
students set in the middle of an all-white, working-class, racist neighborhood.
The scene at my new school reminded me of the bedlam we had just left at
Park Station. There was excitement all over the school grounds. Rose-Innes
introduced me to his classmate Jerry Ntsipe, who adopted me on the spot and
promised to watch over me. Jerry took over and walked me through the maze
of students, arches, buildings, and hallways. He made me promise that if anyone bothered me, I was to come and get him. He introduced me to Xolela
Masabalala. "Xokes," as Jerry called him, was a tall, dark-skinned, humorous
guy with gigantic lips and endless banter that was only surpassed by his friend
Peter "Jeet" Mathlare, a skinny, fast-talking, nervous-acting dude, who complimented Xokes's every word and phrase. Their slapstick slang, which was a mixture of French, biblical English, township Afrikaans slang, and Shakespearean
and Chaucerian phrases, reminded me of Laurel and Hardy, Abbott and
Costello, and Amos 'n' Andy. For the next hour I met other newcomers. The
truck carrying our trunks hadn't arrived yet, so I decided to explore my new
surroundings.

St. Peter's was built in 1916 on a property three blocks long and a block
wide. An open sports field with tennis courts next to it led to the grounds of
St. Agnes's dormitories, where the seventy girls lived alongside the rooms of
their nuns, Sisters Elsa and Elizabeth—the latter came to be known as Sister
Piggy. Next to the boys' hostel stood the priory, the monastery that was the
residence for the monks and novices who were studying for the priesthood at
St. Peter's Theological College. Archbishop Desmond Tutu graduated from
here. It was also here that Father Trevor Huddleston, who was the chaplain of
the entire complex, lived. Fathers Winter and Carter, the founders of St.
Peter's, also lived here, as did Fathers Millington and Jarret-Kerr, who composed all the incidental music for the school's church services. My uncle,
Lincoln "Putugwana" Motsoene, was in his senior year as a novice priest at the
seminary.

Jerry took me to my dormitory, Number Four, "the Fort," named after the
notorious jail in Johannesburg's Hillbrow Section, where the city's best-known
gangsters were incarcerated. Jerry suggested that I choose a bed in the middle
of the hall. Forty boys would live here.

Father Rakale, the warden, was already in his office across the quad from
Number Four. This was the priest Rose-Innes had warned me about. He was

a tall, gaunt, lean man of about forty, very dark in complexion, with a pock-marked face. His features were a cross between Bob Hope and Stepin Fetchit, and when I first laid eyes on him, he was twirling his false teeth in his mouth, jiggling them around with his tongue. He spoke with an Oxford English accent, something he undoubtedly picked up while studying theology in Yorkshire, England. "Masekela," he told me, "we believe in dignity, discipline, hard work, and good manners here at St. Peter's. You better behave yourself or you will be punished, suspended, and possibly expelled." After this sour introduction, I sized up Father Rakale as an asshole.

Damn, I thought, *I just met this man and he's already on me.* "Yes, Father," I replied meekly. Jerry didn't make any eye contact with Father Rakale. After we left the office, he said, "Don't take him too seriously. He's like that with everybody. He's a shitty bastard. Just avoid getting into any trouble with him."

I was one of the first new students to arrive on campus, so I continued exploring my new environment. I watched more of the returning student fanfare and then turned my attention to the girls coming through the gate at the top of the football grounds, heading toward St. Agnes. In a few months I was going to be thirteen. I was beginning to grow pubic hair and hair under my arms; I could smell my body odor and feel that throbbing sensation in my groin. Eyeing those girls made me contemplate the possibility of going further than just peeping under their dresses.

As I was daydreaming about Bessie's thighs, a fat boy walked up to me and introduced himself. *"Heita daar* [hello], I'm Woodrow Lekhela from Potchefstroom." Woodrow told me his father was a school supervisor and his mother was a school principal, and that he came from a prominent family in the western region of the Transvaal. Before I could get a chance to talk a little about my family, we were joined by a group of guys who said they were from Sophiatown. Stompie, Monty, and Lawrence spoke the latest Afrikaans slang with a flare that made me envious. Stompie's brother, Nchi, was a very sharp dresser and an established saxophonist in Johny "Boetie Vark" Selelo's Savoys, one of Sophiatown's top bands. Stompie inherited all of Nchi's hand-me-downs, manufactured by America's most fashionable clothiers and shoemakers. Monty and Lawrence, along with Stompie, carried on endlessly about American clothes, records, the latest dances, and the clothing styles of the Young Americans, Johannesburg's most colorful gang. The Young Americans specialized in robbing goods-trains and trucks. They were the pride of

Sophiatown. All of these guys were sharp dressers. They said I could be part of their clique if I shed my South African clothes. Stompie made it clear: "You can hang out with us, but not wearing those John Drake shoes. Those are for squares, man. You would cause us too much embarrassment. We could get mugged by thugs who might mistake us for country bumpkins." Stompie had a machine-gun-paced banter and an unbelievable gift of gab that was matched only by Monty's. They fed off each other, rattling on about Sophiatown, and how the Young Americans dressed better than American film stars. I was impressed, but with only one pound in my pocket, and my school fees about to take a huge bite of my family's budget, I was thankful for the few clothes I had, even with Johanna's homemade labels stitched in them.

These boys did not intimidate me. I knew I would soon find a group of friends in my class with whom I would feel comfortable. But it was good to get exposed early to all sorts of cliques, clubs, and gangs. I, too, was from the streets. I had known fast talkers, had had my share of fights, and had seen people murdered. I'd lived half of my life in a shebeen where I had heard all kinds of rough talk, had watched my grandmother beat the shit out of rowdy customers, and had heard stories about my father and uncles beating the shit out of thugs during township fights.

The aroma of bad food hanging in the air signaled that dinner was soon. But before my first meal, I was introduced to "Blood," the head prefect and his deputies, Bra T, Vlieg, Abzie, Phungwayo, and Sinuka, a mean-looking, muscular group of seniors. Prefects monitored students in the dorm, dining room, classrooms, and the school grounds in general. They were all basically assholes, especially Vlieg, the assistant head prefect who was assigned to the Fort. I also met students from different parts of the country and neighboring African countries. This group, along with the nerds and the conservative religious students, were considered to be boring squares, especially because they went overboard trying to endear themselves to the school authorities, monks, and nuns. Most of the boys despised them, as did most of the girls at St. Agnes. They were the laughingstocks of St. Peter's. Ironically, they scored the highest academic marks.

When the dinner bell rang, all dormitory and school ground activities ceased. Bad-food jokes aside, I was hungry and it was going to be a long time before I was to taste Polina and Johanna's delicious cooking again. The newcomers were the last to enter the hall. Second-year students ushered us to our places at the back of the dining hall. We all sat on long wooden benches and ate on wooden tables. The servers were students assigned to kitchen duty. Everything was done in precise military fashion. No one sat down before Father Rakale entered the dining hall and took his seat at the head table with some of the prefects and senior students. After countless monotonal responses of "present, Father," to the call of our names, he began his tirade.

"Welcome back to St. Peter's. The year 1952 will mark an even stricter disciplinary code than we had last year. All those who did not answer roll call will be gated [restricted to the campus] for the rest of the year. For those of you who are new, roll call is every day at six p.m., after which the classrooms, the tennis courts, the lab and carpentry shop, the football grounds, the area outside the school grounds, and St. Agnes are all out of bounds. Anyone found in these areas after six p.m. will be expelled. The dormitory lights will go out at eight-thirty p.m. Anyone found outside their dorm, except going to or returning from the toilets, will be expelled. There will be no talking whatsoever after eight-thirty p.m. Anyone caught talking will be severely punished. Visits to St. Agnes will only be allowed after school from three-thirty p.m. until five p.m. on weekdays and after lunchtime to six p.m. on weekends. Anyone found there after curfew will be expelled. You must have an exit permit to leave the grounds to go shopping after school, and you must be back by five p.m. Fighting is not allowed. Only seniors may smoke, and only in designated areas. Prefects are here to help you follow these rules, and anyone who challenges them is challenging me! Your work details will be posted on my office door tomorrow morning before breakfast. Rising bell is at six-thirty a.m., at which time you must go and wash and be ready for breakfast in one hour. Anyone caught in bed after six-thirty will be severely punished. There is a sick bay in my office. The medical officer will attend to your illness. If you are seriously ill, he will report to me and I will make arrangements for medical treatment outside the school. Anybody caught faking an illness will be severely punished. If you don't like these rules, you should leave the dining hall now, go and collect your things, and leave! Let us pray. May the Lord bless the food we are about to receive, Amen."

An eerie silence swept through the dining hall. The tables where the new students sat were especially quiet. I didn't know what to think. All I could hear was the clanking of the spoons against the metal plates and mumbling. I had been at St. Peter's less than three hours and was already homesick. I longed for my mother's cooking.

The bell rang and my roommates and I hurried to our dorm, where we jumped into our pajamas and talked until the lights went out at eight-thirty sharp. It was hard to go to sleep right away. My new friends and I quickly fig-ured out how to break the "no talking whatsoever after eight-thirty p.m." rule. We muffled our laughs in our pillows while assigning everyone a funny nick-name, told quiet dirty jokes, and passed silent farts. This went on until Vlieg came to bed. Then there was silence. The only sounds came from those who were snoring. Exhausted from the excitement of the day, I drifted off to sleep pondering the challenging days ahead and my mother's words ringing in my head: "Boy-Boy, you're gonna be just fine."

The rising handbell was rung by Father Rakale or a prefect at 6:30 a.m., walk-ing in and out of every dormitory. If you were in a deep sleep, the bell would be rung in your ear. Mornings were the most painful time of the day.

My first-period class started with Dr. Benade's mathematics class. He fit Rose-Innes's description to a T. His "you stupid little kaffir" remarks were part of his daily diatribe. I developed an instant dislike for math that persists to this day. In the next period, my algebra teacher was a pompous, sharply dressed, pretty boy. Mr. Dubazi had a habit of whacking you across the back of the neck if you messed up. He, too, was an unpopular teacher, albeit admired for his sophistication.

For English, I had Sister Elsa, a sweet, soft-spoken nun who wore the black, ankle-length religious habit. One hot afternoon, following lunch, I was seated in the front row in the classroom. Sister Elsa was standing by my desk, when in the middle of a sentence she accidentally released a silent yet potent gas bomb. She took a few steps backwards to ease her embarrassment. I and the rest of the class lowered our heads to keep from laughing. I assumed nuns never farted.

Sister Elsa was a welcome change from some of my male teachers. I actu-ally learned something in her class. She opened a whole new world to us, intro-ducing us to Dickens, Shakespeare, Browning, Yeats, and Byron. She actually made learning fun. It was exhilarating, funny, and sometimes complex and mysterious, but generally a new adventure into a world far removed from the township culture many of us had been accustomed to.

As the year wore on, I began taking an interest in the girls from St. Agnes. During one lunch break, Mopedi and her friend Seleke struck up a conversa-tion with me. It turned out that Seleke's father knew my parents. They were both very pretty, and I thought this would be the perfect opportunity to make my move. Suddenly I felt confident; I figured my chances were better than usual because these girls had initiated the conversation.

Ready to display my best adolescent rap, I got tongue-tied. I couldn't believe it. My mouth became dry. I tried to think of something to say. My brain went blank. My palms were sweaty. The girls, sensing my immaturity, left me standing. I watched these two beautiful girls walk away arm in arm, giggling at my weakness. I felt like a fool.

My afternoon classes were a daze. I sat through each class wondering if I was ever going to get another chance to redeem myself. After school we all crowded around the principal's office to check out our work assignments, gather school announcements, and get caught up on the latest gossip. I was assigned to one of the eight intramural soccer teams. Every boy had to play soccer. I was chosen captain of the Benade Dynamites. I figured this would be a way to take my mind off my shyness around girls.

After supper the boys headed to the classrooms for an hour-and-a-half study period under the watchful eyes of the prefects. Our day classes were coed, but we were segregated during study periods. The girls studied in their dormitories. Few of us liked the study-hall prefects. We saw them as spies, Uncle Toms, and sellouts for the school authorities. Blood, Vlieg, Desmond, and Absalom were the most feared and reviled. Bra T, on the other hand, was loved by the students, but mistrusted by his fellow prefects because he would cut us some slack.

After study hall we filed to chapel for evening prayer, called Evensong. The boys sat on the right and the girls would file in minutes later and sit on the left. Following the benediction and closing hymn, both sexes marched to their dorms under the watchful eyes of the priests, prefects, and nuns.

Once the lights went out, we got our second wind. But first we had to wait until Father Rakale made his rounds. Wearing his black cassock and Count Dracula cape, he'd stroll through the dorms shining his flashlight and barking, "Manana go to sleep! Shut up, Shoarane! Mohosh, report to my office in the morning! Masabalala, you will wash all the dorm windows! Mathlare, you are gated! Ngidi, you did a sloppy job on the toilets. Lekhela, I am calling your father in the morning! Molopyane, you are suspended!"

Father Rakale would turn out to be our worst nightmare. While he walked his rounds of the other dorms, we'd giggle, fart, tell dirty jokes, assign more nicknames, make fun of the priests and nuns, and fantasize about the pretty girls and make bad jokes about the unattractive ones. One night after listening outside our dorm window, Father Rakale came bursting through our door without warning. He flicked the lights on and began a rant unbecoming a man of the cloth. He slapped around anyone within the scope of his radar. "I will make certain that you live to rue this night, never to forget my name, and to obey the rules of this hostel." Grabbing one poor soul out of his bed, then another and another, he continued, "Get up this minute and march straight to my office and strip off all your pajama bottoms."

He slammed the door so hard the windows rattled. It was so quiet in the dorm you could hear a rat lick ice. Minutes later we heard a belt tearing into flesh and boys screaming for mercy. "Please, Father, it wasn't me! I'm sorry, Father! I won't do it again, Father!" Some boys refused to cry during their beating. This further infuriated Father Rakale.

I've never figured out how a priest could be so cruel. And worse, how a black clergyman, who claimed to be a servant of God, could be so mean and vindictive. Rumor had it that a student who had been expelled had returned and shot dead Father Rakale's predecessor, Father Bayneham, who had been everybody's darling. I sometimes feared for Father Rakale's life. I was certain somebody would reach the breaking point and kill him. A few months later, Father Rakale did cause, I believe, the death of Godfrey Mochochoko who slept next to me by giving him aspirin for a "fever" that turned out to be brain meningitis. Father Rakale was transferred to another mission in Soweto. After St. Peter's closed in 1956, I never heard of him again.

When Father Rakale was away on a retreat, Mr. Darling, the school's principal and science teacher, pulled triple duty as dorm warden. Generally, he was more pleasant than "Bankbroke." Respected and feared, Mr. Darling relied on the classroom monitors to assist him and the other teachers in keeping order. Vlieg, Blood, Phungwayo, Desmond, and Abzie loved to get us in trouble with half-truths and lies. One day I got into a heated discussion with our Afrikaans teacher, Meneer Mijnhaardt. Both of us were fluent in the language, but we disagreed over what was proper Afrikaans versus street Afrikaans. Since my mother was colored, Afrikaans was her family's first language. We spoke it every day, as did many of her relatives. "Properly," I told Mr. Mijnhaardt, "not with any slang!" I guess I pushed Mr. Mijnhaardt a little too far. He stormed out of the class red-faced and furious. Mongezi, our class monitor, rushed to the office to tell Mr. Darling his version of the story.

"My dear boy, your shabby behavior has come to my attention. I am granting you three options. First, you can receive a blistering caning on your buttocks. Your second option is to wash the windows of each classroom for the next six months. Your third option is the simplest: You can pack your bags and leave." I got six whistling strokes from Mr. Darling's wooden cane. The pain was unbearable. The swollen welts made it difficult to sit down. With tears in my eyes, I apologized to Mr. Mijnhaardt in front of the class and was ordered to take my seat. "That's a good boy, Mr. Masekela," Mr. Darling continued as I eased into my desk chair. "For those inclined to act as Mr. Masekela did, please inquire of him what the consequences will be."

When Bankbroke returned, his temper tantrums returned, and the morale around the campus sunk to new lows. After school, life centered around chores, detention, soccer games, tutoring, ducking and dodging Father Rakale, and getting caught up on the gossip about who got caught and expelled for drinking and which boy from St. Peter's got which girl from St. Agnes pregnant. The exchange of juicy details was always followed by the sadness that the young lovers were caught and, of course, expelled.

Father Rakale loved to flaunt his authority. One night before dinner he cleared up any uncertainty around the latest gossip. "Masabalala and Hatshwayo have been expelled from this institution for breaking the rules. They were caught drinking. It was my decision that they should pack their belongings and leave St. Peter's immediately. Let their dismissals be a clear warning to all of you. I shall not tolerate any wayward behavior in this school. Let us pray. May the Lord bless the food we are about to receive. Amen."

He left the dining hall in a huff. Few of us ate our supper. We were disgusted and showed it by a combined loss of appetite and solidarity with our friends. Even though it meant I was going to have to set two fewer place settings, I was going to miss my friends.

Later that evening one of my dorm mates, Godfrey Mochochoko, complained he was not feeling well. During Father Rakale's surveillance rounds before evening bell and lights-out, we informed him of Godfrey's condition. He checked Godfrey and determined he had a fever. He gave him two aspirins. A few hours later Godfrey was sweating, his body shaking uncontrollably. We got the dorm prefect to call for help. Bankbroke returned only to give Godfrey two more aspirins and assure him that he would be fine by morning. During the night Godfrey became worse. The dorm prefect cursed us for wrestling him from his sleep. By morning Godfrey's bedding was soaked with sweat and shit. He was unconscious. They took him to Johannesburg General Hospital. That afternoon we got word that Godfrey had died from meningitis. Our contempt for Father Rakale had now escalated to hate—and he didn't care. The more we sulked, the more boys he found to slap around. It was as if Godfrey's death had turned him into a bigger monster than he was before. Life in the dorms became unbearable as the prefects, acting as foot soldiers in Rakale's private army, carried out his wrath at will.

Godfrey's funeral High Mass was held that Sunday. Stompie, Solly, Woodrow, and I sat in the first bench on the boys' side of the chapel. The nuns, priests, seminarians, and deacons sat behind Godfrey's family, who were in the front pew. The girls sat on the other side. As the mass began, I remember thinking, *Did Father Rakale really intend for Godfrey to die? Was he so blinded by hate? Should I have gotten up that night, even at the risk of a caning, and demanded that Godfrey be taken to the hospital?* Before I could organize another thought, I found myself crying. Glancing at Godfrey's parents, who were themselves graduates of the school, I wondered how they felt. Had they been told the whole truth about their son's death? About his last night alive? About his suffering? I wondered how my parents would have felt had they lost me in such a way.

Father Trevor Huddleston, St. Peter's chaplain, delivered Godfrey's eulogy. As we listened to him preach in his calm, hoarse Oxford accent, there was not a dry eye in the chapel. Tall, with a lean, muscular frame, angular face, and silver hair, Huddleston spoke about the power of love, hope, mercy, compassion, strength, and forgiveness, as we tried to make sense of our friend's death.

At the end of Huddleston's eulogy, the intensity of the wailing was deafening. Even Father Rakale, who I had been told had been distraught since Godfrey's death, was misty-eyed. For the first time I saw Father Rakale's shoulders droop. On this rare occasion, I felt compassion for him and wondered what was going through his mind while we sang "Abide With Me," Huddleston's favorite hymn. At the cemetery, we filed past Godfrey's grave, dropping handfuls of dirt on his coffin. We said a final farewell to our fallen colleague with an a cappella rendition of "God Is Working His Purpose Out."

That night we went to bed in red-eyed silence out of respect for Godfrey and from emotional exhaustion. Around midnight a thunderstorm began. No one stirred. To me, it was a message from Godfrey, telling us he had reached heaven.

For the rest of the school year I struggled to put Godfrey's death behind me. The school holidays helped because I went home to Alexandra, but seeing Godfrey's vacant bed, school desk, and seat at the end of the dining-hall bench made me miss him tremendously. I began bonding with Stompie, Monty, and

Lawrence, the sharp-dressing guys from Sophiatown. I made sure that whenever we hung out, my shoes were polished and my shirts and slacks were pressed and starched. After I started tagging along with them, the sharp-dressing movie stars they idolized began intoxicating me as well.

Stompie and Monty also knew a great deal about American and South African music. They sang along with all the big bands and knew many of the lyrics to songs by Satchmo, Billie Holiday, Billy Eckstine, and Sarah Vaughan, among others. Soon I was living in a fantasy world of music, movies, sports, clothes, and beautiful women. Studying was becoming secondary. I was even losing interest in my altar-boy and servitor duties. Our jiving became so mesmerizing and animated that we often didn't realize the presence of the school authorities hovering around us.

Father Carter, one of the founder's of St. Peter's, used to admonish us, "If you boys studied the Bible and prayed as much as you talk about these worldly desires, you would know enough to get to heaven." I fell asleep many nights thinking about heaven, Godfrey, beautiful women, nice threads, and music.

5

EW WHITE PEOPLE IN SOUTH AFRICA were as respected and held in disdain as Father Trevor Huddleston. Revered by the downtrodden, he was a pain in the ass to the white government because of his tireless campaign against apartheid.

At St. Peter's, "Die Gerry," as he was also known among the township youths, took an interest in the daily lives of the students. He kept his office door open as a sign that he was willing to assist us at any time. A self-described Christian socialist, Huddleston called everybody "creature" and was always inquisitive about how you were doing and if you were being good. He loved to tousle your hair and look straight into your eyes, always smiling. If there was a social concern that needed attention, Huddleston could be found in the midst of it, listening, giving advice. Helen Navid, the director of Alexandra's Entokozweni Family Center, and a radical antiapartheid activist, once said, "If every Christian in the world was like Trevor, I would join the church tomorrow."

Toward the end of my first year, I was less homesick for my mother's cooking and Alexandra. St. Peter's was beginning to grow on me. It was November 1952, and spring was in the air. I was doing well in my classes, staying out of trouble. However, my lust for girls was beginning to overpower me. I wanted romance and sex. I had had enough of telling and listening to dirty jokes in the dark. I hungered for the real thing.

To my parents' delight, I finished the school year in the top ten of my class. I was glad to be home for the Christmas holidays, but outside of my family, I was bored with the township scene. Even though I was still fascinated by the music of Louis Jordan, Coleman Hawkins, Johnny Hodges, Duke Ellington, and Count Basie, back at St. Peter's the new bebop movement led by Charlie Parker, Dizzy Gillespie, Art Blakey, and Thelonious Monk, to name a few, was beginning to grab our interest—although we didn't quite understand its complex melodies and harmonies. The big jazz collectors were touting this music heavily, with the implication that if you were still listening to swing, you were behind the times. These were the same people who set our fashion standards, and we didn't want to be seen as square and lagging behind in our understanding of things modern. Stompie and my other friends were pretending to understand bebop, and I wasn't going to get left behind. I found myself beginning to follow everything that Stompie said we should be doing to fit in. In the midst of all this, we began to get into trouble with the prefects, Father Rakale, and many of our teachers. And Stompie was getting me into the art of shoplifting. For example, he would start a fight with a certain shopkeeper on the Hill, the arrogant, racist Mr. Christos, who made a lot of money off the student population. While Stompie was riling him up and Christos was distracted, calling us monkeys and kaffirs, I would pocket candies and other goodies. Sometimes Stompie and I would reverse our roles, so as not to establish a pattern that Mr. Christos could detect. Our frequent clashes with Abzie and Vlieg, Bankbroke's favorite lackeys, as well as our talking after lights-out, had the warden calling us to his office regularly.

My second year was dramatically different from my first. Hanging around older guys who were exposed to worldly things fascinated me. I wanted to explore more of this world, but at the same time, the religious presence was very powerful. I was taking a catechism class, getting ready for my Confirmation by the archbishop, so that I could receive Holy Communion and perform altar-boy duties. Unlike most first-year students, Stompie had gotten himself a girlfriend at St. Agnes the very first week of the previous school year. He couldn't understand why I couldn't do the same. He asked his girlfriend, Evelyn, to introduce me to a new student at St. Agnes, Vera Pitso. Vera, a light-skinned girl from Soweto, whose face wasn't that attractive, but had a body to die for. Although Vera never considered me for a boyfriend, she was persuaded by Evelyn and some of the older girls at St. Agnes that I was the guy for her. Soon after our courtship began, we started exchanging love letters and sitting together during movies in the dining hall. Like many of the other couples, we necked and kissed passionately. By the time the lights were clicked on, it was impossible for me to stand up because of the erection Vera had left me with. My short khaki pants would have a large wet spot on the left-hand side of my fly, caused by Vera reluctantly squeezing on my hard johnson while I tried to work my free hand past her squeezed-together thighs. With behavior like this, it was no wonder that I had so many wet dreams. I tried in vain to get her to rendezvous with me at places like the carpentry shop or Happy Valley, a favorite campus lovemaking place, or any other clandestine location around school where we would have had the opportunity to go all the way. After many months of trying, and eventually realizing that I would never get laid, I gave up and we broke up. Vera was heartbroken because she had come to love me very deeply. She was disappointed that I only seemed to want her for her body.

As the school year drew on, interest in my studies waned because of my wild escapades with Stompie. With my powerful high voice, I was still singing soprano solos in the boys' choir. In church, I sat in the front row and sang high tenor. Although the girls thought this was very sweet and cute, they didn't find it very romantic. I now wanted to sing bass like most of my friends and the seniors. Woodrow Lekhela, one of my deliquent friends, told me a sure way to be really "in" was to start smoking and drinking. That way, he reasoned, my voice would change even quicker. Father Rakale had warned us about smoking, but there were certain spots around the school grounds that were ideal for smoking without detection. Behind the boys' dorm was a place called "the Trench," where the disinfectant fumes from the urinals were so pungent that other odors went undetected by the few prefects who ventured around the area. Soon I bowed to peer pressure and smoked my first cigarette. It tasted terrible and made me cough, brought tears to my eyes, and burned my throat. Nonetheless, I quickly overcame these discomforts, and that single cigarette led to a pack of our favorite brand, Cavalla. I got hooked on nicotine. Months later my voice dropped an octave and I started singing bass, with Woodrow smiling proudly next to me.

Upon returning to school the next term, I spent most of what little money I had on Cavallas, and bummed cigarettes from other smokers when I was out. As the habit increased, so did my desire to be even more in with the guys. My wardrobe was still not up to standard, so Stompie and I would use our once-a-month Saturday privilege to stroll through the city, window-shopping and staking out certain stores for potential shoplifting endeavors. One Saturday afternoon, Stompie and I went on a shoplifting mission at OK Bazaars.

Stompie pulled a large coat from a hanger in the men's department, opened it, and held it in front of the white saleswoman standing with her back to me while he directed me to take two light windbreakers he had already folded into a small package and leave the store with them tucked under my shoulder inside my jacket. While he distracted the saleslady with a conversation about the wrong size of the coat, I snuck out of the store. I was scared shitless. I imagined what my parents would think had I got caught. When Stompie caught up with me a few blocks away at the Faraday bus station, my voice was trembling, my mouth was dry, and my heart was beating faster than a tap-dancing minstrel.

When we got back to St. Peter's, I was ashamed that I was becoming a thief—but not that I was stealing from white folks. For decades the only thing blacks controlled, to a great extent, was the underworld. It was heroic for a black person to be good at theft, drinking, burglary, bank robbery, bootleg-ging, selling drugs, and being in a gang whose specialty was robbing white people. Diamond smugglers, numbers runners, and street muggers who tar-geted white folks were township heroes.

The better we dressed, the more respect Stompie and I commanded, but we were getting out of control and being punished for it regularly at school. One spring Saturday afternoon in September 1953, Stompie suggested that we sneak off the school grounds and go to the movies at the Harlem Cinema. He said there was a movie playing called *Young Man With a Horn*, starring Kirk Douglas as Leon "Bix" Beiderbecke, the talented jazz cornet virtuoso, who died in 1931, at age twenty-eight, from bootleg gin and other addictive habits. The film blew me away. Harry James's horn solos in songs like "I'm in the Mood for Love," "Stardust," "My Dream Is Yours," and "I'll Hold You in My Dreams" had me wanting to leap out of my seat. I left the theater not caring if I got caught or what punishment it would bring. My resolve there and then was to become a trumpet player. Kirk's portrayal of a jazz man was so bril-liantly precocious and arrogant that we came out of the movie swearing to spend the rest of our lives as musicians. In the film, Kirk stood in front of the band in his snazzy threads, playing all the solos. He didn't take any shit from anybody, and the women were crazy about him. The only people he showed any respect for were the band's singer, played by Doris Day, and the piano player, "Smokey," played by Hoagy Carmichael. Bix worshiped his black Hispanic trumpet teacher, played by Juan Hernandez, who always came to his assistance when he was in trouble. Everybody else could go to hell as far as Bix was concerned. Harry James's rich, fat, burnished tone on the soundtrack was magical and hypnotizing, bouncing off the cinema walls with so much power that I found my heart skipping a few beats. I struggled to catch my breath from time to time. I was so totally bewitched that I suddenly couldn't imagine myself doing anything else but playing the trumpet for the rest of my life. To be that independent, in demand, and virtually self-employed, never having to work for a white *baas* for the rest of my life; that is what the life of a trumpet player seemed to hold in promise for me. I wanted this with all my heart and being—nothing else would do!

Although I had narrowly passed my exams and was eligible to be promoted to the third-year class, the despicable behavior Stompie and I displayed in and outside of class led the principal and our teachers to recommend that I repeat my second year. The embarrassment of returning to St. Peter's in January 1954 was tempered by the fact that a handful of other boys also had to repeat. Early in the school year, while I was sick with the flu, Huddleston, who was also disappointed that I had to repeat Form Two, came to my bedside with a big smile on his face. "Hugh, what would make you well? What do you really want to do with your life when you grow up?"

Sensing that he was in a generous mood, I said, "Father, if you could get me a trumpet, I won't bother anybody anymore." I still had *Young Man With a Horn* on my mind. Kirk Douglas blowing that horn still had a grip on me.

"Are you sure that is what you want, little creature?"

"Oh yes, Father, that is what I want. I want to play the trumpet."

"You come and see me when you get better, and do get well," he said.

One Saturday morning after I was feeling better, I marched into Polliacks Music Store on Eloff Street in Johannesburg with a letter Huddleston had given me for Bob Hill. An expatriate jazz bass player from Scotland, Hill was moonlighting as a musical instrument salesman. "The Fatherrr is bloomin' crrazy! Whrr did he err hearrr that fifteen pinds could buy a bloody troompet?" Nevertheless, I walked out of Polliacks with a gleaming secondhand horn. Huddleston had asked Old Man Uncle Sauda, the leader of the Johannesburg Municipal Native Brass Band, to give me trumpet lessons. When I returned to school, he was waiting for me in Huddleston's office. We walked across to the Priory carpentry shop, where he proceeded to teach me the C-scale fingering and other trumpet rudiments. He came every Saturday. Every day after school I was back there in the carpentry shop, practicing my lessons like a madman. Four lessons later, I was playing "I'm in the Mood for

Love" on my horn. From my piano-playing experience in Springs, I had developed a natural feeling for instrumental technique. Because I was already familiar with the science of music scales and keys, the hard work I was putting into the trumpet made it relatively easy for me to understand its mechanism. I took to it like a fish to water. I was a natural.

Political events in South Africa began to make it difficult for African students to concentrate on their studies. All African males in their teens and older would be required to carry ID papers on their persons at all times. Rumors were already afloat that Huddleston's beloved Sophiatown was going to be torn down by the government, and its African residents relocated. A few months into the school year, all of the male students at St. Peter's were bussed to the Albert Street government pass office to be issued passbooks. At the pass office there were long lines, thousands of men waiting in the burning summer sun to enter the cursed building, where they would be ordered to disrobe. We were escorted ahead of the long lines outside to join the hundreds inside who were already standing naked in line. It was humiliating for us to stand bare-assed with our clothes hanging from our arms alongside grown men. After eye, nose, throat, ear, and chest checkups, everybody was forced by the belligerent Afrikaner doctors to bend over for rectal and penile examinations. Following that, orders were screamed at us by black security guards to move on to the next section, where even ruder native clerks asked for our birthdates, places of birth, and parents' names and addresses. They measured us for height and weight, photographed us, and herded us into a waiting hall where the completed passbooks, called "reference books," were more or less thrown at us, after which we were commanded to "get the fuck out of here." We were told that we had to keep this ninety-six-page document with us at all times, and that the police had the authority to demand to see it any time they saw fit. It was not unusual to see our paternal elders humiliated in our presence, arrested and paraded up and down the township streets, avenues, and alleys while the police searched for more victims. Beatings were common, and unreported deaths during arrests were something that came with the territory. Failure to produce the reference book on demand usually resulted in imprisonment without trial. Jails often transferred prisoners into the hands of heartless white farmers. These farmers would force them into work gangs to dig vegetables with their bare hands, clothe them in burlap sacks and house them in cold concrete shacks, and beat them mercilessly if they did not

perform. Many a man died on these farms without their families ever knowing what had happened to them. Their corpses were given to medical schools
to dissect. It was the beginning of the horrors of apartheid. The worst was
still to come.

St. Peter's students were arrested regularly for passbook violations.
Huddleston, who opposed the passbook system, usually stormed to Rosettenville police station to get them released. On many occasions the furious priest
was known to strike out at racist policemen with venom unbecoming his station. Huddleston would follow such incidents with days of meditation, confession, and marathon prayer.

The school took on a new character, as the draconian apartheid laws made
us all feel very insecure. We found solace in our schoolwork, soccer, and other,
unsanctioned campus activities. Shortly before my fifteenth birthday I met
Nomvula, a dark-skinned, sixteen-year-old, pear-shaped girl, nicknamed
"Mouse." She was a day scholar. Every day after school I walked Nomvula to
the bus. After a few weeks our courtship really blossomed; there was an alley
near the terminal where we would kiss and fondle each other while we waited
for the bus. I could tell from the way she would rub against my hard dick with
her crotch or hand, and how she would let me put my hand up her thighs and
let my fingers slide inside her, that she was ready to give me some trim. One
day Nomvula agreed to take a later bus so that we could go to Happy Valley, a
prohibited, secluded spot far beyond campus, hidden by hills, valleys, and huge
eucalyptus trees. If you were caught there, expulsion was automatic. Many
babies were conceived on the grassy knolls of Happy Valley. We found a soft
patch of grass where we lay down, and I began to kiss Nomvula all over the
neck, chest, and face as I slid out of my khaki shorts. With my coaxing,
Nomvula wasted no time slipping her panties off from under her school uni-
form tunic. Before I knew it, her legs were high up in the air like the sails of a
ship, as she panted and moaned with the joy of a baby sucking on its mother's
teats. As our out-of-control lovemaking reached boiling point, I suddenly felt
that I was about to die. I began to suffer loss of breath and heart palpitations,
and saw stars. I had an earthquake of an orgasm. I screamed and was about to
faint when out of the corner of my left eye I spotted a rinkaals, a cobralike
snake common to South Africa, raising its head through the grass about three
yards from where we were lying. Out of pure instinct, I grabbed my pants,
yanked Nomvula off the grass, and shouted for her to run up the hill while I
hotfooted in the opposite direction. The last time I saw her, her beautiful little
black ass was disappearing up through the boulders of a hill, her panties swing-

ing in her right hand, her feet nimbler than a mountain goat's. I put my pants on at the top of Happy Valley and calmly walked toward the Hill, where I bought a peanut snack bar from Christo's grocery store and proceeded to walk back to school with a big grin on my face. My mind was completely puzzled, my underpants wet from a mixture of perspiration and residue from our foreplay. Nomvula did not return to St. Peter's after that day, and I was sad that we would never get together again. That was my first sexual experience and, needless to say, the strangest.

Knox Kaloate, a schoolmate of mine and a big jazz record collector, was inspired by my quick mastery of the horn and asked Huddleston for a trumpet. Old Man Uncle Sauda now had two students. We were soon playing the simple duets that our trumpet teacher assigned us. Stompie, who had been taking lessons for a while from Drakes Mbau, the lead trumpeter of the Jazz Maniacs, was now working as an office filing clerk. He visited us on some weekends and showed us some of his new tricks with the horn. Stompie had become a very good player, far more advanced than Knox and me. His prowess made us even more enthusiastic about becoming virtuosos on our instruments. By September 1954, Knox and I had learned even more songs, duets from Sauda's lesson books, popular ballads, and American romantic standards. Of course, our noisy enthusiasm did not sit well with the monks and the residents of the neighborhood. They eventually requested Huddleston to find us more suitable quarters for our practice sessions, where our blowing would not interfere with their solemn meditations and prayers. In an arrangement with Mr. Darling, Huddleston was able to secure us permission to use the school carpentry shop across from the science laboratory.

This music fever became contagious. George Makhene, a senior, put together a partial set of drums from the equipment of the now-defunct Boy Scouts. Huddleston bargained with Bob Hill for more instruments, including cymbals, tomtoms, a high-hat, and a foot pedal to augment George's percussion outfit. We were allowed to carry the rickety upright piano from the school hall into the carpentry shop, where Henley "Bach" Magobiane started to play with us alongside Monty Mahobe, who was now the proud owner of a white, upright double bass that Bob Hill had managed to scrounge from somewhere. "Bach" did not last too long in the band. He was a classical musician with no dance rhythm whatsoever. George, an awesomely muscular weightlifter who had now elected himself bandleader, fired "Bach" and brought in Ivan Mosiah as his replacement. No one liked to disagree with George too much.

We now had a rhythm section. The five of us began playing cover tunes such as "C Jam Blues" and "Tuxedo Junction," and township favorites by groups like the Harlem Swingsters, Ntemi Piliso, and Zakes Nkosi. We tried our best to imitate the recordings we had, but slowly we started to establish our own sound.

Huddleston enjoyed our enthusiasm. He became fascinated with the band as more boys came to him begging for instruments. My cousin Jonas Gwangwa got a trombone; another cousin of mine, Chips Molopyane, and Prince Moloi got alto saxophones, and "Moon" Masemola got a tenor saxophone. We started to get on the nerves of the school's prefects, nuns, teachers, and monks, and many of our male schoolmates were jealous because we were attracting the attention of several fine girls who came by the carpentry shop whenever it was permissible. Some of them were really keen to sing with the band. The school's bookworms found us especially annoying. St. Peter's was coming alive with the sounds of the Huddleston Jazz Band. The only thing we had on our minds was rehearsing. The fact that we had all been avid jazz and mbhaqanga record collectors, who shared the same musical tastes, gave us a pretty large repertoire to choose from as a group. All we had to do was assign each person his part to play. Our experience in ensemble singing in the school choirs and at chapel had honed our harmonic capabilities, which we were able to apply to our band. We became a pretty tight unit in a very short time. By September of 1954 we had put together a hot band augmented by a singing quintet of two girls and three boys. They sang compositions from groups like Glenn Miller's Modernaires, Tommy Dorsey's Pied Pipers, the African Ink Spots, and the Manhattan Brothers. Knox doubled on vocals, joining my new girlfriend, Linda Kieviet, who was also the band's lead vocalist.

One Sunday afternoon, Huddleston loaded fourteen of us into his pickup truck and drove us to a reception at the Donaldson Center in Orlando Township for British Commonwealth flyweight boxing champion Jake Ntuli's homecoming reception. He was the first African to win an international boxing title, and Huddleston had known him from when he was just starting out. Huddleston was very excited by Ntuli's achievement, and thought he'd be an inspiration to all of us. Because we were allowed out of the school only once a month, this chance for an extra outing was like a furlough for a bunch of death-row prisoners. When we got to the reception in the small hall, we sat in the balcony where we could watch the overflowing crowd downstairs thrill to a performance by the Cuban Brothers, a popular Jo'burg singing quartet. The group was great, but all of our attention was focused on the young, velvety-voiced female singer they were featuring, who we were told had just come to Johannesburg from Pretoria. The Cuban Brothers accompanied her with oohs, aahs, and doo-wops on "Nomalizo," a popular ballad about a stunningly beautiful woman who had seventy-two lovers. The singer enthralled the entire audience but left the men completely smitten. She was breathtakingly beautiful, with large brown eyes, high cheekbones, a perfectly shaped nose, a body sculpted by the ancestors with a small waist, and with big, long, shapely legs carrying an ample but beautifully rounded behind. She wore sexy black high heels and a tight, hip-hugging, strapless red dress that allowed us a bird's-eye view into her cleavage from where we were sitting. Her stunning physical attributes were only matched by the beauty of her voice. On the ride back to St. Peter's, all we could talk about was Miriam Makeba. When we got back to campus, the other boys asked us about Jake Ntuli, but forget him; all we wanted to talk about was this tantalizing African goddess we had just seen, with a voice made in heaven, a body by Leonardo da Vinci, a brilliant gap-toothed smile, the dreamiest eyes, and remarkable charm.

Soon we all were fantasizing about being big-time musicians and hanging out with Miriam Makeba, the Cuban Brothers, the Manhattan Brothers, Dolly Rathebe, and the other great South African music giants. Huddleston continued to marvel at our fervor, but reminded us of our promise to him that we would not let the music interfere with our studies. He assured us that if we did, he would confiscate all of our instruments and that would be the end of the Huddleston Jazz Band. We walked the straight and narrow for the rest of the school year, concentrating on our studies, but spending all of our free time on sports and music. Later that year, when she joined the Manhattan Brothers, I cut out all the photographs of Miriam Makeba that I could find in *Drum, Zonk,* and *Bona* magazines, and the *Bantu World* newspaper.

As more guys wanted to join our group, Huddleston had to target other donors. He knew a lot of rich white liberals who salved their guilt by donating to his charities, and was able to get us additional instruments from time to time. Spyros Skouras, a top movie executive from America, visited South Africa and surprised Huddleston by outfitting our whole group with new instruments and band uniforms. However, Skouras insisted that we wear gray cowboy shirts with tassels and black dress pants. We weren't crazy about the uniforms he bought us, but a new drum set, a double bass, an electric guitar, three trumpets, an upright piano, three alto saxophones, two tenor saxophones, three trombones, and five clarinets made it easy for us to tolerate the gaudy outfits. Suddenly more students wanted to join the band. The newspapers began to publish articles about the Huddleston Jazz Band. We were now playing all the monthly dance socials. The girls loved us. We were soaking it all in.

For me, school holidays were no longer boring. I looked forward to spending them in Springs, where, through my uncle Kenneth's hustling, I got to play with Peter Ntsane's Merry Makers' Orchestra. The band's great trumpeters, Elijah Nkwanyana and Banzi Bangani, took me under their wings and worked with me. Once I returned to school, I passed on what I had learned to the guys in our horn section. I began to mimic Elijah's trumpet style, elements that I still use today. He had a lazy way of phrasing, holding long notes to show off his fat, beautiful tone that sounded more like he was singing than blowing the trumpet. Elijah also had a high-pitched singing voice that drove the women nuts. Banzi's style was much more crisp, faster and bright. He was a magician with the wah-wah mute and had a burnished vibrato on his horn that I found much harder to emulate. Elijah's style, on the other hand, just sucked me in. The band only played their own compositions—crisp mbhaqanga grooves that had a touch of Benny Goodman's sextet arrangements, peppered with sprinklings of bebop phrasings and tight harmonies reminiscent of some of Gil Evans's early small band charts. It was irresistible. Playing in the Merry Makers' trumpet section made me proud because there was hardly anybody my age playing with South Africa's top bands. Stompie, who was now playing with the Savoys, was six years older than me.

The Merry Makers played dances all over the townships of the cities neighboring Johannesburg, but I was only playing with them at their nighttime rehearsals in the storefront barbershop that belonged to Peter Ntsane's family. They felt I was still too young to go on the road with them. Besides, my parents would not have allowed it. By now Uncle Sauda had stopped giving me private lessons; I had learned all that he could teach me. My parents were beginning to notice my musical development. Whenever I was home, I would practice in the garage behind our house. Even the naysayers at school, who originally thought we were just making a lot of noise, were now giving us respect. My grandmother called me "Pu-Pu-Ru-Pu-Pu," her imitation of the trumpet sound.

•   •   •

Back at St. Peter's, with the band riding high, and the girls enamored with our rising fame, life had become pure joy. The thought that anything unpleasant might change this wonderful state of affairs never entered our minds. But everything was about to be turned upside down. One night after evening prayer in the chapel, Huddleston asked us to be seated. We thought he had some school announcements or would scold us for some major behavioral infraction. He had done this recently when a student hit a nun in the chest with a brick when he was nearly caught kissing his girlfriend after curfew in a remote corner of St. Agnes's dark courtyard behind the girl's dormitories. Instead, what he was about to tell us was far more serious.

"My dear creatures, the government has introduced a new law which will hereafter require all African children to be given an inferior education in their native languages. This means that when you complete high school, you will be far more inferior to a white child. As a Christian, I find this totally unacceptable. I have convinced the archbishop of the diocese to reject this system of education and to close all African Anglican schools in South Africa rather than agree to this barbaric law. I am happy to say that the diocese has agreed. Our school, St. Peter's, I am afraid, will be the first one to close next December, at the end of the 1956 school term, because this despicable government has already spitefully declared it a black spot. I know this news comes as a great disappointment to you, but it is the only just and humane decision we could reach. Nobody is more shattered than I am, but we have chosen to reject Bantu Education, and there will be no turning back. I will remember all of you always in my prayers and have only the fondest memories of this place. May the blessings of God be always with you. Go in peace. Good night."

Huddleston walked out of the chapel and left us stunned and weeping. We filed out speechless and filled with anger. Our having to get passbooks at the beginning of the school year paled in comparison to this blow.

Adopted in 1953, but implemented on April 25, 1955, the Bantu Education Act was designed to transfer African education from missionary control to the Native Affairs Department headed by Hendrik Verwoerd. As he put it, "I will reform [black education] so that natives will be taught from childhood to realize that equality with Europeans is not for them." Verwoerd attacked the liberalism of missionary education, which gave African children ideas of growing up to live in a world of black and white equal rights. He later explained to the senate that there was "no place" for blacks outside the reserves, "above the level of certain forms of labor." Therefore, "what was the use in teaching a Bantu child mathematics when he cannot use it in practice?" He added: "Education must train and teach people in accordance with their opportunities in life."

African schools were no longer to study from the same lesson plans as those used in white schools; instead they would follow new course outlines based on government-recognized African languages. English, which had been the most common language of instruction, would be scrapped in primary schools and limited in secondary schools. There was mass resistance by African teachers and students to the new law. Arrests were followed by expulsions for the students and firings for the teachers. In one day, seven thousand students boycotted and were expelled. Verwoerd viewed boycotts as criminal acts of rebellion. The government later passed similar laws to control Indian and colored education. Two years later the Extension of University Education Act shut down undergraduate classes to nonwhites in all universities. Ethnic universities were created for nonwhites throughout South Africa. Once the act was implemented in 1959, many African academics quit or were fired. Afrikaans-speaking white professors replaced them for the most part.

The architects of apartheid calculated their strategic moves. Verwoerd recognized that expanding industries in white areas needed a cheap African labor force. He predicted that the nonwhite urban population would begin to decrease in the late 1970s, by which time apartheid would have succeeded in developing the "Bantu" rural reserves as alternative areas of employment. Verwoerd saw the total separation between white and black societies as the final prize of apartheid. African labor in white society, he said, was like "donkeys, oxen, and tractors," which could someday be replaced by other human machinery. White-owned mining companies, white farmers, white commercial and industrial businesses, and white homeowners throughout the country's suburbs had espoused this philosophy for decades.

As the noose of apartheid's fascist terror began to tighten around the necks of Africans, even though most of us were teens, we were becoming more politically conscious by the day. Cognizant as we now were of the bleak future racism was beginning to paint for us, political resistance took center stage in our lives. Verwoerd hated us, and we hated him. He never saw what he was doing as racist, but rather as a scientific philosophy he felt was good for everybody. He believed it was unreasonable to accept Africans as normal, intelligent human beings who could become lawyers, doctors, or scientists. To him,

Africans did not possess the mental tools required for any advanced study. That's why the government spent eight times more on education for whites than for Africans.

A few smaller Anglican Mission schools stayed open, deciding to accept the government's ultimatum, feeling, in Huddleston's words, that "it was better for children to have a rotten education than none at all." But Huddleston and St. Peter's broke ranks, choosing "death with honor." For a long time Verwoerd had been dying to get rid of Huddleston, but lacked an excuse. Now he had Huddleston in his cross-hairs. Soon after the decision by the Anglican Diocese to close St. Peter's, Verwoerd appealed to the leadership of the Order of the Community of the Resurrection in Mirfield to recall our favorite priest.

Huddleston's vow of obedience to his religious order left him with little choice but to comply with his superiors' demand and return to England. His expulsion was headline news in all of the South African newspapers. Many Africans saw his submission as a victory for Verwoerd, but Huddleston had no choice. It was a major blow for the African and political resistance communities, who lost one of their most valued resistance icons. Deflated, yet determined, the African people continued to focus their lives toward finding ways to beat the system that was destroying them. At the grassroots level, they devised sophisticated methods to anticipate where police raids would strike in our communities. These schemes were much more complicated than tossing pebbles on corrugated iron tin roofs. Africans created phantom employment, and forged signatures in the passbooks, to keep the police at bay. They learned how to stay a few steps ahead of the police at all times. They were going through an emotional transformation. But the more they schemed, the more efficient the apartheid system became.

The dragnet of apartheid pulled all of us into a net of treachery, as either victims or informers. The ears of the Special Branch police force were everywhere. Family members became suspect. Lovers became untrustworthy. Names were taken at every political meeting, and many who were hauled in for questioning were intimidated into selling out, or if they stood their ground, they were subjected to torture and round-the-clock surveillance.

In the midst of all this terror, somehow township music was in its golden era, burgeoning as never before.

Dolly Rathebe, South Africa's first African film star, magazine cover girl, and mbhaqanga and jazz and blues singer, used to say that "as evil as apartheid was, it could never completely destroy us because our music was the one thing the white government could never take away from us."

South African jazz orchestrations had their roots in ethnic wedding songs, and a cappella choral compositions, written mostly for school choirs. Marabi, mbhaqanga, and kwela were hybrid styles born from African interpretations of European missionary songs of worship and traditional African folk songs played in the style of American swing.

The township bands and combos were flourishing, especially in the Johannesburg area. Saxophonist Gwigwi Mrwebi's Harlem Swingsters, featuring Chief Manana on the double bass, and Boetie "Vark" Selelo's Savoys, featuring Nchimane Manana on saxophone and Stompie Manana on trumpet, both originated in Sophiatown. From Orlando Township came the Jazz Maniacs, with Ellison Themba, Kippie Moeketsi, Mackay Davashe, and Zakes Nkosi on saxophones, Drakes Mbau on lead trumpet, Jacob Moeketsi on piano, Tai Shomang on double bass, and Boykie on drums; this was South Africa's top orchestra.

Peter Rezant's Merry Blackbirds were the African society band that played such upper-crust functions as prominent weddings, national beauty pageants, and ballroom dance competitions at the Bantu Men's Social Center. From Cape Town came Christopher "Columbus" Ngcukane's orchestra; from the Eastern Cape came Lex Mona's Serenaders; and from Durban, Dalton Khanyile's big band. There were many other big bands out of Vereeninging, Bloemfontein, Port Elizabeth, Queenstown, Benoni, and Kimberley, the diamond capital located in the Northern Cape.

There were innumerable talented female singers including Dolly Rathebe, Thandi Mpambani, Joyce Sineke, Louisa Emmanuel, Dixie Kwankwa, Rose Mathyss, Dorothy Masuka, and Susan Rabashane, and male crooners like Ben "Satch" Masinga, Joey "Maxims" Modise, Isaac Petersen, and Sonny Pillay. And of course there was Miriam Makeba.

My homeboys, the Boston Brothers, led by Sam Williams, featuring "Boston Red," Vandi Leballo, Joey Maxims, and Lawrence Masinga were spending a lot of time with the Huddleston Jazz Band at St. Peter's, mentoring us. There were hundreds of other performers who made up the music community of South Africa at the time. They mostly performed on weekends in the municipal township recreational halls.

The government despised our joy. They couldn't figure out how Africans could still find any pleasure under such harsh social conditions. They were particularly annoyed when Africans jammed with white, Indian, and colored entertainers. Race mingling of any kind was resented by the apartheid government. They didn't even want Africans from South Africa mixing with Africans from other parts of the world. When Sidney Poitier and Canada Lee came to South Africa to film *Cry the Beloved Country* in 1951, they were allowed into the country as indentured servants of the film's director, Zoltan Korda, and labeled "foreign natives." All foreign natives were kept apart from South African–born Africans in single-sex hostel complexes or in the homes or hotels of their employers. Isolating ethnic South Africans from Africans born outside the country drove a cultural and psychological wedge between them that still exists today in the form of the most despicable xenophobia imaginable.

Toward the end of 1954, the Huddleston Jazz Band was on the boil and so was my love affair with our vocalist, Linda Kieviet. Much to my parents' relief and Huddleston's joy, I passed my repeat year near the top of my class. The rest of the band members were equally successful with their studies. I was not so lucky with Linda. Like Vera Pitso, she was adamant about refusing to sleep with me. The frustrating part was that when the girls refused to sleep with me, they never explained why. Even worse, Linda Kieviet later became the lover of our drummer, George Makhene.

My profile got a boost during the holidays, when the Merry Makers hired me to play trumpet in Elijah Nkwanyana's place, who had switched to tenor saxophone. One weekend the group had a wedding gig in Warmbaths, about fifty miles north of Pretoria. We set out in two seven-seater DeSoto sedans with one of the cars carrying the double bass and drum kit fastened to a rack on the roof. Just before sunset we arrived at the bride's home, on a farm on the outskirts of Warmbath's black township. The bride's family fed us well and the brandy began to flow. Much to my surprise, one of the bridesmaids was Miriam Nkomo, a former classmate of mine from St. Michael's. Miriam was about four years older than I, and now a student at Marianhill College in Natal. After playing a pre-wedding rehearsal set for the family, Mankomo, as we called her, and I sat in a corner of the courtyard and enjoyed a pint of brandy, reminiscing about our primary-school days. Soon we were kissing, and after a few more swigs of brandy we lost ourselves in each other. Spurred on by the brandy, Miriam fetched a blanket from inside the house. We made love for hours on top of it near the chicken coop. I'd never known it was possible to make love for so long—it must have been the brandy! Mankomo returned to the house some time after midnight, and I made it to one of the sedans, where

I passed out in the backseat. I had no idea where the rest of the band members had gone, but I assumed they had been kidnapped by local women for horizontal entertainment. The next morning Mankomo knocked on the back window of the car. She had a basin of hot water, some soap, and a washrag for me to wash up. She also gathered my clothes and pressed them for the afternoon wedding while I waited in the car in my drawers. She returned them with a breakfast of a big steak, some fried eggs, and brown bread.

By late morning the rest of the band materialized, one by one, in time for us to play the wedding celebration just before lunchtime. Aside from playing the Wedding March song and other marriage favorites as we marched up and down the street behind the bridal party without a rhythm section and our lips almost numb, we still had to play that evening's wedding reception. Since there was no hall in the township, we set up on the large wraparound porch of the bride's palatial home to play the reception. We did all the township dance favorites: "Tamatie Sous," "Ibhabhalazi," and Elijah Nkwanyana's hit compositions "Siya Giya" and "Thimela." The Merry Makers were a very tight band indeed, and the wedding revelers could not get enough, screaming for encores well into the night. The band let me play many solos, and were knocked out by the style I was developing, a cross-section of Elijah's style with a little of Banzi's playing and a touch of Clifford Brown and Dizzy Gillespie's phraseology. Listeners were fascinated to watch me stand toe-to-toe with the veteran musicians.

After the gig, Mankomo and I made more passionate love with the help of a full bottle of brandy. The next morning I woke to the rooster's crow and a throbbing headache. Painfully hung over, we left Warmbaths sharing stories about our wild weekend while passing around a bottle of Limosin brandy as we headed back to Springs.

Later that day I received two pounds as payment for playing the wedding with the band. I was thrilled, even though I got less than the rest of the guys. They explained that I was still an apprentice, and my day would come. But I had passed my first tests, both as a professional musician and as a lover.

I played a few more gigs with the Merry Makers before the end of my vacation, and was able to save a little money to buy some fine threads. I returned to St. Peter's in late January 1955, energized by my music. I was looking forward to passing on to the Huddleston Jazz Band all the knowledge I had picked up from the Merry Makers during the holidays. My parents were concerned because once again a decision had to be made about which high school I would attend now that St. Peter's was closing, but I also noticed they were more guarded about my musical progress. My father was especially lukewarm. The Batlokwa people, his family clan, prided themselves on education and community service. Music, to them, was something that respectable people listened to, but that was only played by irresponsible, illiterate, drunken layabouts. My parents had never thought that giving me piano lessons and exposing me to jazz records would lead to anything like what was now happening to me. I knew that in their hearts they were very worried.

As the end of the year drew nearer, the thought of St. Peter's closing down and Huddleston's recall to England brought gloom over many of us. Two farewell concerts were organized by a cross-section of community and church activists. We played the dance portion for the second concert, which took place on the first weekend of the December school holidays at the Davey Social Center in Benoni's Twa Twa Township. That concert featured performances by the cream of African music entertainers, including the Manhattan Brothers, featuring their new vocalist, the "Nut Brown Baby," the "Nightingale," Miriam Makeba. This was the second time I saw her, and every time our eyes met that evening, I got a warm feeling inside. The same thing seemed to happen to her, but I dismissed it as a figment of my imagination. After all, she was seven years older than I, and already a national star. When she sang, she bowled over the entire audience—there were endless screams for encores.

At midnight the audience moved the chairs and benches against the walls to make room for dancing. Most of the top musicians from the Merry Makers and the Jazz Maniacs who had played earlier stayed around to catch our set and jam with us for a while. Huddleston and the other dignitaries had left along with Miriam, the Manhattan Brothers, and the rest of the performers. About two hours later a gang of about thirty boys in their late teens, armed with knives and handguns, rushed into the hall, most of them bleeding. The women and young girls ran onto the gigantic stage, shaking and crying with fear. One of the gang members was bleeding profusely from the side of his head and screamed, "Germiston one side, Benoni one side, Springs one side, Boksburg one side, Alexandra one side, Brakpan one side, Orlando one side," ordering people to group with their townships. Some of the Orlando people tried to join the other groups, but were rejected and pushed away. The gang went for the Orlando section, stabbing them mercilessly, as the victims literally slithered up against the wall before they fell to their deaths. Blood was everywhere, gushing from some of the victims like water from sprinklers, splattering on the attackers and all over the floor. People were frantically trying to get out of

there. Some were begging for mercy and crying like babies. The groups from
the other townships couldn't be sure they weren't next in line after the gang
was through with the Orlando section. The weeping, moaning, and fainting
made for a pathetic scene around the hall. Some of the gang members were
waving guns, machetes, long daggers, and tomahawks at the band, forcing us
to play Elijah's "Siya Giya" over and over again as accompaniment to the carnage. "Play, motherfuckers, if you don't want to see your mothers' behinds.
You better play, you fucking shits." Then they would fire a few shots into the
ceiling of the hall. Girls were swooning and fainting all around us on-stage.
Shaking in our funny cowboy uniforms, we played harder than we had ever
played before. Even tough George Makhene had sweat pouring from his entire
body as he sat behind his drums; he banged them like a champ, aware that his
life depended on every stroke of the beat.

When it was over, seventeen people lay in large pools of blood. All of them
had been stabbed to death. The gang ran out of the hall, apparently in pursuit
of some who had gotten away. Much later, as we were packing our instruments, the African police entered the hall, led by several white sergeants with
their disgusted "bloody black savages" expressions on their pink faces. They
looked as if they were wondering why there weren't more bodies. We finished
packing our instruments and got the hell out of there. During the train ride
back to Johannesburg, I wondered why the police had arrived when the carnage was already over. Apparently two rival gangs, the DMGs and the Fast
Elevens, had come to the hall to revenge the fatal stabbing of a Germiston
gang leader who had been killed the week before at a dance in Payneville.
Word was that the police had known about the coming bloodbath but their
attitude was, "Let them kill each other. It's less work for us." The mayhem
obviously marred the debut public performance of the Huddleston Jazz Band.
I was seriously concerned about how my parents would react when they heard
about this, especially my mother, who had periodically warned me of the
fights that took place at township dance concerts. The *Golden City Post*, a
tabloid for African readers, came out the next day with a screaming headline:
GANG CARNAGE AT HUDDLESTON'S FAREWELL CONCERT: 17 BOYS MURDERED IN COLD
BLOOD. When my mother saw the front page of the newspaper, she left her
cooking, sat down at the kitchen table, and began to cry. "Oh no, Boy-Boy, you
have to stay away from this band business. Can you see how dangerous it is?
You will be much better off getting yourself a good education and finding a
good job. Oh no, I can't afford to lose my only son." She continued to weep
quietly. I couldn't answer her. My father came into the kitchen and tried to

make her feel better. "Don't take it so seriously, my dear. This doesn't happen all the time. It was just an unfortunate incident." I was relieved by my father's intervention. It meant I could carry on playing.

Our next performances took us on the road south to Pietermaritzburg and Durban. Following the Benoni riot, our parents were a little nervous about our traveling, and even though we had a chaperone, the parents of our female vocalists refused to let their daughters go with us. But we didn't care; we were mavericks, excited about experiencing the glamorous world of show business. In December the beautiful Drakensberg mountain passes, gorges, hills, plateaus, rivers, and lakes offer splendor to the eye the likes of which I haven't seen anywhere else in the world. Double rainbows arced high up across the horizon where gaps in the clouds showed off a clear blue sky, sometimes with a moon that was visible in the light of day.

The steam engine pulled into the Pietermaritzburg train station, where we disembarked, hung over and reeking of brandy and beer following the overnight trip. We had been drinking hard on the train ride because we wanted to be cool like the seasoned musicians we had read about in *Drum* magazine. Mr. Maphumulo, the head social worker in Sobantu Village Township, met us at the station and we were driven to the township's municipal hall in several cars. A pick-up van carried our instruments and baggage. Following a short reception to meet the local folks, we were taken to a single men's hostel outside the township. At first glance, the place looked clean. We settled in, had lunch, and were given a tour around town. We were delighted to see the posters nailed to the telephone and light posts:

FIRST NATIONAL TOUR

THE HUDDLESTON JAZZ BAND CONCERT & DANCE

FOR TWO NIGHTS ONLY DECEMBER 14TH AND 15TH 8 P.M.

SUNDAY 17TH DECEMBER MATINEE AT 2 P.M.

ADMISSION 2 SHILLINGS AND SIXPENCE.

DON'T MISS IT!

After an early dinner we went to bed, exhausted from the train ride and all the drinking the night before. Around midnight we heard small objects dropping from the ceiling onto our beds, and a scratching noise over the floor. Soon we began feeling bites. I jumped up and turned the lights on. The room was filled with bedbugs scampering down the walls, some coming from behind the cabinets and under the door, while others parachuted from the ceiling. Our white sheets and blankets were marked with bloodstains—ours mixed with theirs. We shook our bedcovers and cleaned our dorm as best we could. The next two nights we tried sleeping with the lights on because the parasites didn't seem as venturesome when the lights were on. Some of the guys drank after rehearsals and performances until they passed out, too drunk to care about bedbugs. But, bedbugs aside, the audiences loved our music. We played many of the mbhaqanga favorites popularized by the Harlem Swingsters, the Merry Makers, the Alexandra All-Star Band, and Zakes Nkosi's Sextext; songs composed by Ntemi Piliso, Gwigwi Mrwebi, Zakes Nkosi, and Elijah Nkwanyana. The revelers always rushed onto the dance floor and went wild whenever they recognized these hit songs. George, Jonas, and I also composed a few catchy songs of our own, like "Motsoala," which we got to record for Gallo Records the following year.

Our next set of shows in Durban, a two-hour train ride to the coast, were poorly attended, so we canceled the final gig, packed our gear, and headed home two days before Christmas. As the train pulled into the station, I suddenly realized that some of us would never see each other again. Some of the guys had graduated from St. Peter's and would soon be off to university. Others, like me, would be attending another high school after the first of the year. Though St. Peter's had closed, we vowed to keep the band together not only as a tribute to Huddleston, but also to earn some money.

One Saturday afternoon in early January 1956, I was standing near the entrance of the Bantu Men's Social Center with Jonas, Monty, George, and Chips, admiring Miriam Makeba, Mary Rabotapi, and Johanna Radebe, then known as the Skylarks, who were standing some short distance away. They were the country's top female singing group at the time, and were absolutely stunning in their six-inch spike heels and tight tapered skirts with slits in the back which allowed for a titillating view of the lower thigh, just enough to make one breathless. With their high-fashion suits and shoulder bags and closely cropped hair, they were a sight to kill for. I caught Miriam's eyes stealing mine a few times and knew they were whispering and giggling about us, just as we were busy flipping over them. I boasted to the guys that I could walk over to the three ladies and begin a conversation. The fellows nearly keeled over—who the fuck did I think I was to dare go over and form my lips to say something to Miriam Makeba? Asking Chips Molopyane to watch my trumpet case, I slowly walked over to the Skylarks, who looked happily surprised that I was approaching them, their faces sparkling with the widest smiles as if to say, "This kid has some fucking spunk to be approaching us, the hypnotizing Skylarks!" Strangely enough, I was not even slightly scared, which was an exhilarating change from my normal terror around attractive women. I usually couldn't come up with anything to say when the time came to make my decisive verbal salvo, but this time I walked nonchalantly, with a little bounce to my lazy strut, and instead of my usual panic, I found myself chuckling softly. I stopped right in front of Miriam and said to her in Zulu, *"Sawbuona Sisi Miriam, u za ngi xolela kodwa be si khuluma ngawe lapha na leya genge ukuthi u cula ka mnandi njani and futhi ukuthi a ma Skylarks a hlabela ka mnandi njani no Kuthi ni bahle njani, ni si bulala blind man."* (Hello, Sister Miriam, please forgive my forwardness but the fellows and I over there were talking about you and how beautifully you sing and also how incredibly beautiful the Skylarks sound. Mostly, we were remarking about how stunningly beautiful the three of you are, and I have to confess without any reservation, that you all are really killing us.)

They burst out laughing. I continued, *"Sa ku bona kuqala e Donaldson nga leya mini kwa ku ne reception Ka Jake Ntuli, wawu cula na ma Cuban Brothers Amadoda a yi seventy-two Sa cula leyo ngoma u ku suka e Donaldson sa ze sa yo ngena e St. Peter's, si phikisana ukuthi u nga thanda bani phakathi Kwethu Sonke."* (We first saw you at Donaldson Center during Jake Ntuli's reception, when you sang with the Cuban Brothers on "Nomalizo had seventy-two lovers." We sang that song all the way back to St. Peter's, arguing among ourselves about who you would choose if you had to pick somebody out of the fourteen of us.) More laughter. "Anyway, I am crazy about music and new in the business, maybe you can give me a little advice and teach me a few things." Still more giggles. Miriam looked deep into my eyes and said, "Go and fetch your trumpet. I want you to come somewhere with me." I was hypnotized. The fellows were dumbfounded when I waved good-bye to them as Miriam Makeba and I strutted slowly down Eloff Street. They couldn't believe their eyes. Neither could I.

As we walked down Eloff Street, people who knew Miriam probably assumed that I was just escorting her somewhere to carry her parcels, since I was practically unknown at the time and too young to be her lover. "Where are we going?" I asked. Miriam said, "I know you love jazz. I am taking you to a friend of mine in Hillbrow who has one of the greatest jazz collections in the world. He's from Switzerland and you will really like him. His name is Paul

Meyer." I was elated. Here I was, walking down Johannesburg's main avenue with South Africa's greatest singer on my way to listen to great records that I could never dream of getting my hands on. On top of that, I was about to meet a great record collector from Switzerland at a time when Africans did not get the opportunity to meet white people, especially from abroad.

Paul was from Basel, a short, blond, blue-eyed man with a film star's looks. He was extremely friendly and spoke with a strong German accent. He fixed some marinated herring and German pumpernickel bread sandwiches for the three of us, and I drank beer with him, which was illegal for Africans at the time. In fact Miriam and I had no business being with Paul at all, because it was illegal to socialize with whites and, with an African woman in the room, we were actually "conspiring to contravene" the Immorality Act. But I didn't care. I was in music heaven. Paul Meyer had every record ever made by Louis Armstrong, Jelly Roll Morton, Ma Rainey, Bessie Smith, Kid Ory, Buddy Bolden, King Oliver, Chick Webb, Jack Teagarden, Count Basie, Sy Oliver, Duke Ellington, and more. I noticed that Meyer did not have any records by white jazz artists. He explained that he knew deep down in his heart that jazz was the music of black folks, and regardless of how much they excelled, white people could never in their wildest dreams capture the true essence of jazz. Paul Meyer's analysis of white people's jazz capabilities really surprised me. I had never heard this angle before. My music colleagues and I had never discussed American or South African music from the perspective of race. We had equally admired Glenn Miller and Count Basie, Benny Goodman and Duke Ellington, Tommy Dorsey and Louis Jordan, Ella Fitzgerald and Rosemary Clooney, the Four Freshmen and the Mills Brothers, Chet Baker, Shorty Rogers, Clifford Brown and Miles Davis, Louis Armstrong and Jack Teagarden—it made no difference to us. We were especially fascinated by the fact that Benny Goodman had included Billie Holiday and Lionel Hampton in his band at a time when racial prejudice was very strong in America. Miles Davis's *Birth of the Cool*, with all those white jazz musicians, Gerry Mulligan, Bobby Brookmeyer, and Zoot Sims, was even more intriguing to us. If anything, we were encouraged that music was being used as a weapon for eradicating racial stereotyping. Paul Meyer's comment burst my little bubble of hope.

It was almost sundown when I let Miriam know that I had better be going back to Alexandra. She wanted me to escort her to Johannesburg Park Station so she could catch a train to her home in Mofolo Township in Soweto. I agreed, and went to take a leak in the bathroom. When I returned, Miriam and

Paul were in a huddle, eyes closed and kissing each other deeply. I was shocked at first, then angry. I didn't know what to do. I went outside and waited on the porch. Miriam came out flustered and apologetic. "Come Sunday" was still playing on the turntable, with Mahalia Jackson singing her heart out in front of the Duke Ellington Orchestra.

I didn't say a word as we walked from Paul's place to the train station. I honestly didn't know where to start. I was hurt and confused. I thought how my friends back at the Bantu Men's Social Center would laugh if I told them what really went down. "What's the matter, Papa?" Miriam said. "Why are you so quiet?" "I don't like being used," I said curtly. "Oh, how can you say I'm using you?" she asked. I said, "You are using me, sister. You knew that it was dangerous for you to go and visit Paul Meyer alone. You wanted to see him badly. You had no one to cover for you because we are not allowed to make love to whites without getting arrested for contravening the Immorality Act. You saw me standing there, all googoo-eyed over you. You figured here was a young sucker you could use to cover your back. So you invited me, knowing I would be excited over Paul's record collection, and I'd just feel privileged to be in your company and that of a foreign white man. Well, my sister, I wasn't born yesterday and I am not impressed, Mama. Don't ever think that you can use me for your little tricks. You better find yourself another fool next time you want to visit your Paul Meyer."

"I'm sorry," she said, wiping tears from her cheeks with a white handkerchief she pulled from her handbag. "I'm sorry, Oupa." ("Granddad," Miriam's nickname for me to this day.)

In January 1956, I began my final year of high school at Holy Cross in Alexandra, but I had lost all interest in my studies. Over my break, I had been dividing my time between our group and the Merry Makers in Springs. The Merry Makers had a huge following. They filled the dance halls more than did most groups in and around Johannesburg. Elijah, the band's leader, seemed to take to me, so we started hanging out a lot. He exposed me to more sophisticated liquor and older, more experienced women. I was finished with homemade brews and schoolgirls. Back at school I was going insane thinking and daydreaming about Elijah, Ntemi Piliso, Kippie Moeketsi, Charlie Parker, Sarah Vaughan, Dorothy Masuka, and Miriam Makeba. I remember sitting at my desk covered with books and notepads, but my mind was recycling chords to the new songs of Thelonious Monk, Miles Davis, and Max Roach.

Pinocchio, South Africa's biggest jazz collector and concert promoter, found me listening to a Dizzy Gillespie album one day at the Coliseum record store in downtown Johannesburg—that's where all the African jazz aficionados hung out and bought their records. He told me, "Don't listen to that man. If you want to listen to some trumpet, you gotta hear Clifford Brown." He said Brown, whose father bought him his first horn at thirteen, was one of the baddest trumpet players on the American jazz scene. My father had just helped me buy a wind-up, long-playing record phonograph. I bought Brown's album, *The Clifford Brown Max Roach Quintet,* and damn near played it to death, memorizing every single note on the album, including all of Max Roach's mind-blowing drum solos. Known as "Brownie," Clifford tragically died in an auto accident a few months later, on June 26, 1956. He was only twenty-five. The newspaper said that Brown, his pianist Richie Powell, and Powell's wife were on their way to meet Max Roach for a gig in Chicago when Powell's car, driven by his wife, skidded off the wet Pennsylvania Turnpike. Brown and his wife, LaRue, had an infant son, Clifford junior, who had not yet turned one.

By March 1956, I had bought everything that I could find and afford by Clifford Brown and Miles Davis. I was also getting into so-called West Coast jazz as a result of my cousin Chips, whose brother Kappie was working at the Coliseum. Chips's brother-in-law, Gwigwi Mrwebi, was also the alto-saxophone player with the Harlem Swingsters and an avid collector of West Coast jazz. When I would visit Chips in Sophiatown, Gwigwi would bombard us with recordings by Dave Brubeck and Paul Desmond, Shorty Rogers, Bob Cooper, Bud Shank, and others. I loved all that jazz, but I remained loyal to Clifford, Max, Miles, Dizzy, Sonny Rollins, and other African-American jazz giants. The West Coast jazz had a much softer style both instrumentally and vocally. Its foremost players, Gerry Mulligan, Chet Baker, Shorty Rogers, Dave Brubeck, Paul Desmond, Bob Cooper, and Zoot Sims, and singers, June Christy, Anita O'Day, and Chris Connor, all had extremely gentle approaches to their arrangements, dynamics, and phrases. The music hardly ever had any loud passages. They were also more colorful in their tropical California dress styles, a quality highly attractive to us clotheshorses. However, the East Coast jazz musicians were all African-Americans who had virtually pioneered bebop. Miles Davis, Clifford Brown, Dizzy Gillespie, Charlie Parker, Sonny Rollins, Cannonball Adderly, Art Blakey, Thelonious Monk, Charlie Mingus, and Max Roach were the leaders of the school of hard bop. They played powerful, driving, loud, and usually very fast tempo music. Their technical dexterity and outstanding wizardry on their instruments was way ahead of the West Coast players. They were the tastemakers of the new music and had a very heavy influence on my playing.

My phonograph helped ease my burning desire to be like my idols. After school I would try to do my homework while the music was playing. The music always won my attention. When the teacher called on me the next day, I was completely oblivious of the question, but daydreaming about music energized me and gave me hope. My trumpet became my personal choice of weapon.

Huddleston was still in South Africa, but about to leave the country for good. He had scheduled a side trip to the United States at the invitation of the South African writer Alan Paton, who was teaching at the Kent School in Connecticut, before returning to England. His order, the Community of the Resurrection, also had a few missions in America. I was very sad, not knowing if I was ever going to see my friend again. I asked if he could help secure me a scholarship to further my music studies, because I knew that if I stayed in South Africa, my career would be doomed. With escalating repression by the apartheid government, and with resistance against it growing every day, I could envision myself being swept away by the powerful currents of radical activism and—given my big mouth and general fearlessness around authority figures—my chances of living very long were rather slim. To progress in my musical career, I would have to get out of South Africa.

"Creature, I'll see what I can do," Huddleston said.

Huddleston visited several American cities. He contacted Dr. Martin Luther King Jr., and discussed the brewing South African situation with the Baptist preacher and fledgling civil rights leader. One night when he was in Rochester, New York, Huddleston managed to see Louis Armstrong backstage before his performance at the Civic Auditorium. Still trying to get us more instruments, Huddleston explained to Satchmo that he had a group of boys in South Africa who were trying to properly learn music. The *Star* reported that Armstrong said, "I figured they'd rather have a horn I've been drawin' a few of those notes on than a new one."

Armstrong's wife, Lucille, a former Cotton Club chorus line dancer, mailed one of her husband's used trumpets to South Africa. The package arrived on April 11, 1956. The whole band gathered that night at the Polly Street Community Center. Press photographers were everywhere. All the band members got a chance to handle Satchmo's horn. The following day the *Star* ran the story in both editions:

LOUIS ARMSTRONG'S TRUMPET ARRIVES—AND A JAZZ SESSION STARTS
HUGH CANNOT BELIEVE HIS LUCK—A TRUMPET FROM THE "KING" HIMSELF

When I opened the package and handled the horn, I was overjoyed. I was seventeen, and for the first time I felt something like a spiritual connection with Satchmo and those musicians back in the states that I idolized to my core. This horn was my connection not just to Armstrong, but to a long, powerful tradition that had crisscrossed the Atlantic from Africa to America and back. It was a sign my direction in life was cemented.

Music was now my everything. A few months later the African newspapers reported that Louis Armstrong was in Accra, Ghana, where ten thousand people had met him at the airport and another fifty thousand had attended his open-air concert. All I could do was close my eyes and imagine I was there shaking his hand, thanking him for sending me his trumpet. I imagined taking out my trumpet and playing a few phrases to let him know that his kindness had been put to good use. Four years later, Armstrong returned to Africa and toured Ghana, Nigeria, the Congo, Kenya, Tanzania, Guinea, and the Ivory Coast. He wanted to visit South Africa, but the minister of foreign affairs said, "It's not in the country's best interest, at the present time, to authorize a visit by Armstrong." When the apartheid government refused Louis Armstrong entry into South Africa, it only deepened my disgust with my country's regime, who were now depriving us of access to our musical icon.

Schoolwork was no longer on my radar screen. Every morning and evening I would help my grandmother, Johanna, with her Fish and Chips shop in Alexandra. On the days I skipped school, I'd play on recordings or rehearse for upcoming weekend gigs with the older musicians like Kippie, Zakes, and Ntemi, who were teaching me more and more. When I wasn't playing gigs with them or the Huddleston band, I was getting steady work with other groups, playing township gigs on what was known as the blood-and-guts circuit—so called because we played in concert halls where fights often broke out. I saw more people stabbed with long-bladed knives than I care to remember. Despite the Paul Meyer incident, a romance began to blossom between Miriam and me. She had a number of lovers, including, for a short time, my cousin Kappie, but we never hid our feelings for each other. After a movie or an afternoon rehearsal at the Bantu Men's Social Center, we would ease between the tall buildings and smooch during our sunset strolls.

It was hard for me to get too angry with Miriam and her other lovers. After all, she was older than I, more experienced sexually, and the darling of the newspapers. I was a relatively unknown teenager of seventeen, and even though our relationship was never portrayed by the media as a scandal, there were obviously adult considerations that I was unable to fulfill for her. And I had many younger girlfriends that I was not about to cut loose. Miriam didn't mind if girls my age flirted with me, but once gossip surfaced that a singer from a rival female group and I were seeing each other, she told me, "If I hear you were with that whore again, or anyone of her kind, I'll kill them." That's how Miriam was. She could unsheath a vicious temper, sharper than an ice pick.

One night Miriam and I slept at Mike "Mazurkie" Phahlane's home. An arts critic for *Drum* magazine and a dear friend, Mazurkie lived in a two-room shack behind his parents' home. The three of us left from the BMSC to Western Native Township, where Mike lived. On our way, we met Boykie and Kit, two members of the township's Corporatives gang. They were bullies who loved to terrorize women artists at concerts. Boykie was a massively built weightlifter who had tried many times to abduct Miriam, but had failed at every such instance, usually because someone bigger and stronger got in his way. When we ran into him on this night, however, we were sure he was going to take her. His one-legged friend, Kit, was dancing about on his crutch, whispering, "Let's take her, Boykie, let's take her." But Mike said, "For the two of you to do that, you're gonna have to kill me first." Boykie pointed at me. "Come on, man, he's only a little kid and has no business being with the babe." Mike repeated, "You heard what I said? I really mean it, you're gonna have to kill me." Realizing that Mike was serious, Kit and Boykie walked away, but not before Boykie screamed, "Yeah, Makeba, you got away this time, but I'll get you one day. My day will come." That night I realized that being Makeba's boyfriend was not necessarily going to be a joyride.

Each morning after leaving my grandmother's fish-and-chips shop, I now went directly to the Bantu Men's Social Center or the recording studios to work with the older musicians. I had to be around music. My skills were improving so much that I was being touted to replace one of my mentors, Elijah Nkwanyana, as the lead trumpet player of the African Jazz and Variety Revue. My only problem was convincing my parents that this opportunity was the gateway to my future.

One evening in late July 1956, I was pretending to be reading my history textbook at the kitchen table when my father came home. At first there was nothing out of the ordinary. He greeted everyone, then asked me, "So, boy, how's it going at school?" I barely got out two words when he kicked the chair from under me. "You little bastard, Sister Michael came by my office today and told me you had not been to school in three weeks. Where do you go every day?" By now I was up against the wall, shaking like a lamb about to be slaughtered. He came at me with fists and feet swinging in all directions. My mother, Johanna, and Elaine started crying. My mother begged him to stop slapping me around. I was dazed.

"Stop, Thomas, before you kill him," my mother said. My father whacked me a few more times before he stopped. He left the house breathing heavily, muttering disgust at my lies and deceit.

My mother sent me to the faucet outside to wash and change my shirt, which was now torn and buttonless. My grandmother fixed me something to eat, but I didn't have any appetite. My father returned long after dark. I heard him park his car in the garage, and counted his footsteps to the kitchen door. The house was quiet. My father went straight to his bedroom, where I overheard parts of my parents' muffled talk. I was too afraid to move. About an hour later, after their light went out, I got dressed, grabbed my trumpet case and a few clothes, and tiptoed to the kitchen, where I quietly wrote a letter to my parents.

> Dear Mama and Papa,
> I am very sorry to be a disappointment to you, but I cannot be what you had hoped I would amount to. I have lost total interest in school. I cannot hear what the teachers are saying; all I hear is music in my ears, nothing else seems to matter. What I am doing is not meant to hurt you. I love both of you very much, too much to want to wrong you, but I have made up my mind to be a musician. I know that I am good at it and that I will achieve great things in the world of music. If you cannot be on my side, I don't blame you. But I am going to follow what I think is right for me. I am leaving home. Do not worry about me. I will be all right.
>> All my love to you,
>> Your son, Minkie

I left the letter unfolded on the kitchen table. Then I eased out the back door, locked it, and slid the key under the door. It was a chilly winter night. I remember the sky, a spooky mixture of stars, scattered clouds, and a quarter moon. I strolled into the night and caught a bus at the corner of my grand-mother's fish-and-chips shop. In town I caught another bus from Diagonal Street to Western Native Township, where I went to Mike's place. Noticing that I was alone this time, Mike didn't ask any questions. He made a bed for me on his floor. I went to sleep without a clue what the next day was going to bring. It didn't matter. The rest of the night I willed my worries out of my soul. Only music rang in my ears.

For the next few nights, Mike and I cruised the shebeens around Western Native Township and Sophiatown, hanging out with friends. Dropping out of school and running away from home meant I had to find means to support myself. Finding work was easy. EMI and Gallo Records had studios and offices next to each other in downtown Johannesburg that attracted a steady flow of musicians who would mingle in front of the buildings, trying to spot a black recording scout who might give them a shot.

Dolly Rathebe was right: As bad as things in South Africa were for Africans, the government could not take away our music. But whites had figured out how to exploit it financially since 1916, when Gallo was established. Africans knew little about the business of music. They played and were paid what whites felt they were worth, which was very little. None of them were paid royalties for their songs. Hundreds of African, colored, and Indian musicians died penniless. Their families were left with nothing. The record companies, meanwhile, made hundreds of millions of dollars off their recordings. It's a practice that continues today, albeit not as badly as before.

Four days after I left home, Bra Zakes Nkosi hired me to play third trumpet in a band recording session at EMI. I was overjoyed. I was sitting in the studio next to my idols Elijah and Bangani and alongside Bra Zakes, Bra Gwigwi, Bra Kippie, and Bra Ntemi on saxophones, Jeff "Hoojah" Cartriers on bass, Zakes Mawela on drums, Lucifer on guitar, and Gideon Nxumalo on piano. This was a dream orchestra. I was smack in the middle of these giants of South African music.

I was given a solo, and while I was in the middle of rehearsing my part, my parents walked in with three of my uncles. I continued playing, but was very nervous. I tried not to make eye contact with my family—especially my father. I couldn't figure out what was going on. My heart was racing, my lips were dry, and my throat parched. Was my father going to snatch me out of the studio in front of all these people? How had they known where I was? Who had told them where to find me? I collected my thoughts and looked around the room. Bra Zakes's smile gave him away. He was a good friend of my parents.

Bra Zakes confessed that he had invited my folks to the studio. He said my parents needed to see me in a musical environment, observe how I interacted with professional musicians, and really hear how good I was. He said that was the only way they could be assured I truly had the potential to be successful in the music business. The session ended about an hour later. Bra Zakes led me to my parents. I stood before them in silence. I still couldn't make eye contact with Thomas. My mother hugged me and gave a big kiss on the cheek. "Come on, Boy-Boy," my mother said. "Let's go home. Everything is going to be just fine. You need to eat a good hot meal." I was relieved. My uncles were all smiling as we walked out of the studio.

Once we got outside, my father tossed me the keys to his new 1956 Chevy Impala. I was confused. He let me drive home. During dinner, no one said a word about my running away, the beating, or my decision to quit school. Because the winter school break had just started, my father had planned a family trip to Durban. Not only did he let me drive, but when we reached our destination, he shared his cigarettes and brandy with me. Although I was enjoying his camaraderie, I was still suspicious about why I was being treated as his buddy and peer. In Durban, we stayed with Aunt Clara, my father's youngest sister, who was the chief administrator of McCord's Hospital. The day after we arrived, we fetched my sister, Barbara, from Inanda Seminary, outside Durban, where she was a boarder. Barbara and I had visited Aunt Clara previously a couple of times. But my parents, my grandmother, Elaine, and Sybil had never seen the ocean before. Johanna was the most overwhelmed by the sea, which to her seemed like a biblical spectacle. She sat on a sand dune, marveling. With tears rolling down her cheeks, she said, "Now I can die. I have seen God at last."

During the vacation, my parents and Aunt Clara reopened the subject of my returning to school, but I stuck by my decision. My parents dropped their objections. I had convinced them I was serious about wanting to pursue a professional music career.

With things settled somewhat at home, I began putting my life plan into action. I continued playing with the Huddleston Jazz Band, with whom we recorded four 78-rpm records for Gallo. There was no contract, and we were paid only twenty-four pounds. I also played with the Merry Makers, and tried getting whatever recording sessions I could find. I kept writing to Father Huddleston, who was now in England, asking him to help me obtain a music scholarship overseas. His replies affirmed his commitment to help me, but I was feeling increasingly desperate.

The government was harassing the shit out of the arts community. My continued association with the deported priest and with his political allies caused the Special Branch Police to keep me under surveillance. All of us African artists, however, carried on the best way we could with our professions. Before Huddleston had departed, he'd started a foundation called the Union of South African Artists, whose mandate would be to assist African artists with the development of their skills and to protect their rights, especially in the case of record royalties. Union Artists, like the touring African Jazz and Variety Revue, promoted a concert series called "Township Jazz" that played for months at the Johannesburg City Hall. The sold-out shows were segregated and didn't have any activist content, because the government would have closed them down immediately and detained everybody. This was a very sensitive period: the ANC's Defiance Campaigns were in full force and many of the organization's leadership were appearing in the country's first treason trials. In Alexandra Township the ANC had just launched a bus boycott that lasted for more than a year, during which time the majority of the township's workers walked ten miles to their jobs in downtown Johannesburg and another ten miles home in the evenings. Because they walked through the city's white northern suburbs, the white residents were pressuring the government to stop this uprising, but it was impossible to break the back of Alexandra's determination.

The Union of South African Artists' headquarters was at Dorkay House, a four-story building next to the Bantu Men's Social Center on Eloff Street. Musicians from all over Johannesburg and the Witwatersrand townships were drawn to there—it was the only creative enclave at that time for African musicians, artists, poets, actors and singers. Bra Gwigwi Mrwebi quit his job at *Drum* magazine to become general secretary of Dorkay House alongside Myrtle Berman, an activist friend of Huddleston, who became managing director. Her husband, Monty, was an ex–concert pianist turned furniture designer who was also a radical political activist. Both were members of the South African Communist Party, as were most of South Africa's other radical politicians. They came in all colors, and had such a strong influence on the direction of our liberation struggle, that in the late 1950s the apartheid government introduced the Suppression of Communism Act, which not only helped it to curtail radical protest in South Africa, but justified murderous incursions into neighboring countries in southern and central Africa in the name of anticommunism. This was at the time when the McCarthy anticommunist witch hunts were terrorizing the lives of many popular artists in America, permanently destroying their careers.

The government, greedy white promoters, and the record companies were uneasy with what they saw as Dorkay House's radical agenda, and kept it under constant surveillance. Because it was now illegal for Africans to be on the streets after dark without proper documents, it was difficult for musicians, who worked mostly at night, to move about.

One night I was hanging out with some of the cast of African Jazz and Variety at Dorkay House. This was before I joined the group, but they were grooming me because there was a possibility that I'd be hired. I was asked to attend a few of their shows so I could learn their music. Before heading for their show at the Orange Grove Hotel, they sent me to buy some Gilbey's Gin from Wemmer Hostel, behind the BMSC, a spot where some of the inmates sold liquor illegally. As I was hurrying back, a passbook raid was taking place right in front of the Bantu Men's Social Center. The cops had a whole line of black men up against the wall, checking their passbooks. Bra Gwigwi's whistling from the fourth-floor window caught my attention. He mimicked to me that I should drink the booze in a hurry because no African wanted to get caught with illegal liquor. I looked heavenward and gulped the whole pint of gin, wiped my lips and chin, and chucked the bottle in some bushes in front of the Jubilee Center. The evidence was destroyed, but my throat and stomach were a rumbling inferno. I flipped my passbook from my rear pants pocket and showed these two Afrikaner cops my passbook without their asking. All they did was look me in the face. I was careful not to breathe on them or make eye contact. A cop shoved my passbook back into my hands, creasing the pages. They saw a cluster of black adults trying to make their way to Faraday Train Station, and hurried down the street like wolves after sheep; they were eager to fuck with somebody else. By the time I stumbled to the third floor, I was a drunken mess.

A few weeks later I got word that Alfred Herbert, the owner of African Jazz and Variety, had finally agreed to hire me. Herbie, as we called him, was the slick-talking son of South Africa's queen of Jewish vaudeville theater; he'd been raised backstage.

I was ecstatic. Soon I would be traveling with fifty-nine of some of the country's baddest musicians and singers. After rehearsing for a few weeks, we left for Cape Town, the first stop on a six-week tour. My Huddleston band buddies were happy for me, but heartbroken at the same time because I was leaving a big hole in the band. Miriam and I were so much in love that I ached at the thought of being away from her for six weeks. Johanna and Polina were at the train station. My mother managed a stiff upper lip, but my grandmother couldn't stop drying her eyes with her handkerchief. The opportunity had finally arrived for me to do what I loved best.

After settling in my compartment, I found some quiet space on the balcony of one of the cars and let my mind roam. As the train made its majestic, solitary passage, I marveled at the never-ending expanses of meadows, rivers, dams, and streams that made up the handsome province of the Orange Free State. The sky was a crystalline blue speckled with clouds. There were bolts of lightning on the horizon where the Drakensberg mountain range rose. I was experiencing the full beauty of this breathtaking land called South Africa, a land whose fertile and mineral-rich soil inspired bloodthirsty greed in the hearts of its European settlers, whose heartlessness and bigotry prevented them from sharing South Africa's bounteous wealth with its native population. My people had been vanquished and manipulated into a cheap labor pool, forced to reside in the squalor of the townships outside the Western architectural monuments of Caucasian conquest. I thought to myself, *I belong to these conquered people whose pride and self-esteem speak to the indestructible fact that you can conquer a people, but you cannot take away their knowledge of themselves or the deep well of pride from which springs poetry, prose, song, dance, architecture, style, cuisine, gait, laughter and courage, a legacy that can't be taken away even in the most demeaning and cruel of circumstances. Rest in peace, Hopane and Mamoshaba and all your forebears and brothers and sisters.*

King Jarvis, the company comedian and veteran vaudevillean actor, came to the balcony where I was contemplating the awesome heavens of my people's land and rudely interrupted my euphoria with his drunken arrogance. He figured since I was so young and new to the troupe, he could bully me. He started poking his fingers in my chest, telling me what a bad motherfucker he was. His sour, alcohol-laced breath was disgusting. I pushed him aside and told him to fuck off. I made my way to the compartment I was sharing with five other cast members. The collapsible table was stacked with about a dozen cans of cold Castle beer and three bottles of South African brandy. My compartment mates and I settled down to some serious drinking as darkness enveloped the countryside. The train's coal-driven engine unleashed a screaming flow of steam that whistled and echoed into the star-filled, half-moon night, possibly pissing off lovemaking rabbits, raccoons, wolves, foxes, bucks, birds, jackals, and other creatures hustling for survival in the eerie night of a racist kingdom whose bloody history they would never know.

6

FTER TWO NIGHTS ON THE TRAIN, our troupe finally pulled into the Cape Town station. We checked into the Tafelberg Hotel, in the District Six section of the Mother City, set aside originally for coloreds. Soon the government would displace this entire community and relocate its members to barren flatlands on the outskirts of town. Our hotel was surrounded by the magical Table Mountain and its mysterious tablecloth of clouds, below which the Atlantic Ocean and the Indian Ocean meet. This place is one of the world's wonders, its coastline lined with mountain ranges, bays, and peninsulas rich in almost every kind of marine life imaginable.

The African Jazz and Variety repertoire comprised covers of popular songs of the time. Ben "Satch" Masinga sang Louis Armstrong's "Blueberry Hill" and "Mack the Knife." He also sang a duet of "Baby It's Cold Outside," with Louisa Emmanuel, à la Ella and Satchmo. Louisa sang Doris Days "Secret Love," Joey Maxim sang Billy Daniels's "Old Black Magic," and did impersonations of Jerry Lewis. Isaac Petersen, whose voice resembled Nat King Cole's, sang "Mona Lisa." The Woodpeckers sang Harry Belafonte's "Day-O!" dressed in calypso dance outfits. Sonny Pillay, the star of the show, sang Frank Sinatra favorites. Dorothy Masuka sang "Let Me Go, Lover," and Dolly Rathebe sang Bobby "Blue" Bland's "It's Gone and Started Raining." Because most of the white audiences were Jewish, all the top stars of the revue had to sing Yiddish tearjerkers like "My Yiddishe Momma." There were forty singers on stage sitting on chairs, minstrel-style, with choreographed hand moves. The men wore beige suits and white gloves. The show was a mixture of vaudeville, cabaret, comedy, musical theater, and smoky nightclub jazz. The only township song was the finale "Into Yam'," which was a vocal dance hit, popularized on record by Dorothy Masuka. Here the cast went wild with all kinds of township dance routines. The highlight of the song came when all the women stood in line next to the footlights downstage, turned their backs to the audience, shook their large behinds up and down in rhythm, and then exited the stage with the male members of the cast lustily dancing in pursuit. This always brought the audience at Sea Point's Weizman Hall to its feet.

From Cape Town, we took a British ocean liner to Durban. The outstanding feature of this trip was that at sea, South African laws did not apply at all. The cast was invited to sit at the captain's table, which had been specially extended for us. The captain welcomed us enthusiastically and assured us that we were as free as any white passenger on his ship. Although the rest of the cast had been on this kind of voyage before, for me it was a special taste of total freedom from segregation and oppression that only exacerbated my hunger to get out of South Africa. That night I wrote Huddleston another long letter of appeal from the ship.

In Durban we stayed at Mrs. Phillips's boardinghouse, the only place that would accommodate black American merchant seamen working on the Farrel Lines, an international shipping company. I moved in with Louisa Emmanuel, her boyfriend Ray Jacobs, and another colored couple. The next day, however, the Woodpeckers persuaded me to move in with them because I would have the freedom to bring women to our quarters after the shows. These guys were the playboys of the company. The day after the first show at the Durban City Hall, they took me to Lamontville Township's supermarket, where they selected a buxom, big-hipped beauty whom we invited to the evening show, after which she came to the boardinghouse with me. The 'Peckers also brought their own women, and after a few bottles of brandy, we each dug into our partners with the lights on. From time to time the crazy singers would leave what they were doing to cheer me on, as if they were watching a soccer game. At first I was embarrassed, but they screamed, "Go ahead and do it, boy. Don't keep the babe waiting. We're with you all the way—yeah!" This bizarre scene was repeated every night with different women. Louisa and her roommates scolded the Woodpeckers, claiming they were corrupting me. But Victor Ndlazilwane, the group's leader, just laughed. "This boy is a man now, and he is having the time of his life. Don't try and turn him into a little pussycat. Go to your room and let the cobwebs envelop you in your dull existence. Leave the boy alone!"

Victor and his colleagues warned me that if I thought Durban was a man's paradise, I was in for a major treat in Port Elizabeth. When the revue hit Port Elizabeth, a coastal city along the Indian Ocean between Cape Town and Durban, we played for two sold-out weeks at the famous Feathermarket Hall. The Durban scene was repeated every night at our boardinghouse in New Brighton Township. After the show closed, we had a few days off before we were to head back to Cape Town. The Woodpeckers hadn't warned me sufficiently about the women of New Brighton. Every one that I had spent my nights with came back to my room in turns. It was obvious that they had arranged it among themselves to give each other a chance, because after one of them had spent a few hours with me, another would impatiently knock at my door. My current partner would suddenly remember something urgent she had to attend to, quickly jump into her clothes, and greet the one waiting outside very cheerfully. This went on for three days, right up until we boarded the bus, which took us to the ship. By then I was a pathetic, worn-out shadow of myself. The Woodpeckers literally helped me onto the ship with Victor laughing, "We warned you, sonny, but you wouldn't listen."

I was only seventeen, and I craved adoration and respect from the Woodpeckers. And they gave it to me. Things had been great, but now my johnson was so sore I had trouble walking upright. I had to sleep on my back because of the pain. Finally I went to a doctor in Cape Town and confessed my sexual antics. He told me, "You have gonorrhea. If you keep doing this kind of thing, you could end up dying or never be able to use your penis for anything except pissing. Does your family know what you're out here doing? This is disgusting!" My johnson had now become a painful scab. I had to take penicillin shots for the rest of the tour. It didn't matter: my addictions to alcohol and sex were well under way.

For the next year I progressed with the group to the point where I was leading the band. We toured pretty much nonstop. The makeup of the troupe would change slightly from time to time as musicians and other troupe members would leave and new ones join. While we were doing a six-week stint at the Johannesburg City Hall, Miriam joined our revue, replacing Dolly Rathebe, who went on maternity leave. Miriam was already, at twenty-five, unquestionably a full-fledged star. She had just quit the Manhattan Brothers because during a concert at the Bantu Men's Social Center, Boykie and Kit had reappeared, pulled out pistols, and tried to abduct her while she was on stage. A shoot-out ensued between Boykie and Kit and the Young Americans, Sophiatown's colorful gang led by Boetie Nkehle, fresh out of jail for a murder rap. Miriam barely escaped with her life, but because he'd saved her from abduction, she automatically became Boetie's girl. Herbie had been after Miriam to join his company for a while anyway, and offered her much more money than she was making with the Manhattan Brothers. More important, African Jazz promised her a safer environment than the Manhattan Brothers circuit, and, of course, my being in the band was an extra incentive. The two of us resumed our romance and lived together on the road for the next few months. This was the first time we experienced this kind of long-term, exclusive intimacy with each other—or, in my case, with anyone.

Dorothy Masuka and Victor, the leader of the Woodpeckers, had an open relationship while we were on the road because he was married back in his hometown of Benoni and had a few women in every city. Dorothy and Miriam were close friends, and when we got back to Port Elizabeth, Miriam went to live with Dorothy at her father's house. I went to stay at the old boardinghouse with my crazy friends the Woodpeckers, where we quickly returned to our debauchery. Miriam was furious and deeply hurt, and made it clear that she would not be as tolerant of my philandering as Dorothy was with Victor. I was too young to understand at the time, but I had just that quickly destroyed a beautiful relationship and broken the heart of someone who really loved me. By the time the show hit Cape Town, Miriam was cultivating a serious romance with Sonny Pillay, the star of the show. I was actually relieved, because Sonny was very close to the Woodpeckers and me, an occasional drinking buddy, and a highly sophisticated gentleman, far more disciplined than us. I was happy for Miriam and glad the pressure was off me.

By September 1957, I had become the bandleader of the show and felt I deserved a raise in pay from ten pounds a week to at least fifteen. Herbie disagreed—he told me I was too young for that kind of money. He said there was no way he was going to give me a raise. He asked, "How much does your father earn?" I replied, "Fifty-six pounds a month." Herbie said, "Now, if I pay you fifteen pounds a week, you'll be earning four pounds more than your father. Don't you think that would break his heart?" That was it. I wasn't going to take that kind of insulting bullshit. I quit on the spot. On the bus ride home from Pretoria, I was fuming but also felt a bit of a thrill. This was my first confrontation with a white man in South Africa, and though Verwoerd was still tightening his screws around Africans, I felt victorious nonetheless for confronting the exploitative Alfred Herbert. When I got home and told my parents, they screamed with laughter. "So, what do you plan to do now, boy?" my father asked.

That night I wrote Huddleston yet another letter. I explained that I was tired of the white shit in South Africa and asked him to please try to get me a music scholarship.

The following morning I went to Dorkay House. The place was buzzing with artists scurrying for appointments, musicians leaning against their horn cases, hoping to land a gig, or just practicing on their instruments playing jazz cover tunes and original compositions in one or the other small rehearsal rooms. In the large rehearsal hall I noticed some of the Manhattan Brothers caucusing with Todd Matshikiza, a gifted composer, journalist, and pianist. It turned out the Manhattan Brothers were going on a Cape Province tour and they needed a trumpet player—I was lucky enough to be hired on the spot.

For two decades the Manhattan Brothers had been South Africa's most popular group. However, their Cape Town concerts were only sparsely attended. Word was that they had stayed away too long and the Woodpeckers, who had also just left African Jazz, were now the new darlings of township audiences. Todd Matshikiza was abruptly summoned back to Johannesburg to begin work on the jazz opera *King Kong*. Clive Menell, the CEO of Anglo-Vaal Mining, who had been working for years with Todd to make the musical a reality, had secured enough investors. *King Kong* was about the life of the controversial heavyweight boxing champion Ezekiel Dlamini, who, while in prison for strangling his girlfriend to death in a jealous rage, committed suicide by drowning himself rather than serve his twelve-year sentence.

Mackay Davashe, Kippie Moeketsi, and Nathan Mdledle, the leader of the Manhattan Brothers, went out looking for a pianist to replace Todd. Christopher "Columbus" Ngcukane, the great bandleader and saxophonist from Cape Town's Langa Township, led them to Dollar Brand (now Abdullah Ibrahim), a brilliant piano player. For the next three months, as we crisscrossed the Eastern Cape, our reception went from fair to spectacular, but we were still not selling out our venues—nor were we making any money. I was spending a lot of time during my days with Kippie and Abdullah Ibrahim around a piano. They would teach me the complicated chord structures for the latest Thelonious Monk and Charlie Parker compositions and songs from the limitless book of Duke Ellington, Abdullah's favorite. Abdullah, who had brought his acoustic guitar along, often regaled us with folk songs from Cape Town's colored minstrel carnival. He was a living reservoir of that genre's repertoire. He also had a rib-cracking sense of humor. If I didn't make any money, at least I received a music education I could never have afforded from these two musical geniuses during our fateful summer tour.

On my return to Johannesburg, my parents along with my two younger sisters, Elaine, eleven, and Sybil, five, met me at Germiston station. When I got off the train, my sisters began to giggle at the sight of me. This continued all the way to our house in Natalspruit. Not understanding the reason for all this mirth, I finally asked my mother, "What is the matter with these girls?" She said, "Oh, Boy-Boy, my poor child, you are so thin. You look like a skeleton." My sisters now shrieked with laughter. My mother finally had to reprimand them. Shortly after moving back with my family, my father hit me with a dose of reality. He told me I was expected to pay a portion of the household bills and help look after Sybil. I was insulted at first, but deep down I knew he was right. I had left school and made the choice to live in an adult's world. Since I hadn't saved any money to get my own place, I had no choice but to live under his roof, by his rules.

My mother spoke to Mr. Hlahatsi, the chief clerk at the Natalspruit Municipal Office, part of the Germiston City Council, to see if he could get me a clerical job. Hlahatsi, who had known me as a child in Payneville, was much loved by the Afrikaner township manager, Mr. Williams, because of his head-scratching, ass-licking, Uncle Tom ways. He and my mother had worked under Buitendacht when he was a young township superintendent in Springs. Buitendacht was now Germiston's manager of native affairs and one of Verwoerd's top advisers. After bowing and cheesing on my behalf, Hlahatsi was able to secure me a job at the municipal office as a language interpreter/housing clerk for Du Plessis, a young, arrogant Afrikaner graduate of Stellenbosch University, the training ground for apartheid bureaucrats. I had to translate Zulu, Sotho, Tswana, Xhosa, and the other indigenous languages into Afrikaans for him. To qualify for a house in South Africa, an African had to prove that he had either been born in the area or had lived there for at least ten years—all in accordance with the government's Urban Areas Act and Influx Control legislation.

Every day I had to work in an office that was one of the principal mechanisms for oppressing Africans. I worked with bigoted Afrikaner administrators and alongside Uncle Tom blacks who looked the other way in order to keep their low-paying jobs. Here I was helping to process papers that dictated where and with whom people could live, translating for my "boss" what their exact status was, and getting caught right in the middle of the decisions that displaced so many Africans out of the areas they and their ancestors had been raised in, and deported them to barren, arid homelands and gulags—the

Siberias of South Africa—where it was next to impossible to eke out a living or even cultivate the hard, wretched earth to grow food or graze cattle. I was working deep inside the very system that engineered forced removals of families, prevented people from being together because of their ethnic backgrounds, and rearranged their lives so that the new Afrikaner hierarchy could dispossess them of their properties, their lands, their livestock, their pride and their humanity.

One of the oldest African residents in Germiston, known to just about everyone in the township, came into my office one day to complain that she had been asked to show proof in order to obtain a new home. She had never obtained any documents because she had lived in the area since the turn of the century and had never felt that such a process was necessary. "Even Buitendacht knows me. You can ask him yourself. Tell that little boy (Du Plessis) to phone Buitendacht now because he will tell him who I am." I modified the translation for Du Plessis, explaining her status and suggesting that he call the manager of native affairs. Du Plessis went crimson in the face. Infuriated, he screamed, "Tell this bloody kaffir old maid to get the hell out of my office. And that if she does not come here with the right papers, it's off back to blerry Lesotho with her black ass." I refused to translate his insult, and told him so. "Then the both of you blerry get out of my office." Du Plessis was now delirious. The old woman wanted to know what he was saying. I just said to her in Sotho, "It's all right. Let's go, Mama." I led her to my office across the corridor and told her that she was better off going to Buitendacht's office herself, because the little white boy didn't understand who she really was. She agreed, and left my office looking very surprised. I immediately went to Hlahatsi's office and tendered my resignation, much to his surprise. Watching Hlahatsi and the other clerks, all much older than me, carrying on like Stepin Fetchit, scratching, tap-dancing, and laughing even when they were insulted— "Oh, but the baas is such a funny baas, such a playful baas, such a kind baas"— was so sickening that I had often wanted to scream or throw up. It was nauseating, but this last episode with Du Plessis was the end of the line for me. I was not prepared to take any more of this shit. I had to get out of there before I killed someone. Mr. Williams, the township manager, summoned me into his office while I was packing my things and asked me to reconsider. He knew the old woman and would rectify the unfortunate mistake, but I told him enough was enough—I couldn't stay any longer, especially for seventeen pounds a month. I was out of there.

To make matters worse, there was no external outlet to vent my frustration. My parents also worked for this system. Even though they were respected because the city council couldn't function without their expertise, they were pissed off by Hlahatsi and his ilk. But they had very little choice—these were the only jobs available for people like them. Their only other alternative was to be political activists and go to jail. They were dedicated community workers, and people like the old lady that Du Plessis threw out of his office needed them all the time. They were not political animals. But I was embarrassed for them. After resigning, I had to watch my back because every township was teeming with government collaborators, and there really was no telling what consequences could befall me. My only consolation was that there were many like me who refused to take shit from racist white folks.

Hardly a week went by before my mother brought me a message to come and telephone Gwigwi from her office. I had caught a tidal wave of good luck. Todd Matshikiza had finished writing the music for *King Kong.* Jonas Gwangwa and I were required to copy the orchestral parts from the sketches, which Mackay, Kippie, Sol Klaaste, and Spike Glasser were writing out. These orchestrations would be the accompaniment charts for the different songs in the musical. South African–born Spike was specially brought from London's Goldsmith Music Conservatory to be the chief orchestrator, and Leon Gluckman, who was resident director at the Windmill Theatre in the West End of London, was chosen to direct the production. Spike and Leon were childhood friends.

This was a colossal undertaking. It was backbreaking work, but it felt good to be part of something that had to do with my craft. And at fifteen pounds a week, the money was delicious. Our team moved into Spike's mother's house in Berea, where the four orchestrators worked around the piano in the living room and passed the charts over to us, page by page, in the dining room, where we did all the copying of the individual orchestral parts. We worked from nine every morning until ten at night, with lunch and dinner breaks. Because we worked long hours, I moved in with the Bermans, who lived in Johannesburg's northern suburb of Sandringham, the reason being that the buses to Natalspruit stopped running at nine-thirty in the evening. When we finished work, we always repaired to Sam Tau's famous shebeen in Western Native Township, a favorite stop for musicians, actors, and journalists. Even if we got home at four in the morning, by eight o'clock we would always be waiting for Spike outside Dorkay House, hung over but ready to go to work.

This was our daily routine, except on Sundays, when we had to find our own way to Berea. There were no days off.

Two months later, in December of 1958, we had completed the orchestrations, and rehearsals went into full bloom with a cast of seventy and an eighteen-piece orchestra, in which I played third trumpet. We practiced in a warehouse not far from Dorkay House. For all of us this was a new experience, a combination of talented people of different races working united in the creation of an exciting project. Living with the Bermans opened my eyes to the ways of white folks. I had seen white opulence from the outside, but these folks had a *fine* house, maids and everything, including many indoor flush toilets. The Bermans were also old friends of my parents. They had met my folks during the Alexandra bus boycott, when they arranged car rides for the elderly and handicapped. Monty and Myrtle were genuine people; they welcomed me into their home and made me a part of their family.

On February 8, 1959, *King Kong* opened at the University of Witwatersrand's Great Hall, the only integrated venue in Johannesburg. The university had legal jurisdiction over its property and facilities, and although the government tried to prevent the opening, they lacked the authority to interfere. It was the first time that my parents and the relatives of the other African performers had a chance to see their children perform in an integrated setting. *King Kong* had a star-studded cast, with Miriam Makeba in the lead role of Joyce, the boxer's flirtatious lover. One of her solo songs, "Back o' the Moon," became a South African classic. Miriam, who had left African Jazz to join this musical, was now married to Sonny Pillay. Following the opening-night performance, the Bermans hosted a cast party at their Sandringham home. The neighbors called the police, who threatened to arrest everybody for conspiring to contravene the Immorality Act, which forbade socializing between Africans and whites. For hours the Bermans were defiant, hoping mass arrests of the *King Kong* cast and their distinguished guests would be good publicity and a further embarrassment for the racist regime. At about five o'clock in the morning, Colonel Spengler, the head of the Special Branch Police, called the Bermans with his final threat. By now we were tired and leaving the party, and the Bermans had once more checkmated Spengler. The party was over.

A few months into the run of the show, Sonny Pillay left African Jazz and Variety for greener pastures in London. I wished him well, though I was envious as hell. He promised to see Huddleston on my behalf, and find out how much progress had been made regarding my scholarship. Once he settled in England, Sonny wrote to me regularly. He also reassured me that Huddleston was trying his best. After a while, Huddleston wrote to the Bermans saying he had asked Johnny Dankworth and Yehudi Menuhin to assist him in finding me a scholarship. Huddleston said in one of his letters that both Dankworth and Menuhin felt that I needed "legitimate" trumpet and music theory lessons from reputable instructors whose recommendations would strengthen my chances of getting a scholarship. The Bermans used their connections to get me a trumpet tutor, Joe Vitali, who played first trumpet with the Johannesburg Symphony Orchestra. Mrs. Bradford, the head of music theory at Wits University, also offered to give me lessons. Both of them waived tuition fees. I felt fortunate because this was probably an opportunity that no African musician had received before.

Following the eight-month Johannesburg run, *King Kong* went on the road for two months to Cape Town, Port Elizabeth, and Durban. Once again, Miriam and I became an item, much to the surprise of everybody in the cast because Sonny and I were such good friends, but Miriam and I didn't let that bother us. Somehow we always found it difficult not to be intimate whenever the chance presented itself—we followed our hearts for better or worse. Besides, when she fell in love, scandal never bothered Miriam Makeba. She was brazen and acerbic with anybody who tried to get in her business. This was probably why the press never wrote about her affairs. No journalist wanted to feel the wrath of Miriam Makeba.

Toward the end of the Johannesburg run of *King Kong*, Miriam fell ill and had to have an operation. Prematurely released from the hospital and still very weak, she insisted on flying to Cape Town to perform. Just before curtain time, Miriam got her heel stuck in a crack backstage and severely sprained her ankle. The wardrobe department had to go and buy her a larger pair of shoes because her ankle was badly swollen. Another night, Dambuza, who played King Kong, was to act as if he was strangling Miriam. He got carried away and flung her across the stage, causing her to exit stage left on her belly. She still had abdominal stitches from her operation. Everybody in the cast gasped with fear that she would be seriously injured. But, resilient as always, Miriam carried on with the show. In October 1959, *King Kong* came to an end. When the train pulled into Johannesburg's Park Station from Durban, we all said our good-byes.

An American filmmaker, Lionel Rogosin, had come to South Africa a year earlier. He quietly shot an antiapartheid docudrama titled *Come Back Africa.*

Miriam, who sang in it, was invited to the Venice Film Festival for the screening. To obtain a passport, Ian Bernhardt, the chairman of Union Artists, had Miriam write in her application that she was invited to Venice to be honored for her role in *King Kong*. Miriam's departure was kept a secret. Only her ailing mother, a practicing *sangoma* (traditional healer), her eight-year-old daughter, Bongi, and Bernhardt knew her departure details. Ian and I accompanied Miriam to the airport. Ian felt that if too many people knew she was leaving, especially the press, the government might start nosing around and find out about *Come Back Africa*. She departed South Africa in November 1959. A week later the country learned that the documentary had been secretly filmed and had now won the festival's award for best film. Verwoerd was furious, and the South African government looked foolish in the eyes of the international community. The Afrikaners wondered how, with their sophisticated intelligence network, a film like that could be made right under their noses. And to rub salt in their wounds, how could Miriam slip out of the country on a bogus visa?

Although the money I had earned from the *King Kong* tour was more than I had made being on the road with the African Jazz, my expensive taste in clothes and other luxuries left me with meager funds. I was hoping for another stroke of good luck that would keep me in money. The last thing I wanted to do was to end up back at my parents' home, doing chores and baby-sitting Sybil. One thing for certain: I was never going to take another clerical job working for racist white folks.

Soon after the closing of *King Kong,* John Mehegan, a pianist and jazz professor from New York's Juilliard School of Music and Columbia University, came to South Africa with his wife, Terry, a beautiful young woman. John and Terry, who came from the bohemian environment of New York's Greenwich Village, were completely outraged by the absurdity of apartheid laws, which had taken them by total surprise. They had heard about discrimination in South Africa, but, not being political activists, they had expected the kind of Jim Crow environment that was slowly disappearing in America because of the civil rights movement. The severity of what they met enraged them. Their newspaper interviews supporting African causes rankled the government. The couple made matters worse by hanging out with us musicians in the township shebeens and walking nonchalantly with us down Johannesburg streets. John gave free music lessons to me, Kippie, Jonas, and other African artists, while charging whites fifteen pounds per lesson. John also featured us on two albums that he recorded for Gallo. The government frowned on any fraternizing with "the natives," and soon got fed up with the Mehegans. Like others before them, they were asked to leave the country. John and Terry soon left, but not until I had bent John's ear, begging him to help me get a scholarship. A month later John sent us copies of *Downbeat* magazine, where he had written an article on his visit to South Africa and the musical talent that was there.

By September 1959, the government was cracking down with spine-chilling vehemence, infuriated by the ongoing Treason Trials and the escalating demonstrations against pass laws. With the formation of the Pan-African Congress, led by Robert Sobukwe, with its slogan, "Africa for Africans," Verwoerd's minions began wielding the hammer of repression with a vengeance. The disrespect that was being hurled at them by the nonracial South African Council of Students and the audacity of Walter Sisulu, Oliver Tambo, Nelson Mandela, and their ANC colleagues, denigrating and vilifying the government's hallowed legislations in their court defenses, was the straw that broke the camel's back. The resulting repression could be felt everywhere.

Work was drying up all over the country, even in Johannesburg, the entertainment mecca of South Africa. Jonas, Kippie, and I got word that Abdullah Ibrahim had formed a trio with young Makhaya Ntshoko on drums and bassist Johnny Gertze, playing to packed houses at the Ambassadors nightclub in Woodstock, next to District Six. We got in touch with Abdullah, and he told us to come down as soon as we could. We took the train to Cape Town and began rehearsing with the trio the very morning we arrived, not even having made any arrangements for accommodation. For the first few nights the three of us slept on mattresses on the floor in the back of the club. I put in a call to Dawn Levy, a radical University of Cape Town student activist with whom I became very close during the African Jazz and *King Kong* days. Her cousin, Tessa Kahn, was engaged to Jackie Marks, whom I'd met on my first trip to Cape Town in 1956, when he had driven me to all kinds of jam sessions around the city. This was also when I met the great saxophonist Morris Goldberg. Jackie came from a very wealthy real estate family that owned luxury properties all along the bay. He was in the middle of renovating an apartment in Camps Bay, one of the peninsula's most beautiful and pristine beach areas. He offered the apartment to us as a place to stay. Of course, Africans were not allowed anywhere near Camps Bay except as domestic help or laborers. Jackie brought us through the service entrance as painters. The house painting had already been completed, but the paint, brushes, rollers, drop cloths, and other equipment were still lying around. Jonas, Kippie, and I had to wear the soiled overalls when we were in the apartment just in case the white neighbors came around asking why there was always a bunch of kaffirs hanging around the place. Dawn was also kind enough to lend us her little Morris Minor car. We would return from the Ambassadors long after midnight, and sometimes Kippie, feeling no pain from the brandy, would be in a boisterous, rebellious mood and start questioning why we had to enter through the back, dressed as painters. "Why the fuck should we come home through the fucking back door? Isn't this our country? The fuckin' Afrikaners should be wearing these fuckin' overalls and coming to our township houses through the back doors to paint our fuckin' places. This is rubbish, man." Jonas and I would beg Kippie to please shut the fuck up until we were inside the apartment. Fortunately, we were never busted.

We performed seven nights a week to packed houses at the Ambassadors. We rehearsed every day from ten to seven, and had a few hours' break before our first show. We played bebop favorites by Monk, Gillespie, Miles, and Charlie Parker, and evergreens by Ellington, Waller, and others. We also composed our own modern tunes, a cross between mbhaqanga and bebop. Abdullah and Kippie were the most prolific composers, although Jonas and I contributed a few songs. Abdullah came up with a brilliant name for us: the Jazz Epistles. There had never been a group like the Epistles in South Africa. Our tireless energy, complex arrangements, tight ensemble play, languid slow ballads, and heart-melting, hymn-like dirges won us a following and soon we were breaking all attendance records in Cape Town. People would sit on the floor and around the edge of the bandstand at the Ambassadors when all the seats were filled. You literally had to walk sideways to move an inch. Reservations had to be made three or four days ahead, otherwise there was no way to get in.

By the Christmas holiday season, the Jazz Epistles were the talk of Cape Town. The tourists, the township folks (coloreds and Africans) from Athlone, District Six, Goodwood, Langa, and all over the Cape Flats, flocked to see us. The wealthy white folks who had suntanned along the sandy beaches all crowded into the Ambassadors nightclub. And the women—*lawd have mercy!*— the most beautiful women of every color and shade filled the joint.

One night Jonas and I kept noticing these two golden, suntanned white girls sitting at the foot of the bandstand in the shortest skirts imaginable—long before the appearance of the mini. They couldn't keep their eyes off us, and every time we looked directly at them, they would flash us the biggest come-on smiles. These babes were fearless, but I was scared shitless. There was no way we could have these girls with the silly Immorality Act staring us in the face. I might have been crazy, but I wasn't stupid. When our break came, Jonas and I rushed to the back of the club, but these girls were hot on our heels. When they caught up with us, they didn't waste any time. Before I knew it, one of them had her tongue almost down my throat. She was kissing me passionately with her eyes closed and one hand on my johnson, while she put my hand on her G-stringed ass. When we finally came up for air, I asked, "Oooweee, what's your name, baby?" "Rosalind, but you can call me Roz. Kiss me," she gasped. We submerged one more time. By now I was about to explode. I can't remember how long it was before Kippie, Makhaya, Johnny, and Abdullah finally came to the back. On hearing their approaching footsteps, we disengaged and the girls slid out of there, but not before Roz whispered, "We'll see you after the show. I'm coming with you wherever you're going."

"Oh shit, man, it looks like you two are fixing to go to jail, hey? Look at your fucking faces, then! Please take me with you," Johnny Gertze joked. All of us burst out laughing as Jonas and I rushed to the bathroom to wash our faces. Roz and her friend, Denise, came to the Ambassadors almost every night. And Roz badly wanted to lay some trim on me. "What are you so scared of?" she asked me. I was too terrified. All I had on my mind was getting out of South Africa. The quest for the scholarship had me too obsessed to fuck around with something as dangerous as Roz. Anyway, one night, Spike, who was now head of the music department at the University of Cape Town, had a party at his house in Wynberg. Roz nailed me in one of the bedrooms. She locked the door and we threw down—except all the time we were getting down, I was more nervous than a broke-dick dog. "What are you so scared of?" she asked me as I kept looking at the window and the door. I just couldn't reach a climax, and after a long time and many of her screams, which I tried to muffle, we joined the rest of the party. Every time she looked at me, she whispered, "Let's go back." All I could do was shake my head.

In early January 1960, we decided to take the Jazz Epistles to Johannesburg. When I got home, my parents and three sisters had a warm welcome for me. Barbara was still on school holidays. It struck me that this was one of the few times that all six of us were together. It was nice having peace in our home. My parents were getting along better, and were now completely comfortable with my decision to be a musician. My grandmother Johanna had moved into her new home in Ennerdale. I was particularly happy to hang out and share confidences with Barbara, who was going to be nineteen in July. Two weeks later she returned to Durban for school. I would not see her again for four years.

After almost four years of hounding Huddleston, I finally heard from Myrtle Berman that he'd written her that through the intercession of Yehudi Menuhin and Johnny Dankworth, I had been accepted to London's Guildhall School of Music. The only obstacle standing in my way now was obtaining a passport.

The Jazz Epistles played a few clubs around Johannesburg. We were also hustled into Gallo's main studio one afternoon to record a long-playing album of some of our compositions. It was called *The Jazz Epistles Verse I,* the first such album by an African group. The only drag was that we were paid a measly seventy-six pounds for our hard work. Even though the recording took only two hours because we knew our music inside and out, we still felt we should have been paid much more. Of course this was a one-time project. Gallo did not sign us to a contract. The quick release of our album shot our popularity through the roof and we were booked into the Selborne Hall, a satellite of Johannesburg City Hall, for six weeks. Tickets for the shows sold out within a few days. This time we were making some good money. We scheduled equal performance days for whites and Africans. In our shows there were no announcements; we just played wall-to-wall songs for three hours without a break. Our audiences were overwhelmed by our "awesome stamina, outstanding musicianship, and most of all, our Bohemian outfits," as one journalist put it. I had already applied for a passport and was phoning the Pretoria Department of the Interior offices almost every day to find out when it would be issued. "We'll call you," was always the curt Afrikaans reply.

We had just finished convincing Ian Bernhardt from the Union Artists to book us on a nationwide tour that was scheduled to begin in April. I was aching to go on the road and make more money so that I would have fat pockets should I leave for England. But things soured that March. I came home one day and my mother told me that she and my father were near the end of their marriage. My mother just came out with it: "Boy-Boy, I am going through hell living with your father. We have nothing left between us and it is painful to be here. I really don't know what to do, my child." The news floored me.

Miriam Makeba was now living in New York, where she had become the toast of America, after making her debut on *The Steve Allen Show.* Following her first appearance at New York's Village Vanguard, where celebrities like Duke Ellington, Sarah Vaughan, Ella Fitzgerald, Mahalia Jackson, Nina Simone, Miles

Davis, Dizzy Gillespie, Marlon Brando, Sammy Davis Jr., Sydney Poitier, and Harry Belafonte, among others, came to see her perform, she went on to play America's top nightclubs and concert halls with either Belafonte or the Chad Mitchell Trio. Miriam wrote to me often, enclosing rave press reviews of her performances. She also sent large packages of the latest U.S. jazz recordings, clothes, shoes, and letters from Dizzy Gillespie. She had told Dizzy all about me, and he started to send me albums by Miles, Monk, the Modern Jazz Quartet, Horace Silver, Duke, Sarah, and Nina. I was overjoyed by Miriam's continuing generosity and deeply moved by her efforts on my behalf. More than that, I was ecstatically happy for her. The success she was achieving filled us all with pride back home. When I read excerpts of her letters to our colleagues and *Drum* magazine reporters at Dorkay House and in the shebeens, they were so overjoyed that they applauded, whooped, and hollered at the end of my reading. Miriam also said she had talked to Belafonte, Louis Armstrong, Dizzy Gillespie, and John Mehegan about helping me get to New York for school.

In early March, my parents took me to see Buitendacht, now Germiston's Manager of non-European Affairs, about using his influence so that I could get my passport. I was ashamed to see how my parents had to grovel at this motherfucker's feet, calling him *baas* and *morena* (king). In Payneville, it was my mother who had taught him the ropes when he was a rookie superintendent fresh out of Stellenbosch University. At the time, he was green and knew nothing about African life. Now here he was, sitting on his high horse as manager of Native Affairs. Sickened as I felt, I was nevertheless helpless. I needed the damn passport. In order to be issued one, an African had to supply a letter of reference from his local police station, the Special Branch Police, his parish priest, his last school principal, a letter from his overseas sponsor, a letter of acceptance from the school to be attended, four hundred pounds in cash in case the applicant was stranded abroad, proof of available funds for a round-trip ticket, sufficient expense money for six months, and a health certificate. They really made it almost impossible for a kaffir to leave the country. Buitendacht told my parents and me that it was a waste of time to go through the trouble of trying to study music overseas. Instead, I should finish school and get a constructive job in South Africa. I looked at the motherfucker like he was crazy, quietly cussing him under my breath. In the end he said he would try his best and telephone my parents with a disposition. We never heard from him.

On March 21, shortly after the visit to Buitendacht, I was at Dorkay House with Ian Bernhardt, preparing our itinerary for the Jazz Epistles' national tour, when we got word that the police had just opened fire on a crowd of Africans in

Sharpeville, who were demonstrating against the town council's raising of rents. More than 69 demonstrators were killed and 250 wounded. Almost all of them were shot in the back while fleeing from the police. I didn't understand the full import of what had happened until the following day. We only had state-controlled radio stations and a few newspapers. There was no television. People in the townships were roaming the streets, furious at this news. An atmosphere of major rebellion was in the air. Robert Sobukwe and many of his colleagues held a demonstration where they all burned their passbooks in public. The entire ANC leadership, with Albert Luthuli at the helm, immediately repeated the same action. More than thirty thousand people marched from Langa Township to Cape Town City Hall to protest the outrage. All over the country, rallies, demonstrations, and marches were being organized. The government rolled out the army and elite police with battle tanks, armored military trucks and vans, and tens of thousands of troops to man strategic points in the townships and other volatile parts of the country. The atmosphere was tense.

The government declared a state of emergency and the country was turned into a military state. Gatherings of more than ten people were outlawed. Because of this new law, Bernhardt told us our national tour had to be canceled. The detention of political leaders of the ANC, the PAC, the Communist Party, and the trade unions, along with other radical activists, went into high gear. Some leaders fled the country illegally. Mandela and Tambo announced the beginning of the armed liberation struggle from Tanzania. Other African leaders sought asylum in the few newly independent African countries. All liberation organizations were now banned. The government was especially incensed that Mandela and Tambo had slipped through their fingers.

Shortly, Mandela returned to South Africa and for the next few years lived as a fugitive all over the country, visiting his new wife, Winnie, while keeping on the run. It was decided that Oliver Tambo should remain abroad, where he would keep the ANC alive, lobby support internationally for the liberation struggle, and arrange for the training of fighters. I was continuing my studies with Vitali and Bradford. After a late lesson one night, I went to sleep over at the Bermans. Just before midnight, members of the Special Branch Police came to arrest Monty. They turned over every drawer and desk and ransacked most of the house, looking for documents. As they led Monty handcuffed out the front door, they were surprised to see me sleeping on the couch. One policeman asked, "What are you doing here in the white people's living room?" I quickly made up some shit about coming to visit my aunt and her boyfriend, but their one room was too small for me to sleep, so the *baas* let me sleep on the couch. The policemen didn't believe me. One of them called Spengler to inquire what should be done about me. All Spengler kept screaming in his ear was: "Fuck the kaffir, do you have Berman?" The policeman would answer in a concerned voice, "Yes, we have Berman, but there is a kaffir in the house." Spengler repeated, "I said, fuck the kaffir, do you fucking have Berman?" One more time the policeman answered, "Yes, we have Berman." "Then, fucking, bring him to me for fucking godsakes," Spengler exploded. The policeman took my passbook details and vowed to follow up on my lie.

After the police left with Monty, it took a long time for us to go back to sleep. The next morning Myrtle, surrounded by her four daughters and her housekeeper, was very cool, but obviously upset for the children's sake. She told me it was best that I go home and lie low, because if the police came back and found me, there would surely be trouble.

When I got to Natalspruit Township, the streets were crawling with black and white policemen armed with machine guns atop tanks, ready to kill. This was the first time I had seen something like this. African policemen had never carried guns before. The previous night, when the white policemen had arrested Monty, was my first time I'd ever seen a white man in handcuffs. When I told my parents what had happened, they agreed that I should stay close to home. I also told my mother that Myrtle had asked that she not call her at work or home, because all the telephones were most likely tapped. In a few days the police came back for Myrtle, leaving her daughters with the housekeeper. Even though I was lying low, I paid occasional visits to Dorkay House, where the mood was pretty glum, especially after Myrtle's arrest. Everyone was very down. However, many Dorkay House members had joined the underground, preparing to go into exile for training, or just helping to organize sabotage squads in their townships. At Whitey's shebeen near the Albert Street Pass Office, where most of the *Drum* magazine staff came to drink, I ran into the journalist Lewis Nkosi, who had written in his *Golden City Post* Sunday column about how I had been found in the Bermans' living room when the police came to arrest Monty. He was with my cousin Ronnie Manyosi, a fellow journalist and crack photographer. I went after Lewis: "You motherfucker, you dirty motherfucker. How the fuck could you write something like that when you know I am waiting for my passport? Whose side are you on, anyway?" I wanted to kill him.

Ronnie stepped between us, as Lewis objected while backing out the door. "I'm just doing my job, I'm a journalist," he said.

"Journalist, my fuckin' black ass," I said. "I swear Lewis, don't let me catch you alone. I'm going to break your head because I don't care anymore. You fucked me up for life."

Somebody pulled him away from Whitey's while he was still protesting, "I'm a journalist. I'm a journalist."

Just in case the Special Branch Police might come looking for me after Lewis's stupid piece, I went to stay at my uncle Kenneth's house in Springs. He put me to work looking after his supermarket while he took off for Durban, claiming he had never been on a holiday. He said there was no way the police would come looking for me in his shop. I would be safe there. This was all tongue-in-cheek, of course.

Three weeks after Sharpeville, Premier Hendrik Verwoerd was shot point-blank, but the assassin failed to kill him. The incident gave him a whole new "messianic" persona. After his release from the hospital and recovery, Verwoerd began wearing white suits. To celebrate the assassination's failure, he gathered his cabinet and staunchest followers to a ceremony where he released a white dove into the air. The dove refused to fly and instead walked away from the ceremony, with press photographers snapping it from every possible angle. It was not a good omen.

From that day on, the apartheid guillotine came crashing down on the country with more venom than ever before. Spengler's Special Branch Police surveillance was intensified; a huge budget was created to pay more agents and collaborators. Political arrests, banishments, assassinations, house arrests, banning orders, accelerated treason trials, and every manner of ploy to get the country under apartheid's foot was introduced into the daily lives of South Africans. Our paranoia had now been upgraded to fear, loathing, suspicion, anger, and hate.

The next month was even tenser. There was no music work. Everyone was on edge. Tired of sitting at home, one day I decided to go to Dorkay House to see if anything was happening. Besides, a few days earlier, Ian Bernhardt had left a message for me at home that he needed to see me. When I arrived at Dorkay House, he told me that Robert Loder of Anglo American Mining, a major supporter of Union Artists, had secured the money for my round-trip airplane ticket to England, plus five hundred pounds in pocket money. I was a step closer to getting out of South Africa. I was thrilled, but stayed guarded. I really had to be cool and stay below the police radar. Kippie and the Epistles were upset that I would soon be leaving the group, but they understood. Besides, we couldn't work anyway.

Around mid-May, my mother called me in Springs and told me it was urgent that I come home because there was something very important she needed to discuss with me. My uncle Kenneth had just returned from his vacation. Worried, I hurried back to Natalspruit, apprehensive and wondering what kind of news my mother had in store for me. When I got to the house, she was still at work. When she came home for lunch, she told me to sit down at the kitchen table. She then pulled a passport out of her bag and put it in front of me. I was so happily stunned and excited that I jumped into her arms and hugged her tight. I rushed in my father's car to tell Ian Bernhardt the news. He quickly called the travel agent to book me on a plane the next day. The night before my departure, I wrote a long letter to Barbara. It was sad having to leave without seeing her. She had been my first friend. The following morning I picked up my tickets and pocket money, drove back home, and started packing.

My parents took the afternoon off from work, and after a light lunch we drove to the airport with my sisters Elaine and Sybil. I waved good-bye to my grandmother, who had come to bid me farewell. She had raised Barbara and me in Witbank, and the reality of my departure hit me full-blast because for the first time I had a strong feeling that this would be the last time I would be seeing my sisters, parents, grandmother, and all the people I had known all my life. Fearing that the Special Branch Police could show up anytime, we had made my departure as low-key and secretive as possible, because the fact of my having been present in the Bermans' house during Monty's arrest hung like a dark cloud over my exit.

My grandmother told me, "I don't care what you do, Mousie, you don't have to send any money or gifts, even if you're very successful. Just always remember one thing: Write to your mother, my child."

Although I was very sad to be leaving, deep in my heart I was excited and relieved to be leaving this cursed, godforsaken land.

Alf Kumalo, a family friend and *Drum* magazine photographer, my uncle Putu, and his three young sons met us at the departure lounge. My flight was announced around four o'clock. After Uncle Putu led a short prayer, we posed for some final pictures. I hugged my dad and kissed my mother and sisters. I was paranoid. I kept thinking the Special Branch Police were going to show up and arrest me. I was anxious to clear immigration. After I passed through the turnstiles and the security officers, I turned and waved to everyone who was now pressed against the fence. Alf somehow got onto the tarmac and was snapping away.

I entered the plane and was shown to my aisle seat by a white stewardess who insisted on calling me "sir." Everybody else on the airplane was white. I was praying feverishly for the Special Branch Police not to show up. When the airplane finally took off, it was as though a very heavy weight had been taken off me—as if I had been painfully constipated for twenty-one years and was finally taking the greatest shit of my life. I said a little prayer for Monty and Myrtle, Robert Sobukwe, and all the thousands of political detainees who were up for treason. Because our flight to London was going via Salisbury, Nairobi, Khartoum, Cairo, and Rome, the pilot announced that it would take twenty hours.

Twenty hours! I thought a bottle of brandy and about six beers should get me to London easily. I realized for the first time that I had never ordered a lawful drink in my life. In the shebeen, when you ordered drinks, you asked for "a straight and fill the table," which meant a full bottle and twelve beers. A "half-jack" was a pint, a "nip" was half a pint, a "honey" was a quarter of a pint. When the pilot announced that we would be landing in Salisbury in thirty minutes, I figured that the honey and one beer would do. But the white passengers were ordering gin and tonic, rum and coke, brandy and ginger ale, vodka and orange juice, whisky and soda water. It all seemed so strange to be drinking lawfully. Back home we didn't mix our drinks; we had to share one glass, and often we had to drink in a hurry before the police came. The trick was to consume the evidence as quickly as possible and then break the empties. The police raids seemed so stupid now that I was sitting in this plane drinking with all these nice white folks who were ogling me unashamed, wondering if this nigger would know how to order a civilized drink.

Sensing the pressure that was now hovering over my social shortcomings, I was able to summon some of my moviegoing memories, and Humphrey Bogart came to me in a much-needed vision of social redemption, sitting in a bar on a high stool, cigarette dangling from his mouth, arrogantly telling a black barman, "A triple shcotch on the rockksh, light on the shoda." I channeled that voice, complete with the lisp, much to the disappointment of the oglers, except the stewardess, who was anxious to lock up the galley before the plane landed. The drink she brought me was fizzy and flat-tasting, and the ice had diluted it. It lacked the shebeen sting of a neat drink—I decided right then that Bogart was a wimpy drinker. However, I ordered the same drink at every stopover and by the time I arrived in London, I should have been sloshed. But I was too excited to get drunk.

We landed in London on Wednesday, May 18, 1960.

PART II

TheWorld

7

FTER LANDING IN LONDON, I took a bus to Victoria Station to meet my friend Sonny Pillay, struck all the while by the uniformity of the architecture. It became immediately clear why the little box houses in the townships in South Africa were all arranged in endless, identical rows—the British had simply transposed their unimaginative town-planning to South Africa. The view from the bus was miles and miles of identical semi-detached homes that made me feel like the same street was repeating itself, as in a cartoon, even though the bus was moving at fifty miles an hour. It was neat and orderly, but dizzyingly boring.

Sonny was waiting with Woodrow Lekhela, the former classmate at St. Peter's who had taught me to smoke cigarettes so I could sing bass; his father was now teaching high school in London. The three of us were young and newly free, buzzing with excitement at our sudden new lives—we were joking and riffing at the tops of our lungs as we rode the underground train back to Sonny's place in Hampstead, alarming and appalling the stiff commuters hiding behind their morning newspapers. They just made us laugh louder.

Sonny had a tastefully furnished ground-floor flat in Hampstead Heath—I could see his singing career was going well. But what fascinated me most was Sonny's television set. I had never seen television before; Verwoerd had banned it in South Africa because he considered it a source of dangerous information. Later that summer we all watched the Olympic Games from Rome. Sonny and I sat drinking whisky, cheering Tennessee State University's "Tigerbelle" Wilma Rudolph win her three gold medals; we jumped and screamed during the marathon as Ethiopia's Abebe Bikila, the skinny barefoot policeman, became the first African to win a gold medal in Olympic history; we were dazzled by an eighteen-year-old American boxer named Cassius Marcellus Clay Jr., who won the light-heavyweight gold medal.

We spent that first evening drinking and reminiscing about African Jazz and Variety, St. Peter's, Sharpeville, Mandela, Sobukwe, Verwoerd, the Spoilers, the Young Americans and Msomi gangs, the BMSC, Dorkay House, international politicians, the girls back home with their gigantic butts, and everything else pertaining to South Africa. Sonny and Woodrow told me about the anti-apartheid protests outside the South African embassy in Trafalgar Square, and the fiery speeches by Trevor Huddleston and other radical activists who led the huge gatherings.

Later we went to a nearby Indian restaurant where we had dinner and drank more whisky. I wouldn't leave my passport behind, and every time I saw an English policeman, I reached for my back pocket the same way a gunslinger reaches for his pistol in a western film. My friends laughed at me and tried to assure me that in England the police were there to protect and not harass me, something that took me a very long time to get used to. Being able to walk around freely, enter any establishment, not worry about curfew, socialize with anybody—all this was new to me. The apartheid laws had become etched into my subconscious. I lived with a private fear of uniforms. Even now, I react whenever I see a policeman; I have to remind myself constantly that I am a liberated human being, more than forty years after I first left South Africa.

Back at the flat, we carried on celebrating. By two in the morning we were unaware of how loud our conversation had gotten, but we must have been screaming at the top of our lungs. Just before dawn, we finally passed out after Sonny went through a painful session of vomiting all the drink and food he had consumed. Later that morning the landlady came and gave Sonny a week's notice to vacate the apartment because of the noise we had made the previous night.

During that first week, I went to greet Huddleston in Holland Park, his church's headquarters. As usual, he was preoccupied with organizing anti-apartheid strategies, but gave me a hearty welcome. He pointed out that Yehudi Menuhin and Johnny Dankworth, to help me get out of South Africa, had only arranged for the letter from the Guildhall School of Music that had enabled my exit—to enroll, I would have to pass the entrance examinations. In the meantime, he told me to call Dankworth, who was keen to meet me.

The following night, I went to Ronnie Scott's nightclub in Soho to see Johnny Dankworth and his band. I was unimpressed with the musicianship in England; my heart was already pushing to go to New York where the real giants of jazz reigned. Dankworth was over the moon that I had made it out of South Africa. We met again the following evening outside the Savoy Hotel to see Sammy Davis's show at the Palladium. Davis did a two-and-a-half-hour show, singing, dancing, and telling jokes, clowning, doing impersonations, and sweating like a long-distance runner. His performance was stunning. Dankworth introduced me to the great entertainer at the backstage party, and Sammy encouraged me to study music in New York. He said he would be looking out for me when I came to America, and that Miriam knew where to get in touch with him. After Dankworth dropped me off at Sonny's flat, I never saw Johnny again. This was no fault of his. I just had America on my mind.

Early the next morning Sonny and I packed our few belongings into an English cab and moved to a two-room flat he had found on Glenloch Road in Belsize Park. I felt immediately uncomfortable with the building because at the entrance there was a sign that read SHHHH, NO NOISE AFTER 9 P.M. At the foot of the stairs were two more signs, one saying PLEASE WALK QUIETLY UP AND DOWN THE STAIRS. The other one said NO VISITORS AFTER 9 P.M. Inside our door was another one: NO BATHING AFTER 9 P.M. We were not too happy living in this flat. From time to time Sonny would go up to Newcastle for the taping of a variety show he sang in. One day he came back from the show with three beautiful blonde dancers. They stayed until five in the morning, drinking quietly with us. We spoke in whispers after nine, but the next morning the landlady came to give us a stern warning that if we had visitors all night again and stayed up drinking with them, we would be evicted. This time we decided to quit before we were fired. Sonny found a beautiful sixth-floor, three-bedroom apartment on Finchley Road in Swiss Cottage. The building was called Bishopscourt. It was fully furnished, and really luxurious. Moving into Swiss Cottage finally gave us peace of mind. Around this time Sonny met Carol Canin, a niece of Myrtle's who was working with a prestigious entertainment company in London.

Early one Sunday afternoon in June, Carol invited Sonny and me to a party in Hampstead where an actress friend of hers would be entertaining. At the party, guests were having drinks and finger food in a townhouse apartment. Among them were three Caribbeans: an actor, the famous dancer Boscoe Holder, who we were told was the brother of the great theater director and choreographer Geoffrey Holder, and a stunningly beautiful, full-figured woman with a face that was a combination of Ethiopian, Indian, African, and

Native American features. Her name was Pat Bannister. On the record player was a Count Basie album—Joe Williams was singing "Every Day." I pulled Carol to the middle of the floor and we started to do the Lindy hop, the bop, and the jitterbug all thrown in together. Sonny stood in a corner of the room with Pat and her boyfriend, the actor. Carol and I got so good on the dance floor that we distracted everybody from their conversations. They stopped to admire and applaud us. I was in the middle of some fancy moves when Sonny came over to me, tapped me on the shoulder, and told me that Pat wanted to dance with me next. I asked Carol to sit out the next song and danced with Pat. She was wearing her long hair up in a bun on the back of her head, and had on a red floral dress that flared from the waist down. The dress rose up into the air like an umbrella every time I twirled her around, allowing me momentary glimpses of her beautiful legs and ample thighs.

"Ooh, this is so wonderful," she said. "I've been wanting to do this for such a long time, but I can never find a partner who can dance. You move so beautifully. I just had to dance with you. I hope you don't think I'm being too forward."

I said, "I am extremely honored to dance with you." She smiled and said, "Then, do you promise not to dance with anyone else but me? Not even the white woman you were dancing with?"

"Not even," I concluded. We danced the rest of the afternoon away in each other's arms. Her long black hair kept falling out of the bun and she kept re-pinning it, saying, "Please hold on to me, don't let me get away." We danced to Nina Simone's "I Loves You Porgy," over and over again. I finally convinced her to let her hair hang loose.

A few hours later, Carol, Sonny, and I started to leave. As we were about to exit, Boscoe Holder invited us to a party later in the week. Pat was waving good-bye with a deeply disappointed look on her face. Suddenly she yelled, "Wait for me, I'm coming with you." She grabbed her handbag off one of the couches and ran to the elevator we were holding open. Pat's boyfriend, a handsome, muscularly built man, was right behind her. "Listen, I can't come right away, but can I join you people later?" he asked worriedly.

"Of course," Sonny volunteered. "Flat 6B, Bishopscourt, Finchley Road in Swiss Cottage. Please do come."

Pat was angry. When the elevator door closed, she snapped at Sonny, "Now why did you have to invite him?" Sonny said, "It's okay, let the poor fellow have a few drinks with us."

Sonny, a genius at Indian dishes, began to prepare a lamb curry and rice supper. My job was to peel the potatoes, cut the onions, and shell the peas. Pat was telling us she was a medical intern at London University, where she would be completing her studies next year, after which she would be returning to Barbados to work at the family clinic. Her brother and father were both doctors—in fact, her father was the surgeon general of Barbados. After a short while, Pat threw Sonny and me out of the kitchen and took over the cooking. She told Sonny that even though he was Indian, he didn't know shit about preparing curry and rice. She wasn't lying—Sonny was good, but Pat's curry was better. Her boyfriend came just as we were about to sit down for our meal.

After dinner we had a few drinks while listening to Sonny's idol, Frank Sinatra, singing "Only the Lonely," "Blues in the Night," "Goodbye," "Autumn in New York," and other classics. We learned a great deal about Barbados and the Caribbean from Pat and her friend, who soon got up to leave. He looked at Pat inquiringly. She did not wait for him to say anything, but looking straight at him and putting her arms around my waist and kissing me on my neck, she said sweetly, "I'm staying with Hugh."

"All right then, I'll be out of the way," he said angrily. He stormed off, taking the stairs rather than ride in the elevator. I really felt badly for him.

Looking at me, Pat said, "I know what you're thinking. You think I'll do to you one day what I just did to him, don't you? The man is not my boyfriend. He's asked me to dinner a couple of times and invited me to this party today. This is only the fourth time I have seen him, and I've never been interested in being intimate with him at all. I really don't like the fellow, you know."

"I didn't say a thing. Let's sit down and relax. I told you I was honored."

"I really like you, you know, not because of your dancing. I'm not that stupid. I really like you," she repeated, looking right through me.

"I really like you too, Pat. I'm so happy you stayed."

We embraced. Sonny interrupted our moment. "Let's drink to this, whatever it is. I think it's absolutely lovely." We poured some whisky and drank to it—whatever it was. It had been a beautiful summer day. Although it was after eight, the sun was still shining brightly in the west as Pat and I walked hand-in-hand to her flat, telling each other as much as we could about who we were, about our families and our friends and what a shock it was that two unlikely people like us should be thrown together.

Pat's sister, Olivia, was even prettier and very different from Pat. Reserved and quiet, she seemed a little surprised that her younger sister was so excited about someone she had just met eight hours ago. Olivia was practicing as a barrister in London and preparing to leave for Barbados.

I spent the rest of that summer with Pat. We had a fairy-tale romance, frolicking and kissing in the parks. We went to the movies and the theaters and even rock-climbed with her friends in Somerset. We went to countless Caribbean get-togethers, dancing cheek to cheek to slow ballads and calypso, looking into each other's eyes, holding hands, and making love every chance we got. We laughed together even when we disagreed intensely about things. Pat turned me on to the kings of calypso, but I fell in love with the Mighty Sparrow. She sang along word for word with all of his records. Our favorite song was "Gimme the Poom-Poom, Audrey," which was our secret signature song when we wanted to go home and get it on.

Todd Matshikiza, who had written the music for *King Kong,* arrived in London in June with his wife, Esme, and their two children, Marianne, eight, and John, six. Todd had come to London to prepare for the West End run of the popular musical. He was being wined and dined regularly, so Pat and I babysat the children two or three times a week. But the big news was that Miles Davis himself was about to come to England for the first time, and the excitement in London among the jazz cognoscenti was at fever pitch. Sonny and I had bought Davis's *Kind of Blue* album, but had worn it out and had to buy another copy. Back home in South Africa I had left a sizable collection of Miles Davis's records, including all the albums of his quintet with Coltrane and the sextet that was augmented by Cannonball Adderley. I also owned *Porgy and Bess, Sketches of Spain,* and *Miles Ahead,* the three classic recordings he had done with Gil Evans. Because of his black pride and fearlessness, Miles was a major township hero back in South Africa. We followed all of his stories and made up some of our own. He was one black man I held in high esteem.

A few days before the concert, Sonny and I stood in line for hours outside the Hammersmith Odeon Theatre waiting for the box office to open so we could buy tickets for his first concert. At the show, word got around as we waited excitedly in our seats that he was refusing to come on stage because all his shows had sold out in England and he was demanding a fifty-percent cut of the profits from Davison, the promoter. Legend has it that as Davison was nervously calling Miles's agent in New York to negotiate the stalemate, Miles sent his colleagues Sonny Stitt (alto and tenor saxophone), who had replaced John Coltrane; Paul Chambers (bass); Wynton Kelly (piano); and Jimmy Cobb (drums) on stage. We roared when they appeared from the wings. Before he hit town, the English press had been extremely critical of Miles's alleged arrogance; Sonny and I assumed that he had just been messing with the promoter's head to give the media something to write about. Miles strolled on stage smiling and waving to the audience—not the arrogant Miles of legend at all. The capacity crowd jumped from their seats and gave him a standing ovation. He counted his band off with a very fast-paced "So What," and for the next three hours played "Milestones," "If I Had a Bell," "My Funny Valentine," "Freddy the Freeloader," "All Blues," "Some Day My Prince Will Come" among his endless repertoire—for all the shows I'd played in and seen in South Africa, this was some of the most exciting *live* music I had ever heard. I never went to another London jazz club. I was in a New York state of mind.

The following week, Miriam came to London to do a BBC television special. Miriam and Sonny were still married, but the communication between them had begun to break down. Nevertheless, Miriam was going to stay with her husband at his new place on Bishopscourt. I had made plans to move in with Pat for the duration of Miriam's London visit. Even though Pat and I visited with Miriam and Sonny a few times, it was always brief.

Miriam asked me to help her rehearse the BBC orchestra she would be performing with. One afternoon she asked me to join her at lunch. She told me it was over between her and Sonny. She had asked him for a divorce, and he was more than cooperative. Miriam also told me that Dizzy Gillespie and John Mehegan had gotten me accepted into the Manhattan School of Music in New York. Her attorney, Albert Geduldig, would be forwarding me the necessary immigration application forms. As soon as the immigration authorities had approved my petition, she would arrange for my air ticket to the States.

Before she left again for the United States, Pat and I went over to Sonny's place to say good-bye to Miriam. The Austin Princess limousine, which had been transporting Miriam around London, came to fetch her and Sonny, who accompanied her to the airport. Pat and I waved our farewell from the sidewalk.

Pat said, "She's still crazy about you," as the limo driver took off.

I denied it. Pat answered me with a knowing chuckle, "You know, Hughie, I'm a woman, and I can tell that woman is still in love with you, mon."

It was probably the greatest summer I'd ever spent. Not once did it rain. The English couldn't stop remarking about the wonderful weather they were having while roasting themselves in the sun until they were beet red.

My visa application had been approved and I would soon be leaving. I informed Huddleston that the Guildhall School of Music option was obsolete now that my American scholarship had come through, but I thanked him for everything and hoped I'd see him again. On September 26, 1960, I said good-bye to Sonny, his new girlfriend Sarojini, and Pat at the Victoria bus station. When the bus finally pulled slowly out of its bay, it was one of the most painful moments of my life. Somehow I knew and Pat knew that this could never, ever be again. It was love lost painfully forever.

This small circle of friends—Pat, Sonny, Todd, and Esme—had been a pillar for me during my summer in London; they had made it easier for me not to miss South Africa so much. Developments back home were just too depress-ing for anyone to miss, anyway. My mother wrote me regularly with updates: members of the Special Branch had been to our home looking for me and had shown unconcealed embarrassment when told that I had slipped away without their knowledge. The Bermans were still in jail along with thousands of other detainees.

After I cleared customs before my flight, I was tempted to call Pat, but felt it would be pointless. Instead, I went to the lounge bar and soaked my sorrows in several triple scotch whiskies. Heartbreak had me so numb I couldn't even get high. I boarded my American Airlines flight with a pounding headache and settled in my seat, crying on the inside for Pat.

As we flew over Newfoundland, my spirits lifted and excitement about com-ing to America flooded me. I realized that I had not had a drop of liquor dur-ing the entire flight. While I was in London, my desire to drink had diminished as I had become closer to Pat. Happiness had helped me to move away from booze without even realizing it.

8

I QUICKLY CLEARED IMMIGRATION at Idlewilde (now JFK) International Airport and, after a nervous walk through the terminal, approached a set of clear glass doors with the American morning waiting for me on the other side. Before I could ponder my next momentous step into a new world, the doors silently slid open on their own and the music of New York chaos breezed in on cool autumn air, an amazement. Miriam had called me before I left London to say that she would be away on tour with Harry Belafonte when I arrived, but that someone would meet me at the East Side Terminal in Manhattan. I was sitting on the bus riding through Jamaica, Queens, a twenty-one-year-old from Witbank on my way to mythic Manhattan, when it finally hit me: I smiled to myself and whispered *die dlladla my ma hoor my*—this is America, I swear by my mother's living soul.

When the bus pulled into the East Side Terminal, I calmly remained in my seat while everyone else disembarked. The bus driver, noticing that my suitcase was the only one left in the hold of the bus, came back into the vehicle and said to me, "Where are you going, buddy?" "I'm going to New York City, sir," I said. "This is New York City, my good friend," the driver said. "You won't find another one."

I stood up in disbelief and slowly stepped off the bus. Nothing around me looked like the sparkling New York City I had seen in the picture books or the movies. Everything was drab, dingy, and dark inside the terminal building. A smiling, light-skinned African man in a navy blue suit with a maroon silk tie over a white shirt walked up to me. He was already holding my suitcase. "Come on, Hughie," he said. "Let's go home."

The man was Mburumba Kerina, a fellow exile and friend of Miriam, who had come to pick me up. I followed him to a cab. He told me he was SWAPO's chief representative at the United Nations—SWAPO, the South West Africa People's Party, was petitioning the United Nations for the liberation of South West Africa (now Namibia). He was married to Jane Miller, an African-American woman from California who was also very active in the Namibian liberation campaign, and together they had two kids, Kakuna, their four-year-old daughter, and Mandume, a boy of two. Jane was expecting the couple's third child. The Kerinas had become friends with Miriam after they attended one of her performances at the Village Vanguard. We rode up Third Avenue to 336 East 82nd Street, between First and Second Avenues, where Miriam was renting a basement apartment.

Driving up Third Avenue, I responded to all of Mburumba's stories about Namibia and the UN and his family with one question: "Is this really Manhattan?" I couldn't believe this was the same New York City I had heard about and seen in movies. From the taxi it was a blur of people in the millions scampering to work, dirty streets, buses, taxis, and shabby tenement buildings, open manholes, and newly dug ditches with hundreds of men in hard hats working on construction sites and street paving gangs. Signs all over read, DIG WE MUST FOR A BETTER NEW YORK. Police cars and fire engines with screaming sirens hurried to one crisis or another, battling to get through the congested traffic. Window washers hung suspended on scaffolding high up against buildings whose windows were sixty stories up in the air. Blaring car horns, stuttering air hammers, screeching tires, screaming voices; street sweepers; garbage collectors running to and from grubby, noisy garbage trucks, toting gigantic plastic bags and cans of trash; cyclists, joggers, and dog shit on the sidewalk— I could not believe the pandemonium. I quietly wondered if I had made the right decision by coming to America. Was this madness worth all the trouble I had gone through?

Since they lived five blocks away, at 77th and Second Avenue, Miriam spent a lot of time with the Kerinas. Bongi, Miriam's daughter, had become like their other child. When Mburumba and I finally arrived in Miriam's pad, Bongi was there—more than excited to see me. She jumped into my arms—"*Malume, Hugh!*"—and launched into a fusillade of Zulu, already broken even though she had only been in America nine months. I had last seen Bongi with her grandmother at Dorkay House, where they had come to make final preparations for her travel plans to New York, so she could join her mother. Bongi was

My grandfather, Walter Bowers, a Scottish mining engineer and shoe cobbler (above left) married Johanna Mabena (above right). Johanna, on the left, is posing with her older sister, Elizabeth Motsoene, in the early 1900s. *Photos courtesy of the author.*

Solomon Khalu Bowers (left), Johanna's son and a cinema manager in Brakpan, was murdered in 1947 by two jealous, racist white men who felt they deserved his job instead. He was thirty-two years old. At the trial, the judge released the killers with a warning "not to go around bothering black people."
Photo courtesy of the author.

My grandparents Mamoshaba and Hopane Masekela at their wedding in the early 1880s, dressed to the nines. The love of good clothes remains in the blood.

Photo courtesy of the author.

My mother, Pauline (Polina) Bowers, was a schoolteacher before beginning a forty-year career as a beloved social worker.

Photo courtesy of the author.

My father, Thomas Selema Masekela, was a noted pioneer sculptor. He also worked as a schoolteacher before becoming a health inspector. After fifty years of community service as an inspector, he retired.

Photo by Alf Kumalo.

Selema and Polina's children (clockwise from top left): Ramapolo Hugh was born April 4, 1939; Barbara was born July 18, 1941; Elaine was born March 23, 1947; Sybil was born September 29, 1953. Sybil died of AIDS in 1998, just ten days before her forty-fifth birthday.

Photos courtesy of the author.

Showing off Satchmo's trumpet (above), which had just arrived in the courier post (1956). *Photo by Jurgen Schadeberg.* The same day that we received the Louis Armstrong trumpet, I took to the streets of Sophiatown, jumping for joy (below left). *Photo by Alf Kumalo, courtesy of UWC-Robben Island Museum Mayibuye Archives.*

Walking down President Street in Johannesburg with my good friend George Molotlegi in 1955 (right). *Photo courtesy of the author.*

Performing with the Huddleston Jazz
Band in the recreation hall at St Peter's
in 1955. *Photo courtesy of Bailey's African History
Archives, Johannesburg.*

My mother kisses me goodbye before
I board the plane to leave South
Africa in 1961. *Photos by Alf Kumalo.*

Playing for Miriam Makeba's second album, *The Many Voices of Miriam Makeba*, at RCA's Webster Hall studios on East 13th Street in 1961. *Photo courtesy of the author.*

Miriam Makeba and me on our wedding day, May 9, 1964 (right). A year later, while the band was performing at Tivoli Gardens in Helsinborg, Denmark, Miriam and I took the band on a picnic on our day off (below). *Photos courtesy of the author.*

In 1968, *Jet* magazine claimed that I eloped with Chris Calloway, Cab's daughter. We were married only three months but the marriage was extremely turbulent and filled with so much substance abuse that it felt like thirty years. *Photo by Jack Robinson/Vogue © Condé Nast Publications, Inc.*

Stewart Levine and me with singer Minnie Ripperton, who was known for her angelic five-octave vocal range, in the early 1970s at Wally Heider Recording Studios in Hollywood. Minnie died of breast cancer in 1979. *Photo by Jim Marshall.*

The Union of South Africa—Ndugu Chancler on drums, Caiphus Semenya on saxophone, and Jonas Gwangwa on trombone—performing at Lincoln Center, New York City, in 1970 (above). Jonas, Caiphus, and I take a break after a gruelling performance in Atlantic City, New Jersey (below). *Photos courtesy of the author.*

eager to hear about her relatives back home, but mostly how her cousins Nhlanhla, Nongobozi, and Thupazile were doing. Unfortunately, I had last seen these kids in 1956 when Miriam and I started our torrid love affair. I could only say to Bongi that I was certain they were all very well, although I couldn't explain why I had not seen them lately. Bongi was crestfallen I had not come bearing any tidings for her from Nhlanhla and her grandmother.

When Miriam was away, Leslie Reed, an aspiring Puerto Rican actress, singer, and dancer, looked after Bongi with the help of Jean Johnson, another aspiring singer from Harlem. The two women were always auditioning, but never seemed to get hired, so Miriam was helping them earn a few dollars by having them look after the apartment and Bongi while she was on the road. Jean was tall, dark, and quite attractive. Originally from the South, she was crazy about B. B. King and Ray Charles. Leslie had light skin, straight hair, and a dancer's body, and spoke with the rat-a-tat relentlessness of a typewriter. Leslie came from a close-knit family, and spoke to her mother on the phone several times a day in breakneck Nuyorican Spanish.

I had been in the house a few hours when Miriam called from Las Vegas. She was excited that I had arrived safely, but would be away for another three weeks. She insisted that I make myself at home, and asked me to help Bongi with her homework because she was just beginning to learn English. With the new, inferior Bantu education for African children back home, Bongi had only been instructed in the ethnic languages before coming to America. My task was to decipher this new world Bongi was entering into Zulu first, and then teach her the English equivalent so that she could cope at her new school, the Downtown Community School in the East Village.

That evening Leslie took me to the Jazz Gallery on East Eighth Street, where Dizzy Gillespie was sharing a bill with Thelonious Monk. When we walked in, the set was already on. Cheeks fully extended, Dizzy was playing with Lalo Schifrin on piano, Rudy Stevens on drums, Mike White on bass, and Leo Wright on saxophone. He had just returned from South America, and you could hear the Brazilian influences in the music his band played: "Desifinado," "One Note Samba," the theme from *Black Orpheus,* and other hot Brazilian compositions. Between songs he spotted me in the audience and smiled at me from the stage, nodding as if he'd been expecting me. Right after his set, he walked to our table and greeted me like a long-lost brother. "Oooweee," he said, "wait till Lorraine hears about this." This jazz legend of bebop and I hugged—he told me how glad he was that I had finally gotten out of the apartheid hellhole and was relieved we didn't have to write each other veiled and coded letters anymore. "Now we can talk about those bastards in South Africa without fear," he said, bursting into his patented laugh and high-pitched "Oooweee."

Thelonious Monk walked in and was heading toward the stage when Dizzy stood up and stopped him. "Hey, Thel, I want you to meet Hughie Masekela. He's the South African trumpet player I told you about. He just got in this morning from London." Monk was wearing his black sunglasses and customary black suit, black shirt, and mini-porkpie hat. He gave me a limp handshake and uttered an unintelligible, high-pitched whine, "Nyiii," then walked away. I never saw his eyes behind those dark sunglasses, just my own confused stare looking back at myself. Dizzy hollered at him, "You was born dead, Thel. You hear me? Born *daaeeiid.*" He turned to Leslie and me, "Don't mind him. He's a born actor. He's got the biggest mouth in the world, oooweee." I was in music heaven, meeting people I had idolized for years. I was dazzled but tongue-tied, especially after Monk's weird introduction.

"Let's pop over to the Five Spot, across Third Avenue. Mingus and Max Roach are playing there. Max really wants to meet you, oooweee," Dizzy said, breaking the awkwardness at our table. "Okay," I managed. Dizzy was in high spirits, bubbling over. He reminded me of my uncle Kenneth back home, who even resembled Dizzy physically, down to the expensive tweed sport jacket, cashmere sweater, brown camel-hair slacks, and English brogues. When we got to the Five Spot, the joint was packed to the rafters. The smoke-filled room was jumping, with Charlie Mingus looming wildly on stage, exhorting, cheering, and scolding his big band all at the same time while playing the hell out of his upright bass. His drummer was shouting back at him while beating the hell out of the skins. The integrated big band was playing their hearts out, intense and on edge, sending up a complex, wailing blues—one section's tight melodies competing with another's seeming chaos—that threatened to tear the roof off. Word was that Mingus was notorious for beating up members of his band when they made mistakes while playing his complicated arrangements, but the finished product was like nothing else, an exhilarating and eclectic mix of bebop, Dixieland, and swing. The band also played many Duke Ellington compositions. Mingus—who had played with the Ellington band for years—worshiped the Duke even more than Abdullah Ibrahim did.

Dizzy led me to a table where I met Max Roach, who seemed overjoyed to see me. He had heard from Dizzy that I was crazy about Clifford Brown, his late partner in the legendary quintet they had led together. Max Roach was an antiapartheid activist, and often organized pickets in front of the South African Mission to the United Nations. He was also a fervent civil rights advocate.

"I know Vusi Make from your country, and Maya Angelou, his wife," Max told me. "They're always at my house. When Miriam returns, my wife Abbey and I are gonna have a party for them. I'll phone and ask her to bring you along. Vusi will be so happy to see you. He talks a lot about you. Welcome to New York. We're gonna win in South Africa, and soon!"

Mingus was still playing when Dizzy checked his watch. He said we needed to get back to the Jazz Gallery for his next set. When we returned, we caught Monk's last four songs, "Ruby, My Dear," "Epistrophy," "Crepuscule with Nellie," and " 'Round Midnight," all compositions that Abdullah Ibrahim had insisted we play with the Jazz Epistles. It was a mind-blowing experience to hear Monk's band with Charlie Rouse on tenor sax, Wilbur Ware on bass, and Ben Riley on drums. My favorite albums were coming alive right in front of my eyes. I could have been dreaming. When Dizzy was preparing to go back onstage, he called over his and Monk's musicians and introduced them. They were all fascinated that I had just come from South Africa, and gave me a hearty welcome—Dizzy had been telling them about me.

Before he took the stage for his next set, Dizzy asked us where we were headed. "Back uptown," Leslie replied.

"No, don't do that," Dizzy said. "Go down to the Half Note on Hudson and Spring Street. Go and catch John Coltrane. Hughie will enjoy that. Don't go home now, oh no, ooowee." We couldn't say no.

We grabbed a cab and headed down to SoHo. While Leslie was paying the taxi driver, I slouched next to her, exhausted, but while the taxi's engine idled I could hear faint rumblings coming from inside the club—Coltrane on his soprano sax, Reggie Workman on bass, McCoy Tyner on piano, and Elvin Jones on drums, pumping away on "My Favorite Things." I leaped out of the cab, itching to get inside. Dizzy was right. The joint was jam-packed. Coltrane had recently formed a new group with whom he was stretching his music into ever greater complexity. But aside from that, his technique on the saxophone was devastating. He could play faster than anyone I'd heard before, and yet when he played slow ballads, his sound was the sweetest cry a saxophone could ever make. Every saxophone player of the time was overwhelmed by the man's genius. After every one of his solos, you could almost hear the clanking sound of players around the world laying down their horns. Trane was really some-thing else, literally, another thing altogether than anything I'd ever seen or heard up close.

During their break, Reggie Workman, who knew Leslie, brought Trane, McCoy, and Elvin over to our table to say hello. They were excited to meet a musician from South Africa. After sitting through their next set, Reggie wrote his phone number down on a drink coaster and insisted that I call him once I got settled. During the cab ride back to Miriam's place, I was intoxicated by the evening's experiences. Leslie was talking, but all I could do was stare at the sky-scrapers on Sixth Avenue and occasionally glance in her direction. "My Favorite Things" kept ringing in my ears. I'll never forget that moment. It was one o'clock in the morning, September 27. I had not had a good sleep since my last night in London, but that night I dreamed I was playing in Art Blakey's band as a member of the Jazz Messengers. In all my years in South Africa, dreaming about what it would be like in America, none of those dreams came close to what I had actually experienced. In only four months since leaving South Africa, I had met Sammy Davis Jr., Dizzy Gillespie, Thelonious Monk, and Max Roach. I'd seen John Coltrane, Miles Davis, and Charles Mingus per-form. I knew I had to work hard to get to the level of the great talents I had just been with, but I was determined to get there.

For all of its wonder, getting acclimated to life in New York was still challeng-ing. Back in South Africa, election campaigns were reserved for the white world. Africans did not participate. When I arrived in New York, I had no idea how that world functioned. I had never had the opportunity to partake in this kind of freedom of expression. It was a bit overwhelming, arriving in America and finding the presidential campaigns between John Kennedy and Richard Nixon at fever pitch, Republicans and Democrats at each other's throats, end-less televised debates, round-the-clock flesh-pumping and baby-kissing, and a lot of character assassination and mudslinging, which all seemed to be in a day's work in the business of politics. My ignorance was obvious to Jean, Jane, and Leslie, who tried to explain what all the madness was about.

As if this were not confusing enough, the annual United Nations General Assembly sessions were winding down. At center stage were Cuba's Fidel Castro, who had just moved his large delegation to Harlem's Hotel Theresa after the Waldorf-Astoria management allegedly accused his group of pluck-ing live chickens and cooking them in their rooms.

Soviet Premier Nikita Khrushchev banging his shoe on the UN lectern and declaring "We will bury you" managed to upstage Castro's exodus to Harlem. The Congo's Patrice Lumumba had come in for one day and returned home to the Congo's murderous turmoil empty-handed. A young Yasser Arafat was also in town, to scream about Israel. I was fascinated by the proceedings. The world's ideological one-upmanship was at its most intense at the United Nations, but basically everyone went back to their country without having achieved any significant victory. The world remained the same.

Meanwhile, the civil rights uprisings were reaching a boiling point in the American South. White people in the South resorted to all sorts of official and mob violence—against black men, women, and children, and their white allies—and it quickly became clear that the freedom we in South Africa assumed existed for people of African origin in America was a mirage. There wasn't too much difference in how most white people felt about black people throughout the West. I quickly realized that while I was in America, I needed to watch my black back and not think this place was that different from South Africa. The methods of racial terrorism might be applied differently here, but the disposition was the same. This was apartheid wearing a different hat.

Imam Elijah Muhammad's Black Muslim movement was also making itself heard in the streets of New York and throughout black America. Malcolm X's fiery speeches at highly disciplined rallies and interviews denounced King's approach and promoted an eye-for-an-eye position. It was obvious that the white media was attempting to create a major division among American blacks by making it appear that Malcolm and Martin were archenemies. McCarthyism was still in the air, and the Communist scare was on the lips of every American, although very few if any could articulate what they were so terrified of. Anyone who stood for liberation from oppression was automatically regarded as a Communist. This was the America I found. This was also the America where Ray Charles's "Wha'd I Say" was the number-one song, followed by Chubby Checker's "Let's Do the Twist," the Impressions' "It's All Right," and Sam Cooke's "It's Been a Long Time Comin'."

I was getting behind on my schooling—Miriam was to help me figure out enrollment and fees when she returned from her tour—but I was thoroughly enjoying my time in the city. During the day, I took care of Bongi and tutored her in English. At night I prowled the jazz clubs with Jean or Leslie, or went to the movies or the Apollo Theater. Back then, the Apollo was still a mecca for black performers, and really opened me up to that world in a new way. I

remember going there to see "The Gospel Train," featuring Reverend James
Cleveland, Reverend Cecil Franklin, Shirley Caesar, and the Five Blind Boys of
Alabama. We also checked out the James Brown Revue. I had never seen such
an intense exhibition of high-level energy. The man made Sammy Davis Jr.
appear lazy. On another day, we grooved to a wonderful rhythm and blues
revue featuring Jackie Wilson, Ruth Brown, Etta James, Solomon Burke, Billy
Wright, and many others. We reveled to the Ray Charles Revue and the Stax
Memphis Revue, featuring Rufus Thomas, Sam and Dave, Otis Redding, and
Booker T and the MGs. I also had my first intense brush with salsa music when
we caught the Latino Variety Revue with Machito's Orchestra featuring his
sister Xaviera; Celia Cruz with Pacheco's band; La Lupe; Tito Puente; Tito
Rodriguez; Willie Colon; Mongo Santamaria; and the Palmieri Brothers. The
Apollo also had a jazz revue with the Horace Silver Quintet, Art Blakey's Jazz
Messengers, the Slide Hampton Orchestra, Les McAnn's trio, Gloria Lynne,
Stanley Turrentine, and the Cannonball Quintet, featuring Nancy Wilson.

These great musicians were a major influence on the jazz and mbhaqanga
groups I'd played with back home, not to mention my own personal approach
to music. I would sit in the Apollo with the animated throngs who screamed
and testified at the players they loved, and all I could think about was how
much I wished some of my friends in South Africa could be right there with
me. Although rhythm and blues, gospel, and salsa were basically new horizons
for me, it all felt like I'd been with all these people in another life. The thing I
wanted to learn most from these genres was an understanding of their language and slang. This was an English I had yet to decipher. The wonderful
thing about music is that, in the end, language don't mean a thing because
when the Latinos hit that stage, I felt I understood everything they were
singing about. My biggest wish was to be able to master their dances . . . shiiit,
those folks can move!

Sometimes when we had overdosed on music, we would catch the comedy
revues and see Slappy White, Lawanda Paige, Redd Foxx, Moms Mabley, and
Nipsey Russell. More than the humor, I took great joy from the fact that people could make fun of just about anything they wanted to ridicule, whether it
was the police, the president, music, dance, white folks, black folks, old folks,
sex, gender, joy, pain, life, death—you name it. Where I came from, people
were so thin-skinned that if you tried to make fun of people and their circumstances, whether you did it on or off stage, you'd be taking your life in
your hands. Back then, admission to the Apollo was only one dollar, and you

could sit in the theater and watch the same show five times from noon until midnight. I was quickly forgetting about the main purpose of my coming to America, which was school.

After about three weeks, Miriam returned to New York. I had not seen her since earlier that summer, when she came to London to do her BBC television show. As usual, Miriam walked into the apartment with her arms full of gifts for everybody. One evening she threw a welcoming party for me. She invited several of her friends, her band members, Dizzy and Lorraine Gillespie, and the Kerinas. This was the first time I met Dizzy's elegant and warm wife. Lorraine told me I reminded her of Miles Davis when he had first come to New York from East St. Louis, twenty years earlier.

While I was enjoying myself, Dizzy asked me to walk with him to the store to get some lighter fluid for his pipe. As we walked around the block, he pulled out his Sherlock Holmes–looking pipe, stuffed it with an aromatic tobacco, lit it, and passed it to me after he'd taken a few draws. I had never smoked a pipe before, but at Dizzy's insistence, I got the hang of it.

"Hughie, is that jacket the only coat you've got? If so, you're gonna freeze your little behind off in that little Italian frock coat, man. It gets colder'n a motherfucker here. You're gonna need a real winter coat if you wanna live until the spring of '61, boy. Tell you what, meet me on the corner of 57th Street and Broadway on Monday around three, at a store called Webber and Heilbroner. You meet me there and let's get you a proper winter coat. Otherwise you gone die in that little thing you wearin' when it starts to snow here. Then we gonna have to dig you out the snow and thaw you out. Oooweee, ha, ha, he, he."

Once back in the apartment, I realized that Diz had packed some mean smoke in that pipe of his, because all I could pay attention to was Ray Charles on the phonograph singing "Just for a Thrill" with mellow strings and voices in the background. I couldn't stop smiling, and I answered everybody with a "yeah" and a grin. Soon I was lost in Ray's "Georgia" and everybody stopped paying any attention to me; they just carried on with their conversations. It seemed like hours later when the visitors said good night. I stood up to shake hands with everybody. When I got to Dizzy and Lorraine, she gave me a big hug and a kiss on the cheek and said, "Welcome to New York, and don't you forget to meet Dizzy on Monday, boy." Dizzy winked at me as he followed his wife up the stairs. "Oooweee, good, ain't it?" Dizzy whispered, referring to the pipe. All the visitors left, and by the time Miriam returned to the apartment after seeing everyone out, I was out cold in my bed in the guest room.

The next day we all went to visit Central Park and some of the city's muse-
ums. Miriam told me that Belafonte was in the process of setting up a nonprofit foundation that would help me through school, but in the meantime she
would take care of my tuition. The next morning we hailed a cab and went to
the Manhattan School of Music. I expected the school to be a sprawling, tree-
lined campus like the ones I had seen in the American movies. I kept looking
for signs of students sporting jackets and sweaters with the school's name
printed on them. When the cab pulled up to 206 East 105th Street, it turned
out to be a pieced-together series of three-story brick buildings that used to be
an elementary school.

I was to study Music Theory 101, Sight-singing 101, Music Literature 101,
French Grammar, English Literature, American History, Brass Ensemble,
Chorus, and Psychology. I would have private trumpet lessons with Mr.
Vacchiano, the first trumpeter of the New York Philharmonic Orchestra. I felt
truly blessed and in immeasurable debt to Miriam, who had paid my fare to
America and was housing me and paying for my tuition, clothing, and living
expenses. When I tried to thank her, all she said was, "Hughie, we are family.
Let's look out for each other. Work hard and let's keep trying our best to find
ways to improve the plight of our people who are suffering back home in
South Africa." Although I found the enslavement of my people by Verwoerd
and his minions sickening, I had never thought I could ever be in a position to
effect any changes against apartheid through music. When Miriam spoke of
improving the plight of our people, it was the first time in my life that I had
been inspired to consider the possibility of ever being able to rattle the com-
placency of Afrikaner racism through my life's work.

Soon after we returned to the apartment, a limousine arrived and Miriam
was off to La Guardia Airport, embarking on a three-week tour with the Chad
Mitchell Trio. Later that afternoon, I went down to 57th and Broadway as spec-
ified by Dizzy, and waited outside the Webber and Heilbroner store. After
about twenty minutes, a tall white man tapped me on the shoulder and said,
"Excuse me, are you Hughie, by any chance?" "Yes," I replied. The man ushered
me into the store. "Mr. Gillespie has asked me to supply you with a warm coat
for the upcoming winter," he said. "Let me show you what we have in stock."

I was still reeling from Miriam's generosity, and now this. I picked out a
modestly priced brown cashmere overcoat, thanked the salesman, and left. As
soon as I got back to Miriam's, I called Dizzy to thank him, but Lorraine
answered the phone. She told me Diz had left that morning for Europe.
"Dizzy's gonna be really happy," Lorraine said. "He's been so worried about

you freezing to death. I'll be sure and tell him that you called. Good luck in your studies, and take care of yourself. God bless you, darling."

The next morning I formally began my life in America. It was a routine that would last a little more than a year. At six-thirty, I'd get Bongi up and get her set for school—fix her breakfast, comb and braid her hair—and we'd be out the door by seven-thirty.

I made friends with some of my classmates: Jimmy Lee, a trombonist from Mount Vernon, who wore thick-rimmed, bebop-style glasses and talked a lot about jazz and came from an allegedly wealthy Jewish family; Tammy Brown, a beautiful black girl from Long Island, who was a voice major studying opera; Fielder Floyd, a black trumpet player from Alabama, whose heavy Southern accent had me calling him "Feelflow" for two weeks until I saw his name on one of his books; jet-black Larry Willis from Harlem, who was already an outstanding opera tenor and basketball player; and John Cartwright, a bass player from Mount Vernon, who was a member of the school symphony orchestra and an accomplished jazz musician. Also in the orchestra was Hugh Robinson, a white trombonist from Jackson, Mississippi, who really wanted to play jazz but only knew classical music. There were a few Asian students from Korea, Taiwan, Japan, and Hong Kong—all outstanding classical musicians.

My fellow students included leading members of the symphony orchestra, opera soloists, top composers, and leading jazz musicians like bassists Ron Carter and Richard Davis, pianists Herbie Hancock, Mike Abene, Dave Grusin, and Larry Willis, drummer Phil Rosen, trumpeters Donald Byrd and Booker Little, and many other young musicians who would later become icons of American music. It was in school that I first met Astley Fennel, a trombonist from the Bronx, whose family originally came from Jamaica; Susan Belink, a mezzo soprano from Long Island, whose father was one of New York's top synagogue cantors; Yoshiko Ito, a great Japanese opera singer; Howie Folta, an outstanding percussionist from Brooklyn; and Sharon Johnson, a beautiful, half-Cherokee French horn player from Cincinnati. The place was like a young United Nations music conference, overflowing with amazing talents and scores of wannabes from almost all over the world. Many of these people would become major influences in my life. Some remain my dearest friends to this day.

On my second morning I was introduced to my trumpet teacher, Mr. Vacchiano, who quickly decided he would be the wrong tutor for me. Vacchiano only taught classical music. I was transferred to Cecil Collins, ex-lead trumpeter for the New York Metropolitan Opera. Collins had lost his front teeth in a hit-and-run car accident at the pinnacle of his career. Most of the non-symphonic trumpet players were assigned to Collins.

For four years I had been playing a German-made F. X. Huller trumpet, the one Louis Armstrong had sent to the Huddleston Band. I had never washed the inside of the horn. On the day of my first trumpet lesson, Collins asked me to play a tune of my choice. After hearing a few notes, he abruptly stopped me. "Your trumpet has leaks," he said. "The only reason you don't know it is because dirt inside is blocking all the holes in it. Come with me and I'll show you what I mean." My stomach sank at his matter-of-fact dismissal of my cherished instrument; I followed him to the bathroom like a sheep to slaughter. He walked over to the porcelain sink, holding my prized Louis Armstrong trumpet like it was a piece of junk. Collins handed me my mouthpiece and then ran a twig through the stem of my trumpet. When he removed the twig, out came loads of green and gray slimy mold. That shit had been stuck up there for years. He then ran water through the horn and foul-smelling, caked gunk came splattering out of the bell in large, green, nauseating blobs. I was embarrassed beyond comprehension.

Back in the practice room, Collins handed me my horn and said, "Now try to blow that thing." I tried, but the horn was leaking like a sieve from around the valves, producing a flat, airy sound more like a leaking exhaust muffler system than a trumpet. I wanted to crawl my humiliated ass out of there and hide.

"You have to go to Manny's Music Store on 48th Street between Sixth and Seventh Avenues and ask for a Vincent Bach trumpet with a 7C mouthpiece of the same name. These will cost you around one hundred and fifty dollars. You also must buy an Arban Cornet Method exercise book, for about twelve dollars. When you have those things, come back to me and I'll teach you how to play the trumpet. With all due respect to Louis Armstrong, that thing is now an old scrap that even he would be unwilling to blow on." Cecil Collins left the room with me standing there holding Satchmo's trumpet in my right hand. I was totally shattered and speechless.

I didn't have one hundred sixty-two dollars, and I had no idea where to get it. Two weeks had rolled by, and I could not take a lesson on the instrument that was my major. Collins kept calling me to his tutorial room to ask when was I getting a proper trumpet. "You are falling behind. This is your major. You are scheduled for brass ensemble, too. By the time you join us, if you ever do, it will be too late because we will be way ahead. Remember, with a new mouthpiece and trumpet, you're going to have to start from scratch. Can't you let me talk to Miss Makeba or Harry Belafonte about the urgency of this matter?"

"No sir," I replied. "I'll figure out something."

My new world was caving in on me. I could never go to Miriam and ask her for money after all she had already done. I had not yet met Belafonte, and the only money I had to keep me going was what Miriam had left for food and transportation for me and Bongi.

Miriam called one day from Canada to check on things, and Leslie told her about my predicament. Miriam was furious that I hadn't let her know. She instructed Leslie to go and see Alfred Braunstein, her accountant. He gave Leslie the money. The next day I walked into Manny's Music Store and purchased my first new trumpet. On the bus ride to school, I thanked my ancestors for their intercession. I also gave thanks to Trevor Huddleston and Bob Hill and Old Man Sauda and Louis Armstrong. I whispered a *very* special thank-you for Miriam Makeba. I got off the bus and marched up 105th Street with a brand-new trumpet in a leather case, complete with the new 7C mouthpiece and the *Arban Cornet Method* book. Collins smiled as I showed him my new prized possessions. I was now a full-fledged student at the Manhattan School of Music.

My American History teacher also taught at Columbia University, and hosted an educational television program on the subject on the Public Broadcasting System, which was shown throughout the U.S. He opened my mind and placed into context many of the distortions I had harbored about the United States. I particularly gravitated to discussions of racism, civil rights, and the other human-rights debates. Discussions of communism, Castro, Russia, Malcolm X, SNCC, and Dr. Martin Luther King fascinated me, as did people and organizations like Strom Thurmond, Jesse Helms, Orville Faubus, George Wallace, the Ku Klux Klan, the John Birch Society, and the white Southern Baptist leadership. As part of the large group of Africans immigrating to the United States to study, I was getting a first-class education in and outside the classroom. A few years later, through Belafonte, I performed a fund-raiser for SNCC.

I will never forget an episode in Mr. Miller's English class. We were discussing George Orwell's *Animal Farm*. Miller began comparing the pigs in the book to Kwame Nkrumah, Jomo Kenyatta, and Patrice Lumumba, among others. My blood began boiling. I raised my hand and objected to Miller vilifying African liberation leaders. I was joined by Astley Fennel and Fielder Floyd, the only other black male students in the class. In the ensuing war of

words, I was branded a Communist and Astley and Fielder were accused of
being disciples of Malcolm X by some of the white conservative students,
while we branded them children of the Klan. We had nearly come to blows
when Mr. Miller, who looked like a U.S. Marines captain, screamed at the top
of his voice, "Stop, stop, stop!" He stormed out of the room and returned with
Dean Whitford, who calmly dismissed the class and asked us to follow her to
her office. They accused me of attempting to create a political forum out of a
classroom discussion, which surprised me—I was just responding to what I
thought were unfair characterizations of the heroes of African liberation. I
stood my ground and told them that I hadn't come all the way to America to
listen to the denigration of people who were dedicated to the liberation of
African peoples. Neither was I in the country to be converted into an American
right-wing patriot. I had come to America to get an education, and I demanded
that Mr. Miller be the one to be spoken to, because he was provoking conflict
and confrontation in his English class. The matter was never brought up again,
and Miller backed off from making derogatory statements. The white students
with whom we had the confrontation never spoke to us again.

Psychology was a class that I could not understand. Freud, Jung, libido—
what in the hell was this shit all about? It wasn't until I went to England thirty-
seven years later for substance addiction recovery that I finally understood
what psychology was all about. It took that long to break down the walls that
had been constructed in my psyche by township life, discrimination, ethnic
cleansing, booze, drugs, and sex. For decades I was certain that psychology
was some white conspiracy to brainwash people of African origin into being
complacent, obedient niggers. I was not stupid; I was just suspicious and not
that keen on the subject.

But all in all, I was doing well at the conservatory. Word had gotten around
about my jazz improvisational prowess, and when I would do my classical
exercises in the basement practice rooms, I'd occasionally break off into some
jazz licks or standard ballads. The room would become crowded with other
students, amazed at this African taking off on their music. Sometimes Mr.
Sokoloff, the treasurer, would burst into the room to remind me that I was in
a school of classical music and those rooms were meant for the furtherance
of expertise in that medium and certainly not for "jazz riffing." I was accused
of reflecting badly on my fellow students and even my home continent! It was
always mentioned that the Ghanaian music professor Dr. Nketia, who had
been at the school during Modern Jazz Quartet leader and pianist John Lewis's
time, had never done that sort of thing. This was odd because so many of the

jazz players of that time had attended the school; in fact, some of its most accomplished alumni, jazz heads like John Lewis and Max Roach, were always mentioned proudly in speeches and conversations by the school's administration. It blew my mind that I had to apologize for playing jazz—but it was just another eye-opener to me of the double standards I'd be facing in American life.

In my class, I got very close to Astley Fennel, Larry Willis, and Fielder Floyd. It turned out that Larry played a little jazz piano. We hung out a lot at Astley's place in the Bronx, where he lived with his widowed Jamaican dad. They had an old piano, and Larry would accompany Astley and me on piano on popular bebop and blues compositions, plus some American standards. Astley had a tin ear, but we hung with him mostly because of the piano at his house. Larry, on the other hand, had great potential.

Fielder and I were sworn disciples of Clifford Brown. We spent a lot of time trading the great trumpeter's phrases and gushing over his incredible prowess on the horn. Fielder was rooming with Marcus Belgrave, who played lead trumpet in the Ray Charles band and had been a personal friend of Clifford's. He was also close to Brown's family in Wilmington, Delaware, a stone's throw away from his home in Chester, Pennsylvania. Marcus and Fielder shared an apartment around 158th Street and Amsterdam Avenue in Washington Heights, where we went after school to pick up pointers from Marcus and ask millions of questions about Clifford Brown. The two trumpeters usually lit up a joint and offered me a drag, but I always cordially declined. From time to time I would notice them going into a nod and rubbing their noses furiously, but at first it didn't occur to me that they were on heroin—their behavior wasn't nearly as severe as that of the addicts I saw nodding on the sidewalks of Harlem around the Apollo Theater. When I first saw those cats, I asked Leslie what kind of booze they were drinking and she said, "That ain't no booze, honey. Those motherfuckers are falling over from shooting heroin." I had never heard of heroin before that. When it finally dawned on me that Marcus and Fieldler were knocking themselves out with H, I was quietly shocked, but I never said anything to either of them. About seven years later, Fielder Floyd died from a heroin overdose.

Jane and Mburumba often brought their children, Kakuna and Mandume, to Miriam's apartment for me to babysit while they went out to one reception or another. Sometimes when Leslie and Jean stayed over with Bongi, I would go to the Kerina flat and babysit there. The Kerinas became like family to me— they were generous and funny and a total joy to be with. Of course, their home cooking and wonderful leftovers gave Bongi and me a very good reason to stop over regularly for a quick hello and good-bye, with the full knowledge that Jane would insist that we sit down and have a quick bite to eat. But their house had more than good eating; I also met many prominent political scientists and activists through the Kerinas, among them the great African-American writer John Henrik Clarke, who was also a radical scholar of international African politics and one of America's foremost civil rights authors and teachers. Then there was the prolific author John Killens; artist/sculptor John Peoples; author Louis Lomax; and Namibian freedom fighters like Kozonguizi, Sam Nujoma, and Ben Gurirab, who were presenting petitions at the United Nations on behalf of their people. Discussions at the Kerina household could go on into the early mornings, with heated confrontations between parties holding different opinions on protest, racism, history, genetics, philosophy, psychology, and liberation.

One night when we popped over, Lomax was holding court. He had just published a book in which he argued that even though he had African blood in his veins, the fact was that he was light-skinned and his closest forebears were of German origin, which made him more a white man than a Negro.

John Henrik Clarke, John Killens, Miriam Makeba, Maya Angelou, Vusi Make, Leslie Reed, Jean Johnson, and a few Africans were at the Kerinas for this discussion. Even though everybody tore into Louis Lomax with scathing and sometimes venomous criticism, he would not stand down. "You are a disgrace to the black race," someone would hiss at him. But Louis Lomax, in his Brooks Brothers suit, Ivy League cordovans, and horn-rimmed glasses, his charcoal-gray, semi-straight hair carefully groomed, would sit back in his chair, flash a very confident smile, and reply, "How can I be a disgrace to a group of people I don't belong to in any manner of speaking?"—a question to which the gathering found it very difficult to come up with a rebuttal except for the stock phrases like "Look in the mirror," or "One drop of black blood makes you a black man," or "Go to the South, hug a white man or kiss a white woman, and let's see how many hours you'll live after that."

Lomax would fire back, "Many white civil rights activists have been murdered in the South. I wouldn't be the first. Stop being racist and emotional. Give me some logical answers." It was a useless case, but Lomax was a grand provocateur—I was still trying to figure out where I fit into all of this, so I just sat back and watched the show. He went on to conduct live debates on television with Malcolm X, other black activists and a number of white conservatives, and with Southern racists who thought he was just a crazy ole nigra.

Even outside of the Kerinas' house, I found myself surrounded by people who were revolutionaries—whether they were African or American, artists or activists, it all seemed to come together magically at that moment. Miriam took me to a party at the home of Abbey Lincoln and Max Roach in honor of Vusi Make and his wife, Maya Angelou. Maya was starring in an off-Broadway production of Jean Genet's play *The Blacks*. Bra Vusi, as we called him back home, had worked at *Drum* magazine and then become a fiery antiapartheid orator in the Vereeniging township of Evaton and its environs. When Robert Sobukwe was detained for treason and sent to Robben Island for life after his death sentence was commuted, Vusi was one of the people from the Pan-African Congress's leadership who went abroad for military leadership training. Vusi ended up in Ghana, where he met Maya. They returned to the United States together—she to pursue her acting career, he to make representations at the United Nations and establish solidarity with American civil rights movements and other activists who were passionate about the liberation of people of the African Diaspora.

Mburumba took me to Harlem one day when he had an appointment with Malcolm X at the Muslim-run restaurant on 116th Street. Harlem always gripped my soul in a kindred kind of way. It reminded me of the communal vibes I experienced in Sophiatown and Alexandra. Just as the townships were cultural kaleidoscopes and key political meeting places for the ANC in South Africa, Harlem, a black metropolis, was the magnet for intellectuals, artists, musicians, black nationalists, and Pan-Africanists. A few years later Langston Hughes invited me to his home in Harlem. Hughes told me that in 1923 he had traveled by freighter to Senegal, Nigeria, Cameroon, the Belgian Congo, Angola, and Guinea. His first published poem was also his most famous. "The Negro Speaks of Rivers" was written when he was only nineteen:

I've known rivers ancient as the world and older than the flow
    of human blood in human veins.
My soul has grown deep like the rivers.
I've bathed in the Euphrates when dawns were young.
I built my hut near the Congo and it lulled me to sleep.
I looked upon the Nile and raised the pyramids above it.
I heard the singing of the Mississippi . . .

He gave me a book of his poems that moved me so much I wrote a song to one of them, "Night Owl."

Contrary to the angry, hostile image the white conservative press had painted of Malcolm X, in person he was handsome, hospitable, and witty—and gifted with an ability to gain your intimacy immediately; Malcolm spoke to me as if he had known me all his life. Following a lengthy conversation, he stood and gave me a firm, brotherly handshake. "One day soon, all your leaders will come out of jail to rule your country and bring peace, love, and joy to your people." His words were not unfamiliar—lots of American activists shared similar sentiments with me all the time—but for some reason, coming from him, they struck me as more prophetic than kind and reassuring. In that era, Malcolm was in the rare company of Miles Davis, Harry Belafonte, Martin Luther King, and Sidney Poitier, an African-American man who seemed to be completely unintimidated by any kind of white people, racist or liberal. His first definition of himself was as a man, one who was only black by biological happenstance and equal in all ways to any man on earth. It was only when people came on as though they were better than he was that he didn't waste time putting them in their place. Malcolm X commanded awesome respect even from people who usually felt superior around blacks. He became, from that moment forward, a model for me of how a man of African origin should project.

When Thanksgiving came around, Miriam took Bongi with her to California, where she was on the road with Belafonte. I was left alone in New York. I really had a rough time understanding the logic of Thanksgiving, watching people become suddenly feverish about buying turkeys. Marcus Belgrave persuaded me to come to Chester, Pennsylvania, with him and Fielder for the long holiday weekend. We boarded a Greyhound bus in New York, and three hours later we were in tiny Chester. We walked from the terminal to Marcus's home, a few hundred yards away, where his extended family was waiting. As soon as we got to the house, they were all over us, happy to see old Marcus and "mighty glad" that he had brought Fielder and me for Thanksgiving.

Marcus's family was from the South, so Fielder was no surprise to them. They were more than fascinated, however, with a real live African. They bombarded me with an unrelenting stream of questions. I was shocked at how little Americans knew about the continent I came from. They believed the outrageous, stereotypical bullshit about Africans still living in the Stone Age gathered from Tarzan films, Nyoka the Jungle Girl, Jungle Jim cinema serials, comic books, and other ignorant portrayals. Black Americans seemed to have been programmed to avoid and deny any historical or genealogical connection with Africa. The majority of them were always quick to say, "No, I ain't got nothin' to do with Africa, man! I'm pure, full-blooded American. You better believe it. Yeah, boy!"

However, most of those from the South were totally different. They easily saw how much we had in common; some recalled their grandparents' folktales, which preserved a connection to Africa. Marcus's parents and aunts and uncles told me about how their own parents had been members of Marcus Garvey's Black Star Movement, which was cruelly sabotaged by the government's intelligence community during the height of the "Back to Africa" campaign. Many had contributed substantial amounts of their earnings over many years so that they could be part of Garvey's revivalist crusade, only to be disappointed when he was systematically railroaded by the American government and totally destroyed. When he was finally jailed on some trumped-up charges, many who had hoped that the "Back to Africa" dream would become a reality were deeply disappointed. Nevertheless, it was encouraging to discover that many African-Americans did not buy the "Africans are savages" propaganda. I found out that a considerable percentage of this community were informed about what was happening in Africa, especially older people with a Southern background and those who had taken it upon themselves to do intensive research on the history of the continent and its people.

It was understandable that there would be such ignorance about Africa in the Western world. There was clearly a concerted effort by the conservative establishment to ensure that people who had African or Native American ancestry knew as little as possible about their history—the past was a portal into anger. On the other hand, we Africans were peddled a vision of blacks in the Americas that suggested they were living the high life—all we ever saw were artists surrounded by glitter and glamour. It came as a shock to my generation, who came to the West in the 1950s and 1960s, to find that wherever black people lived—Europe, the Caribbean, America—they were surrounded mostly by poverty, bigotry, squalor, crime, discrimination, and institutionalized murder. This left many of us wildly disillusioned, but it was also the beginning, for many of us, of a commitment to forge solidarity with these communities.

Marcus Belgrave came from a tightly knit, working-class family. Marcus, Fielder, and I shared a bedroom with three beds on the third floor of their old but sturdy Colonial-style house, which had large downstairs lounges, a wraparound porch, huge landscaped gardens, and a large kitchen that bustled with oversized women cooking beans, sweet potatoes, mashed potatoes, stuffing, rice, hominy grits, cornbread, black-eyed peas, turkeys, hams, gumbo, ribs, sauces, pumpkins, cobblers, cakes, cranberry sauce, and everything else that came with the holiday. The kitchen rang with laughter and gossip, while the men settled on the porch to down one beer after another, drink whiskey, gin, brandy, rum, wine, watch television around the clock, and argue wildly about the state of the world with the little knowledge they had at their command. I was grilled endlessly by preschoolers and octogenarians and everyone in between about Africa.

"What'd y'all eat over there?"

"Y'all got telebision?"

"When'd you learn to speak English so good?"

"You always wore dese clothes an' shoes?"

"Y'all have cars and roads over dere?"

"When y'all gone throw all dem white folks outta dere?"

"D' y'all have fruits and d' y'all live in houses?"

"What yo' daddy do for a livin'?"

"You write yo' mama?"

"How you like it in America?"

"Y'all go to church?"

"Where'd you learn to play music?"

"Show me some a y'all's dances."

Later that evening, Fielder listened to me as I continued talking about my home. With a cynical smile on his face, he said to me, "Tell me somethin', man, how come you talking like a white man all de time?"

"What do you mean?" I asked, rather surprised.

"Man, you always talking dat-tap-de-rap-de-tap kinda shit, man. Why can't you talk like no black man? How come you ain't talking like me and Marcus, man?"

It took some fifteen minutes to try to explain my background, how English wasn't even my language and that I had only been speaking it daily for less than a year.

"Shit, man, that's wild! What you been talking all dis time?"

"Oh," I answered, "Zulu, Xhosa, Sotho, Tswana, Ndebele, Afrikaans, Pedi, Shangaan."

"Wait a minute," Marcus jumped in. "You mean to tell me that you speak all them languages?" Before I could answer, Fielder said, "Say somethin' in dat shit that sounds like you hittin' two woodblocks together, man."

I said some words in Xhosa, and they were mesmerized. Some were laughing, some wanted to look inside my mouth. All of them were trying to imitate me. The laughter started all over again as they hopelessly tried to click their tongues like me.

"Shit, man, that's some wild shit. How'd you do dat? Tell you what, you teach me how to do dat shit wid yo' mouth like you poppin' a cork off a bottle, and I'll teach you how to talk like a black man, okay?"

"Okay," I answered Fielder, as he and the others couldn't stop breaking up from trying the Xhosa clicks. "Sheet, maan, do dat again. Hey momma, come hear what Hugh's language sound like. Hey, Hughie, talk dat stuff again."

Marcus's folks were all stunned when I rattled off a sentence that was full of all kinds of clicks. "Well, I'll be damned," said one of his uncles. "Child, y'all talk like dat back home? Well, Lawd help me out. Hey Lawanda, come down here and listen how dis chile talking dat talk from down where he come from." The fascination about my strange tongues went on past midnight.

The next morning Marcus, Fielder, and I took a twenty-minute train trip to Wilmington, Delaware, to visit Clifford Brown's home, where I got to meet my hero's widow and son. They were fascinated by the fact that I had idolized Clifford from so far away and had taken the trouble to come and see his home. I was treated like a long-lost relation. I was also introduced to Clifford's trumpet teacher, who tried to explain his tutoring methods, but I was too sad thinking about Clifford to even understand what he was trying to say.

We continued on to Philadelphia, where Marcus knew lots of musicians, and we spent most of that afternoon and early evening jamming with them. We worked over Miles Davis compositions like "So What" and "Milestones," standards like "How High the Moon," "All the Things You Are," "Cherokee," and "Body and Soul," Charlie Parker's "Straight No Chaser," Duke Ellington's "A Train" and "Perdido"; the list is endless. The sixties were the golden age of jam sessions—they were very competitive, all about separating the boys from the men when it came to fast tempos and intricate chord structures. They also helped us all get with the latest songs and innovations. This was how word got around quickly if there was a talented new musician on the scene. The sessions were a kind of information service about new talent as well as informal jazz workshops. It was a wonderful day for me, and word got around on the East Coast bebop grapevine that there was a bad lil' trumpet player from Africa who sounded a lil' bit like Clifford Brown.

Thanksgiving 1960 was my introduction to African-American family life. "Y'all be sure to come back an' visit again, y' hear? Don' forgit to write yo' mama," said Marcus's mother, hugging me tightly with a wet kiss on my cheek. "Be sho' to tell her you was wid us over Thanksgivin'. It'll make her feel good to know ya had a decent home-cooked meal." Most of Marcus's siblings and cousins walked with us to the bus terminal and bade us farewell with all kinds of screams and hollers. When the bus pulled off, some of them were screaming unintelligible Zulu and Xhosa words, popping their fingers inside their mouths to make a clicking sound and laughing hysterically. By the time we pulled into New York's Port Authority Terminal at 42nd street, I was talking like a black man and Fielder was " 'sho proud" that he could understand "what de fuck" I was sayin'.

Back in New York, I had Miriam's apartment to myself. I was spending most of my time at the Kerinas' in between going to school, babysitting, club-hopping with Fielder and Marcus, jamming uptown with Larry Willis and bassist Eddie Gomez, trumpeter Larry Hall, drummers Al Foster and Henry Jenkins, and other ex-members of the Music and Arts High School youth band, who were now attending Eastman, Juilliard, or the Manhattan School of Music. Larry and I were regulars at John Mehegan's jazz workshops on the Juilliard campus, and John was now giving him private lessons. Larry was beginning to play the hell out of the piano.

One evening Dizzy invited me to come down to Birdland, a jazz club named after Charlie Parker. He was playing there for two weeks. The place was jam-packed, and a gang of musicians were standing at the bar. During Dizzy's break, the Slide Hampton band, featuring Freddie Hubbard, took the stage. Dizzy introduced me to Horace Silver, James Moody, Errol Garner, Melba Liston, Quincy Jones, Sarah Vaughan, Sonny Rollins, Max Roach, Charlie Mingus, Booker Little, Kenny Dorham, Lee Morgan, Donald Byrd, and many other legends and stars who were in the joint. I was semi-hypnotized from being introduced to all these giants. Then we got to Miles, still my idol. He was surrounded by scores of beautiful women and the musicians from his band—Wynton Kelly, Paul Chambers, and Jimmy Cobb. Miles shook my hand with a scowl and barked at me in his raspy sandpaper voice.

"You from South Africa? You know Jeff?" he asked.

I was tongue-tied. "Jeff. Who's Jeff?"

"Sheeeeet. You don't know Jeff? Diz," Miles turned to Dizzy, "this mother-fucka don't know Jeff. He ain't from no South Africa, man." He growled and then, turning back to me again, he said, "You from South Africa an' don't know Jeff. You full o' shit, man. You don't know Jeff?" His face was almost in mine.

"Miles, who de fuck is Jeff, man? Where he at an' what de fuck do he do?" said Dizzy to Miles in an irritated tone.

"Dis ma'fucker don't know Jeff. He ain't from no South Africa, man. Jeff's in Sweden, baddest bass player from down there, man," Miles replied.

I jumped in quickly, "Oooh, you mean Hoojah. Hoojah got me my first job, man. Hoojah is my uncle, too. I'm sure Hoojah told you off when you first met, didn't he?"

Miles looked at me quizzically. "Hoojah. Who the fuck is Hoojah?"

"Hoojah is Jeff," I said. "Jeff is Hoojah. You don't know Hoojah?" I shot back. "Hoojah can be really tough, can't he?"

Miles smiled. "Hey, you know Jeff? Dat ma'fucker called me a small boy; tol' me I don't know shit, dat Dizzy an' Bird taught me everything. He blew me away. I ain't never met nobody wid da kinda confidence like Jeff. Jeff's one bad ma'fucker. Sheeeet. You know Jeff?"

Miles hugged me and called Paul Chambers over. "Hey, Paul, Hugh here know Jeff in Sweden, say he got him his first gig. Sheeet man, you know Jeff? Jeff a bad ma'fucker." Miles couldn't stop smiling. Paul Chambers gave me a limp handshake, said, "Hey," and then went back to talking with Jimmy Cobb. Dizzy left me standing with Miles and his entourage. He was working the room, greeting friends and laughing his famous "Oooweee" laugh. Miles kept looking at me and shaking his head. "Sheet, you know Jeff? Jeff's a bad ma'-fucker."

On the afternoon of December 12, 1960, I was having a rum and coke with Peter and Bonnie in her apartment. It was cloudy, with a light drizzle. I was looking onto 82nd Street from Bonnie's first-floor window at the drizzle when I noticed that it was not drizzling anymore. These were snowflakes—small ones at first, and then they grew thicker and thicker, slowly blanketing the block, slightly dusting the tarred surfaces with a white carpet of snow—my very first snow.

"Let's go outside and I'll take a picture of you to send home," Peter said. "Get your coat and a scarf so you don't catch a cold." By the time I came back from downstairs, where I could see the snowfall increasing onto our back porch, kids were already making snowballs, hurling them at each other excit-edly as the white stuff came down in bigger and bigger flakes.

We soon got tired of throwing snowballs and returned to Bonnie's for a few more hot rum and cinnamon drinks and watched as the snow came down harder and harder, eventually making the street invisible as it got darker out-side. Even the streetlights were getting shrouded in the heavy storm. I went back downstairs around nine-thirty and shortly after that passed out while watching the news on television. I woke up around seven that morning and it was still snowing. Mayor Wagner was on the television screen, announcing that all schools would be closed until further notice. Snow removers were being brought out to clear the impenetrable streets. The city had come to a standstill. I was lost in the whiteness.

I was freezing my ass off in New York City. I spent Christmas day with the Kerinas, wondering just how many people had been killed in South Africa in car accidents, fights, and by the police. I missed my family, but I wasn't missing my country yet. The weather warmed up a few days after Christmas. I decided to go and catch John Coltrane's group at the Half Note. The snow was melting so fast that torrents of draining water were cascading down the gutters. By the time I entered the club it had begun to rain. I was wearing my Italian raincoat and trademark eight-piece black cap, certain that the warm weather would hold for a few days. By the time Coltrane's group went on for their second set, the rain was turning to snow again. I stayed for two more sets while another snowstorm was developing. As it turned colder, the melting water turned to ice. By closing time at four the following morning, the snow had stopped, but the temperature had gone arctic. People were battling for taxis, shoving and cussing each other. When some of us tried to go for the subway train, we found out that public transportation had been suspended once more. There were more and more desperate people the farther uptown I walked. I tried to go across town, thinking that the East Side would be better. It was worse. By the time I got to Grand Central, I could not feel my feet in my shoes. I walked the next forty blocks home alongside hundreds of people who were freezing just like me. When I finally got home, my hands were so iced I could hardly hold my keys. I rang Peter's bell with tears running down my cheeks. Shocked at the state that I was in, Peter ran a tub of lukewarm water and made me put my hands in it while he made a hot Irish whisky for me. My feet were stiff and my socks were all iced up. By the time I was able to open my apartment door, I had finished my sixth Irish whisky and was still shivering, seven hours after I had left the club. Peter kept reminding me that what I went through was only spring for Eskimos. I didn't think that was too funny. For the next three days I stayed indoors, terrified to venture out in that cold again.

On New Year's Eve, Jane and Mburumba came and yanked me out of the house and took me to their apartment, where we watched on TV hundreds of thousands of people bring in the New Year in Times Square. We stayed up till dawn talking about Kennedy, Nixon, Martin Luther King Jr., the John Birch

Society, the Ku Klux Klan, Mayor Rizzo of Philadelphia, Governors Faubus and Wallace, Barry Goldwater, Che Guevera, Castro, Lumumba, Ed Sullivan, Ray Charles, Chubby Checker, Namibia, SWAPO, the ANC, the Congo crisis, Kenyatta, Nkrumah, Miles, Dizzy, Miriam, Belafonte, Mandela, Khrushchev, Hitler, Native Americans, Langston Hughes, Alexandra Township, John Henrik Clarke, Tito, Lenin, Jesse Owens, Joe Louis, Wilma Rudolph, Sugar Ray Robinson, hair-straightening, silly old Louis Lomax, girls, boys, and our parents.

After some initial struggles in school, I developed a determined routine, which helped me pick up the slack. Every day after fetching Bongi, I would first assist her with homework, then I would practice the trumpet lessons Cecil Collins had given me for the next five hours, with breaks to fix supper for us and walk to the store on the corner for some need or the other. After putting Bongi to bed, I would do my academic and music homework, prepare the next day's clothes for us, and on certain nights do laundry and ironing. Bongi and I always washed the dishes together, with her doing most of the talking about her new school, her friends, her grandmother, and her cousin Nhlanhla, or singing one of the many songs she had composed in her little head.

When Miriam was home, the three of us would sing together the songs of Christina Makeba, her mother, a traditional healer. Miriam and Bongi taught me many beautiful songs from this genre, "Bajabula Bonke" (The Healing Song), "Ngi ya Khuyeka" (I Am Suffering), "Ba ya Jabula" (The Ancestors and the Healers Are Rejoicing), "Dzinorabiro" (I Have Treasured My Traditional Heritage from My Forefathers), "Nyankwabe," "Icala," and others—singing them was itself a healing. I attended John Mehegan's jazz improvisation classes regularly, jammed every weekend with Larry Willis and his friends up in Harlem, did as much club-hopping as I could when Leslie or Jean would stay with Bongi, took in a lot of movies and concerts at the Apollo, Carnegie Hall, City Center, the Palladium, Birdland, the Half Note, the Village Vanguard, the Village Gate, the Five Spot, the Jazz Gallery, and Basin Street East, among others.

At midterm, my trumpet, Brass Ensemble, and French grades improved. I continued to draw a blank in psychology despite the efforts of the teachers, schoolmates, and friends like the Kerinas, who all tried their best to explain the concept to me. I just could not get it.

In the spring of 1961 we moved to Park West Village, a new apartment complex on the West Side. Some of the tenants were Ray Charles, Joe Zawinul, Horace Silver, Lee Morgan, Ray Bryant, and a host of authors, poets, designers, and visual artists. A few weeks later I finally met Harry Belafonte at his offices on 57th Street. He introduced me to his production manager, Bob Bollard, who immediately assumed developmental custody over my life. In the back of the offices was a large library with stacks of tapes, tape recorders, and a large working desk. This would become my workplace for the next three years. It was the library of Harbel and Clara Music, the music-publishing wing of Belafonte Productions. Over the years they had acquired hundreds of calypso tapes and recordings of chain-gang music. Researchers who had visited prison work gangs in the South in the early part of the twentieth century and recorded the music had sold the latter to them. Belafonte already had a sample of this genre on a record titled *Swing Dat Hammer,* which his company produced. This album captured the poignant beauty of chain-gang prisoner musicianship, the power of its militant cry for fair prisoner treatment, and the painful cries of men whose lives were filled with hopelessness. My job was to transcribe this taped music onto paper so that it could be copyrighted. I would be paid five dollars an hour, working after school. In addition to my salary, Belafonte's foundation awarded me a stipend of $190 a month to supplement my living expenses.

Belafonte was far better looking in person than the pictures of him on his countless album covers, or the movies I had seen him in, like *Carmen Jones.* Tall, athletic, and with golden porcelain skin and pearly white teeth, he also exuded the compassion and humility of the activist and philanthropist he was, with no pretensions of glamour or stardom. When he spoke, he looked you straight in the eye and spoke with simple eloquence. He was very unaffected—and this was at the time when he was among the most famous entertainers in the world. Most of his staff addressed him as "Harry" or "Mr. B." Even though he joked around with everyone in the office, there was no doubt he was a very focused and serious person. His impeccable taste was evident in the paintings by Charles White and other great African-American painters that hung on the office walls, and his elegant furnishings. Harry came and left in a taxi, rushing to pick up his daughters from school after affectionately speaking with his wife, Julie, on the phone. His simple lifestyle was a pleasant surprise because I had expected a lot of flash, glitter, and fanfare around him. Instead, the people who worked for him were like family. That he was able to keep such a low profile, in spite of his box-office successes, millions of record sales, and sold-out performances all over the world, was amazing. Over the years Harry came to be more than just a benefactor to me. He has been a father to me, the strongest influence on my stage presentation, my community activism, and my commitment to the fight for human rights. Even though it took me a long time to finally come around to it, Harry always tried very hard to teach me self-respect, compassion for others, and, more than anything else, never to forget the people I came from.

Over the weekends Leslie or Jean looked after Bongi. Although everything was going swimmingly for me, I would get terribly homesick at times, and there was still a dark cloud over my memories of home. I had lost touch with all of my Alexandra and St. Peter's friends. Monty and Myrtle Berman could not write because they were still under detention and not allowed any correspondence. The only person who was writing to me was my mother. She kept me abreast with as much news as it was permissible to send me.

I would often go to Central Park across the street from our new flat, find a solitary area, and talk to myself in all the different home languages I could muster. On one such Sunday afternoon I was talking township slang to myself in the park, with all the choreography that comes with the territory, hands waving, torso angling to get the point just right, totally unaware that a group of people who were watching me from a distance thought I had lost my mind. Concerned for my sanity, they had called a black policeman, who startled me out of my township dialogue by tapping me on the shoulder. "Hey, buddy, are you okay?" I was so taken by surprise that my heart was pounding violently against my chest. I was also scared to see a policeman. For a moment I had a flashback of South African police brutality. "Sir, officer, I am quite all right. I'm from South Africa. I've been here for six months and have not spoken my language too much. I was talking to myself, pretending to be conversing with some of my buddies back home."

The policeman laughed. "Oh, you're from South Africa. It's pretty bad back there. You're very fortunate to be up here in New York City, my friend. Welcome." With those words he stuck out his hand to shake mine, told me why he had approached me, and pointed to the group of people who had alerted him to my solo performance. The cop and I walked around the park, talking about New York and South Africa, and two hours later he shook my hand in front of our building and wished me the best of luck. I never saw him again, but his friendliness did remind me how fortunate I really was to be away from South Africa, where my people were being imprisoned every day for activism—and some just for being black and in the wrong place at the wrong time. Members of the liberation movements were leaving the country for Botswana, Swaziland, and Lesotho. From there they went on to Zambia,

Tanzania, West and North Africa, Russia, and Eastern Europe, seeking an education and military training. Others were recruited by Cuba and China. Nelson
Mandela and many of his comrades were on trial for treason. Word was that
the CIA had assisted in nabbing Mandela after he had reentered South Africa
from his trips all over the world, including Central Africa, where he and Oliver
Tambo had established the military wing of the ANC, Umkhonto we Sizwe.
Among those fleeing the country or being imprisoned or murdered by agents
of the evil administration were many of my friends, relatives, schoolmates,
friends of my family, and people I had looked up to all my life.

I was in Mrs. McLaughlin's dictation class one morning when a bespectacled,
distinguished man in his early thirties walked into the room and asked to speak
to her outside. Mrs. McLaughlin came back inside and said, "Masekela, your
services are needed. Please take your trumpet and follow the man, he's waiting for you outside."

"Hello! I'm Al Brown," the man said shaking my hand and smiling. "Harry
sent me to come and get you. He is recording Miriam at RCA's Webster Hall
studios, and wants you to come and play some horn on a few tracks."

That afternoon, I played muted trumpet on "Strawberries," "Umqhokozo"
(My Little Red Xhosa Dress), and "Ntyilo-Ntyilo" (The Love Bird) for Miriam
Makeba's album *The Many Voices of Miriam Makeba*. Harry produced it, and
was bursting with creative energy, enthusiasm, and jokes—clearly enjoying
what he was doing. He was driving Bill Salter (bass), Archie Lee (percussionist), and Sam Brown (guitarist) to the limit. The album was a huge success and
garnered major radio play, especially by Symphony Sid on his WEVD-FM
nightly program, *Jumping With Symphony Sid*. He targeted the three songs I
played on, which transformed my rep around the city. Suddenly I was starting
to command a little bit of respect, especially around the school. The young
ladies were now extra-friendly, and in the cafeteria, people were asking me
how it was working with Miriam Makeba and Harry Belafonte. "Do you really
know Dizzy?" "Have you been with Miles?" "Do you know Coltrane?" "What
is Louis Armstrong like?" The questions never stopped. The people proudest
of me were Miriam and Harry. They were more than convinced that they had
made the right move by helping me to come to America.

Ron Carter, Donald Byrd, Richard Davis, David Izenzon, Richard Williams,
Herbie Hancock, Mike Abene, and all the other successful musicians who were
going to the Manhattan School of Music became friendly. Ron Carter especially took a liking to me.

• • •

Jean Johnson had basically taken over from Leslie Reed, and had more or less moved in with us by now because Miriam was getting busier, going out more on her own tours, and beginning to perform a lot abroad in Europe, the Caribbean, South America, and Asia. With my part-time job at Clara Music, I was finding it harder to spend as much time as I had with Bongi. She was really growing now. Her English was better than ever, and she was doing well in school and was crazy about music. She was blessed with the sweetest singing voice, had natural talent for composition, and always sang new songs for me when I was at the piano. One song, "Nhlanhla," which Bongi had named after her favorite cousin, I later recorded as an instrumental arrangement with my first band. I knew Bongi was destined to become a great musician.

Astley had an aunt who lived on Manhattan Avenue in Harlem, between 112th and 113th streets. Some days I would go with him to visit Mrs. Miller. She would lay some serious Jamaican dishes on us: rice and beans, sweet plantains, jerk chicken, fish stews, and homemade ginger beer, with the meanest meat patties this side of Montego Bay. Astley suggested to me one day that I should move out of the Central Park West arrangement and get my own place. "How can you live there with all these women, man? Why don't you take a room over at my aunt's place? These women are stifling your shit, man. You oughta move your ass outta there and get some space, ma'fucker."

Later that spring it occurred to me that with my working after school at Clara Music and the $190-a-month stipend from Harry's foundation, I could afford a small place. I took Astley's advice and rented a room from Mrs. Miller for forty dollars a month. I can't say Miriam was happy with my decision, but it was time for me to find my own space. What I really liked about my new place was that I could practice my trumpet long into the night. I'd sit in my room and practice my scales and then play some of Clifford's, Miles's, and Dizzy's licks. A drunken tenant from across the alley would be my audience. "Blow dat horn, ma'fucker, blow dat ma'fucking horn. You one soulful nigger. Blow dat horn, ma'fucker!" he'd yell out to my dicey new neighborhood, which was teeming with heroin junkies, pimps and prostitutes, numbers runners and drug dealers.

Around this time a new influx of South African exiles began migrating to the Northeast and Mid-Atlantic United States. Miriam and I were overjoyed about this addition to our growing South African community. She really enjoyed for all of us to come over for dinner, have drinks and bury ourselves in nostalgia, and end the night singing songs from home, followed by a grand finale with Bongi, Miriam, and me singing the traditional ethnic chants. Miriam was the toast of New York's African community, and America in general was fascinated by her charm and seeming simplicity, as well as her exotic looks, magical voice, and overwhelming personality.

Miriam, Mburumba, and Jane introduced me to people from all over the world. Miriam had performed at John Kennedy's inauguration, at the opening of the Organization of African Unity in Addis Ababa, at Carnegie Hall, at the Hollywood Bowl, and in almost every prestigious arena, forum, night club, amphitheater, auditorium, and stadium in the world. Even more amazing was the fact that all this had occurred over less than two years.

Although Mrs. Miller was warm and motherly and treated me like a son, she did not allow me to have female company in my room. I was beginning to feel caged in. After a few months I went looking for places to rent below Harlem, but was always rejected for any number of reasons. I was a foreigner. I didn't have full-time employment. I was a student. I soon figured out that the problem was the color of my skin.

One afternoon I walked up 57th Street with Belafonte to the Russian Tea Room, where we had lunch with his guitarist Ernie Calabria, Diahann Carroll, Anthony Quinn, and Sidney Poitier. Harry had wanted to host an evening of poetry reading at his home—nothing elegant, just an artistic, creative, fun-filled evening with his close friends and musical accompaniment by Ernie, John Cartwright, and me. Walking back to his office, I told Belafonte about my problem finding an apartment. He turned me on to Millard Thomas, his other guitarist, who lived at 310 West 87th Street, between West End Avenue and Riverside Drive, where there was indeed a one-bedroom flat for rent on the ground floor. The proprietor, who lived on the floor above, was Mrs. Edith Marzani, a radical socialist who had been blacklisted during the McCarthy witch hunts. She liked me right on the spot and told me to move in as soon as I wanted. She was in a wheelchair, having been paralyzed from the waist down, but her spirit was dynamic. Mrs. Miller was sad that I was leaving. She liked my midnight horn serenades. I would miss her wonderful cooking and motherly care. "Be sure to come and visit me, you hear?" she said, misty-eyed.

I took off from school the next day and bought a bed and other household goods from the Salvation Army. I painted the apartment walls flat white and the window frames glossy black. Miriam gave me some sheets, pillowcases, a bedspread, and a few kitchen items. That Friday night I slept in the first bed I had ever owned in my life.

I got a telephone and regularly spoke with Sonny and Pat in London. Pat told me she'd be coming to New York to spend a few weeks with me before continuing on to Barbados. Sonny had secretly warned me that Pat had been living part-time with Ben "Satch" Masinga, who was in the cast of *King Kong,* which was now a big hit in the West End. Although we had been apart for almost a year and I also had had my fair share of dalliances, still I felt betrayed, mainly because Satch was an old friend from African Jazz and Variety days. However, Pat had a very logical explanation—she described their relationship as purely biological. The tables were turned.

Still, we had a very enjoyable two weeks together. I took her to see Miles, Belafonte, Dizzy, Miriam, and a Duke Ellington and Ella Fitzgerald concert at Carnegie Hall. We also had a few dinners at Miriam's, and when we left her place, Pat brought up an old subject again.

"Hughie, she still loves you," Pat said. "Remember what I told you before? I'm a woman. I can tell."

"It can't be anymore, Pat, come on," I replied. "Since I've been in the States, Miriam's been having affairs with Pernell Roberts, Horace Silver, Max Zollner, a West African diplomat, and Kenneth Dadzie, a United Nations officer, all of whom she has introduced to me as her lovers. That is ample proof that she's gotten over me a long time ago."

"On the contrary, Hughie," Pat continued. "She's doing all of this to make you jealous. Can't you see?"

My head was swimming in confusion as our cab meandered back to my apartment. I was over Miriam, and she was over me. She had her lovers and I had mine. I had just lived with her for more than six months and we'd never spent a night together. What was Pat tripping about? If there was anyone I had strong feelings for, it was Pat. Regardless of Satch, I was still madly in love with her. Belafonte saw that I was crazy about her, and thought Pat was the ideal person for me. "Why don't you marry her, Hughie?" Harry's question had gone over my head at the time, but checking out Pat staring out the taxi window, I began wondering if I should seize the moment.

One night Pat and I had just returned from a movie when the phone rang. It was Millard, asking me to come upstairs for a minute. As soon as I walked in, Millard put five fat marijuana joints in my shirt pocket, lit the one he was holding, and said, "I know you are accustomed to only the best where you come from. All along I didn't want to waste your time with the bullshit smoke I been holding. Last night a friend of mine scored me a couple of ounces of Panama Red, the connoisseur's smoke. I know you'll love this, Hughie," he said. Without waiting for an answer from me, he passed me the joint and I proceeded to savage it, passing it back to him from time to time. When the joint was finished, Millard said, "Hurry back to your lady, man. I know you're gonna enjoy yourselves tonight." He wasn't lying.

Pat and I made torrid love until morning. I asked her to marry me a few times during the course of the night, but she just giggled and kissed me all over my face. I passed out until midmorning, when Pat asked if I was ready to get up and eat some breakfast. She was weeping. "What's the matter?" I asked. "Nothing," she replied. "I'm just sad because I'm leaving in a few days and we are having such a wonderful time together. Shit, man, go and wash so we can eat." It was a beautiful summer Sunday morning. I suggested that we take a stroll through Central Park. Again, Pat started crying. "What's the matter, baby?" I asked.

"Hughie, I want to marry you so badly," Pat began, "but my parents will not hear of it. I have already asked them, but they say I can't marry some musician who has no future to talk about. My father is the head of Barbados's hospital system and the medical association, and all my siblings and cousins are doctors, lawyers, bankers, judges, and ministers of state. I am expected to marry into such a family, and they refuse to listen to why I want to be with you. I just don't have the strength to go against the grain, Hughie."

A few days later we took a taxi to the airport. We said very little during the ride. This time there were no tears when we said our good-byes. We both knew that we most probably would never see each other again. Back at the office a few days later, Belafonte asked me about Pat. I told him she had left for Barbados. "You should go fetch her back, man. You'll never find another one like her," he said. "Not for a long time." He was right.

During the summer of 1961, Miriam and Bongi left for an extended tour of Europe, Asia, Canada, the United States, and the Caribbean. With school out, I worked full time at Clara Music and kept up my private horn lessons with Cecil Collins at his home in Tenafly, New Jersey. Bob Bollard thought I was doing so well that he recommended me to Hugo Montenegro, Belafonte's new music director. At the time, Hugo was arranging orchestral music for Harry's upcoming summer tour, which would include a large dance troupe selected by the great choreographer Walter Nicks. Among the dancers were Paula Kelly, Altovise Davis, and one of New York's greatest dancers and choreographers, Pearl Reynolds. Hugo hired me to notate Nicks's dance sequences as a guide for him to translate them into an orchestral score for the concert tour. For me, this was the biggest challenge I'd faced since *King Kong*. I managed to pull the task off over three days and became good friends with the dance company, especially Pearl. Hugo Montenegro was so impressed with my work that he proposed I work with him as his orchestrator.

Around this time I met Valentine Pringle at the Belafonte office. He was Harry's new protégé. A tall, ebony-complexioned, bass-baritone singer with a voice very much like Paul Robeson's, his spirituals and folk songs made him popular on the club and concert circuits. Val's guitar player was Bruce Langhorne, a curly haired, light-skinned musician with a delightful sense of humor. The three of us hit it off hard and started hanging out at my apartment, where we would listen to music, drink a lot of cognac, and laugh our asses off. Sometimes we hung out at Bruce's apartment on 48th Street, where he lived with Georgia, his dancer wife, who was a product of the Katherine Dunham dance ensemble and a close friend of Pearl Reynolds. Although Bruce worked with Val from time to time, his regular gig was as an accompanist for Odetta. He played on recordings for folk-music giants like Phil Ochs, Judy Collins, Bob Dylan, and Pete Seeger.

One evening Pearl, who had just returned from a Belafonte tour, invited the Langhornes and me over for dinner along with Ernie Calabria, Belafonte's guitarist, who came with his wife. Pearl was very heavy into African tradition, culture, and dance. She was also crazy about Cuban music, which she played throughout dinner, especially the Juajuanco music of Tito Rodriguez. We drank a lot of sangria wine, and then Pearl pulled out some of that Panama Red smoke, which we had with dessert. Before I knew it, I was helping Pearl wash the dishes and saying good-bye to the guests as if I had been the host. With the doors firmly locked, we sat in the candlelight, deep in discussion about African liberation, art, and dance while we graduated to some fine cognac and more Panama Red with Tito Rodriguez. This night was the beginning of a long and beautiful friendship and love affair.

One day Jimmy Lee, the hip trombone player from Mount Vernon, who was also in my class, invited me to a penthouse loft party where Prophet, the great artist and designer, was having a farewell party for Quincy Jones's band, which was leaving the following day on a European tour with Dizzy Gillespie. He asked me to bring my horn because there was going to be a jam session, but there were so many gate-crashers and musicians trying to sit in that I lost the desire to play. Instead, I enjoyed the 360-degree view of the Manhattan skyline, Brooklyn Bridge, the Battery, the East River, and faraway New Jersey, across the Hudson River from Prophet's wraparound penthouse porch. Jimmy Lee introduced me to a tall, blond, mischievous-looking young musician by the name of Stewart Levine. Right away Stewart and I were rapping about Africa, Asia, and the rest of the world. His girlfriend, Susan Carp, was a leader of the Young Socialist Party, which is how he came to know so much about Cuba, China, South Africa, Vietnam, North Korea, Nkrumah, Sekou Toure, Lumumba, and so many other elements that had become troublesome to America's political and business establishments.

During our discussions, Stewart corrected me on many issues with facts that let me know he was very well read—a quality that distinguished him from most Americans, who knew nothing about matters outside their little neighborhoods except the anticommunist propaganda they got from the national media. Stewart was different.

On the first day of my second year of school, Stewart walked into Music Literature class and sat next to me. Right away, we sensed that we were on the way to becoming friends for life.

My reputation as a musician was beginning to grow. I was getting work as a session man on recordings and club dates with the help of Al Brown. The extra money helped toward my tuition. Mrs. Marzani offered me a larger apartment on the same floor for only fifteen dollars more a month. I took it.

Jimmy Lee and Stewart came over to help me paint my new place. Stewart asked me if I smoked grass—a question he first hit me with at Quincy's party. He found it very odd that a musician from South Africa didn't smoke dagga, when that country was one of the world's biggest exporters of the herb. But I was suspicious; Millard had once been set up and busted for marijuana, and warned me to keep my habit a secret because the penalty for possession was stiff.

We drank vodka and orange juice while my friends helped me with the painting. Sloshed and exhausted, we finished on Sunday morning, passed out, and woke up that afternoon with painful headaches. Later, Frank St. Peter, a saxophonist friend of Jimmy and Stewart, came over and, without asking, lit up a joint and began to pass it around. It was strong Colombian smoke. I had totally forgotten my denial.

"You bullshit motherfucker," Stewart admonished. "I knew you were full of shit when you told me you didn't smoke. I said to myself that you definitely must have been putting us on, you jiveass motherfucker. Light up another joint, Frank."

• • •

Toward the end of 1961, Belafonte thought I was ready to record my first album, especially after the success of Miriam's last album. That night I walked to my apartment oblivious of the twelve blocks in the subfreezing temperatures; my thermal underwear and the cashmere coat Dizzy had bought me kept me warm. Inside, my soul was fired by the prospect of recording. I was very excited.

Around Thanksgiving, the first wave of South African students from the PAC and ANC refugee camps in Tanzania arrived in America to attend school at Lincoln University in Pennsylvania. I had been very close friends with some of them back home. At the beginning of the Christmas holiday season, Joe Louw, Willie Kgositsile, and Peter Davidson came to visit. George Molotlegi, who had been studying at Howard University in Washington, D.C., since 1959, also arrived. They all laid down their bags and made themselves at home. They had come to celebrate the festive season with me. George was a family member of the Royal Bafokeng Nation, recognized globally as one of Africa's richest tribes. His family ruled a kingdom of more than 300,000 people spread over 750 square miles in South Africa's Northwest Province, home to some of the richest platinum deposits in the world.

Schools had closed, and they had nowhere else to go for the holidays. I was the only person they knew would welcome them. At first I was worried about how my landlady would react to my boisterous guests. On the contrary, Mrs. Marzani stopped by my apartment as was her custom, greeted my friends heartily, and welcomed them to America. But the arrival of my holiday visitors didn't go unnoticed by federal authorities. To my surprise, an unmarked car suddenly appeared and stayed parked outside my apartment building. In South Africa, I had grown used to being shadowed by the police and informers. One day I asked one of the trenchcoated men in the car why they were always parked in front of my place. I was abruptly told, "None of your business." I reported the matter to the police and was told they were the FBI, and that their surveillance superseded local police jurisdiction. Although this brought back memories of South Africa's Special Branch Gestapo, we decided to ignore them. And throughout the holidays we partied openly, showing that we were not intimidated by their arrogance. My friends returned to their respective schools following the Christmas holidays, but the FBI, the Internal Revenue Service, and U.S. drug enforcement officials would keep an eye on me. My telephone was bugged for the next three decades that I spent in America.

9

IN EARLY 1962, Belafonte asked me why I hadn't started on the record
we had discussed. I'd started selecting the material, but I'd made a mistake
choosing Hugo Montenegro as arranger. Coming as he did from a
Lawrence Welk/André Kostelanetz background of very Muzak-like arranging,
Hugo had no knowledge of African music except what I had exposed him to
thus far. The choice of songs for my album was basically gleaned from the
repertoires of Harry and Miriam Makeba. The excitement of working with a
big band composed of top session musicians whom I had idolized for years
took precedence over actually coming up with a style that fit my background.
The closest we came to my musical roots was Miriam Makeba's famous
lament "Umhome" and "Merci Bon Dieu," a Haitian folk song from one of
Belafonte's previous albums. That I didn't tap into my township dance band
experiences with Zakes Nkosi, Ntemi Piliso, Elijah Nkwanyana, and the Merry
Makers, or even my Huddleston Jazz Band beginnings boggles my mind to this
day. What was I thinking? Harry had assumed that because Hugo was an
orchestral arranger, my album would at least have taken a more traditional
African dance band route.

The outcome was an album called *Trumpet Africaine,* and it was a disaster,
an unlistenable mixture of elevator and shopping mall music. Belafonte was
disappointed—and infuriated. After the album's release, he ripped the project
to pieces, calling it "antiseptic, jive, white music." It received poor reviews and
very little radio play. Sales were dismal. Embarrassed, I shelved my album
dreams for a while, and began working hard on losing my stupid fascination

with all things American and developing a style that better fit my skills and tastes, based on the African music I was raised on back home.

My disappointment didn't dampen Miriam's confidence in my abilities. She asked me to do the arrangements for her next two albums, *Voice of Africa* and *Makeba Sings.* The reviews of both albums were great, but they didn't set the world on fire. All the songs were South African traditional and township favorites. I infused the music with a back-home flavor, but once again my arrangements smacked of the Hugo Montenegro influence. RCA Records persuaded Miriam to consider other arrangers for her future projects. I had been given a chance that many other deserving musicians would have killed for, and had failed in my first three attempts. I immersed myself in my studies and worked feverishly with Cecil Collins at improving my trumpet technique.

That Easter, my student friends returned to New York for their spring break. They brought several new arrivals from the Tanzania camps. The late-night partying, dancing, and loud music resumed—my apartment was once again transformed into a township commune, with most everyone sleeping on the floor and couches. I kept my bedroom private because Pearl Reynolds was a regular overnight visitor. Of course, the FBI car, which had gone away after the Christmas holidays, returned and parked in front of 310 West 87th street again.

I was finding it difficult to feed all of them and satisfy their booze appetites. I appealed to Miriam for help, and as usual her generosity was abundant. The students warned that many more were on their way to America. This was obviously going to be a heavy load for both Miriam and me. They told us of the difficult conditions in the refugee camps, where many of the young people lacked adequate clothing, medicine, food, and other commodities, and were contracting all kinds of diseases. This information raised Miriam's concern. She suggested that we form a nonprofit student organization that would raise funds to help these young people with their needs in America and in the camps. She spoke to Harry about the idea, and he promised to bring in friends like Sidney Poitier, Lena Horne, Diahann Carroll, and Marlon Brando to become patrons and trustees of the South African Student Association (SASA). At the launch of SASA, the students performed freedom and resistance and liberation songs that were being sung at rallies and in the refugee camps. Belafonte was deeply moved, and proposed that he and Miriam, along with the students, record an album from this repertoire.

• • •

Later that spring, Jonas Gwangwa arrived from London to begin attending the Manhattan School of Music. South African saxophonist Morris Goldberg, who had been playing on a cruise ship between London and New York, had also been accepted by the school. Jonas and Morris became my roommates. As if that weren't bad enough, Sonny Pillay arrived. He stayed with us for two months until he found a place of his own.

My apartment quickly became a meeting place for many of my musician friends who were attending the Manhattan School of Music. I rented an upright piano and transformed the place into a music lab with regular week-end jam sessions, where we developed a wide repertoire of bebop classics and American standards. We composed new songs and worked on arrangements for Sonny's nightclub engagements. Instead of complaining about the chaos, Mrs. Marzani totally embraced the constant bustle and hubbub taking place below her apartment. By now even the FBI agents were becoming fascinated with the human traffic of musicians, fine women, students, and Africans in traditional robes. One of them asked me one day, "Tell me, what's really going on in there?" I said, "Good times, my man, good times, yeah!" I told them they could drop in anytime. "Unfortunately," one of them said, "our job does not allow that." I felt sorry for the FBI.

One day Miriam asked me to go to Los Angeles so I could meet with Marlon Brando and explain the idea of the South African Student Association to him. He was anxious to get more information about the organization. She felt I, as the newly elected president, could best articulate the group's mission. I stayed at the Chateau Marmont Hotel on Sunset Boulevard, where I met with Brando. I was struck by his knowledge of what was happening in South Africa. He shocked me when he asked about the possibility of breaking Robert Sobukwe, the president of the South African Pan-African Congress, out of Robben Island prison. He was serious. He said he had the means and the contacts to make it happen. I was skeptical—Brando's idea sounded like a Hollywood adventure-film scenario.

Following the 1960 Sharpeville Massacre, Sobukwe was arrested and sentenced to three years for incitement, and imprisoned on Robben Island. The apartheid government, fearing his fiery oratory would influence an already incendiary African community, instituted the notorious Sobukwe Clause, which allowed him to be kept on Robben Island without being charged with a crime. He was kept in isolation from the other political prisoners. Nine guards watched his movements, but they were never allowed to speak to him, so he lived in solitary confinement for six years without ever hearing the sound of a human voice. In 1969 he was released and then banished to Kimberley, a mining town where he had never lived. Before his incarceration, Sobukwe was a lecturer in African Studies at the University of Witwatersrand in Johannesburg. During his imprisonment he obtained a degree in economics from the University of London and started his law studies via correspondence. He finished law school in Kimberley, and in 1975 he started his own law practice. Although he was offered several teaching posts at American universities, the government prevented him from traveling overseas. The years of isolation must have caused him severe mental anguish. Sobukwe, who had been under house arrest for twelve hours a day, died in Kimberley at age fifty-four, on February 27, 1978.

I gave Miriam a full report of my meeting with Brando, and, moved by his concern, she resolved to consult with the Pan-African Congress leadership on his plan during one of her upcoming trips to Africa. In 1964, A. B. Ngcobo, the PAC's chief representative and a close friend of Robert Sobukwe, came to New York and had dinner with Miriam and me. We told him about Brando's interest, and he was very keen to meet the actor. Miriam took Ngcobo to Los Angeles, where she introduced him to Brando, who later gave him $20,000 as seed money to plan for Sobukwe's rescue. No one ever heard from Ngcobo again, and Brando lost interest and confidence in our cause.

Miriam had contributed a hefty amount of seed money toward the formation of SASA. Our activities had not gone unnoticed by some high-ranking U.S. State Department officials. On July 16, 1963, she addressed the United Nations Special Committee on Apartheid. The press reported Miriam's remarks, and the South African government immediately banned her albums. Miriam had also grown close to Kwame Nkrumah, Sekou Toure, Jomo Kenyatta, Tom Mboya, Muammar Qadaffi, Julius Nyerere, Kenneth Kaunda, Edwardo Mondlane, Amilcar Cabral, and Fidel Castro, to name a few. She'd sacrificed her highly lucrative career at the pinnacle of her international successes to highlight the plight of her people. But her actions prejudiced the entire establishment of the Western countries against her.

In February 1963, I opened *Playboy* and saw one of the most beautiful women I'd ever seen. She wasn't the centerfold, but a dark-complexioned, sculptured black panther, part of an eight-page "Chicks of *Cleopatra*" pictorial that was part of the publicity for Elizabeth Taylor's upcoming movie. I kept that *Playboy* opened to her page on my living room table. I couldn't stop looking at her—if only I could find her.

One evening, Bruce Langhorne and his wife, Georgia, were at my apartment for dinner when Georgia began thumbing through my *Playboy* magazine. Seconds later she let out a scream. "Hey, Bruce, check this out. This is Barbara Alston standing at attention in slave threads at the feet of Elizabeth Taylor's royal throne! Can you believe this shit?" I moved closer to see what the hysteria was about, only to find out that they were laughing about the girl I wanted to meet. I asked, "You guys know this woman? I want to meet this girl." It turns out they'd known Barbara for years. Georgia had worked with her on a number of dance projects.

Bruce promised he'd try to locate my panther. Two weeks later he called and told me she was working as a dancer in a tropical revue at the African Room nightclub on 44th Street, where she was part of a show headed by Johnny Barracuda, a young calypsonian from Trinidad. She was even more beautiful in person than in *Playboy.* After the performance she came over to our table, where we were introduced. I invited Barbara, her dance colleagues, Johnny, and their conga player, a tall, genie-like giant named Big Black, over to my apartment for drinks. At the house, Johnny seemed insecure every time I spoke to Barbara, and Big Black told me they were an item, even though Johnny was living with another woman. This news was encouraging.

A few days later I was on my way to work at Clara Music when I bumped into Barbara on 57th Street. She was coming from a dance class. I asked her to dinner. She accepted and gave me her telephone number. The next evening, Barbara and I had dinner at Maharajah, an Indian restaurant on 92nd Street, after which we went to the Village Vanguard to see Miles Davis. She seemed very impressed that I knew Miles when I introduced them. Afterwards, we took a taxi to Harlem where Barbara was living with her mother. She gave me a passionate good-night kiss, the beginning of an affair that lasted years, over many breakups and reconciliations, and of a friendship that still endures.

At this time I was still dating Pearl Reynolds, and she began to sense a change in me. She soon found out about Barbara Alston, and although Barbara's name never came up, one morning Pearl left my apartment in tears. It was the end of our love affair.

Sonny and Morris had found their own places to live, leaving Jonas and me as roommates. By now Jonas had pretty much established his own lifestyle and had his own circle of friends. My Lincoln University friends returned for Easter vacation. One day Big Black was telling us about this place in New Jersey where we could buy tripe, intestines, and live goats. The guys became excited about the prospect of some genuine, home-style cuisine—goat meat, cornmeal pap, onion-and-tomato gravy. We just had to get a goat. I pointed out that there was no way we could slaughter a goat in the backyard because it was illegal. "We'll slaughter it in the bathtub," one of my friends said. Late one night, three of them returned from New Jersey with a billy goat dressed in a jacket, a cap and a scarf fastened tightly around its mouth to muffle the animal's moans. They had sat with the goat disguised as a passenger in the backseat between two of them so they wouldn't have any problems with the attendant at the George Washington Bridge tollbooth. Thank God the FBI car was not there when they returned to my apartment. We had the music up loud when the goat was slaughtered in the bathtub, but during the process Mrs. Marzani called from upstairs to find out what all the commotion was about. It was unusual for her to call, because she had never complained about noise coming from my apartment, but she apparently seemed to sense that something weird was going on. She never found out. We feasted on that goat for almost two weeks.

One evening Barbara decided to spend the night with me. Jonas was away, and I looked forward to being alone with her at 310. I met her after her dance class, and we had an early dinner and caught an early Miles Davis set at the Village Vanguard. On the way home we picked up some groceries and a bottle of Courvoisier. It was an evening both of us had been looking forward to for a long while. Shortly before midnight, when we were hurriedly walking down 87th Street toward my place, I noticed at least a dozen guys waiting at the entrance to 310. One screamed, "Hey, Hugh, hurry up, man, it's cold out here." Barbara said, "Who the fuck are those people?" I explained that they were my homeboys from Lincoln University, and that my place was the only one they knew to stay in New York.

Even though they were polite and affectionate when they introduced themselves, Barbara was livid. "Hughie, are you trying to tell me that these people are going to sleep in your apartment? Where are you going to put all of them?" she whispered. Once inside, we resumed the debate in my bedroom. Barbara continued, "Hughie, I love you very much, and I like your friends, but I ain't sleeping in this house with all these niggers. This was supposed to be our first night together. I am not going to do it with all these people in the house. How am I gonna go to the bathroom if I wanna take a leak with all these Negroes looking up all over my ass? I'm sorry, Hughie, you're just gonna have to take me home."

"Okay, Barbara, I understand," I said. "Don't worry, baby, I've got a solution." I called the Paris Hotel on West End Avenue, where Barbara and I spent two undisturbed, blissful days.

My final school year was halfway gone and I still had not begun to understand what psychology was all about. My passion for study began to disappear. My club-hopping, pot-smoking, cognac-guzzling, and dalliances with countless women were also beginning to take a toll on my schoolwork. The pain of being unable to return home was becoming unbearable. A certain recklessness was creeping into my lifestyle.

My parents' recent divorce triggered a new restlessness in me. I began to develop an aching desire to return to South Africa, teach music, and help my mother cope with her new responsibilities of having to care for my sisters on her own while my father prepared to take a new wife. The periodic visits from people back home and the recordings they brought us by outstanding new groups such as the Dark City Sisters, Mahlathini and the Mahotella Queens, and veterans like Zakes Nkosi and Ntemi Piliso, made me more homesick than ever; I was aching for the township life and decided that I would return to South Africa. I felt very strongly that I had learned everything in America that I needed to know, and it was time to share my experiences back home. I had made enough money to kick-start a new life in South Africa. When I told Harry Belafonte about my plans, he sat me down and said, "Hughie, this is not a good time for you to go back home. Nelson Mandela and all of his colleagues are sentenced to death. With your mouth, you have exactly the kind of temperament that will place you in direct confrontation with the apartheid authorities. If something bad happened to you, there would be nothing much we could do to help you. There won't be any international outcry to intervene on your behalf. On the other hand, if you remain here and continue to make a name for yourself, you will eventually have access to the media so that when you talk about your country's problems, people all over the world will listen." I appreciated Harry's concern for my well-being, but I had made up my mind to go home.

Miriam Makeba, after having made her United Nations General Assembly speech against apartheid earlier that year, was deeply concerned about my plans to return to South Africa.

Jonas planned to go as far as London with me, where he would stay and visit friends and then return to New York in the fall. We explained our London plans to Mrs. Marzani, who allowed us to leave the apartment in care of Willie Kgositsile and Joe Louw. In London, Myrtle and Monty Berman, who had left South Africa on exit permits, warned me that if I returned to South Africa, I would be arrested immediately. Myrtle said, "Are you crazy? Spengler will be waiting for you with open arms."

My mother sent me a letter warning me not to set foot on South African soil. She reminded me of a previous letter in which she'd mentioned that the Special Branch Police had come to our house looking for me after I left the country. They were not pleased that I had slipped through their fingers.

My sister Barbara had also taken an exit permit from South Africa. She had married an American who was her professor at Roma University in Lesotho. He went to teach at Legon University in Ghana, where Barbara enrolled to study. Shortly after their arrival in Ghana, they broke up. My sister had just come to London to enroll at the university. It was truly a pleasant surprise, because I hadn't seen her in more than four years. She let me know I was completely insane for wanting to return to South Africa. All of this made me reconsider my decision to go home.

By coincidence, a telegram arrived from Miriam. While on tour in Los Angeles, she had become ill after complaining of a lack of energy. She was hospitalized there and had been diagnosed with cervical cancer. She didn't know if she was going to survive or, if she did, how long it was going to take for her to recuperate. She asked me to return to New York and help look after Bongi. I was in a state of confusion. I had now been thinking about staying in London where I was getting many lucrative offers. But Miriam was in trouble. I sent a telegram to Mrs. Whitford requesting reinstatement to school and my need for a student reentry visa. When I got back to New York, Miriam had been released from Hollywood Community Hospital and had been given a clean bill of health. She was back in New York, and thrilled that I had returned.

I found 310 in shambles. Willie, Joe, and the Lincoln University gang had trashed the place and left an eight-hundred-dollar telephone bill. Barbara Alston and I spent two days shampooing the carpets and cleaning. I noticed that the unmarked FBI car had returned to its usual spot. For better or worse, I realized, America was home.

In January 1964, Miriam and I unexpectedly found ourselves rekindling our romance. I was now playing one-nighters around New York on a fairly regular basis with pianist Larry Willis, bassist Hal Dodson, and drummer Henry Jenkins. Our quartet was beginning to attract major critical notice. Because I sang to the musicians when teaching them South African songs, Miriam and Larry persuaded me to add my singing to our live act. Larry threatened to refuse to play if I didn't sing. At first I was reluctant because I felt my voice was not good enough, but I tried it. The audiences seemed to enjoy my singing, especially on tunes I had learned from Bongi and Miriam.

The first song I wrote for this group was "U-Dwi," my mother's nickname. It was an uptempo mbhaqanga shuffle, which had a heavy bebop and merengue groove, an ideal vehicle for Larry and me to show off our dexterity on our instruments when we were soloing. Miriam's mother's "Dzinorabiro" (I'm Possessed by the Spirits of My Ancestors) and "Abangoma" (The Traditional Healers Are Rejoicing) were up tempo songs. Here, Larry and I did traditional call-and-response vocals before jazzing up our solos. "Bajabula Bonke" (They All Rejoiced at My Illness), another song from Miriam's mother, was a slow lament in which Larry harmonized my vocals. "U' Nhlanhla," a composition by Bongi about her cousin back home, was a mid-tempo shuffle. "Ntyilo Ntyilo" (The Bird Song) was a classic South African love ballad.

Then we would break into a furious double tempo with Henry and Hal playing feverishly against Larry's vamping and my solo, reminiscent of Coltrane's quartet. "Mixolydia" was a tribute to Miles and Coltrane, a cross between the former's "All Blues," and 'Trane's "Favorite Things." Larry's "Con Mucho Carino" was a fast-paced Juajuanco-jazz kind of salsa. I also wrote "Child of the Earth," an ethnic-sounding chant about a beautiful young rural woman walking with a tempting, rhythmic gait on her way to fetch water from the village stream. All of our songs were a hybrid of traditional and ethnic chants, township dance, and Caribbean, calypso-like grooves mixed with jazz and Brazilian sambas. It was a potpourri of the music of the African diaspora. All kinds of jazz critics and music experts have tried to categorize it, but have been unable to pin it down. I haven't either. One thing is for sure, it has gotten me where I am today. Village Gate owner Art D'Lugoff was so knocked out by the group that he hired us to open every time female artists like Nina Simone, Gloria Lynne, Buffy St. Marie, or Carmen McRae headlined.

In February, Miriam asked me to escort her to the Grammy Awards, held that year at the Hotel Astor in New York City. It was a big night for the Beatles, who won Best Performance by a Vocal Group, and Barbra Streisand, who won Best Vocal Performance, Female for "People." Miriam spotted Louis Armstrong and his wife, Lucille. Armstrong had won Best Male Vocal Performance for "Hello Dolly." She introduced me to the couple. I finally had a chance to meet one of the people who had first sparked my passion for music. I must have talked him to death about how his trumpet made the Huddleston Jazz Band the envy of South African musicians because of the news coverage. Satchmo kept smiling. Here I was standing with the man whose banning from South Africa when he visited the continent had angered me so deeply because I had lost a chance to shake his hand in person and thank him for the trumpet. I had envied so much all those people I saw shaking his hand in press photographs. But now here I was, alone with the great Satchmo. It was more than a dream come true. The only thing I've always regretted is that I didn't have my picture taken with him right then.

He eventually got in a few words. "Well, lemme tell you sumtin. Lucille packed that horn and took it personally to the post office to make sure you got it." I thanked him again. Armstrong just kept on smiling. I was so glad he didn't ask if I was still playing his trumpet, although I suspected he knew the truth. Miriam also introduced me to Sam Cooke, Phyllis Diller, Tony Bennett, Barbra Streisand, Count Basie, Ella Fitzgerald, Mahalia Jackson, Dick Gregory, Steve Lawrence, and Eydie Gorme, among others—once again, I was struck dumb in awe.

I had come to New York as a bebop musician, hoping to one day become a member of Art Blakey's Jazz Messengers or Horace Silver's Quintet, or to play in Les McAnn's group, but when I broached the subject with any one of them, the answer was always, "Hughie, why don't you form your own group?" This frustration was lightened by Belafonte, who said to me, "Why don't you play music from your home? Look at what it's done for Miriam." Dizzy Gillespie told me the same thing, and Miles Davis always said to me, "Hughie, there are thousands of us jazz musicians in this country. You're just gonna be a statistic. But if you play some of that shit from South Africa and mix it with the shit you know from here, you gonna come up with something that none of us can do. Fuck jazz, man. You don't wanna do that shit, ma'fucker. You know what I'm sayin'?" Bebop was at a crossroads, and Dizzy and Miles were both already experimenting with new styles. Their encouragement was a turning point for me.

For the six months after my return to New York, Miriam and I were inseparable. We had candlelit dinners in New York's finest restaurants, took walks hand-in-hand through dimly lit Greenwich Village streets. We went to movies, plays, concerts, awards shows, and banquets. One spring evening, while we were out having dinner, Miriam said, "Hughie, why don't we get married?" I was stumped. We had a beautiful romance, but marriage however never entered my mind—I had not been expecting that as I thought that at any time Miriam might start to drift away from me as she had before. But somehow, this time, we seemed to need each other more than before—it felt urgent that we hold each other up at a time when we were both vulnerable. I was so desperately homesick, I'd nearly walked back into the jaws of apartheid, and Miriam's near-fatal illness had shaken us both. Most of all, Bongi had never been happier than when we were together. The prospect of a family never felt more natural. I told Miriam I would be honored.

I moved back into Miriam's Park West Village apartment, and we made wedding plans immediately. But before exchanging vows, we had to purge the skeletons from our closets. I spent the next few weeks trying to break off my relationships, but I overlooked telling Susan Belink, with whom I had carried on a torrid love affair when we were both students at the Manhattan School of Music. Our relationship had rekindled in recent months. She was a fiery opera singer, and I knew she wouldn't take my impending marriage lightly.

I told Belafonte about our upcoming marriage. He didn't say a word, but became visibly upset. He looked straight into my eyes with a big question mark on his face. I had always considered Belafonte a father, and was deeply grateful to him for having given me my first opportunities in America. As I was telling him about our marriage plans, I couldn't help remembering the time he'd chastised me after catching me smoking pot with a group of musicians. Belafonte lectured me with the gentleness of Father Huddleston, but with the firmness and concern of a parent. He was right. Had I got caught smoking pot, I could have been deported and my future would have been sidetracked. But I felt that it wasn't his place to advise me this time.

The night before our wedding, Miriam and I had a terrible argument that almost derailed everything. She had waited until the last minute to tell actor Pernell Roberts their relationship had to end. She went to his hotel the night before our wedding to break the news, and didn't come home until after midnight. I flew into a jealous rage. She said all they did was have dinner, but I couldn't imagine it took that long to tell the motherfucker she was getting married. I was pretty sure they were having one last bang. We both ended up screaming at each other into the night, but the next morning our tempers cooled and all was right in our world again. That day, a few weeks after my twenty-fifth birthday, I wore a black suit and my bride wore a white two-piece ensemble. The ceremony was held at Priscilla and Bob Bollard's home in

Stamford, Connecticut, with just a few close friends. We didn't go on a honeymoon, but eased into New York's social scene as newlyweds. Miriam gracefully saluted us one evening while she was performing at the Village Gate. "Ladies and gentlemen, this is my husband, Hugh Masekela." Resounding applause, mixed with screams of joy, shook the club. The staff were especially thrilled because they had been there when I first started performing at the Gate, where Miriam had also performed early in her career. I stood up and blew my wife kisses.

Miriam and I were settling into a nice family rhythm when one evening, a week later, the telephone rang. Miriam answered the phone. It was Susan Belink. Their conversation was far from pleasant. Almost immediately, Miriam started screaming. It was obvious that Susan was goading Miriam into an argument. I stood by her as she kept screaming at my ex-lover. When she finally hung up the phone, I asked what was going on.

"Fuck you, motherfucker," Miriam replied. "Don't fucking ask me what's going on. You have the nerve to tell me not to see or talk to any of my ex-boyfriends and then have the nerve to have one of the whores you used to fuck call our house and insult me? Put on your fucking coat. You are taking me to her house. I am going to beat the shit out of that white bitch."

I replied, "Zenzi, I don't even know how she got our number. I don't even know hers, or where she lives. I haven't talked to her in months." This was a lie.

"Damn you, man," Miriam continued. "The fucking slut gave me her goddam number and fucking address. She even said she was waiting for my ass. You call that bitch and tell her never to call my house again, you hear me? You keep your stinking dogs from my door."

Miriam dialed Susan's number and, before the first ring, shoved the receiver in my face. "Here, you tell that bitch I'll kill her if I ever lay my hands on her."

With a dry mouth, I whispered to Susan, "Why are you calling my house and insulting my wife?"

"Fuck you and your wife, Hugh," Susan said. "I was calling to congratulate you, and she goes off on me! I can cuss too, you know."

Miriam started crying and hyperventilating. Bongi came out of her room, asking what was going on. "Go back to your fucking room," Miriam snapped.

Susan continued, "You think you can just fuck me over and then abruptly go off and marry this bitch who has the nerve to insult me?"

Before I could respond, Miriam yanked the phone from my ear. "Fuck you, you white slut. I'm coming over there and beat the shit out of you."

Before she hung up, I heard Susan scream, "Fuck you too, you black whore. I'll be waiting for your ass."

Miriam banged the phone down and screamed, "Come on, Hughie, you're coming with me. I want you to see what I'm going to do to all of your fucking bitches who don't want to accept the fact that you're my husband."

I tried to calm her down, but Miriam had the door to the hallway open and was screaming so all our neighbors could hear. "Come on, motherfucker, let's go."

I followed her meekly down the hallway into the elevator and out onto 97th Street. We were walking so fast, we looked like a couple of Olympic race-walkers heading down the Upper West Side.

"I am Zenzi of Makeba, Ka Qgwashu," she ranted. "We are the demolishers of anything that stands in our way. When we finish eating, we just kick the dishes away. She'll find out who I really am today, this dirt of yours. I'm gonna beat her till she shits."

I was walking a few strides behind Miriam, and she would occasionally yell, "Come on!" while people gawked in amazement at the great Miriam Makeba. I was thinking to myself, *We've been married for only a week, and we're already on our third major fight.*

Miriam walked straight past the doorman and into the elevator with me on her heels. Before the man could say a word, the elevator doors closed in his face and we were hurtling up to the fourth floor. Miriam went to Susan's apartment door and began banging with both fists. "Open the door, you fucking bitch," she screamed. "I'm gonna show you. Come on out and talk that fucking shit you were talking on the phone. Come on!"

I guess Susan hadn't expected that Miriam would come to her building. A muffled voice shot back from behind the door, "Go away. I'm calling the police." By now the doorman and Susan's neighbors had gathered. The doorman pleaded with Miriam to leave. She finally relented.

Walking back to our apartment, Miriam began to cry. When we got home, she became eerily quiet. All she did was play some Billie Holiday and Dinah Washington records. A mournful air descended on the house. Sitting on the living room carpet, Miriam began writing me a long letter. I went to bed with Dinah Washington and Billie Holiday still singing in the living room, "Am I Blue."

The next morning, Miriam was still quiet. She washed, dressed, and left the house. I said good-bye to Bongi, who was leaving for school, and watched her walk to the subway from our balcony. I went to rehearsals with my band, wondering where it was all going. That afternoon I read Miriam's letter. She complained about her generosity and how she was always trampled on, my cruelty, her ill health, her late mother, and how she only had Bongi left as family; how everyone took advantage of her, and on and on and on. I really regretted not having leveled with Susan, but this was now water under the bridge. I braced myself to weather the storm.

When I came back from rehearsals, Miriam was cooking up a storm, playing happy songs on the phonograph and friendly as ever—as if nothing had happened. Jean joined us for supper and stayed to babysit Bongi while we went out to a movie. All was well—or at least that's what I thought. This would become the pattern of our marriage when we were together for more than a week at a time.

When Miriam was happy, no one in the world could match her generosity, affection, sympathy, goodwill, charity, warmth, and humor. Her laughter would ring through the house, the gossip delicious and delightful, her impersonations and miming flawless, and her loving the sweetest a man could ever wish for. But when she lost her temper or was in a bad mood, she had the fury of an erupting volcano accompanied by an earthquake and a hurricane. Sweet as she can be, when Miriam is pissed off, the most advisable thing is to simply run for the hills and not come back until the storm has subsided and she is humming again, telling her funny stories and singing her happy songs.

Dizzy Gillespie had just moved to Englewood, New Jersey, a short drive from the George Washington Bridge. This was after he had spent almost all of his New York days in Flushing, Queens. Dizzy was like a foster father to us, and I relied on him for all kinds of advice from music to every facet of life. Dizzy always had a solution to my problems, no matter how complex—he always had the shortest and simplest answer, embellished with crazy jokes and unbelievable anecdotes.

Miriam, Bongi, and I were outgrowing our New York apartment. The African community, especially the diplomatic and exile population, was growing in leaps and bounds, and our place had become a home away from home for many people from these groups. Students, ambassadors, musicians, actors, writers, dancers, and activists, all felt a deep affection and love for Miriam. The civil rights and African-American communities held a special place in their hearts for her. More than that, people of all nationalities and every ethnic group worldwide recognized and loved her with a sincerity I have seen reserved only for a few very special people in the world. Miriam was extraordinarily special then, and always will be. But it didn't make for a peaceful apartment.

In February 1965, Miriam won a Grammy Award for the album *An Evening with Belafonte & Makeba*. Jonas Gwangwa mostly produced this project. In only her sixth album and just six years out of South Africa, Miriam had made it to the top of the music world, becoming the first South African to win a Grammy.

A few weeks later, on Sunday afternoon, February 21, word spread like wildfire throughout New York City that Malcolm X had just been assassinated. He was giving a speech arranged by his Organization of Afro-American Unity at the Audubon Ballroom in Harlem, when three black gunmen shot him in front of his wife and children. There was an outpouring of grief and anger by many blacks. The first thing I did was call Mburumba Kerina, because he had introduced me to Malcolm. He had already heard the news, and was staggered. All the African liberation movements had embraced Malcolm X even before he made his pilgrimage to Mecca. I never forgot the prophetic words he had spoken to me when we met, foreseeing the liberation of all African people.

Around this time, the South African musical *Sponono* opened on Broadway to lukewarm reviews, and closed after a short run. About half the cast remained in New York and formed a group called the Zulus. They were hired by the New York World's Fair as part of the African Pavilion. Caiphus Semenya and Douglas Xaba decided not to join the group, and with Miriam's assistance they rented an apartment not far from our place.

Caiphus never stopped lamenting over how much he dreamt of bringing his childhood sweetheart, Letta Mbulu, to America. Letta had been a member of the Swanky Spots, a teenage singing quintet that had captured the hearts of South Africa's audiences in the Township Jazz concerts, and had gone on to play the parts of some of the children in the *King Kong* musical. During the run of the musical, Caiphus's singing group, the Katzenjammer Kids, had featured parts in the play, and the couple became close to Miriam and me. After U.S. immigration granted her a work visa, Letta finally arrived in New York during the spring of 1965, and the couple moved in with us at Park West Village.

Miriam agreed with me that we needed more living space. Dizzy introduced me to a real estate agent who found us a house across the street from the Gillespies, at 372 North Woodland Drive in Englewood, New Jersey, just across the bridge from New York. Shortly thereafter, the five of us—Letta, Miriam, Bongi, Caiphus, and I—moved out there and adopted a new suburban lifestyle.

This was a wonderful period in my life, and is the source of wonderful memories. Caiphus and I worked on developing some of his compositions. At that time, his "Bo-Masekela" was a mainstay of my band's playlist. It was a beautiful rhythmic ballad in the harmonic style common to the folk music of the Tsonga, Pedi, Venda, and Ndebele people, peppered with blues chordal progressions, a prominent contrapuntal bass line, and a sweet trumpet melody. There are very few recordings of mine that do not contain one or two of Caiphus's compositions—I consider him one of Africa's greatest composers. The basement became our music studio. We held all of our rehearsals down there and gave some jumpin' parties that lasted into the early morning and helped keep the nighttime raids of the raccoons on our garbage cans down to a minimum. Often Caiphus and I would go for morning runs through the luxurious neighborhood and marvel at the palatial estates, manicured lawns, and lush gardens that surrounded Englewood's sprawling mansions. In the evening we gathered around the fireplace when Miriam was home, and the five of us would sing the songs she, Bongi, Caiphus and Letta taught us—ancestral classics that would have us chanting nostalgically through the night.

I drove Bongi to school every morning. She was now attending the High School of Music and Art in north Manhattan. Letta started to rehearse for her debut engagement at the Village Gate. Dizzy, who had never learned to drive, would walk over from time to time, needing a ride. It gave us a chance to smoke a spliff, since Lorraine and Miriam were dead set against marijuana. Our rides were then naturally riotous, while Dizzy spun out an education for me in African-American music history, laced with his storehouse of hilarious band-on-the-road stories. He was a walking history book of black ghetto humor and lore, but his life also touched on the signature names and moments in his people's musical history. His first band had featured Sarah Vaughan on piano, singing duets with Billy Eckstine. He told me that John Coltrane had just come out of his teens when he joined his band. He had stories about his State Department tours with a wonderful big band playing Quincy Jones arrangements all over Europe and Asia. In India he sat down with the snake charmers and got the cobras dancing to his trumpet playing. For me, his funniest story was how Cab Calloway claimed to have fired him for shooting a spitball in his direction, but according to Dizzy, he quit after refusing to continue babysitting little Chris Calloway. The little girl drove him crazy, and he couldn't take any more. I would discover how right he was about Chris a little later. Strangely, Dizzy never talked about Charlie Parker. I once asked Lorraine about Bird. She detested him and never allowed Parker in her home. She thought he was morally bankrupt and a terrible influence on all the musicians around him. I suspected Lorraine's venom might be the reason Dizzy eventually stopped playing with Bird. Lorraine was a staunch Catholic; Dizzy even had a private chapel built for her in their home. She had no time for diplomacy. She was a straight shooter, with the most hilarious guttural guffaw, as well as a fiery temper. And like Miriam, she also had an unbelievably generous disposition. We loved the Gillespies—I still miss them.

Around this time, my sister Barbara came on vacation from London to visit us. After a few weeks I began wondering when Barbara was returning to London, because she never mentioned her plans. One day Miriam dropped the bomb: "Hugh, Barbara is expecting a child very soon, and she won't be returning to London just yet." I was surprised because Barbara didn't look pregnant, but nevertheless, on July 26, Miriam and I rushed Barbara to Mount Sinai Hospital in New York. I had hardly parked the car and made it to the delivery ward when Mabusha Dumisa was born. Two days later we were back in Englewood with the new master of the house—my nephew. Barbara said nothing about who Mabusha's father was, and we were so excited over the new arrival that we didn't ask.

A month after the baby came along, a disagreement exploded between Miriam and Barbara, and Barbara moved in with a girlfriend of hers in Lower Manhattan. A few months later, Caiphus and Letta found an apartment in Harlem, where Bongi began to spend a lot of time because it was not far from her school. Their moving out didn't sit well with Miriam. She enjoys being surrounded by people. She still lives with a lot of people in her house. It is her style. She enjoys cooking and caring for everybody.

That summer Miriam and I toured Europe with our bands, playing Copenhagen's Tivoli Gardens for a month. We also went to London for a joint BBC special. We played with Jack Jones in San Francisco, and spent a week at the Apollo Theater and a sold-out week at Hollywood's Huntington Hartford Theater. For the first time we brought to American audiences traditional South African folk songs, gumboot dances, and our liberation songs with Letta, Caiphus, and Philemon Hou, another *Sponono* alumnus, joining us on the tour.

After the bad experience with *Trumpet Africaine*, I was determined to establish a definitive African character in all the music that I played. I recorded my second album, which was produced by Ed Townsend for Mercury Records. It featured Morris Goldberg, Larry Willis, Jonas Gwangwa, the legendary guitarist Eric Gale, and tuba player Howard St. John. The repertoire was pure township dance band songs like "Johannesburg Hi-lite Jive," a favorite classic, Douglas Xaba's "Emavungwini," The Dark City Sisters' "Iya Hlupeka Le Ngane," "Ntyilo Ntyilo," and other township favorites. It was another nerve-racking experience. The record company didn't even know that my album existed. I blew up at Mercury's president Irving Green, who had been wining and dining me and was now suddenly unavailable after my album was released. One day I got fed up and told his secretary to tell Green I said, "Fuck him." Not surprisingly, I was released from my contract very shortly after that. The album was not released until after I'd had my first number-one album with another label. The record suddenly appeared with a toy baby tiger on the cover, titled *Grrrrr!*

Tom Wilson, who had produced Simon and Garfunkel, Eddie Harris, Terri Thornton, and Bob Dylan at Columbia Records, became MGM Records' first black vice-president. After my Mercury release, Wilson, who never missed any of my performances at the Village Gate, signed me to MGM. We recorded my first live album, *The Americanization of Ooga-Booga*, at the Village Gate, featuring the songs I had learned from Miriam and Bongi, along with compositions by Larry Willis, Caiphus, and me. The band had become very tight. The music was kicking, and the album turned out great. Tom was over the moon and had my album released right away. It began to receive major play in California and I was hopeful I was on my way to my first hit.

One day I went to visit my friend Stewart Levine. He had just married Susan Cederwall, a dancer from Wenatchee, Washington. Stewart and Susie lived in a second-floor apartment at 58th Street and Second Avenue. During my visit with the newlyweds, Stewart and I decided to form a production company. We called it Oo-Bwana, pronounced "double-o Bwana," a named inspired by the James Bond films. We noticed that many young musicians and record promoters we knew of or were close to were beginning to achieve success by forming independent record and production companies. So, we decided that we were talented enough to do likewise, especially because we had access to all the untapped talent of our ex-schoolmates and the people from the *Sponono* cast who had remained in America. Initially inspired by Stan Getz and Joao Gilberto's collaboration on "The Girl From Ipanema" and other Brazilian music, we figured that if Stewart assumed a similar kind of persona on his saxophone and fused South African township music with American jazz, we would come up with a popular hybrid.

In late November, Miriam was on tour in Europe. As a sixteen-year-old teenager, Bongi was developing an interest in boys, and I felt she needed to spend more time with her mother. I was doing my best to be a good parent, but with my professional engagements, it was difficult to give her the attention she needed. By February of 1966, Miriam had been away from home too long, and I felt that she needed to deal with my concerns about her mothering. Bongi and I boarded a plane for Stockholm, where Miriam was performing at the famous Bernes nightclub. We arrived in minus sixty-five-degree weather. Throughout our marriage, I never thought of entertaining any dalliances. I was completely loyal to Miriam and our family. And I believed that Miriam, too, was fully committed to our vows. Even during her long absence, she'd call home regularly. Our lives were so intertwined that there would never have been a moment to think of anyone else, or so it seemed.

There was a *West Side Story* company playing in Stockholm. Some of the cast members would catch Miriam's second show, and afterward we'd all hang out. One of the lead actors, who would come to Miriam's shows, was a Latino from New York. I soon sensed that something was going on between him and my wife.

After about a week in Sweden, I told Miriam I had to leave because of some upcoming club dates at the Village Gate—also, I was getting anxious to get Oo-Bwana off the ground. I explained I would be leaving Bongi with her. Miriam showed no interest in keeping Bongi with her in Sweden, and was very critical of my attempt to develop a production company.

She said, "How could you try and go into the record business, when people like Belafonte have been unable to succeed at it? You recorded for his production company, and your record went nowhere. You are just wasting your time, man. You and your Stewart are just playing games." I didn't pursue the matter any further, but deep down I was a little hurt.

After we agreed that she would send Bongi back to New York the following week, I asked Miriam when she thought she would be returning to the States. I told her Bongi needed her mother's guidance on womanly matters that I could not handle. Miriam told me that after her Bernes engagement, she was first going to Paris for shopping and that she would return to America when she was good and ready. I could tell that she was trying to coax me into a confrontation. Already feeling betrayed and disappointed, I decided not to show my anger and hurt. I didn't want to cause a scene, but my heart was sinking— I bade her farewell, feeling this was the last time we were going to be a family. And somehow I really felt sorry for Miriam.

Edith Nozipho Grootbroom, who was also in Sweden with Miriam, working as her personal assistant and traveling companion, returned to the States with me. En route to New York, I said, "Zip, you don't have to tell me anything, but I am more than certain Zenzi is having an affair with that Latino boy. What beats me is that she thinks I would be so naïve as not to notice. I've known Miriam closely for more than ten years, and in the past she would behave just like she's been behaving this week when she would try to hide a lover from me. I always caught her, and she caught me, too, when I fucked around. But this time is different. We are married, and I'm not going to let it go by without doing something about it."

Nozipho was quiet for a long time, then finally sighed and said, "Hughie, I'm glad you said it. I'm not saying a word. She told me to mind my own business, and I'm staying out of this. I'm going back to New York to start my life afresh. I wish you all the luck." Ten days later, Bongi arrived—alone! Miriam called soon after, and I gave here an ultimatum that if she didn't return by a certain day in March, I would drop Bongi off at our lawyer's office and walk away with my horn and the clothes on my back. Miriam insisted she was still going to Paris and would be back when she was ready. I informed Max Cohen, our lawyer, of the situation. He tried to get me to rethink the matter and be more patient. I refused to be dissuaded. Explaining to Bongi was the most painful thing I ever had to do. *"Malume* [uncle] Hugh," Bongi said, "I'm gonna miss you, but I'll come and visit you wherever you are." My ultimatum date arrived. There was no sign of Miriam, and she hadn't called. I dropped Bongi off at Cohen's office. I held back my tears until I reached the elevator. When the doors closed, I wept openly.

I caught a cab to Susie and Stewart's apartment. We smoked a couple of joints and listened to some Miles Davis records behind a few shots of cognac. For the next few nights I slept on Jonas's living room couch at 310. Of course, in my determination to walk out of Miriam's life, my pride and pain blinded any rational thinking on such matters as where I was going to live. Jonas, seeing my predicament, laughed at my lack of planning.

Peter Davidson, a fellow South African, was living in New York. He had graduated from Lincoln University and was now studying for his economics degree at Manhattan College in Queens. He lived in a rented loft at 65 Warren Street, near Wall Street. Jonas asked Peter if he would take me in. Peter gladly agreed. I was very grateful to both of my friends. Besides my horn and the clothes on my back, all I had was an American Express credit card. And, of course, a completely broken heart. I bought two pairs of blue jeans, some T-shirts, socks, a cap, and one pair of sneakers.

Ernie Altschuler, the head of artist repertoire at Columbia Records, introduced Stewart and me to Lee Eastman, a noted lawyer who looked after the interests of Picasso and Miró and was on the board of the Museum of Modern Art. He also had a publishing company, Cherio Music, which owned the catalog of Louis Jordan's compositions. He agreed to represent us, incorporated Oo-Bwana, and said, "If you boys have the talent that Ernie claims you have, I will take you all the way. I've always wanted to be associated with something that would have the same impact on the world as the Beatles. Can you guys do it?" Of course we agreed, signed a publishing contract with Cherio, and received a substantial advance from Eastman to start recording.

We signed a girl trio made up of Bongi and two of her schoolmates, along with Letta and the Safaris, Stewart's instrumental group, and the Bwanas, led by Caiphus Semenya, with Philemon Hou, Ernie Mohlomi, John Sithebe, and Douglas Xaba, and some of the other former members of the musical *Sponono*.

Tom Wilson introduced us to Ed Rice. At his studios in mid-Manhattan we began cutting rhythm tracks. Ed taught us the fundamentals of recording techniques. Stewart, Caiphus, Jonas, and I were the songwriters and arrangers, and Stewart was executive producer. Our rhythm section consisted of John Cartwright on bass, Eric Gale on guitar, Charlie Smalls on piano, and Herbie Lovell on drums. Jonas, Stewart, and I played all the horn parts. With fifteen hundred dollars each from Stewart and me, and the advance from Lee Eastman, Oo-Bwana Productions became a reality, and soon we were walking around with demos. Ernie loved the music, and three single 45-rpm records were released on our new label and distributed by Columbia. Letta and the Safaris received major radio play with a Jonas Gwangwa composition, "I Wanna Go Home Now." The song entered the singles top-100 charts in both *Cashbox* and *Billboard* magazines. We were on our way.

• • •

By the time Miriam returned from Paris, Oo-Bwana was moving at full throttle. One late March afternoon, Miriam and I met at the Russian Tea Room, next to Carnegie Hall. Our meeting was cool and short. I could tell she was seething with anger because I had called her bluff. I was past caring. She was clearly in a hurry to get out of a bad situation. We agreed that Max Cohen and I would go down to Mexico right away to arrange for a quickie divorce. Two weeks later Max and I were on a plane to El Paso, Texas, along with two of his other clients—Gail, a stunning Irish beauty, and Ingrid, a Swedish scorcher whose black psychiatrist husband had left her for a relationship with a man. We arrived in El Paso on a Friday night, and that evening, along with hundreds of other Americans soon to be divorced, we dined and danced to the tequila-and-mescal strains of the hotel's mariachi music. I spent the weekend sleeping with Gail and then with Ingrid. We needed consolation.

We arose early that Monday morning and took the hotel shuttles to Juarez, Mexico, where the divorce cattle-call formed. Long lines of American men and women waiting to get into the town's divorce halls, where you sign a form before a magistrate and your lawyer, and before the ink dries you're divorced and heading back over the border to your El Paso hotel to pick up your bags and drive to the airport to fly back to your new life, stunned, hurt, and empty inside. I wondered how all those people were feeling after being ogled by the Mexican peasants from their decrepit shacks. With their Catholic rosaries under their ponchos, they no doubt marveled at their country's hypocrisy—a nation of Catholics opposed to divorce, raking in millions of dollars from all those immoral Americans sleeping with one another in El Paso hotels over the weekends and then crossing the border on Monday mornings to sign their marriages away without even going to confession.

Ingrid flew back with me. She was shattered and wept all the way to New York, heartbroken and overwhelmed that her rich ex-husband had left her for another man. Ingrid stayed with Peter and me for a few days. Ten months later, after she had returned to Sweden, I received a letter from the Child Welfare Office in Malmo, Sweden. It read, "You are the father of a baby girl. You don't have to pay any maintenance or support for this child, because Sweden looks after its children." For almost forty years I have tried unsuccessfully to locate my daughter and her mother. I suspect they have eluded me on purpose. I would give anything to meet my daughter before I die.

What's amusing is that to this day Miriam swears my daughter was conceived while we were still married. A few weeks later, Jean Johnson called and said Miriam was distraught and needed to talk to me. She said Miriam's Latino lover had turned out to be a heel, and he had done Miriam badly. Jean asked if I would consider reconciling, because Miriam really needed me. Miriam came to the phone and told me how sorry she was about our breakup. I consoled her and assured her of my friendship for life, but told her our marriage could not be rekindled.

Miriam wrote in her autobiography that the reason our marriage didn't work was that I was too young, naïve, and immature, and that I was jealous of her career. I was never jealous of Miriam. She was one of my greatest inspirations, both as an activist and a professional artist. If it hadn't been for her belief in my talents and her generous assistance to get me a music education, I could never have reached the place where I am today. But I don't know many marriages that could have survived that degree of daring infidelity. Although Miriam and I remain dear friends, and occasionally shared intimacy for many years after our breakup, I never regretted divorcing her. But I will always love her.

10

J OE WESTERFIELD, AN ECCENTRIC artist who lived most of the time
in Hampton Beach, Virginia, with his beautiful wife, Priscilla, owned
Peter's loft apartment. Westerfield's specialty was painting nude pictures of
Priscilla along with other women entangled in erotic, orgasmic positions. One
day Peter told me one of Westerfield's fantasies was to paint a picture of me
fucking his wife. At first I thought Peter was pulling my leg. But one afternoon
we got a visit from Westerfield. He proposed the idea, explaining it would be
an honor if I did this for him. He assured me that his wife would also be honored. I couldn't believe my ears. I graciously turned down his request, but he
insisted that I not close the book on the idea. This was my introduction to the
sixties, not the actual decade, but the era marked by, among other things, wild
decadence in America and global culture. And in my life in particular.

My confidence in the recording *The Americanization of Ooga Booga* began to
crystallize into reality. Tom Wilson called one day to tell me the album was
breaking out big in Los Angeles. Around this time I couldn't play any gigs
because I didn't have a band. I started calling around, trying to reassemble my
old band. Keeping a band together can be difficult because musicians gravitate
wherever there is a steady flow of income. Larry Willis, with whom we had
started my first group, was unavailable. He had gone back to Denmark to
marry a woman he had met when we were playing the Tivoli Gardens. By
coincidence, John Cartwright called me that evening to say that he had quit
playing with Harry Belafonte, and wanted to know if I knew anyone interested
in a talented bassist. I immediately roped in Cartwright, who told me about a

gifted pianist who had just graduated from the New York High School of the
Performing Arts. "Let's bring Charlie on board, too," I said. I also discovered
that Henry Jenkins, our drummer on *Ooga Booga,* was available. In no time we
had assembled a new group. This was the season for a lot of rich music in
America and around the world. It was the era of Motown and Stax records, of
the Impressions and Jerry Butler, of Simon and Garfunkel, the Young Rascals,
the Beatles, the Stones, Jefferson Airplane, Janis Joplin, James Brown, and Otis
Redding. The music of Motown and Stax had the strongest impact on me at
that time. I had become an avid collector of rhythm-and-blues albums and was
slowly moving away from a jazz-based approach to something that combined
more of an R&B feeling. The new white musicians like the Beatles, Simon and
Garfunkel, Tom Jones, and the Mamas and the Papas had a very heavy effect
on me, too—mainly for their compositional excellence as songwriters. The
compositions of that time had a universal appeal that had not been seen since
the days of Strayhorn and Ellington, Cole Porter, Fats Waller, the Gershwin
brothers, and Hoagy Carmichael in the 1930s and 1940s. My next album was
crammed with selections from these new songwriters. The record was called
Hugh Masekela's Next Album.

I rented a piano and we started rehearsing in earnest at the loft in preparation for an album of songs that would include "Loving You" by Stevie Wonder,
the Beatles' "Norwegian Wood," Paul Simon's "Sounds of Silence," and Tom
Jones's "It's Not Unusual." I walked into Tom Wilson's office for an appointment to finalize our recording schedule and found Paul Simon playing selections from his new album for Tom—this was the first time I met Paul. He kept
playing "Scarborough Fair," which struck me as a brilliant piece of work.

My band went into the studio for one week, in which time we finished the
whole album, including the overdubs, the liner notes, and the cover shot,
which was done early one Sunday morning in the middle of Broadway and
44th Street by Chuck Stewart, the famous jazz photographer.

Ooga Booga was climbing the charts, but I still hadn't received any royalties,
nor had Oo-Bwana Productions generated any income yet from the acts we
produced. Peter and I began experiencing some serious cash-flow problems.
He was receiving a small allowance from his parents, and the little money I had
saved from gigs before I broke up with Miriam was about gone. New York was
an expensive place to live, then as now. Dizzy Gillespie called one day and
invited me to come and catch his performance at the Metropole Café on
Broadway. "Bring your horn," he said. I sat in with him during one set. When
I was leaving, he gave me a big hug and slipped an envelope into my jacket

pocket. He said, "I know it's kinda uphill these days. Here's something from Lorraine and me to tide you over. Oooweee! Be strong and take care." On the subway I opened the envelope. It was a check for a thousand dollars. My ancestors had intervened once again, and through the kindness of Dizzy and Lorraine, Peter and I were able to pay a few bills and buy some groceries. A few days later, MGM advanced me five thousand dollars. Now Peter and I bought a few threads and started to party.

With *Ooga Booga* doing well out West, I became concerned that months had gone by and there was no radio airplay on the East Coast. Tom Wilson advised me to go to Mort Nasatir, who was the president of MGM, and pressure him to get the company's sales department to promote my album. I didn't want another "fuck you" confrontation like I'd had with Mercury Records. I was cool and relaxed, but Nasatir was brittle and unpleasant. He said, "Your music will never sell, Hugh. It's pointless wasting funds to push it. People just cannot get with your type of music." I left his office pissed off and determined that if MGM wouldn't push the product, I would do it myself. I had connections, so I had Tom arrange to send me a box of twenty-five albums that I would take to radio stations and try to hustle some airplay.

The next morning I stopped by the apartment of Richie Druz, a drummer I knew who also dealt a little smoke on the side. I gave him an album and picked up an ounce of grass. He and his roommate were in a strange, giggly, bubbly mood, imitating everything I said. Richie pulled out a little vial and asked me to sniff the white powder off a miniature spoon. It was cocaine. I had seen the stuff before, but hadn't tried it.

Richie gently pushed the spoon up to my nose. I asked, "Richie, is this shit gonna fuck with me like those junkies I always see nodding on the sidewalks of Harlem?" Richie and his roommate started laughing at me. "Come on, Hughie," Richie said, "just take a little bitty in each nostril. You'll love it." I sniffed the coke up each of my nostrils, paid for my grass, and left them giggling. The cocaine hit me when I came out of the elevator into the street. Boom! Suddenly I was all energy and enthusiasm, totally invincible. It was a sunny spring afternoon in late April of 1966, and I was ready to take on the world.

I went to the nearest telephone booth, called Del Shields, the managing director of radio station WLIB, which was in Harlem, not far from the Apollo Theater, and asked if I could bring my album by. "Come on up, Hughie," he said. I did on-air interviews with Shields and later on with Billy Taylor on his own show. That evening I was with Eddie O'Jay at WWRL in Queens. After that, I went back to the loft and collected more albums. I laid records on who-ever I thought could help me get the word out about my music. With the cocaine still in my system, I thought I could shake up the whole world. I came home around midnight totally exhausted, but exhilarated from the blow. I knew I was gonna love the stuff.

Tom Wilson was disappointed with Mort Nasatir's reaction to the album. He figured that the best plan of action should be focused on Los Angeles, where *Ooga-Booga* was having an impact. He knew an agent at the William Morris Agency who was booking most of the Motown groups out there. His name was Wally Amos, and he later became "famous" for his "Famous Amos" cookies. Wally was well connected with promoters and club owners. The rhythm-and-blues and jazz circuits were his specialty. Two weeks later Wally came back with great news. We would be playing the first Watts Jazz Festival in Compton, outside Los Angeles, near where the 1965 riots had taken place. The idea behind the jazz festival was to help cool tempers and spread goodwill throughout the community.

We arrived in Los Angeles on August 4, rehearsed for a few days, and on Saturday, August 9, 1966, we went to play at Jordan High School in Compton. More than ten thousand people showed up for the last night of the festival. We played most of the songs from *Ooga Booga* and *Hugh Masekela's Next Album*. The crowd loved us so much they wouldn't let us off the stage. They sang along on most of our songs. No group had ever played in South Central Los Angeles that could bring together ordinary people of all colors from every part of the county to a neighborhood that had just endured a massive civil distur-bance. After the show, I called Peter Davidson and told him I doubted we would be returning to New York anytime soon. I also called Stewart Levine and told him that if Oo-Bwana was ever going to take off, it would most likely happen in Los Angeles, where the people had taken a serious liking to our music. New York was still not biting, and it was obvious we would have to conquer it from the West. Once the East Coast realized it was being upstaged by California, a state it considered musically inferior, the radio people back in New York would want to catch up. I was not prepared to wait for slick New York to let me in when we had already garnered such a large following in Los Angeles. Radio station KBCA played *Ooga Booga* and *Next Album* around the clock. Three of their top DJs—Tommy Bee, Les Carter, and Rick Holmes—had been the masters of ceremonies during the Watts Jazz Festival. Wolfman Jack of XERB radio, which had the largest listenership on the West Coast, was another DJ playing the albums on regular rotation.

Our success at the festival got us an engagement at the Living Room, a club on Sunset Strip, a hangout spot for hustlers, stars from the film world, and rock-'n'-roll royalty. Before we left for Los Angeles, Dizzy had given me some fatherly advice about the seedy side of club life in La-La Land. He had warned me about the waitresses. "Hughie, if they gonna give you some pussy, you'd better figure they been fuckin' cats from other bands, too. When Miles first went to L.A., he was about your age. I gave him the same advice. He didn't listen and ended up with a mean case of de claps. Ooowee." Of course I forgot all about Dizzy's advice. When we opened at the Living Room, I spotted a stunning waitress. She not only found some grass for me, but one thing led to another, and by the next afternoon I had a screaming dose of de claps. During the Living Room gig, our drummer Henry Jenkins told me that he needed to get back to New York, because he just could not get with L.A., it was too strange for him. Trombonist Wayne Henderson of the Jazz Crusaders introduced us to Chuck Carter, who replaced Henry.

Dave Nelson, our local agent and Wally's man on the West Coast, booked us into the Montecito Hotel, where many of the "blaxploitation" movie actors of that era like Yaphet Kotto, Louis Gossett Jr., Max Julien, and Raymond St. Jacques stayed. I had already met Lou through my sister Barbara in New York, when she was roped in by director Dore Schary to be his language coach when he played a leading role in the Broadway play *The Zulu and the Zayda*. Lou introduced me to his fellow actor friends when we were sitting around the hotel's swimming pool. They claimed to have been regulars at my shows at the Village Gate and seemed genuinely excited that I was breaking out in Los Angeles. I became longtime friends with many of them. Charlie Weaver, who was Bill Cosby's stand-in on the set of the *I Spy* series, took me to the set early one morning because he and St. Jacques felt I had acting potential. Bill Cosby remembered me from his Basin Street engagement with Miriam Makeba, and promised to get in touch with me. I knew then that I could never be in films because the working hours started too early, around the time when I was coming home to sleep, usually pumped up from booze, blow, and pot.

Consistent radio play of our records made it easy for Nelson to book us at more concerts and clubs, while back in New York, Stewart Levine was making plans to move Oo-Bwana to the West Coast. Before I left New York, Tom Elius, a top agent and a friend of Stewart's, had hooked Stewart and me up with Henri Gene, a friendly, very well-connected old wheeler-dealer and real estate mogul. Gene and Frank Sinatra were on a first-name basis, and Gene was very tight with top people at Sinatra's Reprise Records on the West Coast. Gene called Mo Ostin, the president of Reprise, and recommended they sign our production company. Gene gave Stewart a few thousand dollars to come to L.A., and by early fall, Stewart arrived in Los Angeles. A few days later he went to meet Jimmy Bowen, the artist and repertoire boss at Reprise. Stewart had copies of our Oo-Bwana recordings that he wanted them to sample, but Bowen was not interested in listening to our music—he just wanted to sign us on because Henri Gene had said he should. Stewart stormed out of the meeting, offended. There was no deal.

Stewart had previously made some major contacts in Los Angeles, one of whom introduced us to Larry Spector, a very successful young businessman who at that time was managing the affairs of the Byrds, Dennis Hopper, and Peter Fonda. Larry advised us to start our own independent record company. He registered Chisa Records, the label through which we would be releasing our recordings. He then introduced us to Danny Davis, who was running Phil Spector's record company. For a fee of five hundred bucks, Davis promised to teach us the ropes of the record industry.

Dave Nelson booked us into the Tropicana, a very popular club in Compton that my band would pack to the rafters every weekend for many months to come. It was from here that we established our California base. Musicians and celebrities like David Crosby and Peter Fonda came out to see us. We slowly became the toast of Hollywood. Through Crosby we met Alan Pariser, who dealt the best grass in California. He was supplier to all the smoking stars of the movies and rock 'n' roll, many of whom we met at his house in the Hollywood hills. Of course, Alan became a very close friend of ours. Pariser was the heir of the Solo Cup fortune in Detroit. He had moved to Los Angeles out of his love for the music business. Realizing that pot lovers in the industry did not have a decent source of good grass, he made it his business to fill this void. Pariser's "ice pack" grass was amazing, specially grown in Mexico under the supervision of agronomists that he brought in to train the Mexican farmers he was in business with. This distinction endeared him to all of Hollywood's elite smoking community.

All our new acquaintances became very crucial in popularizing Chisa in the Los Angeles entertainment community. David Nelson booked us into the Both And, a jazz club in San Francisco, where we quickly established ourselves as strongly as we had in Los Angeles. One night Big Black, the percussionist who played at the African Room behind Barbara Alston's dance troupe, walked into the club with his congas, set up on stage, and started playing with us. From then on, he became the fifth member of the band. Our group stayed in a couple of houseboats across the Golden Gate Bridge at the heliport in Mill Valley. In this neighborhood were a couple of warehouses where Janis Joplin and Big Brother and the Holding Company and the Grateful Dead rehearsed. Through David Crosby, we became friends with them, as well as Jefferson Airplane and other Bay Area groups. They all regularly dropped in at the Both And.

I was really fascinated by San Francisco. The Haight-Ashbury neighborhood was teeming with young and old druggies walking the streets like mummies, flying high on acid, along with an assortment of eccentrics, drifters, and crazies. It was no different than the mayhem in Sodom and Gomorrah. I was intrigued.

Sausalito, where we stayed, was the very beehive of the psychedelic philosophical movement, and marathon debates on "the meaning of life" took place on the sidewalks, in restaurants, on college campuses, and in the homes of all the wealthy people who had come there to "drop out." The No Name Bar on the main street was where I learned to throw down multiple Irish whiskies, philosophizing while tripping on acid with total strangers who were transfixed by anyone who had mastered the art of verbal diarrhea. It was a time when panties were seldom worn, bras were out, and high women wondered scornfully why men talked so much instead of fucking the hell out of them.

Just about everybody around us was getting high. Charlie Smalls, John Cartwright, our new drummer Chuck Carter, Stewart Levine, Big Black, and I were already seasoned admirers of good marijuana. Between gigs and on days when we were not performing, I would pop an LSD tab with my friend Luigi Alfano and go sit atop Mount Tamalpais, up above the redwood forests of Marin County, and trip on being American Indians or medieval sages. Giggling uncontrollably, we traveled through all kinds of hallucinogenic euphoria and out-of-body turbulence; we moved the mountains and juggled the forests, the ground rumbled under our feet, and the plants spoke to us in tongues.

When you came down from an LSD trip, you were so exhausted that you needed a few days to return to earth. Like the Dead Heads, however, some of us became so accustomed to the drug that we didn't need the rest anymore. We could trip every day. I was forgetting New York and Miriam, and even home.

Letta, Caiphus, Philemon Hou, Ernest Mohlomi, John Sithebe, and Mamsie Gwangwa, Jonas's new wife, arrived in Los Angeles, and it wasn't long before Larry Spector organized the launch of Chisa Records at the sprawling estate of

one of his movie-mogul associates. It was a star-studded night, with Henry
Fonda, Peter Fonda, Dennis Hopper, Jimmy Stewart, Hoagy Carmichael, and
many other luminaries in attendance. Luigi Alfano, my tripping partner from
Sausalito, arrived dressed in regal Pueblo finery. That night our African sounds
and rhythms had their coming-out party, and we would soon become an inte-
gral part of the fabric of the tradionally lily-white Hollywood scene.

In 1966 Los Angeles was by far one of the most affordable big cities to live
in. Everyone seemed laid back, with a have-a-nice-day disposition. Everyone,
that was, except Stewart and me. We were two cocky, rambunctious, fearless
motherfuckers who drank like pirates and smoked pot like Rastas. We stuck out
like sore thumbs in Ronald Reagan country, and began to attract the attention
of the Los Angeles Police Department. Fonda, Crosby, Hopper, and Alan
Pariser, the godfather of gourmet mind-altering substances, liked Stewart and
me for our maverick spirits and the laughter we brought to their otherwise
tight-assed lives. But we rubbed many people the wrong way, especially the
police, who delighted in pulling us over for bullshit reasons. We came to be
known to the entire Los Angeles system, from the highway patrol and the sheriff's department to the notorious LAPD. Larry Spector was always bailing us
out of jail.

Through David Crosby, who was a dedicated antiwar organizer, we got to
play many free "Stop the War" concerts in Los Angeles and San Francisco
parks and arenas, alongside Jefferson Airplane, the Grateful Dead, Pacific Gas
and Electric, Jim Morrison and the Doors, Steven Stills and Buffalo Springfield,
Big Brother and the Holding Company with Janis Joplin, Eric Burdon and the
Animals, the Hollies, the Byrds, and many other "love groups" around
California. We were part of the sound and the fury of the Flower Power era.

Susie, Stewart, and I rented a house up on Queens Road off the Sunset Strip,
where I slept in a back cottage. We were now getting so seriously high, the
only time that we were straight was when we were sleeping. One night I got
so bombed, I fell asleep with a cigarette in my hand. When I awoke, everything
around me was on fire except for the spot where I was sleeping. I jumped up
in a drunken stupor and ran back and forth from the bathroom several times
with a glass of water, trying to put out the flames. Realizing the futility of my
drunken efforts, I rushed out of the cottage stark naked to awaken Stewart and
Susie. They came out with large buckets of water to help extinguish the
flames. It took us the better part of thirty minutes to contain the fire. We had
to repaint and refurbish the cottage. With so much pot in the main house, we

dared not call the fire department. We were having so much fun, we didn't even notice our stupidity.

Wally Amos landed my group a week-long engagement with Bill Cosby at the West Covina Theatre-in-the-Round. We were the opening act. One Saturday I arrived ten minutes late for our backstage call, which is traditionally thirty minutes before showtime. Our old Thunderbird had a flat and the spare tire had a puncture, too. Roy Silver, Cosby's manager at that time, was sympathetic, but Cosby decided we would not play that afternoon. I overheard Cosby telling Silver, "He's not playing, and that's final. Let this be a lesson for Hugh Masekela. This is a business. You cannot succeed if you don't have discipline. He won't be playing the matinee. And that's final." Cosby let us play the evening show, but canceled us for the rest of his tour. It was a shattering blow that I never forgot. Stewart and I felt that Cosby was overly conservative, acting like a square white boy, and being unfair. I felt bad about losing the opportunity of getting exposure to the enormous following he commanded, and I was certain he never wanted to see me again. To my surprise, a few years later Cosby called and asked me to join him and Sarah Vaughan at Redd Foxx's Club. He was trying to help keep Redd's club from closing. We played there for a week, during which time neither of us mentioned the past incident. Redd kept us in stitches the entire time. He was so appreciative of our efforts to help save his club that he always talked about it when we were together in the company of his friends. I became very good friends with Redd till he passed away.

In 1967, MGM Records forgot to pick up their option on my contract. This left me free to start recording for Chisa, my own label. Stewart rushed us into Gold Star Studios in Hollywood to record *The Emanicipation of Hugh Masekela.* It contained our current stage repertoire, with songs like "Desafinado," the great Brazillian classic by Antonio Carlos Jobim, "Ha Le Se Le Di Khanna," the second of Caphius Semenya's many compositions that I would record over the years, and several other selections.

Our new album broke out nationally, finally putting Chisa Records on the map. We were getting calls from all over the country. In a month Stewart and I hit all the major cities and met everybody in the record business who mattered. At that time few independent record companies entered the market with the impact Chisa had. *Emancipation* was climbing the charts, approaching the 100,000 mark in sales. Even though we had a hit record, we were pressing and shipping at our own expense, and payment did not come from distributors until after a ninety-day period. We were sinking deeper and deeper into debt.

Larry Spector was beginning to cry that the earnings from my engagements were insufficient to support the Chisa campaign and cover the expenses of promoting the recordings. We began to owe everybody we did business with—the record-pressing plants, the label printers, the independent promotion agents—not to mention rents, car payments, and telephone bills. The shit was coming down all around us.

Luckily, Universal Studios wanted to branch into the record industry, and assigned Russ Regan, an old soldier in the record business, to sign Chisa Records. Russ approached us with a deal under which Universal's new label, UNI Records, would pick up our debts. UNI had only signed one act on their label, Strawberry Alarm Clock, a rock-'n'-roll group. They needed a marquee artist like me to help build their brand. We signed with UNI and handed over their check for $100,000 to Spector to clear our debts and get him out of the hole. We shook hands on it and thought all contractual issues had now been resolved. The only remaining business requirement was for us to sign a management release from Spector. He refused to sign because he wanted to keep making a management commission from our future earnings. Spector eventually signed our release papers, but not before Stewart grabbed him by the ass and hung him out the window of his sixth-floor office. Spector begged for his life, cried like a baby, and apologized until Stewart pulled him back in. We learned a little later that Spector had actually coerced us to make the deal with UNI Records when we could have waited another month and received royalties that far exceeded our debts. We had agreed to sign right away because we were told that Spector's mother was on the verge of a stroke, and if the deal wasn't made, she could die. We were slowly learning the hustle of the music business.

Ned Tannen, a young vice-president of Universal Studios, introduced us to Joe Glaser, the head of Associated Booking Corporation in New York. Glaser booked just about every leading jazz legend. He was revered and feared by every concert promoter and club owner in America. Tannen made Glaser promise to get me high-profile engagements that would match the kind of money UNI Records was about to invest in me. I was assigned to Oscar Cohen, who was Glaser's heir apparent. Glaser immediately took a liking to Stewart and me, claiming that my humorous and outgoing personality reminded him of the young Louis Armstrong. "Satchmo" had helped Glaser to represent most of the greatest black jazz artists as his clients, and he was Armstrong's lifetime business partner and manager.

Before long I was appearing on the Mike Douglas, Pat Boone, Johnny

Carson, and Merv Griffin television talk shows. The two kings of teen-hop shows, Dick Clark and Jerry Blavat in Philadelphia, invited me on all the time. I was the new kid on the block, and luckily I had the goods that gave Joe Glaser and Oscar Cohen the credibility to muscle the music industry on my behalf.

Oscar put us on the road, where we now opened for such acts as the Supremes, Marvin Gaye and Tammi Terrell, Stevie Wonder, the Temptations, B.B. King, Martha Reeves and the Vandellas, and the Four Tops. One of our first engagements was a concert with Stevie Wonder at Lincoln Center in New York.

Alan Pariser had convinced the owners of the Whisky à Go Go in Los Angeles to book us. We were a smashing success, with lines stretching way up Sunset Boulevard. The club had always been a white preserve where rock groups broke in their acts, and the home of rock royalty. Most of the big groups fine-tuned material for their upcoming international tours at the club. My group was only the second black outfit to play the club, shortly after Otis Redding had baptized it with his funky brand of soul music. No one seemed to care about race at the Whisky. It was a revelation to see how open white kids—at least some white kids—had become on the issue. I had long ago crossed that stupid line. The open doors of the Whisky led to the first influx of African-American clientele from South Central Los Angeles into the Sunset Strip neighborhood. Until then, the racist character of Los Angeles had made it a no-go area for black people.

At the time, John Phillips of the Mamas and the Papas was lining up the Monterey Pop Festival. Again, Pariser got us on the bill. The people at UNI thought this was the gateway to a completely new audience for us. But of course there were problems. After the Stevie Wonder concert in New York, John Cartwright and Charlie Smalls told me that they would not be returning with us to California. They were disgusted with the manner in which we were handling our business, and had nothing but contempt for Stewart Levine: "Your fucking white boy," they sneered in my face. This posed a grave problem because we were due to play the Monterey Pop Festival the following weekend, and then go for a week's engagement at the Whisky, during which time we were scheduled to record a live album for UNI Records. Back in Los Angeles we recruited South African pianist Hotep Galeta, who had come with the Oo-Bwana entourage, saxophonist Al Abreu, and bassist Henry Franklin. We began to rehearse feverishly in preparation for the recording and the festival.

It was at the Monterey Pop Festival that Otis Redding, the Who, Jimi Hendrix, and Janis Joplin became international household names overnight with their riveting performances, which became legendary with the release of the concert film. The three-day festival also featured Simon and Garfunkel, the Mamas and the Papas, and Tiny Tim. Ravi Shankar played a stunning three-hour closing set, during which ten thousand people sat enthralled, in total silence. Almost everybody in the audience was tripping on LSD. It was the largest group high I had ever witnessed. Our band also had a wonderful reception, and the engagement brought attention to us from the massive psychedelic community and international audiences who caught it live or through the film. It was here also that my friendship with Jimi Hendrix started.

We recorded the music for *Alive and Well at the Whisky* over three days with Stewart running back and forth between the mobile studio parked behind the club and the stage. The set included the Fifth Dimension's "Up, Up and Away"; Procol Harum's "A Whiter Shade of Pale"; "Ha Le Se Le Di Khanna"; "Coincidence," an antiwar lament that I composed while on acid one day; and "Son of Ice Bag," an ode to Pariser's wonderful smoke. The resulting album became a huge favorite with radio stations. "Up, Up and Away" flew to the number-31 spot on the *Billboard* singles charts. The people at UNI Records were beside themselves, and so were Joe Glaser and Oscar Cohen at ABC.

Marvin Gaye and I became good friends when I worked with him at the Apollo Theater. It was a very sad time for him because Tammi Terrell, an outrageously talented singer, had been diagnosed with a brain tumor. Maxine Brown was her replacement. One night after a show, Marvin's percussionist, Eddie Bongo, invited me to a freak party in Harlem. Marvin had warned me not to go. "Hughsky, don't go there. Edsky is a bad boy. Believe me, man." I thought he was just joking. When we got to Sugar Hill up in Harlem, Eddie led me into a luxury apartment where three fine, big black women had been impatiently waiting for him. They even got more excited at the sight of me. I was an unexpected delight. On the table were a magnum of cognac, ready-rolled joints, and a large bowl of pure cocaine. After gulping a large cognac and taking a few snorts of coke, I realized that the women had rather abruptly undressed and were pulling the clothes off Eddie and me. Before I knew it, I was being twisted and stretched into all kinds of contorted positions—getting fucked to smithereens. Time flew by, because I kept dipping into the bowl, the cognac, and the babes. When Eddie said we had to go to work, I couldn't believe that it was almost noon—showtime at the Apollo! On stage I was so exhausted that when we counted off our latest hit, "Up, Up and Away," I went to blow my horn and nothing came out, my lips felt like they were hanging, still frozen from the cocaine and the night's other activities. I managed to play a short version of the song and motioned my band to leave the stage. Marvin was standing in the wings and said to me softly, "Hughsky, go and get some sleep. Come back for the third show at six. You should have listened to me. I told you about Edsky. That brother is bad." Eddie Bongo was smiling at me from the other side of the stage. I was too wiped out even to be embarrassed, as I staggered out of the Apollo and hailed a taxi to my hotel.

Did I learn my lesson? No! I felt as if I were unleashing a lifetime's worth of suppressed energy, and I wanted to pack in as much as I could—it's a cliché, but I literally lived as if each day were my last. When I got money, I spent it. When I found love—or lust—I pursued it with everything I had. When I was offered a new drug, a new high, a new indulgence, I took it. I was thousands of miles from home, as displaced as the miners I grew up with in Witbank, and eager to find a way to forget a home I wasn't sure I'd ever see again. I was drunk on money—when I could find it—drugs, which were never hard to find, love, lust, and music, and in no hurry to sober up. In fact, it would take me several decades more to wake up from it.

Potent grass, LSD, and cocaine supplemented my craving for booze and cigarettes. I had more out-of-body psychedelic experiences than I cared to admit. My very first LSD trip was at David Crosby's Beverly Canyon Drive home. His girlfriend had worked all evening on a sumptuous spaghetti dinner, and when we sat down to eat, the pasta began talking to me. I answered, "You are so beautiful. I can't eat you." We went outside, where the red roses and white carnations in his landscaped garden also spoke to me. Crosby and Stewart were right behind me, giggling at my silliness. I looked up to the sky, and the stars came raining down on us. "The stars are raining," I shouted. My two friends ran back into the house, thinking I had finally lost my mind. Three days later, the science section in *Time* magazine published a photograph of the meteor shower that had occurred that night, with an accompanying article that claimed this was a phenomenon that would not occur for another ninety years. On one flight from Chicago to Los Angeles, after taking LSD, I knew I had died because the airplane had turned into wax and all the passengers looked like Disney characters, including Al Abreu, who was sitting next to me, unable to speak because he was just as high as I was. When Stewart met us at the airport, I told him that the world had ended, and he drove me to his Malibu home, where Susie gave me a very strong barbiturate and suggested a walk on the beach, where the moisture and the sea breeze would help to bring me down. When we came back from the walk, I had something to eat and then passed out. I didn't wake up for two days.

In January 1968, I decided to travel to Lusaka, Zambia, a country north of South Africa, to visit Barbara, who was now attending the university there and working with the exiled African National Congress in the office of its president, Oliver Tambo. My problem was I didn't have a passport. In 1964, after my first one expired, I went to the South African consulate in New York and applied for a new one. Every time I inquired about its status, I was told an answer had not yet come from Pretoria. After several years I got the message and stopped trying. To get around the passport problem this time, I asked Rupiah Banda, the Zambian ambassador in Washington, to arrange for me a one-journey travel document that would enable me to go to Lusaka via London and reenter the United States with my permanent residence green card. I planned to see Barbara, and Rupiah set up a special meeting for me to see President Kenneth Kaunda about the possibilities of establishing Chisa Records in Zambia. Formerly northern Rhodesia, the country had won its independence from the British in 1964.

Stewart traveled with me on the London leg of my trip. Rather than stick to the script—which was to attend a few business appointments—we got side-tracked partying, and got so high on grass and hashish that I missed my flight to Zambia and, most important, my scheduled meeting with the president. When I arrived in Zambia three days later, there was no one at the airport to meet me. President Kaunda had left the country on business, and Barbara was very disappointed by my lame excuse. I was terribly embarrassed because I had just blown a major opportunity to bring modern production and recording technology to this part of the world. This would have been an ideal platform for fledgling African talent to get international exposure. That night we went to see Dorothy Masuka, who was performing with her band from Zimbabwe at the city's famous Woodpecker Club. The following day I went to visit her in the township where she lived. It was truly heartbreaking to see her living in such squalor. Situated in a rundown neighborhood of gravel streets, her small, four-room home was sparsely furnished with old, thrown-together benches and chairs. The cooking was done on a brazier in the backyard. The house was packed with all kinds of people, ranging from little children who were her nephews, nieces, and cousins to uncles, aunts, and her grandmother. I had last seen Dorothy when we were both members of the African Jazz and Variety Revue. She was one of the revue's big stars.

The next morning I went to see the president's secretary and politely asked him to convey my sincerest apologies to President Kaunda on his return, and thank him for scheduling time for me to see him. At the ANC offices I greeted Uncle Oliver Tambo and some of the other South African exiles. It was wonderful to see so many of the friends I had grown up with in Alexandra Township, many of whom were now top guerrilla commanders in the liberation army Umkhonto We Sizwe (Spear of the Nation). In downtown Lusaka, I bought many of the latest recordings by South African groups like the Dark City Sisters, Mahlathini and the Mahotella Queens, Zakes Nkosi, Ntemi Piliso, Betty Khoza, and others. Some local musicians gave me demo tapes of their material in the hope that I might use some of it or help them advance their careers.

The evening before my return to London and then on to Los Angeles, Barbara took me to see Todd Matshikiza, the composer of *King Kong.* He was on his deathbed. Esme, Todd's wife, tried to put on a brave face, but I could see in her eyes the strain she was under, watching her husband wilt away. Todd could barely talk. He offered me something to drink, and as badly as I wanted a shot of brandy to anesthetize the pain of seeing him in that condition, I declined because at the time I just could not partake of something that I felt was partly responsible for his condition. During the ride to the airport, I knew I would never see him again. A great musician, pianist, composer, and author, exiled from his country of birth, was waiting to die in a foreign land, far from his friends the Manhattan Brothers, who were now living in London, and away from Mackay Davashe, Kippie Moeketsi, and many others who I knew would have walked to Zambia to be his pallbearers, if not for the travel restrictions imposed by the South African government. Once again I was filled with contempt for the apartheid government. It was galling that such great talents as Todd had to leave South Africa and struggle to achieve recognition abroad when they came from an environment that would have given them the glory and good life they deserved. Mackay, Kippie, Dorothy, Dolly Rathebe, the Woodpeckers, and the Manhattan Brothers could have reached glory in a free South Africa, but they were all either struggling to make a living abroad or still suffering the humiliation of the internal oppression they were subjected to. In light of all this, the success Miriam and I found in America would always ring hollow as long as our people were enslaved. As I looked down on Lusaka from the porthole window of my plane, the thought of Todd Matshikiza in that bed brought tears to my eyes. He died the next day.

Stewart and I returned to Los Angeles from London to record a fourth album for UNI Records. I had some tapes and recordings from Lusaka, which I gave to Philemon Hou, one of the Bwanas from *Sponono,* who had come out west with Letta and Caiphus. Philly was now staying with me. He listened to the tapes over and over again, and soon began to make up little compositions inspired by the music. We titled the new album *Promise of a Future.* The high-lights on it were Marvin and Tammi's "Ain't No Mountain High Enough," Stevie Winwood's "No Name, No Number," and Al Abreu's "Señor Coraza," which was our ode to cocaine. Russ Regan came to the studio and felt that we needed one more song to complete the album. Al Abreu insisted that we do one of Philemon Hou's songs inspired by the music of southern Africa. Because of the simple melody and the easy bass, piano, and guitar lines, we learned the song in half an hour and recorded it in one take. Bruce Langhorne was doing an album with Phil Ochs in an adjoining room at Gold Star Studios. We called him in to play the guitar part because of his background knowledge of South African music from our days at 310 West 87th. After he played his part, he held the cowbell for me to play on with two drumsticks. The entire song took less than two hours to record, overdub, and mix. When Russ Regan heard it he said, "Shit, this is a smash." We titled the song "Grazing in the Grass."

The album and the single immediately began getting huge airplay on radio across the country, and soon both were climbing the music charts. Peter Davidson had recently graduated from Manhattan College in Queens and was getting ready to return to South Africa. Stewart and I sent Peter an airplane ticket so he could come to Los Angeles and join in celebrating our success. Little did I know that my world was beginning to take off in directions I never imagined and couldn't control. With "Grazing" approaching number one on the charts, the gigs were flying in. The phones never stopped ringing and the telegrams kept coming in to ABC, which led to bookings all over the United States. We needed a road manager, and I asked Peter Davidson to postpone his plans. He agreed, and stayed with us for two years. We crisscrossed the coun-try headlining festivals and concerts, playing the top clubs and selling out everywhere.

In Philadelphia we played the Quaker Jazz Festival at the Spectrum arena. I was leaving the venue when a beautiful woman stepped out of a limousine parked next to mine. It was Tammi Terrell. She said, "Release your driver. You're coming with me." She whisked me off to a suite she had reserved for us at the Marriott Hotel, where we spent the rest of the weekend together. Tammi spoke about how saddened she had been by not being able to join Marvin and me at the Apollo Theater. She had had an operation earlier that month, and the doctors were hopeful that they'd successfully removed the tumor. She would be going for X-rays later in the month to see what kind of progress was taking place. This was the beginning of a very tender relationship with the beautiful Tammi. I went to Philadelphia to visit her at her parents' home whenever I could. I would take her out for dinner or lunch, but as time went on she grew progressively weaker. The chemotherapy and several more operations did not help. I continued visiting her right up to a few weeks before she died. After she passed away, Marvin was so distraught he did not tour for three years.

On my twenty-ninth birthday, April 4, 1968, I was in New York City, having played a concert the night before in New Jersey. I had just left the Village Gate, where I had stopped for a few cognacs before heading uptown to my hotel. While I was driving a rented Cadillac up Sixth Avenue, an announcement came over the radio that Martin Luther King had been assassinated. I was shocked. A few seconds later, while I was stopped at a red light, a car plowed into my rear. I got out of the car to talk to the driver, a gray-haired old white man. An elderly woman, who I assumed was his wife, was seated next to him. They were both shaking like tree leaves in a storm, and suddenly they began to cry and begged me not to hurt them. I told them to go home and get some rest, and they drove off in disbelief. When I got to my room at the Mayflower Hotel, I turned on the television and saw there were riots going on in almost every black ghetto in America. No wonder the white couple had been crying and begging for mercy. I had not wanted to involve the police in my fender-bender because I had been drinking and snorting cocaine all day. I had two grams of cocaine in my jacket pocket, had been smoking a joint in the car, and was carrying a pocket full of rolled joints. This had become my lifestyle. I wasn't alone in this; all over the world, not every participant in the struggle for liberation was sober. In fact, the stress of it all drove many radicals into their graves either through booze or drugs, and even through sex.

Miriam was far more active than I in civil rights causes. She even attended Dr. King's funeral in Atlanta. I stayed so high that I missed many historical events that were taking place right under my powdered nose. We played Symphony Hall in Chicago during the summer of 1968, on the day that the riots were at their full fury, yet we didn't learn about the events that had taken place until we landed in Cleveland the next day and read the morning papers. Stewart and I had been prohibited from entering Mister Kelley's, where Cannonball Adderley was playing, because we were not wearing ties. We cussed the manager, jumped back into our limousine, and returned to our hotel to get higher, while the riots were taking place all around us. Many delegates to the Democratic Convention stayed in our hotel. The hotel manager tried to impress us by telling us he had rejected the Mississippi delegation and booked us in their place. We didn't understand what the fuck he was talking about.

The spring and summer of 1968 turned out to be one of the most insane periods in my life. I went totally nuts. We hired the accounting firm of Pilger and Dubey to manage our finances. Except for my Jaguar, Philemon Hou's MG roadster, and Peter Davidson's car, our clothes, the hi-fi set, bedroom linens, housewares, a few pieces of furniture, and my trumpet, everything was leased. Lou Pilger assured us that this was the wisest way to manage our money. All of my earnings were paid into Chisa Record Corporation, whose sole directors were Stewart and myself. We were making money hand over fist, but we hardly owned anything. Many people tried to coax me into buying property and invest in other businesses, but I wasn't listening. Some people warned me that Stewart, Lou Pilger, and Paul Dubey were exploiting me, but I was convinced that my funds were being managed properly. The only thing I put my foot down about was that once every month, my accountants send my folks money back in South Africa. Other than that, I followed their advice. I was too preoccupied with getting high and getting laid and having a good time. Like so many artists before and after me, I didn't think the windfall would ever end.

Around this time I took Mabusha, my nephew, from Miriam, who was now married to the activist Stokely Carmichael. Miriam had taken Mabusha from Barbara in Lusaka because she was having a difficult time minding him, working in the ANC office, and going to school. Peter, Philemon, Mabusha, and I lived in a big mansion on Queens Road. Out on the road I was having too much fun to mind the handling of my finances.

Shortly after the release of *Promise of a Future*, I was in New York playing the last night of a sold-out, two-week engagement at the Village Gate, when Jimi Hendrix came backstage. At this time Jimi's career was flying high. He was the god of the guitar and jammed every night at The Scene, at 49th Street and Eighth Avenue, where he always invited me, but I wasn't into rock jam sessions. The most beautiful women always surrounded Jimi. It was wonderful to hang out with him because he had a calming effect on me, and all the beautiful women around him made for some wonderful pickings. But unlike me, he had a cool and calm demeanor, spoke very little, and was very laid back. We had met at the Monterey Pop Festival and always talked about going on the road together. Jimi felt that most of his audience was white, and because I had such a large black following, the combination of Jimi, Sly Stone, and me would be a great way of integrating audiences.

After my last set at the Village Gate, Jimi and I ended up at a place called the Salvation. It was a beautiful basement club and disco with a stage, booths, a glass dance floor, great snacks, and waiters who were waiting to be discovered as singers, actors, dancers, songwriters, authors, and poets. In one night, just about everyone who had a top-ten record, or was in a hit show on Broadway or in a movie, would pass through the joint to network, cruise, meet a top drug dealer, or just plain hang out. Just about everyone who came to the Salvation was good looking and a sharp dresser. We loved the Salvation because it was a "members only" establishment. We were not members, but our celebrity was our entrée. Most of all, the food was gourmet quality, the drinks were top-shelf, and the women were some of the world's most beautiful, cosmopolitian to the bone.

Thelma Oliver, a stunning black woman who played opposite Gwen Verdon in the Broadway hit show *Sweet Charity,* came to see us perform at the Village Gate one Sunday, her night off, and I invited her for a drink at the Salvation. I had seen posters of Thelma, and like many others, I was an admirer of her coffee-brown beauty and dancer's body. That night we had drinks, and in the days that followed I became absolutely besotted. She was alarmed at how little time it had taken me to fall completely in love with her, but after a week she opened up and seemed to develop similar feelings for me. Then, hardly two weeks after we met, she told me she was leaving with the show for Paris. I was devastated. This was the first time I had really fallen boots and all for a woman since my divorce from Miriam, two years earlier. Saying good-bye to Thelma was painful, especially because she was still smiling that beautiful smile of hers as she waved to me from the taxi on her way to the airport. For the next two days I didn't feel like leaving my hotel room. For a while there, I lost my appetite for the smoke, the blow, and the drink. The guys in the band couldn't figure out what was the matter with me, and I wasn't saying anything. I felt lost and alone again. It was only when we played that I revived.

11

ONE OF THE WAITERS at Salvation, Mario, a young gay lyricist who claimed to be working on songs with Ashford and Simpson, had been telling me for weeks that a girlfriend of his by the name of Chris was dying to meet me. I never paid much attention to him. I was hanging out with Jimi again, hitting the night spots, dance clubs, and restaurants around New York with his entourage of beautiful women. He would say, "Hey, forget about Thelma, she's gone, and she ain't coming back no mo', but dig it, there's a whole lot of them where she came from. Let's hang and have a good time. You gotta bring your horn and blow with me at The Scene." But I just couldn't bring myself to go and jam with Jimi.

One night Jimi and I were at the Salvation, enjoying the funky music of the house band, the Chambers Brothers. I had been slipping out to the bathroom for a hit of coke between cognacs. Mario knew that I didn't like my glass to be empty, so he kept coming around to top me up. Around midnight, he sidled over to our table and whispered, "Hughie, can you come over with me for one second? I want to introduce you to someone who wants to meet you desperately." I followed Mario to a booth where Toma Gero, a famous designer who used to make clothes for Miriam, was sitting with this light-skinned, freckle-faced, bubbly beauty, dressed in an elegant black pantsuit.

"Hughie," Mario said, "this is Chris Calloway." Chris took my hand in both of hers, smiled her bewitching dimpled smile, and asked me to sit down. Mario brought a bottle of Dom Perignon to the table and uncorked it with a loud bang. After a while, I looked over where I had been sitting and Jimi was gone.

We ended up at Toma's spacious eight-room apartment in Chelsea, where Chris lived with Toma and her two little daughters. After more than three hours of nonstop conversation about Chris's Broadway show, *Hello Dolly*, and all of my questions about her father, Cab Calloway, whom I was dying to meet because I had seen him in so many of those half-hour sepia shorts in the movies back home, I left their flat when the sun was already up. Chris and I had not taken our eyes off each other the whole night. I thought I had found the cure for my Thelma Oliver blues.

The next night, Chris and I had an early dinner before her performance in *Hello Dolly*, which starred Pearl Bailey and her father, Cab. Chris was playing the comedic role of Miss Marmelstein in the show, which had the audience rolling in the aisles with laughter. After the show, we went back to the Salvation and enjoyed another long evening of endless conversation. The following morning I had to catch a flight back to Los Angeles. We phoned each other several times a day. Whenever I had a few days off, I flew to New York to be with Chris. It must have been a month or so after we met that we fell madly in love. I would rent a limousine that would take us to White Plains, where we hung out with Chris's dad and mom, their neighbors Moms Mabley, the Gordon Parks family, Ossie Davis and Ruby Dee, and many other Mount Vernon luminaries. Moms Mabley was a pure joy and affectionate, but Chris's mother, Nuffie, was very guarded, just like Pearl Bailey when Chris introduced me to her backstage. They both extended their arm from far away to greet me, their brows furrowed. Chris told me not to mind them. Chris took me to the Parkses' home—she had grown up with Gordon Jr. and his brother, David, who were extremely funny. Gordon and his wife treated Chris as if she were their own child. Ossie and Ruby were just as cordial. By the looks of the gigantic homes they lived in, I assumed that these were all very wealthy people—I was being introduced to yet another hidden stratum of American life, a black elite that I hadn't ever really seen before.

Cab and I hit it off hard. He loved when I told him about the movie shorts I had seen him in, especially when I imitated how he sang, did some of his steps, and described his zoot suits to a T. He would laugh and set me straight on his contributions to this game: "I was the first hip cat and I introduced the hip language, like 'slap me five' and 'yeah, daddy-o.' You know what? Them young bebop cats stole a lot of my words, like 'hep,' which they changed to 'hip.' They'll never admit it, but if it wasn't for me, we'd all still be square."

Nuffie would just look at her husband and shake her head, while Cab and I were roaring with laughter and throwing back that Dom Perignon. None of these folks seemed to care about my number-one hit or my newfound celebrity because they had been celebrities for decades. They were more interested in South Africa, my parents, whether I wrote my mother, the languages I spoke, when I would be going home, and all the rest of the stuff that Marcus Belgrave's people had asked me back in Chester—only in more refined English.

Toma Gero was preparing to leave for Europe with her children to visit their father for the summer. Chris was going to have the apartment to herself. I moved in with her right away. By the beginning of May, Chris was visiting me regularly in Los Angeles, where we would spend most of our time at Stewart and Susie's Malibu Beach home getting high, laughing, and loving. A few weeks later I asked Chris to marry me, because I wanted to be intimate with one person and have a real home. It was too easy playing around with a lot of women and hanging out with Jimi from club to restaurant to after-hours joint. I was keen to have some children and raise a family. Chris came from what looked like a stable, secure family background, and that appealed to me. I pictured us driving the kids to visit their grandparents in White Plains, my in-laws fussing over them, Cab and me shooting the breeze, sipping champagne on the porch, and going fishing. I ached for a stable environment, something I knew I couldn't find in South Africa, because I wasn't going back there anytime soon. With Chris, I felt the potential of that kind of warmth in our lives. Besides love, it was with this larger vision of a *life* in my mind that I proposed marriage to Chris Calloway. She accepted.

Word spread quickly of our whirlwind romance and upcoming wedding, but rather than a chorus of congratulations, I was surprised when I got warnings and catcalls. Friends started telling me, "Hughie, this is one move you are going to regret for the rest of your life." "Hughie, Chris is crazy, man. Everybody knows that. Where you been?"

Billy Dee Williams, who used to date Chris, warned me, "Hughie, I lived with her, man. She is insane. She's gonna drive you up the wall, brother." I had met Billy Dee through Chris's manager, a young black accountant named Dennis Armstead, who also managed the affairs of several other actors. Dennis accompanied us to many dinners, shows, parties, and clubs. Before long he and I became good friends—we shared a healthy appetite for XO cognac, vintage champagne, prime weed, and pure blow. Most of all, he loved fine women. A few other friends tried to warn me, but I was totally deaf to them on the subject.

On the other hand, Stewart, Susie, and the guys in my band liked Chris. With all my blow, smoke, uppers, downers, cognac, champagne, and wine, I never noticed any unusual behavior. To me, she was always cool, soft-spoken, sweet, and funny. And believe me, if she could keep up with the amount of substances that Susie, Stewart, and I were consuming, the girl was okay by me. We were convinced everybody was slandering her out of jealousy and envy.

The Calloways were excited about our wedding, which would be at their White Plains estate. Nuffie had grown to love me, and Stewart was going to be my best man, my band members the ushers. Bernard Johnson, Broadway's top designer of clothing at the time, would be doing the men's outfits. We planned to fly in Toma from Europe to do the maid of honor's and brides-maids' clothes. Nuffie marched us through the motions in the gigantic gardens of her estate, briefing us on how the ceremony would go down, from the back porch through the trellises to the gazebo, where the minister would marry us. The guests were going to be the who's-who of the entertainment business, Mount Vernon's upper-crust black families, and my hanging partners. My blood relatives were all back home, and Barbara was in Zambia. I had lost touch with the South African community in New York since beginning my new life in Los Angeles. My family back home was so preoccupied with their own problems and trying to survive the apartheid nightmares that all they could wish me was happiness. They were very appreciative of the monthly check I was sending, and never tried to tell me how to live my life. My mother prayed for me every day.

Although Chris was happy, she seemed detached from the wedding plans. Her younger sister, Cabella, spent a lot of time with me in her upstairs bed-room, where we could view the entire estate gardens while we smoked spliffs and philosophized about life. Her older sister, Lael, was very quiet and spent most of her time with her mother. I spent hours drinking with Cab and talk-ing about his band and all the people he'd trained, especially Dizzy Gillespie, whom he said he'd fired for his practical jokes. Dizzy always told me about how crazy Cab used to be, and vice versa. Cab assured me that Dizzy had learned everything he knew from him—scatting, humor, bebop, you name it. Cab could really run his mouth until Nuffie entered the room, at which point he'd straighten up and behave.

Cabella asked me one day, "Hughie, are you sure you want to marry my sis-ter? My sister is crazy, Hughie, believe me. Chris is out of her fucking mind. You'll see." I was stunned to hear Cabella talking like this about her sister. I said, "Cabella, this grass is getting you all fucked up." All she said was, "Believe me, it's not the grass." I was a little startled, and all the negative voices started echoing in my mind, but I was too far gone on this journey. I could have walked out, but I didn't have the balls. *Chris had the balls!*

One Sunday night when I was scheduled to fly from New York to Los Angeles, Chris rode with me to JFK Airport in a limousine for our usual romantic farewell. When it was time for me to board, Chris began to weep very emotionally. She said she could not stand the separations anymore. At this time she was the toast of Broadway and I was the golden boy of the record world. Everybody more or less knew us all over New York. Chris's weeping pulled on the airline crew's heartstrings as we stood by the gangway. They were preparing to shut the doors, and we were delaying the departure of the plane. Because the crew found the whole scene so romantic and encouraged her with their sighs, by the time she walked me to the airplane door, Chris was weeping hysterically. The flight captain and crew were waiting at the first-class door. Chris wailed, "I want to go. Don't leave me." I told Chris that she didn't have a ticket. By now the tears had completely caused her freckles to vanish. Her eyes were bloodshot and her lips crimson-red. The captain said, "Let her come along." I told the captain that I didn't have my credit cards or that much cash on me. He interrupted, "She can come as our guest." The crew broke into applause, sighing, "Aaahh" in unison. Chris was now chuckling through her tears. We were the only two people in first class. The crew spoiled us during the flight. We had completely forgotten about the limo driver back at JFK Airport, who was supposed to take Chris back to the city.

On Monday afternoon as the sun was beginning to set on Malibu Beach, we were lying on sofa benches, drinking in the cool sea breeze, sipping Dom Perignon, smoking the best weed in California, and occasionally snorting a whiff of prime cocaine. Susie and Stewart had been fussing over us as usual, and all four of us had nothing on our minds except chilling. It was getting late. I told Chris we needed to get back to my place in Beverly Hills, so she could get ready for the red-eye flight back to New York. Chris abruptly said, "I'm not going back." Surprised, I took a few deep drags on a joint before responding. "You've got a gig on Broadway, a whole cast that depends on you, and a contract with David Merrick. He will flip out if you don't show up tomorrow night. Are you crazy?"

"Fuck David Merrick," she said. "That motherfucker is just exploiting us with this black *Hello Dolly*. Pearl and my father are not getting the kind of money Carol Channing and the white cast got. Plus, the people in the company hate my guts. I'm miserable in that show, and if you love me like you say you do, then you won't send me back to those motherfuckers."

Susie leaned over and embraced Chris. Stewart, who was high, chimed in. "Yeah, baby, fuck David Merrick and them Broadway motherfuckers. Hughie, the poor girl doesn't deserve to be with those lowlifes, man. She's happy here with you. Fuck those New York people." I thought everyone was losing their minds—or maybe I was the stupid one, because I was outnumbered. I should have stood up to them and taken Chris to that plane, but instead I said, "Yeah," topping our glasses and passing my joint to Stewart as Susie and Chris attacked a coke vial. "Let's break open another champagne and celebrate this moment. You ain't goin nowhere, sweetheart. Let's get high, goddamm it!" How quickly I lost my will.

My attorney settled Chris's contract with the David Merrick Company for fifty thousand dollars. He told me many times how crazy he thought I was. The cast of *Hello Dolly* started spreading the bad word around about Chris. It became apparent that she would never work on Broadway again. By the end of the week, the tabloids had done an about-face. We were no longer the darlings of the media. CHRIS CALLOWAY ABANDONS HIT BROADWAY SHOW TO ELOPE WITH AFRICAN JAZZMAN HUGH MASEKELA, rang one of the headlines. Cab and Nuffie were livid back in Mount Vernon. To them I had become the devil incarnate. Meanwhile, back in California, Chris and I were so anesthetized, our only reaction was "Fuck 'em all. They can kiss our black asses."

We decided to skip the Mount Vernon ceremony and have a quiet, private wedding in a Hollywood chapel. We went to the license bureau in downtown Los Angeles and got our marriage certificate. On our way out of the building, we discarded what we thought was junk literature in a garbage basket at the foot of the stairs. Jumping into a stretch limousine, I ordered the driver to head for the chapel. During the ride we smoked prime Oaxaca ganja we had mixed with some top-grade opium, drank champagne, and snorted pharmaceutical cocaine, while singing and laughing our asses off.

Outside the chapel, we calmed down at the sound of the soft, piped-in solemnity of wedding music and held on tight to each other as the woman minister, with Marilyn Monroe looks and a Colgate smile, began the ceremony. With Susie and Stewart as our witnesses, the minister asked Stewart for the marriage certificate. She looked down at the papers we'd handed her and said, to our surprise, "This is not a marriage certificate. These are the forms on how to apply for a marriage license." Chris and I looked at each other in amazement and realized that we must have accidentally thrown our marriage license out with the other papers back at the license bureau. We apologized to the minister and ran out of the chapel into the waiting limousine. During the ride back to the State Office Building, Chris and I couldn't stop laughing, while we stole the moment to resume our smoking, snorting, and champagning, much to the driver's amusement.

It was nearing five o'clock when we approached the license bureau. Office workers were already streaming out of the building. There was a garbage truck parked outside, and men dressed in orange overalls were busy collecting trash containers from inside and outside the building. We ran up the stairs to the wastebasket, and at the bottom, to our relief, was our certificate. As we rushed back to the limo, I began to worry if this was an omen of doom. Back at the chapel, we continued the ceremony. Susie, Chris, and I cried. Stewart kept a stiff upper lip, and the minister wiped her designer tears and proclaimed us man and wife. Chris was twenty-two. I was twenty-nine.

We spent the following week dining, laughing, making love, getting high, shopping, and driving around Los Angeles planning our future. We were going to make kids, build a house in the country, buy a town house, and enjoy life together to the fullest. I started a new tour, and we moved back to Toma's house in Manhattan. It also seemed that we had re-won the hearts of Americans and we were soon appearing in the country's leading magazines—*Vogue, Life, Jet, Cosmopolitan,* and national newspapers—as a lovable and exciting couple. Invitations to parties came from everywhere. I often remembered all the naysayers like Billy Dee and the others who had warned me about Chris. Their attitudes, as well as the cast of *Hello Dolly,* Nuffie, Cab, and Pearl Bailey, became the best source material for our private jokes when we were getting high, enjoying the last laugh.

One evening, after spending the afternoon with Stewart and Susie, we were driving back to our Hollywood Hills home in my new Mercedes, taking in the sweet Pacific breeze while an orange sun set on the California coast's beautiful golden horizon. "Grazing in the Grass," which was still number one on the record charts, was playing on KGFJ, the local R&B station, when suddenly Chris let out a shrill shriek and started to kick in the dashboard. I pulled over in total disbelief. "Chris, what the fuck are you doing?" "Hit me. Hit me!" she screamed back, continuing to kick at the dashboard, shattering the glass in the speedometer, gas gauge, oil gauge, thermometer, and clock. I grabbed both her arms and tried to get her to look me in the face.

I said, "Stop it, Chris. Stop it." But she kept screaming and kicking.

"Hit me. *Hit meeee!*"

I had promised my grandmother and mother that I would never strike a woman, but this one was begging for it. I reluctantly gave Chris an open-handed smack across her left cheek. She stopped immediately. My heart sank from what I had just done, and my head spun—I had no idea what to expect next. She looked me straight in the eye and whispered, "Thank you, Hughie, I love you so much." Then she clung to me, crying, "I love you. I love you."

Now I was really worried. As we resumed our drive back to Queens Road in silence, the roar of the ocean had lost its charm. With dusk turning into evening and the Santa Monica lights beckoning us toward the twilight zone of Hollywood's weirdness, I was deep in thought. I figured it might be better to return to New York, that maybe the Los Angeles environment was not her piece of cake. She didn't have a circle of friends in California, and for a person like Chris, who loved to get around, L.A. was a nightmare because she didn't have a driver's license, and even if she had, she didn't know her way around. Most of all, Chris had very little if any rapport with Philemon and Mabusha, who were living with us. When she was around Philly and Mabusha, they would go to their rooms. They just couldn't be in the same space with her, and this spooked her, even if she didn't say it. On the other hand, Chris and Peter Davidson got along fine, and she was tight with Susie, Stewart, and the band. But the rest of my Hollywood scene was anathema to her. After about fifteen minutes of total silence, which I needed to calm my nerves, especially when I noticed the shards of glass all over the car floor, I decided to attempt a sympathetic inquiry into Chris's mental state.

"So tell me, Chris, what was that all about?" I asked cautiously, so as not to provoke another psychotic explosion. She was furiously biting her cuticles. I noticed that she had bitten off all her nails, and two fingertips were bleeding. For the first time I realized that I had a major problem on my hands. With tears in her eyes, Chris began to explain how dominating Nuffie was, and what a wimp her father could be, out of fear of his wife. She said she despised her father and resented her mother's domineering nature. This, she said, was the main reason why she didn't want us getting married at their White Plains estate. "It would have all been a show for our neighbors and not much to do with us."

I was flabbergasted. We stopped at a Beverly Hills restaurant for coffee. I decided that perhaps we should go on a two-week honeymoon. The idea seemed to return Chris to a happy, tranquil mood. She apologized for the dashboard and assured me it would never happen again. On our drive into the hills, she changed to her bubbly self again, to my temporary relief.

She told me stories from her childhood—about her godmother, Lena Horne, who would sit young Chris on her lap and tell stories and sing to her; about cruises to Europe on the *Queen Elizabeth*, ski trips to Switzerland, and train journeys on the *Orient Express*. She loved it when she and her sister Lael would go on tour with Cab's band and Dizzy would babysit them—but mostly she was very lonely. When they'd get back from their tours and trips, her sister and mother would spend time together, leaving Chris to fend for herself.

At this point, my heart went out to her. She was clearly miserable. I was determined to make her happy.

I told her about my youth in Witbank, Springs, and Alexandra, and by the time we reached home we were laughing and joking again. We had some champagne, coke, and other goodies, and ended the night with torrid lovemaking. We decided to take a honeymoon on the *Queen Elizabeth* from New York to London. We would then travel across Europe on the *Orient Express* and take in the romantic sites of Rome and Paris before I returned for the Newport Jazz Festival tour, where I was headlining a bill that included Dizzy Gillespie, Sarah Vaughan, Max Roach, Nina Simone, Miles Davis, Duke Ellington, Cannonball Adderley, and Thelonious Monk. Things seemed to be looking up again.

My travel agent in Los Angeles made all the bookings for our transatlantic cruise and European honeymoon. With the album and the single still sizzling, I was doing back-to-back interviews in New York, so I put Chris in charge of the travel logistics. A few days after our arrival in New York, we had tickets, visas, hotel and car vouchers, traveler's checks totaling about fifteen thousand dollars, and a happy marriage to take on our honeymoon. When I suggested— on the day before our voyage—that we begin packing, Chris began to cry. She said she had lost her bag with the tickets, traveler's checks, vouchers—everything. She didn't know how, when, and where. After I called American Express to cancel the traveler's checks and my travel agent to cancel our cruise and European tour, I consoled Chris, telling her that perhaps our trip wasn't in the stars. She became furious with herself, biting her nails again, and stormed out of the house crying. I didn't run after her, but instead called a friend of mine in St. Thomas and arranged for us to travel to the Virgin Islands the next day.

When Chris returned later that evening, I was all packed and told her about the St. Thomas alternative. Although she didn't appear too excited, she agreed to the plan, but seemed disappointed that the cancellation of our European honeymoon had not sent me into a ranting and raving tantrum. Later that evening she told me that she had visited a clairvoyant who had assured her that I was going to die soon. I just shook my head in absolute wonder. After a couple of snorts of cocaine, some cognacs, and a big spliff of opium-laced ganja, I laughed myself to sleep while Chris downed a cocktail of barbiturates.

The next morning we were off to St. Thomas. My friend Jimmy Davis, a successful businessman, radio personality, and concert promoter, and his wife met us at the airport, invited us to their home for lunch, and took us to our villa on a secluded beach, situated in a quiet part of the island. The villa came with a cook, a valet, a maid, and a groundsman. When Jimmy was about to leave us in our room, he pulled me aside and asked why my wife was so unsociable. I explained that Chris was still upset about our botched European honeymoon. At dinner at their house that night, she was worse—nasty and rude to our hosts. She left the table in a huff, and went and sat in the Jeep I had rented. On the way back to our villa, I was too pissed to speak to Chris, and all she did was chew her nails. She later took some downers and passed out. The next morning, when I woke up, Chris was already up and gone. Worried and dressed only in a pair of swimming trunks, I went looking for her. The gardener told me he'd seen her walking up a nearby hill. I followed his directions and spotted Chris wearing a white cotton nightgown, standing on a jagged precipice with the ocean below splashing up against the cliff. Her gown was drenched from the ocean spray. She looked down at me and screamed, "Go away! Go away!" I ran up the rocky incline like an Olympic athlete in a hundred-meter dash, all the while thinking how the media would report the whole incident: HUGH MASEKELA MURDERS YOUNG WIFE DURING CARIBBEAN HONEYMOON: PROSECUTOR SEEKS DEATH PENALTY. Chris was still screaming "Go away!" when I reached her and proceeded to drag her down the mountain with a tight grip on her arm.

"You should have left me to die, you idiot," she said, with tears streaming down her cheeks. I could hardly talk, I was so out of breath, but I was relieved by our narrow escape. Back at the villa, the staff, which had witnessed the spectacle, was thanking the Lord for Chris's life.

After I calmed down, I decided to try to get to the root of Chris's problem. At this point I was trying out the therapeutic route, convinced that from what she had told me about her unhappy childhood, some sympathy and understanding from me might help turn her toward normalcy. By midday she was laughing and we were snorkeling, diving, and cavorting in the waters of our private seaside alcove, blending in with the fish in the sea. Life seemed once more fat with bliss. Even though I had no experience in psychotherapy, and had flunked psychology miserably at the Manhattan School of Music, I put all my heart and mind into a deep desire to cure Chris's ailment. I saw it as the only way to save our marriage. Wading out of the water for a late lunch, I felt a sting in the sole of my left foot, but I ignored it. By the time I came out of the shower, I was walking with a limp, my foot had begun to swell, and the pain was excruciating. I called Jimmy, and he referred me to a doctor at the Bayside Clinic. Even though he suspected Chris had something to do with it, I was mum on what might have happened. The drive to the clinic was torturous. The doctor told us that I had torn the tendon in the sole of my foot, and he advised me to return to New York for treatment. We had to cut the honeymoon short.

Jimmy came to the airport to say good-bye. He never said one word to Chris. Pulling me aside, he whispered in my ear, "Be careful of this woman. She's gonna kill you, man." I told Jimmy that he didn't understand, that Chris had had a raw deal and that I was trying to help her. "She's beyond help, Hughie," Jimmy continued. "This girl is mean and crazy. Go well, Hughie, and lots of luck, man. Believe me, you're gonna need it."

My doctor in New York bound my foot with bandages, gave me a couple of injections, prescribed some anti-inflammation medication, and ordered me to keep my weight off my foot for three weeks. My next gig was in Philadelphia the following week, at Eagles Stadium, where we would kick off the Newport Jazz Festival. I stayed off my foot as much as I could in Philly, though Chris had me hobbling in and out of limousines, assisting her on endless shopping expeditions. My injury attracted considerable attention, but we lied to everyone about what had happened. I did tell Stewart the truth—that I'd probably injured my foot running up that mountain barefoot, trying to stop Chris from jumping.

"She is crazy, Hughie," Stewart said. "Damn, she really had us fooled. What you gonna do, man?"

I told him, "I'm gonna try and help her. She really deserves a shot. She had it so tough."

"Tough, my ass, Hughie," Stewart said. "She's Cab Calloway's daughter, man. Dizzy told me what a fucking brat she was when he used to babysit her.

She ain't never gonna change. And you can't do shit for her. Cab has always been a happy millionaire. There's no way Chris could have ever suffered except by her own doing."

Like they say, love is blind. I know now that sometimes love can be stupid, too.

The following week, Chris's disposition improved. She was back to being a loving, attentive wife. Her mood swings had dissipated. One evening we had her parents over for dinner, which even gave us the opportunity to reconcile with her family.

There were forty thousand people at the kickoff of the Newport Jazz festival. Because I was still on crutches, when it was my time to go onstage, Chris escorted me onto the gigantic platform. At the microphone, she curtsied to the riotous applause of the stadium. She exited stage right with a fulfilled look on her freckled face. Al Abreu, our saxophonist, came over to my ear and whispered, "Your old lady loves that you're hobbled. She gets to be in the spotlight." It had never entered my mind that Chris could be that manipulative, but Abreu's comment stuck with me as I started to count off our opening song, "Son of Ice Bag." The crowd went berserk from the very first eight bars we played, and as the clouds gathered above us, the entire stadium went into a frenzy.

When we got to our second-to-last song "Bajabula Bonke—the Healing Song," I began to introduce the band: "On bass, from Riverside, California, Henry Franklin; on drums, from Watts, California, Chuck Carter; on piano, from Cincinnati, Ohio, Billy Henderson; and on sax and everything else, from the Bronx, New York, via Puerto Rico, Alfredo Abreu." The crowd went bananas. From the corner of my eye, I caught Dizzy and Stewart sitting in the back of our limousine behind the stage, toasting me with a vial of coke they were passing back and forth between them. They were dying from laughter every time I looked their way with envy. Lightning and thunder struck when we broke into "Grazing in the Grass." It began raining hard when I went into the first solo of the song. The crowd never left; they just kept on dancing, bumping and bouncing and hollering, under the torrential showers. When the song ended, they hollered for more. It was pouring rain, but we played "Grazing" again. Still that wasn't enough. The crowd wanted it a third time. We obliged, then bowed and left the stage to their thunderous applause.

Back in the dressing room, Peter Davidson walked over to Chris, who was helping me change into dry clothes.

"Chris, I'm confirming seats for our flight tomorrow for Pittsburgh. I need to know now if you are traveling with us. It's summertime, plus it's the weekend and the planes are usually full. Do you want to come?"

She declined, saying she wanted to go shopping and would be waiting for us when we returned to New York on Monday.

"Okay, Chris, don't change your mind."

The next morning Peter, Stewart, and the band picked me up at the hotel for the flight to Pittsburgh. We were at the departure lounge waiting to board the plane when Henry Franklin, our bassist, started in on me.

"That Chris is really something else, Hughie. I'm telling you, you married a hell of a chick, brother."

Balancing myself on my crutches, I said, "Henry, why the fuck would you be thinking of Chris right now? Can't you give us a little break from that girl?"

"I wish I could, Hughie, but she just ran by us." The whole band and some of the other passengers who were waiting in line with us turned around, and running down the terminal was Chris in a floral minidress, doing a slow trot so as to make sure somebody would catch her if they gave chase.

Peter and Stewart instinctively shot out after her, bringing her back, as if they were the policemen and she the fleeing thief. She was sobbing. I said, "Chris, you kept the limo so you could go shopping. Peter asked what your plans were. You never mentioned coming to the airport."

She said, "I waanna go. I wanna *gooooo.*"

I said, "Peter told you the plane would be full on Sundays. Now you are here, causing a scene. Chris, what the fuck is the matter with you, baby?"

She insisted, "I want to go, goddammit, Hughie. Talk to the fuckin' captain. I'm comin' with you, man." By now everyone within earshot was focusing in on this tragicomedy. I told her again that the plane was full. "Full, my freckle-faced black ass. You got influence, Hughie," she said, biting her nails and shaking nervously. I said, "I've got work to do, Chris, and you are wasting my time, good-bye." I hobbled onto the plane with the band behind me. Airport security came and pulled her away from the gate while she kicked and shoved, protesting vehemently.

Inside the first-class cabin, Stewart looked at me sadly. "Whatchoo gonna do about this bitch, Hughie? She seems to be losing it more and more every day." I just shook my head in utter amazement. I had not thought about the possibility of cutting loose from Chris until right that second. But I said nothing to Stewart.

When the plane pushed away from the boarding gate, Henry started laughing. I said, "It ain't funny. Just cut it out." He quickly replied, "Oh yeah, it's funnier than a motherfucker, man. This shit is too funny. Just look through your window, Hughie. Man, this Chris is just too fucking much. I'm telling you." Everyone in first class jumped for the windows, to see Chris being chased by six security officers. She was running toward the plane screaming, "Stop! Stop! Stop!" with her hands waving high over her head and her dress up to her stomach in the breeze, with only a skimpy pair of panties covering her ass. The security officers lifted her off the ground and onto their shoulders. Even I had to join the laughter on the plane, but truthfully I felt badly for Chris. I thought to myself, this poor girl is really suffering.

My band, Stewart, Dizzy, Ben Riley (Monk's drummer), and some of the members of Blood, Sweat and Tears were seated in my dressing room suite, smoking "ice pack" at the Pittsburgh Convention Center before the show, listening to Cannonball Adderley tell us stories about past music-business antics. We were all laid back and laughing when Henry started up again about Chris. But before he could get in full stride, in walked Chris, her fingernails bitten down and bleeding, her freckled face red with remorse. She looked me straight in the eye and said, "Yeah, so you thought I couldn't get here, right?" Within seconds the group disappeared as if the narcotics squad had arrived. Only Henry stayed back, not wanting to miss any potential fireworks, but I asked him to leave, too.

I was filled with so much anger and bitterness for the first time, and I wanted Chris to understand just how I felt. I said, "Chris, I don't know what you are trying to do, but this is my livelihood you are upsetting here. I have been kind and patient with you, and have tried to understand whatever it is that is bothering you. But this disruption is beginning to anger me deeply, and if you don't stop, I am going to have to turn you loose, baby. I am very sorry, but you are busting my balls, man. And I am not prepared to take this shit anymore. Do you understand what I am saying to you?"

"I just want to be with you, Hughie," she said. "Why are you pushing me away?"

I stood up and she rushed to hand me my crutches. I took them and continued, "Chris, I am going to get someone to go and find you a seat in the show. From there, I expect you to enjoy the festival without disrupting anything. If you do, I will have you legally and forcibly removed. Now, are you gonna cooperate with me, or should I have you thrown out now?"

I think Chris understood that the game she was playing had gone far enough. She didn't give anyone any trouble the rest of the evening. After the show, she returned with me to my hotel suite, where I spoke with her almost till dawn. I told her that she had to pull herself together. She promised to change her ways, and apologized to me and to the band. Later in the day, Chris and I flew back to Philly to pick up our things from the hotel. We took the limo back to New York. Our driver was shell-shocked from the Sunday airport experience. He hardly said a word to us during the ride. We never saw him again. I suspect he must have begged his company never to assign him to us again.

For the next three weeks Chris was extremely well behaved, except when she would sneak out to consult with her clairvoyant, who kept telling her that I was going to die soon. I finally told Chris that I was going to have her clairvoyant murdered. She stopped talking about my imminent death, and probably warned her fortune-teller about my threat. I never heard about her again.

Now and again Chris would sleep for two days without waking up. I suspected that she was on some serious downers. I soon discovered that she was taking Placidyl, a barbiturate that I really got to like because after I took it I could easily go to sleep when the cocaine kept me up. Around this time Stewart introduced me to Artie Ripp and the other executives at Buddah Records. Even though "Grazing in the Grass" was still number one, and I was signed with UNI Records, these guys were hellbent on signing me for their label. Ripp was also fascinated by my reported prowess with women. He said he knew this chick named "China" who could bust my balls and put me away in bed. He swore "China" could tame me. I thought all of this was odd, and perhaps Stewart was behind all this because he wanted me to get away from Chris and her madness and disruptive behavior. With Chris sleeping most of the time, I began to hang out with "China." Iris—her real name—was a pretty blonde with a beautiful smile and the body of a Congolese Amazon who had been raised in the depths of Zululand. Stewart would lend me the keys to his suite at the Drake Hotel, and there I would rendezvous with Iris during the day when Chris was on downers and sleeping away, sometimes for days on end. Instead of "China" bringing me to my knees, she fell madly in love with me and the joke was on Artie Ripp, or maybe on me. By this time I had had it with Chris and didn't care anymore about our marriage because she didn't seem to give a shit. I was seriously contemplating ways to call it a day, but she kept begging me to give her another chance. "I'll get well, Hughie. You'll see. Believe me."

When the Newport Jazz Festival resumed, I left Chris at home, but occasionally she'd come along. And for a while, I must admit, she conducted herself properly. But as in the past, her good behavior didn't last long. During one of our flights we were caught in a nasty and turbulent electric storm. The plane was bouncing every which way and the passengers were terrified—everyone, that is, except Chris. Staring at me with wide-open eyes, she hissed, "You are scared, right? We're gonna die. It's all over." Stewart and I looked at each other in amazement. He was shaking his head in disbelief. While our plane was being tossed about and bouncing what seemed like one hundred feet at a time, Chris sang out in a deep, ominous voice, like Dracula's in those vampire films, "It's all over, Hughie." We reached Louisville, Kentucky, safely, but I was now wondering about Chris. Where was she coming from with all the shit she was talking on the plane? Could she really be that weird?

Other than Susie, Stewart, Peter, and the members of the band, Chris did not have any friends. Aside from Toma Gero, Dennis Armstead, and the Gordon Parks siblings, whom she grew up with in White Plains, Chris spent most of her time shopping, traveling, or getting high alone or with me.

Toward the middle of July, the Newport Festival was winding down. We only had two more venues—Newport, Rhode Island, and Montreal. When we arrived in Newport, we rented two station wagons and drove to our motel near the festival venue. It was a beautiful, sunny summer afternoon and all of us were in a hilariously happy mood. We had a mountainous stash of about an eighth of an ounce of pure coke, a half-pound of prime Oaxacan "ice pack," a slab of Afghani hashish, Valium, Placidyl, Courvoisier, Dom Perignon, half a fist of Thai opium, three books of Bambu giant rolling papers, and some amphetamines. At the Newport concert, there must have been more than fifty thousand jazz fanatics in attendance. It was late in the afternoon when we jumped into our first song, "Son of Ice Bag." After four tunes, we played Marvin and Tammi's "Ain't No Mountain High Enough," which was one of the most beloved songs of the season. By the time we got to "Grazing in the Grass," all hell broke loose. People started dancing as if possessed by African demons of rhythm and voodoo—frenzy and abandon unleashed. I couldn't stop shaking my head in delight, really amazed that music could have so much power. All of a sudden, in the middle of my solo, the crowd stopped dancing and began laughing and pointing to the stage. I couldn't understand what was going on until I glanced over my right shoulder. Standing beside me was Chris, cool, calm, and flashing the audience her freckles and toothy grin. Stunned, I said, "Abreu, take a solo." I turned around and hugged Chris gently around the waist. She followed my lead and we floated offstage, Fred-and-Ginger-style. I handed her over to Stewart, who was standing at the foot of the stage. "Hold on to her," I said, rushing back on stage. After the show, Henry weighed in with his usual jabs. "Hughie, I just love that Chris."

This was the last straw. Once we returned to our motel, I told her, "I would appreciate it if you would just go back to New York in the morning. I want you out of my life because you are driving us all insane, and nobody needs that shit here anymore. We've all had enough of your drama. I'm certainly not taking you to Montreal tomorrow."

She snapped back, "Oh, shut the fuck up, Hughie. There you go whining again. Nobody else is complaining, man. Everybody enjoyed the show. What is your problem, anyway?"

"Fuck you, Chris! I've had enough of your bullshit. Can't you get it? I'm not going to take any more of your shit, baby. You are going back to New York tomorrow and out of my fucking life, and that's it. I don't give a shit what you do with your life, but you ain't going to fuck mine up anymore. It's all over, baby. That's it. You're out of here, goddamnit."

She studied me for a few moments, then replied, "Well, fuck you too, Hughie," and walked out of the motel suite. About two hours later, around ten o'clock, she came back. No one paid her too much mind, but Henry greeted her with, "Hey, Chris, you're really too much, baby."

She brushed Henry off and addressed me. We were all seated on sofas and armchairs, passing joints and vials of cocaine and drinking cognac and Dom Perignon. Chris said, "Well, Hughie, since you don't want me around here, give me the fucking keys to the car and I'll drive to New York and get out of your fucking life. Come on, give me the fucking keys."

I said, "Chris, you don't have a driver's license and you are fucking high out of your mind. You wouldn't even get out of town without getting stopped by the cops. Do you think I'm crazy?"

Determined, she persisted, "Give me the fucking keys. I can drive, and no cops are gonna stop my fucking ass. Just give me the fucking keys."

I said, "Go to hell, Chris. I ain't giving you shit, and I don't care what you do. I'm tired of your shit. You hear me?"

I stood up and began to walk toward her, but she walked out and hollered over her shoulder, "Fuck you, asshole, I'll hitch a ride back to New York. I don't need your ass. Fuck you, Hughie." With that, she disappeared into the night as we continued our party. Around midnight, Chris returned, stared at us, and mumbled something. Her speech was slurred.

"Oh shit," Stewart said. "She's OD'd on some downers. Somebody get lots of black coffee." He went over to Chris and caught her just as she slumped into his arms. Realizing we needed to call for help, I began shouting orders to hide the drugs. Al Abreu rushed in with a jug of coffee from where I don't know. It was a messy situation, and we were panic-stricken. Soon the police arrived, along with paramedics who took Chris to the hospital. We were relieved that the cops didn't have time to sniff around. Stewart, Susie, and I rode with Chris to the hospital.

As she was being wheeled to the emergency room, Chris suddenly came to and began screaming and kicking. "Don't help me. I want to die. I want to fucking die." A nurse gave her a shot and she passed out. Susie stayed with Chris because Stewart and I had to catch our flight to Montreal. I was exhausted and I had to go to work. She was in good hands with the hospital staff and Susie standing by. That morning as we flew to Montreal, Dizzy said, "Man, I used to babysit that girl when I was in her father's band. She was always throwing all kinds of shit in my face. The girl's always been out of it, man. I wish you luck, boy. You're gonna need it. Oooweee." Periodically, Henry Franklin would shake his head and whisper, "Man, oh man."

On our flight back to Newport from Canada, Stewart and I sat alone, exhausted from the gig, yet relieved that Susie had called and reported that Chris was doing fine and would be ready to travel to New York. Stewart broke the silence. "Hughie, whatchoo going to do with this girl, man? She's completely out of her mind and driving you up the wall. You're beginning to look like a skeleton. You're hardly eating anymore. All those uppers and downers the two of you are taking. The endless coke and cognac, man. You are looking really bad, Hughie."

I had no idea what to do. I knew I couldn't leave her in that condition, but I was exhausted by the thought of Chris. Deep down, I wanted to leave her. I had had it. Stewart then hit me with some heavy news. "I'm cutting Susie loose. We're getting a divorce. Susie is going to an ashram somewhere in upstate New York, where she's joining the Maharishi and going to find herself. I can't get into that shit, man. She's really deep into it. We're calling it quits. No hard feelings." All I could say was "Damn."

Chris and Susie were waiting at the motel. "How do you feel, Chris?" I asked, not so much because I was interested, but for lack of anything else to say. I was exasperated with her by now.

"Hughie, I'm sorry. I am really sorry. I don't know what came over me.

Please forgive me, Hughie. I'll be really good. I swear I'll be good. Please take me to New Orleans." Nuffie was from New Orleans and Chris had always wanted to go there to see her mother's hometown. She somehow felt there was something magical she would find in the Crescent City.

Listening to her beg, then cry those crocodile tears, I said, "Listen, finish packing so we can check out." At the front desk, Stewart asked me if I was going to take Chris to New Orleans. "I have to, man. I can't leave her alone at the apartment. I'm afraid that in the condition she's in, I just might come back to find her dead."

Chris was excited that I'd had a change of heart and decided she could come. We found my band at the Roosevelt Hotel, where Billy Eckstine was also staying and performing in the hotel's famous lounge. After our concert, the promoter Larry McKinley treated us to dinner at the hotel while we enjoyed Billy's performance. It turned out that Billy was some kind of godparent to Chris and very close to her folks. He invited us to his suite. Larry had found us some of the best grass and the best cocaine money could buy. We had some pure Sandoz LSD from Switzerland with which we spiked everybody's Dom Perignon as we partied in Mr. Eckstine's suite. The guys in the band were all with foxes. Everybody was getting ripped, and feeling no pain.

At about 2:00 a.m., I came up with a suggestion that had obviously been prompted by the LSD in combination with the cocaine, weed, cognac, and Dom Perignon. "Let's go down to the Mississippi and check out the river." All of the revelers agreed, except Billy. "You people are all crazy. I ain't going to no river at this time in the morning. Ain't nothin' happening there. Y'all go ahead. I'm going to bed."

In a convoy of about six cars, we got to the river, walked to the edge, and just stared at the magnificent river. The acid was really beginning to kick in. "Wow," I said. "I can actually hear the trumpets of Buddy Bolden and King Oliver playing under the river while a chorus sings 'When It's Sleepy Time Down South.' This is beautiful, man." Chris was bored stiff.

"Come on y'all," she said. "If you really want some excitement, let's go to the graves. That's where it's really at, man. Not this Mississippi River bullshit." Everybody rushed back to their cars, while I hung back for a minute, still checking out the beautiful voices and trumpets of King Oliver and Buddy Bolden.

When we reached the graveyard, Chris took my hand and led me through the cemetery, cackling and hissing and moaning and groaning, trying her best to scare me. "Come on, Hughie, I know you're scared." We walked deep into the graveyard, while the others stayed at the cars, smoking and snorting. All I could hear was the music from the Mississippi River, and Chris was really disturbing my vibe with all her boring graveyard shit. Suddenly she came upon a partly open grave. "Hey, Hughie, come nearer to this one. This is gonna blow your head off."

I stood at the edge of the grave, took out my johnson, and began to pee into the grave. Chris let out a piercing scream. "He's gone crazy. He's lost his mind," she yelled as she ran back to where the others were. I came out of the cemetery still smiling to the music of the Mississippi River.

Stewart asked, "What happened, Hughie?"

"Nothin', man," I replied. "I just peed on a grave and Chris flipped out." It was nearing dawn and we all left for the hotel. Before we left New Orleans, Chris asked me to take a last walk with her through the French Quarter. I was still tripping. I listened to her blabbering throughout the walk, but my mind was somewhere else, I don't know where. On the drive to the airport, I told Chris that I was returning to Los Angeles and hoped to never see her again. I had finally had it. I had reached the end of the line. I recounted all the madness of the past three months. Chris tried to say something to me during our flight to New York, but I wasn't listening. I was coming off the high and was really beginning to get angry.

When we got to the apartment, Toma Gero was there without her children. I told the limousine driver to wait for me. I greeted Toma and went to pack my belongings. I could hear Chris and Toma whispering in the kitchen. A few minutes later Toma came into our bedroom and said that I had broken a lot of her things and destroyed some of her antiques. Not wanting any confrontation, I told her I would pay for anything she claimed was damaged. "These things are priceless," she fumed.

The doorbell rang. It was Dennis Armstead. Chris huddled with him, and I could see she was trying to pit Toma and Dennis against me. I had finished packing and was making my way toward the front door when Toma pushed me in the chest. She said, "Look here, Hugh. You just can't walk out of here after taking advantage of my kindness and destroying my house." I was confused. Nothing had been destroyed. During the short time that Chris and I had lived there, we took care of her place. I figured she was just bitching because I was leaving her friend. I said, "Toma, I told you I would pay for anything you think was destroyed. There's nothing else I can do. I wish you'd get out of my way and stop pushing me." Dennis could sense the mounting tension. Chris was smiling, enjoying every minute of the action. "Come on, y'all," Dennis said. "Let's talk about this like sensible grown-ups."

"Fuck it, Dennis," Toma said. "This nigger has fucked up my house. Who does Hugh Masekela think he is?" That was it for me. I realized that I was being set up, and I decided that the only way that I was going to get out of there was to call their bluff and show them just how crazy I was. Laying down my bags, I grabbed anything that I could get my hands on—vases, glasses, lamps, and furniture. I was throwing things against the wall, screaming, *"Fuuuuuck yooooouu!"* as they shattered all over the floor. I overturned dressers, couches, and chairs. Toma was beating and scratching at me while Dennis tried to get between us.

Chris was standing on top of the living room table, screaming, "Watch out, Toma. Be careful. He's an African savage. He is a wild man."

Toma kept attacking me. "You motherfucking barbarian. You black motherfucking African beast. You fucking asshole."

I turned around and smacked Toma hard in the face and watched her fall to the ground. "I'll kill you," was the last thing I said. Picking up my horn and luggage, I left the house with my neck and face bleeding. I didn't give a shit about what I did to the place and Toma. Had Dennis not been there, I had been prepared to do enough even to go to jail. I only got scared when I was outside and realized that I had been psychotic in there.

When I reached Los Angeles a few days later, I told Peter Davidson, Philemon Hou, and Stewart what had happened. They were agape listening to me describe that scene, but relieved I'd finally been able to cut Chris out of my life. Throughout the next few weeks, Chris would show up at some of the hotels we were staying at on the East Coast. She'd try to gain access to my room, but management had been alerted not to let her in. Once Henry woke me up. Chris was standing outside screaming, "Hughie, let me in. Take me back. I'm your wife." Hotel security came and led her away.

I asked my attorney, Albert Geduldig, to file for divorce. Her lawyers demanded alimony. I told Geduldig to tell them that I would stop working and become a beggar before I would give Chris a penny, because I felt she didn't deserve shit from me. She had tried to destroy my life in every way she could. I really would have had to be very stupid to want to have anything to do with her, or help her in any way. In early August 1968, I went to Juarez, Mexico, for a quickie divorce from Chris Calloway. It took a load off my mind. She later showed up at a concert I was playing in New York, and after getting high backstage, we spent the night together. I guess I wanted to see if she was still insane, but it was no use. The following morning, I let her know that I would never get back together with her.

I ran into Iris a few weeks later. She vowed she was not going to let me go. Two weeks later, after finishing some East Coast gigs, I flew home to Los Angeles—with Iris. This turned out to be another bad decision.

I didn't see Chris again for eleven years. One day Dennis Armstead, who was now managing Miriam Makeba, told me Chris was anxious to see me, that she wanted to bury the hatchet. I invited her to my apartment in Riverdale. I cooked us dinner and then we made love. Later that evening, as Chris was leaving, she said, "Hughie, I really got you, didn't I?"

It didn't matter to me anymore, and as I laughed along with her I said, "Yeah, Chris, you reeeeally got me."

She seemed satisfied. I kissed her good-bye at the elevator doors. Before the doors closed, she said once more, "I really got you." She smiled as the elevator doors closed. From my eighteenth-floor balcony, I watched her drive away into the September New York night. That was the last time I saw her.

12

I WAS LOSING MY PRIVACY at the Queens Road house, where I was living with Philemon, Peter, and Mabusha. Al Abreu spent every day there with me, mostly working on music arrangements at the piano. The band's rehearsals also took place at the house. This was all okay by me. The problem was all the baggage that came with it: the women we were dating or sleeping with casually and all their friends and relatives, not to mention the hangers-on and groupies. The traffic was a nightmare. Every, Tom, Dick, and Mary was constantly at my house for one reason or another, from free drugs and booze to just hangin' with Hughie. I got an apartment for Peter somewhere around Hollywood, and another one for Philemon at the bottom of Laurel Canyon, where Mabusha stayed with him when I was on the road. A real estate woman from Malibu got me an intriguing house just above the sheriff's station off Pacific Coast Highway. The house was way up on the top of a hill. It had a long living room with glass walls on both sides, which met at the apex of a triangle where the room ended, almost jutting into the ocean, which was visible from both sides of the room, about seven hundred feet below. The only way to get to the house was by a cable car that operated with a special key. I brought all kinds of beautiful women to spend the night with me at my mountaintop haven—sometimes two at a time. A shock wave went through the female community when Iris moved in with me.

Stewart and I were enjoying our lifestyle with Susie (who was still around), Iris, Philemon, and Peter almost always by our side. We were rolling in money. Stewart and I were reckless; success had given us swollen heads, and nobody detested us more than the Los Angeles Police Department. One evening Iris and I went out to have dinner with Stewart and Susan. Mabusha and Philemon were staying at my place for a few days and watching television. The four of us returned and were sitting out in the garden enjoying the full moon and the roar of the ocean. Shortly after midnight I noticed flashlights around the house. Stewart and I rushed into the house, and when we got to the door, three Los Angeles police detectives were on their way out of the house with a shoe-box top containing a few grams of grass, half a vial of cocaine, a piece of hashish, and some Seconol sleeping pills.

"Hi, Hugh, look what we found," one of them said, shoving the box top in my face.

I replied, "Let me ask you something. Do you have a warrant? How did you get up here, because I don't remember sending the cable car down for you."

They all drew their weapons at the same time. The one in front shouted, "Get in here now and lay on the floor, on your stomach."

I screamed, "Iris, Susie, run, go get a lawyer. This is an illegal bust." The cops had us on the living room floor and handcuffed our hands in the back. Philemon and Mabusha looked on in amazement. They let us stand, but wouldn't let us use the phone. I went into a cussing rage. One officer was Lebanese. I kept cussing at him and calling him a sellout nigger. He was almost on the verge of tears.

For the next eighteen hours we were handcuffed in the living room. From time to time we were allowed to go to the bathroom or to check on Mabusha. Finally, by evening of the following day, a lawyer called the house and insisted we be brought to the Malibu sheriff's department and charged. At the station they wanted to send Mabusha to a children's home. But I refused. I called friends of mine, Richard Alcala and Carrie White, Beverly Hills hair salon owners, who soon arrived to take Mabusha with them.

After I knew that Mabusha would be looked after, I went ballistic. The police took us to a cell and locked us up; all the while I kept cussing them out. Stewart pushed me against the wall and said, "Sshhh." He then pulled a three-gram vial of cocaine from inside the swimming trunks he was wearing under his pants. We washed our faces in the cell's sink and hurriedly snorted the cocaine, then threw the empty vial through the barred window in the back of the cell and started cussing the cops all over again. By this time I was foaming at the mouth and on the verge of going crazy. Twenty-four hours later, our lawyer came and bailed us out. I found out afterwards that the chief arresting officer was an FBI agent from New York.

When Stewart and I got back to the mountaintop house, we were shocked to discover how much cocaine and grass the police had failed to uncover—in the refrigerator, the bedroom, the closets and drawers, the bathroom cabinets and kitchen cupboards. It was hilariously embarrassing. I suggested to Iris that she return to New York and lie low for a while. After snorting the cocaine we found in the house, I became extremely paranoid. I could not stop peeping through the curtains. I knew I was hearing police coming up to the mountain house from all sides. I couldn't sleep. Susan and Stewart suggested I crash at their place. I took some downers and finally went to sleep after three straight days of being up from cocaine, booze, grass, hashish, opium, acid, amphetamines, and lunacy. I woke up the following afternoon and began accusing everybody I could of setting us up.

We had been scheduled to go on a major college tour, but the promoters canceled nearly the entire concert series after our bust. We were not the only ones busted that night. Sly Stone, Stephen Stills, and Barry McGuire were also busted then. John Lennon and Jimi Hendrix were busted in London. We thought it might have been a concerted Interpol exercise. A few promoters kept us on their schedules. We played Howard University's Homecoming with a young pianist-singer and Howard University graduate named Roberta Flack, whose "The First Time Ever I Saw Your Face" was a big hit. Roberta had been a cocktail lounge pianist at the famous Mr. Henry's restaurant in Washington, D.C. Al Abreu had gone to see her act there a few times, and had really loved her show. She would always drop by the Bohemian Caverns after her gig and catch our last set. In the Homecoming audience at Howard were Adam Clayton Powell, Stokely Carmichael, Julian Bond, and many other activists from SNCC and the Black Panthers. We were still reeling from the bust and from a fiasco at Hampton Institute in Virginia, another predominantly black college. After that show I had found Stewart surrounded by some of the members of the school's football team and their coach. They were accusing him of giving me drugs, and were refusing to give him the money due us for the concert performance. I started yelling at them.

"You motherfuckers are fixin' to lynch my friend because he is white, at a time when the Ku Klux Klan is lynching your asses all over the South just for being black. Now y'all are turning into a black Ku Klux Klan. Get the fuck out of my dressing room, you black motherfucking rednecks. Give us our fucking money and let us get the fuck out of here." We got paid and left Hampton, Virginia.

By now the U.S. newspapers were reporting my drug arrest and those of the other musicians. Back in South Africa, the government seized the moment, and the white press condemned me mercilessly. I had truly set myself up, and they dutifully went to town on my screw-up. I felt awful for my parents, even though they remained supportive. But I was getting higher than before. By now I was a confirmed drug and alcohol addict, and the fear of the legal consequences my bust would bring led me to try to drown the pain by getting high. I was angry with the laws that had led to my arrest, angry at myself for being so careless during the preceding months, ashamed over the bad publicity I was receiving and the loss of many lucrative engagements, and most of all feeling guilty about my reckless ways. All these feelings were powerful catalysts for deeper addiction. The more I drank and took drugs, the more ashamed, angry, and guilty I felt. Because none of the mind-altering substances took away my pain, I reached out for more.

Stewart and I decided that I should move out of the house on the mountain in Malibu and spend more time in New York City. We had first met Ray Lofaro in the early 1960s back in New York through Richie Druz. Ray was president of PGL films, a company that had won international awards for top-flight television commercials, for a few of which Richie wrote the music. Ray had become a very close friend, and over the years we became almost like family. He was well connected in New York. Through Ray we met a classy real estate woman who found Stewart and me a beautiful penthouse apartment on 82nd Street and Riverside Drive, with a 360-degree wraparound terrace view of Manhattan, New Jersey, Brooklyn, Queens, the Hudson River, the East River, and the Harlem River. It was breathtaking. We moved right in.

I went to my first court case before the end of November at the Santa Monica courthouse, where Harry Weiss, my attorney, requested a motion for dismissal because there had not been a warrant for my arrest. The court rejected his motion. "Law and order" was a theme of Richard Nixon's presidential campaign at the time, and his friend Ronald Reagan, the governor of California, had been promising his constituency that he would be cleaning up the state and ridding it of all criminals, drug dealers, and addicts. I didn't stand much of a chance. Shortly after my first appearance, Harry Weiss was arrested for possession of cocaine. His partner, Peter Knecht, took over. I was in and out of court just about every two weeks. Knecht kept seeking continuances, fishing for a sympathetic judge. Every time I appeared for a hearing, there was a seedy, middle-aged wire service reporter present who I suspected was working for the South African government's international public relations network.

They made sure that every time I made an appearance, this man sent a report back to South Africa. The actor and former football star Jim Brown always seemed to be there too, for a hearing about an assault charge against him by one of his girlfriends. We would stand around the corridors and blame our woes on the racism of the day. This was the time when the Chicago Seven were on trial, as were the Black Panthers, Angela Davis, and several other antiwar and antiestablishment activists. Miriam Makeba was now living in Conakry, Guinea, with her husband, Stokely Carmichael. Stokely's criticism of Israel's position in the 1967 war brought the couple condemnation from many Western countries and their allies around the world. Her recordings were no longer available in American record stores, and life in America had become unpleasant for her. Of course, I didn't even realize how ludicrous it was for Jim and me to compare our self-imposed woes with the politically motivated trials of others. I obviously couldn't see past myself.

The summer of 1968 had started with a number-one record for me. "Grazing in the Grass" helped to catapult my name into international fame, but I was not equipped to handle success. The constant drugging, endless drinking, and pussy-chasing warped me. I became obsessed with pleasures of the flesh, which only led to lonely sleepless nights, mind-boggling immorality, dishonesty, broken hearts, and hung-over mornings.

In 1965 I met Johnny Nash and his partner, Danny Sims, through singer-actor Adam Wade, who was a regular at my Village Gate performances. Johnny and Danny had a luxury apartment at Lincoln Towers on West End Avenue at 68th Street. It was always bubbling with beautiful women. I recruited quite a few scorchers from there over the years. Now that I was living in the penthouse, it was only a five-minute drive to Johnny and Danny's flat.

Johnny and Danny also owned a studio in Kingston, Jamaica, where they had a mansion in the Blue Mountains. One day I flew down to Jamaica with Danny and spent a glorious week at the Blue Mountains house, which was always full of stunning women and Rasta dudes who kept ganja pipes "full and fired up" during every waking hour. Johnny Nash was then working on his hits "Stir It Up" and "I Can See Clearly," ushering in his reggae phase. Working closely with Johnny and Danny's company was a young artist named Bob Marley, whose compositions they were publishing. On several occasions I played the trumpet on Marley's tracks. During the very first Marley session, I was sitting with Johnny Nash's co-producer, Reggie, who was from the Bronx, and Danny in the control booth, and I noticed that when Bob was singing at the recording microphone, he would do his fancy jump-up dance steps and often get out of range for the mike to pick up his voice. I finally said, "Bob, the mike don't pick up the dancing, mon. Try to stand in one place." Later, I asked Danny and Reggie why they hadn't told Bob to stand in one place, and they told me that it had never entered their minds; besides, they hadn't felt like disturbing an artist at work.

Back at the house we never stopped smoking the ganja, which made me cough deliriously. It amazed me to watch Bob and the other Rastas take huge puffs out of the pipe. When they blew the smoke out, they would disappear behind the cloud that formed in the room. I just couldn't get the knack of it. Anyway, we would get so high that we would be speechless and just sit there watching or listening to the rain. I didn't see Bob Marley again until a few months before he passed away. He was sitting in his manager's office in New York, looking weak and sad. We shook hands and said a heartbreaking hello.

Back in Los Angeles, I was renting an apartment in the complex where Philemon Hou was living, at the bottom of Laurel Canyon. Mabusha was now living with Big Black and his wife, Ginger, and their four kids. UNI Records wanted me to record a new album to follow up *Promise of a Future,* so we went into the studio at the end of 1968 and recorded *Masekela.* Because of my drug bust, I had developed a very deep anger toward America's collaboration with the South African government and their concerted methods to punish everyone who criticized their anticommunist and racist campaigns. The songs in *Masekela* all addressed their evil partnership and condemned it because I felt that the apartheid administration was painstakingly working with U.S. intelligence agencies to make my life a living hell. I laid the blame for all my troubles and madness at their doorstep. During a three-week, standing-room-only engagement at the Village Gate in the spring of 1968, the chief international public relations officer for the apartheid regime came backstage to greet me. He said, "Hugh, you are condemning us very unfairly on television and radio, and in print, and consequently turning many people against us. We want you to come home as our guest and live at the Carlton Hotel so that you can witness all the marvelous changes taking place at home."

I countered, "Why should I stay in a hotel and be your guest in my own country? My father has a beautiful home where I can sleep."

"Oh no, you will be surrounded by the fans, and this would be a security risk. Besides, you should enjoy the country like Percy Sledge, who is there as an honorary white and having the time of his life," the white Afrikaner replied.

"You have the nerve to come into my dressing room and ask me to visit my country as an 'honorary white' while you persecute, jail, banish, and murder my people in the name of white supremacy? You must think I am stupid. Get the fuck out of my dressing room. Get out!" I had Peter Davidson call security, who ushered him out of the club while he continued to explain, "You really don't understand, Hugh. You must come and see for yourself."

In our recording, we paid tribute to Robert Sobukwe, the leader of the Pan-African Congress. He had made it very clear that his organization did not recognize the government of South Africa and had led the pass-burning demonstrations shortly after the Sharpeville massacre. Sobukwe was rotting on Robben Island's prison, where he was incarcerated without trial. The song "Sobukwe" was a haunting instrumental very much in the style of John Coltrane and Miles Davis's late 1950s stylings, inspired by the modal, dark melodies featured on their *Favorite Things* and *Kind of Blue* albums. "Mace and Grenades" lamented the fact that at the time, if you disagreed with the U.S. administration's policies or those of the South African regime, you were in prison even if you were walking free in the streets, fighting in Vietnam, demonstrating for civil rights, or working for the establishment. The lyrics screamed, "I'm in jail in here. I'm in jail out there. I got the warden to protect me, feels like it's safer to be in jail." The song had me screaming the melody over the tom-toms, a recurring booming bass line, thumping piano, and blaring brass ensemble, reminiscent of Coltrane's loudest passages on *My Favorite Things*. "Gold" was about the exploitation of African cheap labor to dig tons of the mineral for export when none of the wealth it brought reached the homes and families of the laborers. "Riot" was very much in the groove and sound of "Grazing in the Grass," but not as joyful in color and sound. It was much darker and more ominous, with the bass line doubled on the acoustic piano. The dark texture, thumping piano chords, blaring horns, and scathing, anti-racist, antiwar lyrics gave the album a very radical and militant texture. It certainly did not endear me to the distributors, radio stations, and concert promoters, even though "Riot" went to the Top 20 on the *Billboard* charts.

Russ Regan begged us to change the title of "Riot," assuring us that if we agreed, the song would shoot through the roof. He felt it would do better than "Grazing in the Grass" because of the audience we had amassed. He might have been better off trying to suck water from a desert stone. I was not only adamantly opposed to changing the title, but I was high out of my mind all the time. I thought Russ was crazy even to suggest such a thing. Ray Lofaro went ballistic. "You motherfuckers are seriously bent on self-destructing. You have really fucking lost it."

Eric Clapton walked in the studio with Alan Pariser, who, as usual, was holding some prime coke. I was standing in front of the microphone, exhausted from lack of sleep and hung over from the previous night's partying. My voice was hoarse from the all-night pot-smoking and coke-snorting. I was overdubbing my vocal solo for "Is There Anybody Out There Who Can Hear Me?" This was a lament about police brutality, racism, and unfair imprisonment of black males, the suffering of the Vietnamese, and the conscription of innocent young men into the army to fight and kill people who had done nothing to harm them. I was just barely managing to sing. During the playback Eric suddenly said to Stewart, "Shit, I wish I could get my voice to sound like that." We all looked at him in amazement.

Around this time, Al Abreu became seriously addicted to heroin. We suggested that he go to his parents' home in Puerto Rico to clean up. We were getting ready to go out and play a series of year-end, holiday-season concerts, and Al wasn't showing up for rehearsals. Worried, I called his brother in Boston. He told me Al had been driving with his girlfriend and another couple in his new car down in Puerto Rico, when he fell asleep at the wheel from an overdose of heroin. The car went over a cliff. All four of them died. We were shattered by the news. This was the beginning of the disintegration of our stellar group. I had lost a dear friend, colleague, and music teacher. As a replacement, we brought Big Black back into the group, but it wasn't quite the same.

On New Year's Eve in 1968, Big Black and his wife, Ginger, invited Stewart, Peter, and me over to his house for a party. I knocked on the door and when it opened, standing there was the most beautiful smiling face I had ever seen, surrounded by ginger hair. She was slightly taller than me, green-eyed and light-skinned, bubbling with a sweet, gentle charm. Jessie La Pierre and I liked each other immediately, and danced together for the rest of the night and into the early morning, unable to tear ourselves apart. Jessie was a friend of Ginger's niece Terry. The two of them had graduated from high school in New York and come to check out career opportunities in Los Angeles. Jessie was from a Haitian immigrant family but, now about to turn twenty, was looking to establish an independent life away from her New York beginnings.

She found work as a saleswoman at Robinson's in the Beverly Hills Mall, and I was there every day when she finished work to drive her back home. I was now living with Peter Davidson at Stewart's old Malibu beach house. Jessie was spending a lot of time with me, and not too long after we met, perhaps three months later, I persuaded her to resign from Robinson's and move in with me at the beach house. When I went to the penthouse in New York, Jessie came with me. I began to establish a quieter lifestyle because of her— although I was still reckless on the concert tours.

Over a year after my bust, my new lawyer, Larry Cohen, found a precedent to my case in another case he'd had dismissed a few years earlier, and was confident that he could repeat the feat. On the morning that we were due in court, Larry's wife telephoned Stewart at 7:00 A.M. Weeping and distraught, she told him that Larry had died suddenly that morning from a heart attack. I was shocked, and getting suspicious that all the calamities my lawyers were experiencing were not a coincidence. Paranoia set in.

My next lawyer, Harry Ransom, found the right judge and made a deal for me to plead guilty to a minor charge of misdemeanor possession of a nonprescribed Seconol barbiturate tablet. We rehearsed the entire proposed court scenario in the judge's chambers. The key was that after the prosecution and defense had rested, I was to say, "I'm sorry, Your Honor, and I ask for forgiveness." We went to lunch and came back to the court. All went according to plan until it came time for me to make my one-sentence statement. I completely blew it.

Having just smoked some strong ganja and snorted a little coke, I fell into a state of amnesia after returning from a great lunch of seafood on the Santa Monica Pier with Jessie and Stewart. I had become infuriated over the prosecutor's opening remarks, and had totally forgotten the earlier agreement we had reached in the judge's chambers.

"Your Honor," I said, "this unfair trial has caused me to lose many engagements. It has cost me a very large amount of money in legal fees and wasted a lot of my time." The judge's face had turned scarlet red. Harry Ransom ran over to me and put his one hand over my mouth while the judge screamed at me, "You ungrateful little slob. I sentence you to two years' probation. Court dismissed." He stormed out of the courtroom in furious disbelief while Ransom attempted to explain what he thought I was trying to say.

Jessie and Stewart were looking at me in openmouthed disbelief. "What happened here, man?" Stewart asked.

I answered, "I just don't know, man. I felt so angry about all this shit, I just couldn't get myself to apologize."

We had paid Harry a hefty amount in advance. He walked away dazed.

I spent the next two years signing weekly letters for my probation officer, a Mexican-American office clerk who was also a trumpet player. I could not leave the state of California without his written permission. However, he was very lenient with me and let me send the letters to him from wherever I was. Still, it was a very unpleasant two years during which I was not allowed to leave America.

Without Al Albreu, the group just wasn't the same anymore. After a concert in Miami, Big Black had a major showdown with me over my drugging and drinking. He cussed out Stewart and me at the top of his voice and threatened us with physical violence, then quit on the spot. The other band members, drummer Chuck Carter, bassist Henry Franklin, and pianist Billy Henderson, had also come to the end of their tether with our madness. The Miami date was the last engagement with that wonderful band. Though we were constantly working, my funds ran low again because of the legal fees I had amassed over the previous two years. Stewart's Malibu house went up for sale, and we all had to move out. Peter Davidson soon left for South Africa because his father was very ill.

Jessie and I moved into a large house at the top of Coldwater Canyon situated inside a large cul-de-sac where Gloria Foster and her husband, Clarence Williams III, were our neighbors. I didn't know the couple; I'd only seen them on film and television. Gloria was very sweet and neighborly, but Clarence was very distant and aloof. He hardly ever spoke to us except for the occasional nod. Many conservative artists kept me at arm's length after my drug bust. We fetched Mabusha from Big Black's to come and live with us.

Not long after we moved in, I received a letter from my sister Barbara, who was back living in Zambia. She had been in a car accident, and was traumatized by the crash. My immigration lawyer, Albert Geduldig, helped me obtain a visitor's visa for her, and until she finally came to live with us a month later, I was terribly worried about my sister's well-being and safety. We were relieved when she landed in Los Angeles. Except for a small scar on her forehead, she was her usual self. Nothing else was wrong with her.

Since my arrival in Los Angeles, Wayne Henderson and Wilton Felder of the Jazz Crusaders had played on quite a few of Chisa Records studio sessions, and I came to be dear friends with Wayne. They later introduced us to pianist Joe Sample, another Crusader. We persuaded the three of them to reunite and begin recording for Chisa Records. They contacted their drummer, Stix Hooper, who was winding down his tour with George Shearing. When Stix came back to Los Angeles, the four of them signed a deal with Chisa and went straight into the studio to record their first album as simply the Crusaders, without the "Jazz."

Running short of money, we went to UNI Records to demand our royalties. Russ Regan gave us a story about how they needed to show end-of-the-year profits as a corporation, and asked if we could give them another three months, at which time all our money would be paid to us. Instead of remaining calm, we lost our cool. High out of our minds, we demanded to be paid on the spot or given a release. It was not a pleasant scene. Ned Tannen, who had introduced Stewart and me to Joe Glaser at ABC, and a number of the company's top executives were present. In hindsight, they had nothing to lose. We were no longer any use to them. We had turned into arrogant, radical alcoholics and drug addicts. Russ looked at me with disgust. "You ungrateful little shit. I worked so hard to get you where you are today. I've been your booster, motherfucker, and you thank me like this."

"Fuck you, Russ," I shouted back. *"We* boosted *you.* We made UNI Records. This fucking building is here because of us. You had no fucking record company before you had us. Give us our fucking release now."

This screaming opera went on for a while and then, to our shock, the company gave us our release. We walked out of the Universal Building feeling victorious, oblivious of the reality that we had just given away *everything.* In the end, all our lawyer could get for us was a release without any money. Suddenly we were not living so high on the hog anymore.

Barbara's arrival came at a time when my star was on the decline, and I was slowly mutating into an ugly little asshole. My group had finally disintegrated and I was playing all of my concert bookings with my old friend Larry Willis on piano, bassist John Williams, and drummer Al Foster. Life was getting progressively grimmer. Chisa had managed to get a distribution agreement with Motown Records. We had just completed an album by the Crusaders and another one with Letta Mbulu. I was also in the studio, completing an album titled *Reconstruction.* We went down to San Francisco for Motown's tenth-anniversary celebration. The Motown artists were all present, including their sensational new group, the Jackson Five. The Crusaders, Letta, and I, along with the Jacksons, the Four Tops, and Gladys Knight and the Pips, performed at the gala dinner. Then one day I got a call from Caiphus Semenya that Jonas had come to Los Angeles and was staying with him. The three of us formed a group called The Union of South Africa. We went right into an intense rehearsal schedule every day at Caiphus's apartment in the Pico neighborhood.

Barbara found it difficult to stay with us because of my behavior. She was fond of Jessie, and it saddened her to see how I was mistreating her. She went to stay with Philemon in his Laurel Canyon apartment. Not long after Barbara moved out, Jessie, Mabusha, and I moved from Coldwater Canyon because we couldn't afford the high rent anymore. We found a house in the San Fernando Valley, around the corner from the Universal Studios offices where I had so brilliantly ruined my career at the screamfest with Russ Regan. Our coffers at Chisa had dwindled down to a trickle. This led to Stewart turning a section of our Sunset Strip office into an apartment for him to live in, since he couldn't afford the rent on his Malibu apartment. Wayne Henderson found a small office building out on Western Avenue near Compton, where we held all of our rehearsals and pre-production sessions.

One day I was visiting hair salon owners Richard Alcala and Carrie White at their Benedict Canyon hilltop house, when a musician from the South, Jimmy Ford, told us he was working in the studio with Sly Stone at Wally Heider's on Cahuenga Boulevard, the place where we were making our records. I told Jimmy how much I would love to see Sly. Stewart and I had met him in Oakland back in 1967 when he was a DJ on a Sunday-morning program on the town's largest black music radio station. At the time we were promoting Chisa's first album, *The Emancipation of Hugh Masekela,* and Sly had spent his entire show playing music from my album and talking to us on air. After the interview, Sly took us to lunch with the station owner. We had a great day with him, and he told us about his group, which was just then getting off the ground. We promised to keep in touch. Little did we know that Sly would become an icon. I drove Jimmy Ford to the studio where Sly was overdubbing a bass part for a song called "Family Affair." He had a saucer full of cocaine on top of the console. It began to rain, and every time I tried to leave, Sly would insist I stay. We were snorting coke with Jimmy and a group of Sly's friends for hours while he kept playing the bass over the same eight bars of music on the track between large snorts of blow. Just before midnight, Stewart burst into the studio, high out of his mind. He asked to borrow the keys to my green Jaguar so he could go up to Laurel Canyon to pick up this girlfriend. He promised to bring my car back. Stewart never came back. I kept calling Jessie to tell her I was with Sly and would be home as soon as Stewart returned with my car. We snorted ourselves silly. Around ten o'clock the next morning, one of Sly's friends dropped me off at my place. After coming down from the cocaine, I finally went to sleep. Still no word from Stewart. He called the next morning and asked me to meet him at the garage across from the Whisky à Go Go. My Jaguar was parked on the far side of the workshop, festooned with branches and hedges and covered with mud. Most of the windows were broken and its once-beautiful exterior was peppered with dents. I spent over ten thousand dollars remodeling the car.

"Wow, what happened, Stewie?" I asked in disbelief.

Stewart explained in detail how he went looking for his friend's house at the top of Lookout Mountain Drive, but couldn't find it in the pouring rain. He tried to make a U-turn and lost control of the car. He jumped out of the rear door and it went spinning over a cliff. The car slid down the muddy hillside and ended up in a swimming pool. The homeowners wanted forty thousand dollars in damages to their pool and hillside garden. We settled the mess out of court for about half that amount. My uninsured Jaguar was destroyed. I was upset, but never had a confrontation with Stewart about it because throughout the years we had both put each other in badly compromising situations on several occasions. Our friendship was strong enough to survive these outrageous incidents. We always ended up shaking our heads in disbelief, grateful to have escaped another life-threatening episode and finding humor in our madness. We were both quite insane.

Shortly afterwards, Caiphus, Jonas, and I went into the studio to record our self-titled debut album, *Union of South Africa*. Wayne Henderson, the Crusaders' trombonist, played drums; the group's saxophonist, Wilton Felder, played bass; and pianist Joe Sample and guitarist Arthur Adams rounded out the group. After the recording, Wayne introduced us to what would become our road rhythm section: Lannie Johnson, a gifted pianist, bassist Kent Brinkley, and a seventeen-year-old drummer, Ndugu Chancler, who was later replaced by Thabo because his mother felt he was too young to go on the road with us. *Union of South Africa* was completed over two weeks, mainly because we had rehearsed so intensely for at least three weeks. The results were a masterpiece. Caiphus wrote most of the songs for the album. The outstanding selections were "Johannesburg Hi Lite Jive," an adaptation of Christopher Sonxaka's hit mbhaqanga instrumental we picked up off a tape a friend had brought us from home; "Hush," an old Negro spiritual, which had been popularized by Miriam Makeba and the Manhattan Brothers back home; "Caution," a brisk instrumental in six-eight time, which Caiphus based on traditional Pedi and Tsonga rhythms and harmonies from northern South Africa. When we were rehearsing this song, its complexity drove pianist Joe Sample to wonder where the first beat of the song was. "If someone can just tell me where one falls in this song, I'm gonna play the fucking shit out of it."

The songs were based on South African urban or traditional jazz adaptations, with us playing and singing different three-part harmonies. Jonas and I played all the solos, and Caiphus played alto saxophone and sang the vocal improvisations. Jonas's mbhaqanga "Shebeen," a traditional Xhosa folksong groove, was the highlight of the album.

Not long after the album's release, tour bookings started pouring in. We were playing one night at the Whisky à Go Go, where author-poet Quincy Troupe came to see the Union. He was knocked out by our performance. Troupe, an English literature professor at Ohio University in Athens, Ohio, was also an outstanding member of the Watts Writers' Workshop. At a meeting he had requested with us, he told us about how he and some other members of the workshop were planning to stage a free festival for the Watts community. He asked if we would be willing to headline such an event. We agreed, and the hugely successful festival, which also featured the Crusaders and Letta Mbulu (both of whom offered their free participation after we asked them), marked the beginning of a lifetime friendship for Quincy and me. Around this time, Troupe and my sister Barbara became good friends, and he was instrumental in helping her continue her studies at his campus.

After the Zambian incident, Barbara still needed time to be comfortable on her own, and establish a foothold in Ohio before taking on the responsibility of parenting. Mabusha could have stayed on with us until she was ready, but I was only thinking of myself. The day Barbara and Mabusha left for Athens was a tearful one for Jessie, my sister, and my nephew, a day that conjures deep guilt and remorse in me. I was at my ugliest then.

I didn't know that Jessie was pregnant. She had been afraid to tell me, and it was only when she turned down snorting some cocaine with me that she told me the reason why. Jessie could not stand marijuana and refused to drink, but under pressure from me she had finally succumbed to doing a little coke with me from time to time. This was another one of my ugly creations. Ironically, when I heard the news, I got very excited about being a father. Jessie and I drew even closer, and for a while I began spending more time at home. Our house in San Fernando Valley was inside a large square with a sports ground and running track. I began an intensive exercise regime coupled with a daily barefoot run of three miles around the track. Although I became fit, I continued my romance with cocaine and booze, albeit to a much lesser extent. Our bliss was short-lived because a few weeks prior to Jessie's delivery date, she had a miscarriage. We cried all the way home from the hospital, and for the next few days we occasionally broke down in tears. It seemed as if life had become just one big downhill slalom ever since Jessie and I met. It wasn't long after this misfortune that I suggested to Jessie that we should break up and that she should return home to her mother in New York.

But Jessie stayed, found a job as a store manager at Carrie and Richard's hair salon, and moved into an apartment in Beverly Hills. By this time I had moved into a house at the top of Lookout Mountain in Laurel Canyon with Stewart. It turned out that at the time Jessie and I parted, she was already pregnant again, which was one of the reasons that she did not return to her mother in New York. She still wanted to be near me, especially now that she was carrying our child—she was also not that keen to go back home. I moved in with her and restored an old bicycle I found in the storeroom. I was riding it every day to Caiphus's house for our Union rehearsals. Everyone who knew me and saw me riding thought I was on a health kick. I was riding my bike down Sunset Boulevard one day when I ran into Charlie Weaver, Bill Cosby's perennial stand-in. He was driving with actor Rupert Crosse, who was now married to Chris Calloway. We pulled into a parking lot and smoked some grass and had some laughs. Rupert died not too long after that from cancer. Weaver was impressed with my fitness. "Shit, Hugh, I'm really knocked out that you're getting your health together." I quickly changed the subject because I didn't want him to discover that my bike was my only means of transportation at that time.

Our Lincoln Center show with the Crusaders was sold out. The Union had become a hard-hitting, tight-knit group. The reviews were great. I thought we were going places. But financially the situation was not good. Still, the Union's momentum continued, and we played a series of gigs, including the first "Operation Push" festival that Jesse Jackson put on in Chicago, where we played with Quincy Jones, Cannonball Adderley, Nancy Wilson, and *Shaft* composer Isaac Hayes, who was riding high on his *Black Moses* success. That same night Stewart called me from Los Angeles to say that he had taken Jessie to the hospital. We were the parents of a boy, whom we named Selema.

After the Lincoln Center concert, the band worked many gigs using New York as our main base. At the time, Amiri Baraka was the "Imamu" of a spiritual black organization headquartered in Newark, New Jersey. This group set up a series of concerts for us around the East Coast, headlined by Miriam Makeba. A day before we were to go on this tour, Jonas was hit by a car while crossing the street in the Bronx. He was very badly injured and wouldn't be able to perform for several months. We went on the tour without him, but the group wasn't nearly as tight. After playing the concerts with Miriam in Boston, Philadelphia, Washington, D.C., and Pittsburgh, we were obliged to break up the Union and return to Los Angeles. Playing opposite Miriam's group was especially difficult because they were very well rehearsed and had been together for years. Without Jonas, our efforts paled against her sizzling performances. Baraka's organization was especially disappointed in our lame sets, because the organization's primary focus was to bring African cultural education to the African-American communities they were working with.

When we returned to Los Angeles, we terminated our Motown agreement and signed our Chisa music operation to Bob Krasnow's Blue Thumb Records. Krasnow loved the Union of South Africa format and wanted a new album right away, so he suggested that we fill the space left vacant by Jonas with other South African musicians. We went to London so we could record with famed South African saxophonist Dudu Pukwana. We brought in Larry Willis from New York, Makhaya Ntshoko from Zurich, and bassist Eddie Gomez, who was playing with Bill Evans at Ronnie Scott's in Soho. Based mostly on instrumental compositions by Caiphus, the double album, *Home Is Where the Music Is,* had such outstanding performances by my fellow musicians that to this day it is in very heavy demand by jazz lovers all over Africa, Europe, and America. But at the time of its release, it didn't sell much. My career had come to a dead end.

When Jonas came out of the hospital, we tried to go back to the studio to record a new Union of South Africa album, but the harmony among us was gone. We couldn't even get one song done. That was the end of the Union of South Africa. Jonas and Caiphus may have felt that doing the album in England while Jonas was still recovering was a betrayal. The fact that I was still recklessly getting high did not help to endear me too much to them. From the very first attempts to sing the first song, we just couldn't get into the mood.

I was now drifting around without a band and hanging out at jazz clubs in the hope of finding the right musicians to play with. One night I dropped into Shelley's Manhole, where my old friend trumpeter Freddie Hubbard was holding fort. In the audience were a few of my acquaintances from New York. Among them was the great jazz singer Abbey Lincoln, whom I had first met when she and her ex-husband Max Roach hosted a party for Maya Angelou and her husband Vusi Make. Abbey was now single, and she gave me her business card, held my hand tenderly, and insisted that I should give her a call. She invited me to dinner, and thus began a torrid relationship. She and I spoke a lot about Africa. Like a lot of African-Americans of her generation at that time, she was looking for Africa and passionate about finding it.

I tried to form a group with Ronnie Laws on saxophone and the old rhythm section from the Union. We played some dates around the West Coast, but I was just too out of it, hanging a lot with Sly and some of my many other friends who were also cocaine fiends. Sometimes Sly would fall by the way after midnight in his luxury tour bus. He would be with a bevy of coked-out young ladies and a couple of male friends. We would stay up sometimes until the following afternoon. Sly had a small violin case in which he carried a variety of prime blow, along with designer barbiturates to help him come down if he got too wired. Many times he would bring his guitar and sing some of his new compositions for us. He would sing parts of songs, two times here, three times there, a bridge here and an introduction there, a hook here, a chorus there, laughing and joking in between. Sly was a very funny man who improvised funny lines off anything most people around him said. He kept his life extremely private, with a very small circle of friends, mostly people he was raised with. He was crazy about his family, his sister Rose and brother Freddie who played in his group, his mother, and the other members of his band. Outside of these, his whole life was centered around his music, regular horseback riding, and walking his killer pit bull around his estate.

All the time that I used to hang out with Sly either at the studio, his house, or mine, I never saw him around other musicians. Although I was also high most of the time, it nevertheless saddened me how many great opportunities Sly missed because he wouldn't show up for performances or appointments on account of the blow. Just before I was to leave for Africa, I tried to encourage him to come with me so he could take a break. He wanted to, but could never get his passport and visa requirements together. We slowly drifted away from each other. After I left for Africa that first time, I never saw Sly again until we were on Broadway with *Sarafina* in 1989 and the great musician and producer James Mtume came backstage to tell me Sly was staying with him. They were working on an album, and I went out to visit them at Mtume's studio in

Orange, New Jersey, just outside Newark. Sly was happy to see me, but he couldn't finish a sentence or a music phrase. The nonstop partying had taken its toll. It saddened and terrified me.

Jessie had had enough by this time. I had bankrupted the little remaining compassion and friendship she had invested in me. Jessie found solace in the doctrines of the Jehovah's Witnesses. She joined the church and soon moved out with Selema to go and stay with some fellow Witnesses.

Barbara had graduated from Ohio University and was now an English literature professor at Staten Island University, living in an apartment near the campus. After hearing about the turn my life had taken, she brought Jessie out to live with her. Shortly after that, Barbara transferred to a post at Rutgers University in nearby New Brunswick. She moved to Manhattan and left Selema and Jessie with the Staten Island apartment. This was the closing chapter for the hectic and unpredictable life I had subjected Jessie to. Without any acrimonious feelings for me, she began to carve out a spiritual path for herself and build a new life. She soon met Manny Gonzalez, a fellow Witness. They were married, and Manny forged a terrific bond with Selema, encouraging him to take up gymnastics and pointing him toward an athletic life in which he would subsequently become very successful. Manny is a gentle, loving soul. Selema and Jessie were truly blessed the day he came into their lives. At this time, even though I was happy that Jessie had chosen a new life, I felt like a total failure. I had destroyed my life with drugs and alcohol, and could not get a gig or a band together. No recording company was interested in me, and I had gone full circle from major success to the point where my life was worse than when I had left South Africa eleven years earlier to seek a music education and a professional career in America. I had lost a treasure, an irreplaceable companion, and a wonderful human being. Jessie's mother, the sweetest soul ever to take a breath, had asked me many times, "Hugh, why don't you marry Jessie? She loves you so much." My answer was always, "I don't think I'm ready for marriage, Mama." It was true. I was such a drug and alcoholic addict. Selfish, immoral, reckless, and insensitive, I would have made a terrible husband. I felt like shit.

Back in New York, we had long since forfeited the beautiful penthouse on Riverside Drive because of our financial disasters with Chisa and the crazy life Stewart and I had brought into our business dealings. Ray Lofaro, on the other hand, was doing extremely well with his advertising film company. Ray, whose ex-wife and their three children had a home in Woodstock, always rented a house there from the end of the summer until the beginning of the following year. Ray had become a big brother to me and Stewart, always trying his best to lead us gently back to the way we were before we became such psychopaths. Sometimes we would join him in the rental house and split the expenses. We spent the fall and winter of 1971 as Ray Lofaro's housemates in a house that was a six-bedroom architectural masterpiece.

Over the years, our favorite Woodstock hangout was the Joyous Lake, a restaurant-nightclub that was owned by Dr. Ron Merians and his beautiful wife, Valma, fun-loving friends of Ray's whose joint was always packed with artists, musicians, young New York business sharks, filmmakers, Big Apple beauties, famous beatniks, bikers, and bohemians. There was also a hot group playing there over the weekends, led by Paul Butterfield, the harmonica virtuoso and blues shouter from Chicago, or other groups from the blues, folk, and rock worlds. The Joyous Lake was a good place to meet beautiful, independent young women who were almost always very keen to round off the night at our place before heading home. One night we were playing some of our favorite records by Marvin Gaye, Aretha Franklin, Jobim, Bird, Sarah, Billy, Miles, and Monk, talking as though we knew everything, when out of nowhere this song began to ring in my ears. Suddenly I ran to the piano and began to sing a song about a train that brought migrant laborers to work in the coalmines of Witbank, my birthplace. Ray and Stewart followed me to the piano and stood transfixed as I sang. Ray said, "That's a mean song. When did you write it?" I said between phrases, "I didn't write it. It's coming in now." The song was "Stimela/The Coal Train." I sang it from beginning to end as if I had known it for a long time. By now, everybody was standing around me. None of them believed that the song had just come to me. It still remains the most requested song when I'm performing. For me, songs come in like a tidal wave, and if I don't get to a piano there and then, they're lost forever. At this low point, for some reason, the tidal wave that whooshed in on me came all the way from the other side of the Atlantic, from Africa, from home.

PART III

Africa

13

I FIRST MET THE MBATHA FAMILY in 1962 at 310 West 87th Street when the anthropologist Mphiwe Mbatha and his wife, Beatty, a nurse, moved to the United States with their five daughters, Jabu, thirteen; Busi, eleven; Ntathu, nine; Buhle, seven; and Mpozi, five. Even then, it was easy to tell that they were pretty little girls who were going to become beautiful women when they were grown up. Mphiwe had stopped over to greet us after he learned that many South African students used 310 as their base during the holidays.

I teased little Jabu that one day I would marry her as Jonas and I walked the family to their car. They were driving to Hartford, Connecticut, where Mphiwe was to take up a professorship at the university. I would often take Bongi to Hartford for a few days during the holidays. She would visit the home of Professor Vilakazi, another South African academic who had two daughters Bongi had befriended. I would see little Jabu and her sisters and always repeat the little joke about marrying her one day. It used to make her blush while the other girls giggled.

I didn't see her again until we came to play Lincoln Center with the Union of South Africa. She was now a grown woman of twenty-two with a librarian job at the *New York Times*. I wasn't joking anymore. I was now very keen to get next to Jabu. She attended more of our concerts, and following one of the post-concert parties, I escorted her to her apartment in the Bronx, where she let me sleep over, but would not allow me to go any further. I told Willie Kgositsile, one of my homeboys from our days at 310, how I felt about Jabu. He turned out to be very tight with her and her family. Willie took me to a

party at Jabu's Bronx apartment, where many of the old 310 gang were present, along with several very fine young ladies from South Africa and other
parts of the continent and the Caribbean, all friends of Jabu and her sisters. I
had a wonderful time dancing with all the pretty women, but it was obvious
that Jabu was cautioning all of them to lay off me because I was hers. The
party ended in the wee hours of the morning, and I invited Jabu to drive back
to Woodstock with me.

The usual get-together was planned for that evening. Exhausted, Jabu went
to bed, but woke up a few hours later to come and spirit me away from the
dancing and drinking to what would become our bedroom for the rest of that
wonderful week.

Quincy Troupe was now teaching at Staten Island Community College and living at my old building in Park West Village. We were spending a lot of time
together—doing clubs, restaurants, and poetry readings and taking long walks
around Manhattan, marveling at the vibrancy of the city, its beautiful land-
marks, crazy people, and fine women.

Quincy had just returned from Nigeria, where he had spent considerable
time with Fela Kuti. "Hey, Hugh, Fela wants you to get in touch with him,
man. He told me he looked for you in 1969 when he was in L.A., but couldn't
hook up with you. He gave me a beautiful time in Lagos. Make sure to get in
touch with him. This is a *baaad* brother."

Quincy didn't have to convince me—I already wanted to meet this *baaad*
brother. A year younger than I, Fela Anikulapo Kuti was the child of professional parents—his father was an Anglican pastor, principal of a grammar
school, and an accomplished pianist and his social-activist mother wanted their
son to become a doctor. They sent him to London in 1958 for a medical education, but Fela registered at the Trinity College of Music instead. He grew
tired of studying European composers, and by 1961 he and his band, Koola
Lobitos, were a fixture on the London club scene, playing a hybrid of Nigerian
folk and urban dance music with a touch of jazz. His sound was strongly influenced by "highlife," the popular Ghanaian dance groove, with which he mixed
a diaspora's worth of influences, including big-band swing arrangements, folk
chants, a touch of calypso, ska phraseology, and South African township
mbhaqanga. Fela returned to Nigeria in 1963 and started another version of
Koola Lobitos that added into his crazy musical mix the James Brown–style
singing of Geraldo Pino from Sierra Leone. Combining this with elements of

traditional highlife and jazz, Fela dubbed this infectiously rhythmic hybrid "Afro Beat," partly as a critique of African performers who he felt had turned their back on their musical roots in order to emulate American pop music trends. Besides being a vocalist and a prolific composer-arranger, Fela played the saxophone, keyboards, horn, and guitar (he had given up on the trumpet, which he had played for many years). A frequent performer in the United States, Fela absorbed the political principles of black consciousness and the civil rights movement in America, which helped define the Africanism in his music. I wrote Fela's address and phone number on the front page of my address book and resolved to get in touch with him when I was ready to go to Nigeria. Although Fela's name was on the lips of many of my West African friends, I had not yet heard any of his music.

In New York City, Quincy had become a major organizer of poetry readings, which would take place mostly on Saturday and Sunday afternoons at neighborhood community centers or downtown lofts in Manhattan. At those readings Quincy introduced me to the stars of the black literary scene, which was now, through the movement called Black Arts, becoming a strong force for political and social change. Jayne Cortez, Toni Cade Bambara, Vertamae Grosvenor, Amiri Baraka, Ishmael Reed, Toni Morrison, James Baldwin, Terry McMillan, Sonia Sanchez, and other dynamic writers would read, and on most occasions I would also have a slot where I would play solo trumpet—riffing out passages that I drew from plantation field hollers, chain-gang work songs of the American South, and chants of my father's clan. I drew on the suffering of impoverished or misplaced people of African origin all around the world. On some days the World Saxophone Quartet, featuring Julius Hemphill, Sonny Murray, and Hamiett Bluitt, would play while marching behind poetesses like Ntozake Shange or Nikki Giovanni, who read their stunning, syncopated verse at full throat. I was captivated. This poetry—unlike the poetry I was schooled on—used the language of everyday black folks to tell the story of a full range of emotions: outrage, joy, love, passion, resistance, disgust. It was the language of an internal revolution that had spread all over the world, the liberation of voice. It sparked in me a deep urge to become a writer and reminded me of the underlying urge of my own art—the impulse to change the world, right the wrongs, and tell the truth, through the power of my voice.

Whenever I was with Quincy, we listened to a lot of African music and rapped about the continent's issues and its artists, especially Fela. Quincy encouraged me to visit Africa because it was clear that even though I was from South Africa, I knew little or nothing about the rest of the continent—which was at that very moment going through a phase of intense postcolonial flux. I was recharging my batteries in New York, but my star had clearly stopped shining. Making a musical and personal pilgrimage to Africa began to appeal to me. My idea was to get away and try to rediscover some missing piece of myself, something I'd lost. I also thought I could scour the continent for interesting new sounds and musicians and put together a new kind of group, which had become impossible in America, given my ruined reputation in the music industry. I decided that this pilgrimage was the answer to most of my problems, especially cocaine, which would be totally inaccessible on the continent. Back in Woodstock, I told Ray Lofaro and Stewart Levine about my plans, and they encouraged me to take the plunge. It was as obvious to them as to me that for me the sun had set on the United States. It was time to leave the country.

The problem with leaving the country was that at this point Letta, Caiphus, Jonas, Philemon, and I had been rendered stateless. We were South African artists who could not travel outside America because the South African government had long since canceled us from their travel document registers. Miriam Makeba had now been living in Conakry, Guinea, for more than five years, and I told her about my plans and our difficulties in finding a way to travel. She persuaded President Ahmed Sekou Toure to issue passports to us.

Back in Los Angeles, I put what few belongings I had together and prepared for my new adventure. I got a release from my recording contract, telling Bob Krasnow that I would not be returning to America. He was very unhappy with my decision, and told me how full of shit Stewart and I were, before he agreed to let me go. I told my friend Herb Alpert at A&M Records about my impending African expedition and how I intended to put together a group somewhere on the continent along intense ethnic lines. Herb and I had a little mutual admiration society going as fellow trumpet players and Clifford Brown aficionados. Herb was also becoming interested in African music, and expressed interest in collaborating with me should I develop a project during my sojourn. He promised that his company would be keen to sponsor such an undertaking.

Toni Cade Bambara, the great poet and novelist, had been a regular participant at Quincy Troupe's weekend poetry readings. During this time we became very close friends because of her intense fascination with African culture. We spent many hours talking about my upcoming pilgrimage to Africa, which intrigued her for its complete lack of planning, except the pretty vague idea that I would try to put a group together. Back in New York, Toni hosted a farewell party for me at her Harlem penthouse, and many of my friends, including Jabu, attended. I spent the next two days at the Essex Hotel with Jabu. We thought we might be in love.

I arrived in Conakry, Guinea, one morning in early 1972 to begin a new life. Not expecting me that soon, Miriam was pleasantly surprised to see me. To my amazement, Abbey Lincoln had finally realized her dream of coming to Africa, and was visiting Miriam. When Sekou Toure discovered how happy Abbey was to finally visit the continent, he held a small ceremony to rename her Aminata Moussaka. When our eyes met, the idea of rekindling our romance was tempting, but we were not about to resume it on this new terrain.

It was common practice in all socialist African countries of the day for visitors to have a guide. Conteh met me at the airport. He told me he was officially assigned to me during my stay in Guinea. I was not to leave his side. I was registered at the Hotel de France, but would be spending my days at Villa André, a gated community, where Miriam lived in a luxurious cottage. Villa André, named after Sekou Toure's wife, was a series of thatched-roof lodges where guests of the government and other dignitaries stayed. On my first evening there was a major drink fest at Miriam's place. Some of her musicians attended, as well as Colonel Kouyate, a jazz lover in the Guinean military, my guide Conteh, and the filmmaker Gilbert and his wife Audrey, both of whom I had met in Los Angeles when he was in film school. Philemon Hou, who had arrived a few months before me, Kante, the country's sports commentator and cultural organizer, and a handful of other friends of Miriam were also there. Stokely Carmichael, her husband, was in the States on a Black History Month lecture tour.

During the course of the evening a heated political debate developed, which was all in French. I was completely in the dark as to the exact subject matter. I was able to grasp only bits and pieces because the only French I remembered was the little bit I had learned at the Manhattan School of Music. Around midnight, everyone was getting quite drunk. Jet-lagged, I tried to persuade Conteh to escort me back to my hotel. With their political debate now at fever pitch, my guide could not tear himself away. I finally lost my patience and decided to walk back to my hotel by myself. Little did I know there was a citizens' militia guarding the city because of the ongoing Guinea-Bissau war raging next door, a war of liberation against the Portuguese. Bissau's many freedom fighters were staging their battle from Guinea. Strangers were watched like hawks. Collaborators were summarily executed. There had been a few raids by Portuguese insurgents, and every citizen was armed to repel them whenever they attempted to attack the coastline. Even schoolchildren carried arms to class.

I was stopped at a few roadblocks during my drunken walk back to my hotel. At each stop, I asked if I was walking in the right direction toward the Hotel de France. I was within a few blocks of the hotel when a Land Rover materialized out of nowhere. The driver asked me in perfect English, "Where are you going?" I explained I was near my destination. He said, "Listen, I am a close friend of Madame Makeba. Jump in. We will stop at my house, drink a few cognacs, listen to some good jazz, and then I will drop you off safely at your hotel." It sounded okay to me—jazz and a few cognacs were not things I usually declined, even with a stranger on my first day in a new country. He drove for about five minutes, then stopped in front of a well-lit house that he said was his home. I followed him through the front door into what turned out to be an army office, where he handed me over to a couple of elderly, high-ranking soldiers who began to interrogate me in what sounded like French. The English-speaking driver vanished before I could protest, and it struck me that I was in deep shit. A soldier demanded, *"Ou est vôtre guide?"* (Where is your guide?) In my most fucked-up, terror-filled, broken French, I tried to tell them that I was a guest of the president, a brother of Miriam Makeba, a musician, and whatever else I could come up with. I noticed that all I was causing for the old colonels was a great deal of mirth. Somehow the fact that my French was more fucked up than their own illiterate patois amused them and the other soldiers who were gathering around. Soon this room, its dingy walls splattered with blood, was filled with soldiers laughing every time I opened my mouth. As the colonel raised his voice to terrify me even further, my lips went dry. I sobered up quickly when I realized that I could possibly die in this room where others had obviously lost their lives.

The bizarre interrogation went on for the remainder of the night. By sunrise the soldiers had had enough fun, and the colonel ordered one of them to drive me to my hotel—and, if they found no Guinean passport there, to bring me back for God knows what. When we got to the hotel I gave the driver my passport and slept like a baby in my bed until evening, when Conteh came to my hotel and scolded me for leaving his side. I never saw him again. He was apparently transferred to a remote part of the country for failing in his duties.

Two days later, Miriam took me to meet Sekou Toure, Guinea's president. He invited me to the People's Palace for the customary evening of national cultural entertainment. When the president was in Conakry, the capital city, he sat in the front row of the People's Palace (Palais de Peuple) next to the stage and recorded every performance. Protocol dictated that all guests were obliged to sit through the performances with the president; these included drama sketches, choral singing, bands, drummers, acrobats, and gymnasts, and went on until two or three in the morning and sometimes longer. The next morning or anytime during the day, Sekou Toure could go on national radio and call a people's meeting in the national stadium. In less than an hour the seventy thousand-seat Conakry Stadium would be filled with citizens, schoolchildren, members of the government, the military, journalists, members of the diplomatic corps, farmers, and others—mostly dressed in white. Whoever wasn't in the stadium had to listen on radio as Toure addressed the nation—sometimes for as long as seven hours. When the president left the country, people would have to line the route to the airport and sing and drum and wave the national flag as his motorcade passed by. The pageantry was repeated again when he returned from a trip. Athletes, artists, and musicians all received a monthly salary from the state; ordinary citizens who did not work for the government were supplied food coupons and commodity rations from their committee headquarters. Committee leaders kept tabs on everybody. Those who were reported as not toeing the Socialist line were in danger of being categorized as cinquième colonne (fifth-column antisocialist collaborators). The punishment for this infraction was indefinite imprisonment or, in extreme cases, execution. Nestor Bangoura, Miriam's English-speaking band manager, had been jailed and his father had been executed for collaborating with the enemy. Toure was a passionate lover of his people's culture, but could also be a paranoid tyrant. Guinea was a beautiful and terrifying place.

Ashkar Marof, who had been Guinea's ambassador to the United Nations, and Diallo Telli, who had helped us form the South African Students Association when he was Guinea's UN representative in New York, had been summoned home a few years earlier. One morning when the people of Conakry woke up to go to work, these two men, along with seven others, were hanging by their necks in the town's main square, put to death for collaborating with the enemy. Such drastic measures terrified the populace into realizing that stepping out of line could put one in the graveyard. Sekou Toure and vice-president Lansanah Beyavougi ran the country with an executive council of ministers. It was a tight ship and you didn't fuck with it. The buck stopped at the president's office. He cared for all the families whose heads had been executed. Their wives, who were humorously referred to as the "joyous widows" in French, all tried to endear themselves to Toure and Beyavougi if they wished to continue peacefully living in the country. Several folks who were dissatisfied moved to Senegal, Ivory Coast, Liberia, Mali, or Sierra Leone, but many returned because of new obstacles in lands where they knew no one.

Prêt pour la Révolution (ready for the revolution) was the patriotic greeting everyone used, and it had to be expressed with enthusiasm. It was a regimented life, but it had its consoling pleasures. The president was the executive producer of all performances, and was blown away by my trumpet playing when I performed with Miriam's group at the People's Palace. I was assigned to teach music theory to the local band members any way I found possible. The president ordered that I be transferred from the hotel to a chalet next to Miriam's villa, where for a short time I was furnished with an upright piano. But after a few days, committee members picked it up. I was told the piano was needed for some other purpose. I didn't question it. Guitarists Sekou and Kemo Kouyate and percussionist Papa Mor Thiam were my most ardent students. They taught me Guinean songs like "Nina," a love song about a very beautiful girl. It was a national favorite that always brought down the house when I sang it at the Palais de Peuple. The popular music of Guinea was very much like the griot songs of Salif Keita, the world-famous albino singing wonder from neighboring Mali, and one of Sekou Toure's favorite artists.

Sekou Kouyate became my best friend. He knew where to find marijuana. Word was that if discovered, the punishment for smoking pot could be brutal, but Sekou assured me that the president knew about musicians and athletes' smoking habits and turned a blind eye because he was partial toward these communities. Nevertheless, one had to be secretive about it, because flaunting the practice could result in dire consequences.

Philemon and I shared the chalet. Miriam and I revived our intimacy. This led to many nocturnal visits by her to my chalet. When Stokely returned from his U.S. lecture tour, he began to spend a lot of time with Colonel Kouyate and me, smoking, drinking, philosophizing, and laughing. If Stokely suspected that Miriam and I were sleeping together, he certainly didn't act as if he did. But then he too was quite a nibbler in that field. Stokely was a power swimmer, and he swam in the ocean every morning. Sometimes I joined him. Villa André was right on the beach.

I had come to Guinea holding an airline ticket that went as far as Zaire, with Liberia, Gambia, Ghana, Ivory Coast, Nigeria, and Cameroon as stopping points. I also had one thousand dollars in traveler's checks and a couple of thousand in cash. But one could not just leave Guinea. Special permission was needed. With my French still minimal, Miriam explained to the president on my behalf that I wanted to go on a music pilgrimage throughout the continent, starting in Zaire.

Sekou Toure favored the idea, but insisted I take Sekou Kouyate with me. Sekou spoke perfect English and French, and knew his way around Africa. We left two weeks later.

On our arrival at Kinshasa International Airport in Zaire, the immigration officials detained us merely because we were coming from Guinea. We spent the whole day sitting on a bench outside their offices without being told why we were being held. Whenever I stood up and asked what the hell was going on, I was shouted down and told to shut the fuck up and sit down. Sekou figured that the reason might be that many Guineans had been deported from Zaire a few weeks earlier for being involved in diamond smuggling.

Twelve hours later, just before sunset, Sekou recognized an airport officer who was coming on night duty. Three months earlier Sekou had been in Zaire with Miriam when she had performed there. Sekou asked the officer if he could help, and a few minutes later he told us all we needed to do was give the man who had detained us five dollars. We complied, and five minutes later we were given our baggage and were on our way. Sekou felt very stupid that he had not remembered the custom of greasing officials' palms. But he blamed the oversight on the fact that my argumentative nature had thrown him off. We checked into the Intercontinental Hotel in downtown Kinshasa, and hit the spots with Sekou leading the way. First we stopped at the Ange Noir (Black Angel) club, where love balladeer Fonseca sang mostly French love songs with a trio. After supper we hopped taxis to various venues where bands played Congolese music. By eleven o'clock, we were at Tabu Ley Rochereau's gigantic nightclub, dance garden, and restaurant, on the outskirts of town. Tabu Ley's drummer, Cheskien, was very tight with Sekou and came with us after their performance to Matonge, where the great "Franco," Luambo Makiadi, and his TP OK Jazz were holding forth at his famous Un Deux Trois dance paradise. This was the very heart of the Congo's music soul. The singing, the playing, the dancing, the ambience—everything—was just too delicious. The Congolese women were statuesque and friendly. They wore colorful cloth bustiers or blouses and matching ankle-length cloth skirts, loosely tied at the waist around their ample lower bodies. At the beginning of each song, one could just amble over to any of the ladies and ask her to dance; no introduction was needed. The first parts of the songs were always slow rhumbas where you could talk to your partner and get familiar. The bands timed this part so well that just as you'd gotten familiar with your partner, they would break into a double tempo of furious guitar, bass, drums, percussion, and vocal riffs whose contrapuntal rhythms and interweaving harmonies rendered the revelers on the dance floor and around the tables and bars totally out of control, clapping their hands, cheering the band, singing along, screaming unrehearsed chants in remarkably tight unison. The dancers were lost in a frenzy of hip-swerving bumps and grinds, designed to get the limpest person hornier than a broke-dick dog. As they gyrated, pumping and grinding their asses, the women would unfasten their clothes at the waist, giving their dance partner a quick flash of ample thighs and other merchandise under their skimpy underwear. This is the phenomenon that is the Congo. We danced until dawn and ended up at a roadside café where a band was playing to customers who were having their last drinks before setting off to work. It was shortly before seven in the morning when Sekou Kouyate and I said our good-byes. It was a night to remember; these people lived for music. The bands staggered their performances in traffic-light fashion so that the fans could rush from one venue to another without missing any of the shows—from a couple of hours before midnight until it was time to go to work the next morning.

Cheskien took us to all kinds of musical happenings—urban, rural, spiritual, and traditional—it was absolutely scary how much music of superlative quality proliferated in the Congo from one end to the other, bubbling and boiling in the midst of a population that had seen exploitation and suffering to equal or surpass any manner of cruelty that had ever been visited upon the human race. And all this great music was exploding in the middle of a period when one of Africa's most dictatorial despots, Mobutu Sese Seko, was ruling the country with an iron-fisted military machine, and the entire Western industrial complex was supporting his regime and sucking the Congo dry to the bone while Mobutu siphoned his share into banks all over Europe's wealthiest countries.

In Zaire I was introduced to Franco, one of the greatest bandleaders in all of Africa, whose guitar licks sent listeners into hysteria. He popularized the music of the Congo and was used by Mobutu as a conduit into the hearts of the entire Zairean population. Later on, when Mobutu's stranglehold on the people was secure and he had no more need of Franco's assistance, he turned against him, driving him into exile, where he eventually died, a lonely man in Belgium.

Right away Franco took to me. He made a furnished apartment available to us for rent, across the giant circle from his club. Franco also provided us with a rehearsal room with all the equipment I needed to put a band together. Cheskien put a few good musicians together, and with him on drums, Sekou and I began to rehearse a group. But after two weeks of rehearsals we were still struggling with the first song because when it came to music, the musicians could only express themselves in Lingala, one of the most commonly spoken languages in the Congo, which Sekou and I didn't understand. It was terribly discouraging. But our nights were spent grooving hard, hopping from one garden club to another, and always ending up at Franco's club, Un, Deux, Trois, with a bevy of fine women following us to the flat. Around lunchtime, those who had frolicked with us would awaken us with a large bowl of local cuisine, which they had gone to their homes to prepare with the "taxi fare" we had given them. After lunch they would request more "taxi fare" and go home to fix another dish for the evening, taking our laundry along to wash and iron as well. But always the matter of "taxi fare" came up. Sekou explained that because the Congolese had been deprived of almost any meaningful education by the colonial Belgians, when the country finally won its independence in 1960, there were only six African doctors in the country. Their leader, Patrice Lumumba, had himself only been a schoolteacher, and the first people to be educated were the male population. As a result, when mass migration to the big cities took hold, the only people who had money were men. The majority of the women were very possessive of their men because that was the most accessible way to the cash. It was not so much prostitution as much as an industry born of their reduced status. A boyfriend, when found, was kept close to the family. And if the dude crossed a woman, the girls would not fight each other. The rivals would gang up on the man and scratch the hell out of him. This explained why Cheskien had such a scratched-up face. He was most instrumental in introducing us to the young ladies we were hanging out with—all siblings or cousins ready to rotate around us as long as no outsider was brought into this inner circle. With endearing smiles and unparalleled loyalty, they nonetheless watched us like hawks.

Months of endless reveling with different women, dancing into the early morning hours, drinking and smoking pot, and enjoying the people of Zaire and their music became too much. The original intent of putting a group together had failed miserably. The morning we were preparing to leave, there was a knock on our door. Six soldiers toting Uzis entered and ordered Sekou and me to dress. They bundled us into an army van, drove us to their head-quarters, placed us in an interrogation room, and told us to wait there. Within a few minutes, Tabu Ley Rochereau entered the room resplendent in an haute couture suit with matching black tie, shirt, and cuff links. His designer moc-casins were shining from a recent spit-polish. He sat across the table from us with a gloomy expression on his face and addressed us in high French.

"There has never been a world-famous celebrity to come into my country without being received and entertained by me. Yet you have come to Zaire and have hobnobbed with a lowly drummer from my band. He is responsible for lowering your status and treating you like just another ordinary visitor. I object vehemently to this state of affairs, and this is why I brought you here. Tonight you will come to my club, where you will be honored properly with wonder-ful dining, a great performance by my band, the best champagne, and other drinks. But most of all, my other guests will be great people of your caliber. I will send a car for you at seven. Please be on time. Thank you."

Rochereau left the room and us with our mouths agape. The soldiers returned us to our flat. That night we were wined and dined and fêted at his garden club until after midnight. It was one of the most wonderful evenings I had spent in my life. A few days later, Sekou and I returned to Guinea, where a reply letter from Fela Kuti had been waiting for me.

Dear Hugh,
Just come to Lagos as my guest and we will take care of it from there.
Whenever you are ready, you can sit in regularly with my band, and you
will meet other musicians from whom you can pick people for your
proposed band. I will meet you at the airport when you come.

                                               Sincerely, Fela

14

In January 1973, a summit meeting took place in Guinea of all the leaders of ex-Portuguese colonies of Africa. It was attended by Samora Machel of Mozambique, Amilcar Cabral from Guinea-Bissau and Cape Verde, Eduardo Dos Santos from Angola, and many other delegates, to discuss the way forward in their liberation campaigns. Sekou Toure was chairman of the conference. Following the talks, a celebration was held at Payotte, the capital's most famous nightclub, with all of the VIP delegates and their spouses. We were dancing up a storm when word came from the presidential palace that everyone should immediately return to his or her hotel or villa.

When Philemon, Miriam, and I returned to Villa André, we heard that Amilcar Cabral had just been assassinated in the city. We later learned that a traitor by the name of Innocentia Candia, an agent of the Portuguese colonialists who had infiltrated into the ranks of the government three years earlier, had killed Cabral, who was only forty-nine. Philemon, Miriam, Bongi and her two children Zenzi and Lumumba, and I sat dejectedly in Miriam's lounge. Samora Machel soon walked in with three members of his delegation. He squatted on the carpet and began to regale us with stories of Frelimo's success in the Mozambican war against Portugal. Frelimo was the most popular organization fighting for liberation of the Mozambican people, who had been colonized by Portugal for over five hundred years. Machel talked about his beloved late wife and his young fiancée, Graca, who was a top commander of the women's corps. Before long, he had us singing South African work songs he had learned when he worked in Johannesburg's mines. Machel ended by singing the South African liberation anthem, "Nkosi Sikelela."

By the time he left, just before dawn, our spirits had been lifted, and despite the death of a great African freedom fighter, we were left feeling positive about Africa's future. For the first time we understood that many freedom fighters would lose their lives before all of Africa would be liberated, and that one fallen hero should not derail our determination to continue our quest regardless of inevitable setbacks.

By the first week of April, preparations were under way for a national cultural festival that would be taking place all over Conakry. The following week the great singer and composer Aboubacar Demba Camara, one of the most loved and popular performers in West Africa, was killed in a car accident while in Senegal for a series of concerts. Demba's music was a blend of Mandingo musical traditions and Cuban and Congolese influences. When his body was returned to Conakry, the entire country, already saddened by the news, went into public mourning. Flags flew at half-mast and just about everybody lined the streets from the airport to the city to view his cortége. Women were weeping, and drums thundered everywhere. His body lay in state at the Palais de Peuple, and for two days mourners from all over Guinea came to view Demba, while griot singers took turns singing over his coffin. Demba was given a state funeral, attended by government officials and musicians from all the neighboring countries, including sixteen-year-old Salif Keita from Mali. During and after his funeral, the streets were packed with drummers, dancers, praise-singers, and orchestras—millions turned out to bid him farewell. When I first met and hung out with Demba before going to Zaire, I didn't realize what a giant he was in the hearts of so many people. His band, Bembeya, didn't perform for three years following his death. Sadly, Demba had been very keen on us collaborating on recording projects when he returned from Senegal.

The national cultural festival was a two-week spectacular. As executive director, Sekou Toure had organized the country into fifty federations, each of which had a ballet company, a theater company, a griot ensemble, a series of bands, traditional drum ensembles, athletes, acrobats, choral groups, children's groups, poets, and magicians. It was mind-boggling. There were performances around the clock at the Palais de Peuple, in the town squares, along the streets, and in other cities around the country. The president attended many of the events. The country's top movie director, Gilbert, commissioned me to write the soundtrack for a film he would be making that linked the different events. I wrote several songs that I recorded with a cross-section of Guinean artists.

In neighboring Liberia, President William Tolbert was energetically pushing a project called "Higher Heights." He wanted to galvanize Liberia's citizens into contributing physically, financially, and spiritually to uplifting the morale and economy of the country. After seeing Miriam's show during the Guinean festival, especially how we performed together, President Tolbert invited us to Liberia to perform and help raise funds for his initiative. Stokely had just returned from another U.S. trip, in time for the Guinea festival, with his younger sister Madeline in tow. A few days before we left, Madeline and I hit it off and were spending romantic nights at her chalet. Stokely found out about us, but turned a blind eye.

Our entourage was welcomed at the nursery/floral park of Gertylue Brewer, whom everybody called Sister Gertie, in the Congotown section of Monrovia, the capital of Liberia. Sister Gertie and Miriam had become close over the years, so naturally, Miriam stayed at her estate with Stokely and Madeline. The band stayed at the estate's motel, which was surrounded by a beautiful drinking garden, a huge bar area, and a patio facing the sprawling landscaped gardens below the double-story mansion. The house had a wraparound porch filled with tables laid out with all kinds of drinks and Liberian cuisine. Invited were government officials and the cream of Monrovia's social elite, including some of the most beautiful women I had seen since my return to Africa. Cecil Dennis, who worked in the president's Office of Home Affairs, had chosen Sister Gertie's home for our reception because she was reputedly one of the country's finest chefs and a generous hostess. Dennis was the coordinator and executive director of the "Higher Heights" project. A tall, humorous character with movie-star features and a mischievous smile, he officially welcomed our delegation and briefed us on our itinerary. He introduced me to a beautiful young lady whom he announced to the guests would be my official escort for the duration of our stay. This brought laughter from all the guests except Miriam. I was leaning up against a far patio wall, drinking with some of my new acquaintances and being briefed by my escort, when Miriam walked over to me while I was in deep conversation with my escort. Miriam asked her to excuse us because she wished to have a word with me in private. The young lady said, "Oh, pardon me, Mrs. Masekela."

Miriam slapped the woman across the face, sending her staggering to keep her balance. "I am Mrs. Carmichael, you little bitch, and that man standing over there is my husband, Stokely Carmichael. Don't you ever forget it, you little bitch!"

Miriam turned and stormed off into the house. The whole place went silent except for Sister Gertie, who gracefully tried to restore calm. "Everybody, the food is ready," she said. "Come and dish up for yourselves." I looked at Stokely, who was pouring himself some wine and knew better than to follow his wife until after she cooled down.

After the reception, Madeline rode back with me and was checked into a suite next to mine at the Ducor International Hotel on downtown Monrovia's highest hill, with a breathtaking view of the city and the Atlantic Ocean. The "Higher Heights" fund-raisers at the E. J. Royce Auditorium and the national stadium were a resounding success. Although Miriam had previously performed in Liberia, this was my first time. The crowds were particularly enthralled. When the guitar introduction to "Grazing in the Grass" was kicked off by Sekou Kouyate, the crowd went insane. When the song ended, they screamed for an encore. We obliged several times to their demands. They especially loved Miriam's universally acclaimed "Click Song." They tried singing along, excitedly clapping their hands to the rhythmic arrangement of the song's fascinating Xhosa tongue-clicking. Many of them were trying to make the sound, but only ended up laughing at themselves. When Miriam went into "Pata Pata," the stadium went totally insane with excitement. They knew the words to this song and sang it with so much spirit that they would not allow Miriam to finish. She had to repeat it a few times.

Back at the hotel, Madeline and I had another week of passion and laughter. At the end of our stay, President Tolbert gave a farewell dinner for us at his official residence, where he awarded me full citizenship and a passport from the government of Liberia. When Miriam and her group left for a European tour, Sister Gertie invited me to extend my visit and move to her palatial home in Congotown, a suburb of Monrovia. A few days later, Sister Gertie brought in Nga Machema, a South African guerrilla fighter who had gone to Michigan State University with many Liberians in the 1960s while I was studying at the Manhattan School of Music. This was a pleasant surprise because we were old drinking buddies. Nga was on sabbatical from fighting alongside Roberto Holden against the military forces of the colonial Portuguese regime in Angola. Holden was the leader of Falana, one of the three liberation movements fighting against the Portuguese insurgents in Angola. Nga was one of Holden's chief commanders. Nga Machema was his *nom de guerre*. Although his real name was Manelisi Ndibongo, we all called him Nga.

My old friend began to show me the exciting life around Monrovia, where the scene was the exact opposite of Conakry. Monrovia never went to sleep. The people partied around the clock, and all of Nga's fellow Michigan State alumni were in senior government posts or were top business moguls. There was a heartbreaking disparity between this community, who called themselves Americo-Liberians, and the ethnic population, which was obviously living in abject poverty. Liberia was the oldest independent African country. Freed American slaves who wanted to return to Africa were resettled there by the United States government starting in 1822. Surprisingly most of them reverted to more or less the same behavior of their former slave masters by treating the natives like dirt. I felt uncomfortable with this state of affairs, but strangely Nga, his friends, Sister Gertie, and all the people I was hanging out with brushed me off nonchalantly every time I brought it up. Miriam and Stokely, however, did privately express their disgust to me, but pointed out that it was futile to pursue it, and not a politically correct topic to broach with our hosts if I wanted to remain in their country.

Unfortunately, throughout all of Africa the cruelty of the colonial regimes and the tyrants who came in their wake caused the people to seek solace in mind-altering substances—mostly alcohol. Marijuana and the mouth-numbing kola nut and khat are most widely used among non-Christian communities and where famine is rife because in the latter cases, they kill the appetite. In Africa, as in many other parts of the world, the military is notorious for abuse of alcohol. In South Africa, alcohol was only legalized for native consumption in 1961; prior to that date, abusive drinking became a heroic form of militant protest that, unfortunately, turned into a national culture. It's no surprise that most of the liberation cadres of that country arrived at training camps already seasoned alcoholics. Sexual decadence was always part of the package, owing to the fact that most of the world's military community is morally bankrupt and its respect for women is almost nil. Anywhere there is suffering and oppression, the same situation exists. In its alcoholic and sexual decadence, Liberia's elite society was no different from any other society where the guilt of oppressing the disadvantaged haunts those who are in power.

Political reservations aside, I was having a ball and not too keen about returning to Guinea. We were hitting all the clubs, and the women of Monrovia were as friendly as those in Kinshasa, except that many had their own businesses, homes, and cars. The "taxi fare" request hardly ever came up.

One great quality that both Guinea and Liberia had in common was that government ministers, upper-middle-class big shots, and dignitaries, including the diplomatic corps, all basically hung out in the same bars, clubs, and restaurants as the working classes, and most people were on a first-name basis. There was very little of the "Your Excellency," "Mr. Minister," and "Your Honor" bullshit that you find in so many African countries today. There were also very few if any of the noisy, irritating sirens of police motorcycles and countless bodyguard convoys that go harassing pedestrians and motorists all over the roads, bringing traffic to a standstill. In Guinea, everybody, including the president, was addressed as "Comrade." Although William Tolbert was called "Mr. President" formally, he privately loved his nickname, "Speedy." In Liberia, people addressed each other as "mate," "buddy," "bubba," "my man," or, in the case of females, "my child."

Two weeks later I returned to Guinea, but soon I became a man of two cities, splitting my time equally between Monrovia and Conakry, which made for a wonderful contrast in lifestyles. Conakry was the regimented home of strict socialism and rules, militancy, political slogans, discipline, fierce loyalty, one-party solidarity, and the iron-fisted rule of Sekou Toure's committees. The Guinea-Bissau war was ongoing, and there was constant anticipation of an insurgent raid by Portuguese mercenaries. The population, ninety-nine percent Muslim, was armed to the teeth and ready to defend itself. Monrovia, on the other hand, featured round-the-clock bars, a thriving international tourist trade, and American currency. It was governed by a Christian minority of the descendants of American slaves, who treated the indigenous population almost like slaves. Americo-Liberian opulence and vulgar wealth existed in the midst of embarrassing ethnic poverty, ritual secret societies, and deep superstition.

Comrade Sekou Toure and President William Tolbert shared the most unlikely mutual admiration, given the contrasting qualities of their political agendas. The irony was that although one country was capitalist and the other socialist, their regimes were similar in their autocratic and totalitarian suppression of their peoples. They shared a common interest in ensuring that the masses did not have the opportunity to voice their grievances. This was also tactically very crucial, because the borders between the two countries were colonial inventions. The people in the region originated from the same ethnic groups, and family ties dated back many centuries.

In the summer of 1973, I flew back to New York to fetch Mabusha, after convincing my sister Barbara that it would be good for my nephew to learn the indigenous languages, customs, traditions, and culture of West Africa. The people of this region lived together like one large extended family, a quality not present in a city like New York. Mabusha jumped into Guinean life with gusto, making friends quickly and learning how to play soccer and bonding with Lumumba and Zenzi and all the other children in the vicinity surrounding Villa André. They would start screaming for him to come out and play early in the morning on holidays, weekends, and after school. We often took trips to Miriam's villa in Dalaba, way up north in the Fouta Djallon mountain region, the home of the Fulani people, where the weather is temperate and the nights are cold. Sekou Toure refused to allow mining multinationals and other industrial giants to exploit the raw materials of his country. As a result, the ecology of the country remained pristine. Guinea was a country of many small towns and villages; even Conakry was really only a hamlet. Migration to urban areas was not permitted, and development of village communities and feverish agricultural activity was heavily encouraged and sponsored by the state.

As a result, there were great expanses of virgin land covered by native flora and fauna. On our trip to Dalaba, we actually had to stop for a community of hundreds of gorillas crossing the road. In July the rains came, and because Guinea is so rich in minerals, the lightning and thunder were awe-inspiring. When it rains in Guinea and Liberia, it's like standing under a waterfall; umbrellas and raincoats are a joke, because the rain penetrates right through them. The rain is so torrential you cannot see more than a few inches away from your own face. And the rains can come down for weeks without end. The average rainfall is about three hundred inches a year. Tropical fruits such as bananas, mangos, coconuts, dates, pawpaws, and plantains grow wild. Fruit bats darken the sky. Tropical vegetables, fish, and forest animals are in ridiculous abundance. That there is famine in Africa from time to time is perplexing, given these limitlessly abundant gifts of nature. It is unfortunate that almost all of Africa's regimes are run by greedy bastards who think only of their personal well-being and the amassing of wealth at the expense of the masses, without harnessing the available resources. Enough natural resources are available to supply every family on the continent with sufficient food, but the selfishness of those living at the top makes it impossible to create an infrastructure that could extract such value. The needs continue to exist, but the will to solve many of Africa's problems is absent among the majority of Africa's ruling and wealthy classes. They are the only ones who have the capabilities and resources to achieve this end.

• • •

Soon after I recovered from a short bout with malaria, I received a message from Fela, asking again for my presence in Nigeria. Stewart Levine, who was still my partner in Chisa Records, flew to Liberia from Los Angeles and together we took off for Lagos, where he would help me assess musicians for future recordings. Finally I was to meet the legendary Fela.

As promised, Fela met us at the airport. Standing about five feet seven on a taut and muscular frame, he strutted toward us like a matador approaching a crazed bull before the kill. Head held high, Fela stepped out in his white moccasins, wearing light green, tight-fitting toreador-style pants and matching shirt. Laughing, he welcomed us to Nigeria.

The welcoming lounge in Lagos was totally insane, with scores of people there to meet arriving passengers. Taxi and bus drivers were hustling; self-appointed porters and security personnel were jostling and screaming hysterically over each other's heads. About twelve strapping young men with rippling muscles were pushing and shoving each other in a tug-of-war to carry our bags to Fela's car. As they pulled our bags hither and thither, their body odor was so strong it almost knocked me out—I was dizzy and my eyes watered uncontrollably from the stench. Fearing they would destroy our luggage, we looked at Fela with anxiety. He assured us our bags were safe. He said, "Oh! Oh! Don't mind these fools. They will bring the bags to the car. Hugh, this place is fucking crazy, man. You haven't seen anything yet." When we got to the car, our self-appointed porters kept yanking our bags in all directions. Fela yelled, "Put the bags in back of the car, you stupids." He then gave them a naira each (about one dollar) and told them to go away, as they tried to hit him up for a bigger tip, praising him by screaming, "Black president! Chief priest!" Everyone who saw Fela's convoy echoed this chant throughout our trip into town. We crossed a bridge into Lagos proper, and the madness began right away. There were traffic jams everywhere. What seemed like millions of people were screaming at each other in the packed streets and sidewalks, hanging out of apartment windows, and trying to keep from falling off overloaded trucks. Cars were honking endlessly; Nigerian juju and Afro-beat music was blasting from storefronts and little kiosks. At the taxi and bus terminal, a long line of people were waiting to slap the face of some man who had allegedly been beating his girlfriend. In the back of the line, some potential slappers were asking what the man had done, even though they were spitting in their palms in enthusiastic anticipation to whack the poor motherfucker silly.

Passing us some robust marijuana spliffs, Fela said, "They will slap that man till he dies, and if his family doesn't find a traditional diviner to come and pray over his body, his carcass will rot right there on the sidewalk because it is bad luck to touch it. Even the ambulance and mortuary folks will not go near it until the diviner has come. If they try to move it, the crowds will kill them too. This is a crazy place, Hugh." I looked at the victim in amazement as our vehicle inched its way through the heavy traffic and stifling heat.

Lagos was the dirtiest place I had ever been to. The stagnant water in the open sewers running down both sides of every street was pitch black. The stench changed in odor just about every fifty yards, unexpectedly surprising the nose and causing Stewart and me to moan painfully at every new, pungently unbearable aroma. The smell of urine and feces came rising from some of the sewers at unexpected intervals. Majestic mansions reared their fancy parapets and verandas in the midst of millions of hovels, shacks, and corrugated iron storefronts, kiosks, and improvised dwellings in and out of which ran snotty-faced, bare-assed toddlers and preschoolers, dogs and midget goats, dirty chickens and dried-up cats. Women of all sizes, wearing headscarves, their torsos wrapped in colorful fabrics with matching blouses, pounded cassava and yam in giant wooden mortars with long pestles made from tough timber, and prepared meals on outdoor braziers. The men, muscular and taut, lingered about or walked hurriedly to some destination. Everybody was screaming, arguing, or yelling at one another. Millions of restless souls, reeling from the heat, irritable from the discomfort of their conditions, pissed off at government neglect but somehow still laughing from their souls between shows of violent temper: social schizophrenia at its most intense permeated the atmosphere.

"Fela, why is everybody screaming at each other and so short-tempered?" I asked.

Fela said, laughing, "Hugh, these people are very happy. These are Nigerians, man! This is their nature. They don't hold anything back."

The rich men were dressed in bright-colored lace, silk, or linen ankle-length *boubou* and *agbada,* layers of long gowns that they nervously adjusted into place over their shoulders, matching caps tilted to one side on their heads. Their women, often wives dressed in similar overflowing robes and gowns, walked submissively behind them. The bright, rainbow-colored outfits most people wore sparkled with cleanliness, seemingly dirt-resistant in spite of the filth. Amazing.

Fela checked us into the Niger Hotel in Lagos, where the bar was full of men loudly debating about God knows what. The rooms were funky. The whole place smelled like shit. As Fela prepared to leave us, I said, "Fela, there is no way we're going to stay here. This is just too funky, you know what I mean?"

Fela laughed and said, "But, Hugh, I thought you wanted a typical African atmosphere."

"That I want, but this shit is not it."

By this time we were all bent over with laughter.

"Okay, Hugh, it's too late now," he said. "But first thing tomorrow morning I will take you and your man to a place where the white people stay, okay?" He continued, "I'm leaving you with these two girls." Fela handed me four more pregnant spliffs. He walked away laughing, and two young ladies materialized out of nowhere.

The next morning Fela moved us to the Mainland Hotel, which was clean and full of international tourists. We spent the rest of the day at Fela's house in Surulere, across from his garden club, the African Shrine, located in a suburb deep inside the confines of Lagos's poorest and most overcrowded slums. When we entered Fela's house, it was full of scores of women huddled on the floor panting, *"Fela, Fela, me wo! Fela!"* He ran past them to a side room, yelling at us, "Sit down, guys, make yourselves at home. I'll be right out." He emerged a few minutes later dressed only in bikini briefs, and joined us at a small table. Every time he ran to the bathroom, the women would stampede to get in there with him, as he fought to lock the door from the inside. "Me, me, me, I beg!" they screamed. One or two managed to get inside with him, where apparently they would bend over as he fucked them from the rear. We could hear their screams of passion, while the unfortunate ones left outside the bathroom listened at the door, panting, *"Oh, Fela, oh, Fela, wo."* All I could say was *damn.* Stewart was looking at me, shaking his head.

After a while Fela came out with a big smile on his face, wiping his brow with the palm of his hand as sweat poured down his face. He panted, "Hugh, it's a rough life, I tell you." Before we could say anything, Fela screamed, "Smoooke!" Eko, one of his acolytes, showed up with a cigarette pack full of marijuana spliffs. We each got one, and the girls fought to light them for us. "Boooze!" he now shouted, and Ywami, his finance man, appeared with cognac, ice cubes, Coca-Cola, and bottles of beer. The girls poured. "Foood!" he shouted, and more girls entered with bowls of food and dished it into plates for us. It was an impressive demonstration of Fela's power in his private kingdom, which he'd dubbed "the Kalakuta Republic."

Although Quincy Troupe had briefed me about Fela, his report had been rather understated compared to what I was seeing now. Perhaps Fela and his people had behaved differently around Quincy; maybe the great musician felt more at ease around me, and just let it all hang out. Listening to his records and stories that I had heard, my perspective about him was strictly music-related. Never had I expected to arrive at the madhouse of a stud-in-heat and his sex-hungry harem.

Fela's commune consisted of about a hundred men and women who made up his inner circle. These were members of his thirty-piece orchestra, the girls who did furious, ass-wiggling dances on the stage very much in the style of the old go-go clubs of the sixties, where women danced half-naked in knee-high boots. Fela's women, however, danced barefoot in skimpy, tie-dyed, rainbow-colored loincloth skirts made from animal skins. Their bodies were painted with multicolored mud, and their faces made up like ethnic masks. Draped over their shoulders and bare breasts hung traditional African beads. And then there were the drivers, bodyguards, stagehands, and sound and lighting crews. Eko and Ywami and J.K., his manager, were his closest associates. The bodyguards monitored the behavior of the troops, and took down names of transgressors, who were later called to Fela's court of law, where sentences ranged from lashes with a whip made from dried cow-blood vessels, to detention in the cramped chicken coop that was dubbed "Kalakusu Prison." Band members who were late for rehearsals and performances, or who missed their music cues on stage, were subjected to similarly harsh punishment.

Beyond this group were Fela's second tier of followers, posses, and groupies. They were known as the Young Pioneers, and numbered close to thirty thousand. They always shouted "Black President! Chief Priest!" wherever Fela showed up. Fela's origins were in the Yoruba center of Abeokuta, from where his surname, Kuti, had its genesis. "Kalakuta Republic" and "Kalakusu Prison" were both derivatives of the name Abeokuta. He ruled his kingdom with a very tight fist. His word was law, but his style of governance was rib-cracking improvised humor. Kalakuta Republic's specialty was the butchering of the English language as intensely as possible to create the ever-changing pidgin slang that the troops spoke.

That afternoon Fela invited us to a photo session for his new album, *Africa 70*, which contained the classics "Lady" and "Shakara." The scene was a garden club on whose dance floor was drawn a large map of Africa. Topless girls were kneel-

ing all around the map's outline. We went up to the roof with Fela and the photographer. Fela then told the girls, "When I say smile, you must smile. I don't
want you to grin. You have to smile. You understand me?" "Yes, Fela," they
chimed in unison. "Okay. Ready? Smiiiiile!" he screamed. They all obeyed while
the photographer shot feverishly. The new album was playing in the background while we smoked large spliffs and Fela directed the shoot from the roof.

An old Sierra Leonean friend, Frank Karefa-Smart, who worked with the
diamond company of Maurice Templesman, joined us at the end of the session.
He was working from Nigeria, Sierra Leone, and Niger, where he had homes,
aside from his Riverside Drive apartment in New York. We rode back to Fela's
compound in his slick Mercedes. More food, smoke, and booze. Fela always
traveled in a convoy with a minimum of fifty people. That evening we went to
a club called the Gondola. Our entourage must have totaled seventy-five people, mostly women from his concubine stable. An Afro-beat combo was performing, featuring a very talented mulatto vocalist. At the end of the set, Fela
took me to meet the singer. He warned me, "This guy loves you so much, he
might jump on us and kiss you, Hugh. Watch out." He stopped the young man
and said, "Hey, you, you've been bothering me so much about Hugh Masekela.
Here he is. I brought him to you." Stunned, the young singer responded,
"Who?" Fela repeated, "Hugh Masekela. Here he is." Confused, the young man
said, "Ah! Wow. Me, I no sabie um at all." (I don't know who you are talking
about.) Fela whistled the first few notes of "Grazing in the Grass," and the
young man went wild. "Hoojie, Hoojie Makaselaaah." He embraced me and
then lifted me high into the air. He couldn't stop screaming "Hoojie
Makaselaaah." He ran back to the stage and started his next set earlier than
scheduled. "This is for my greatest idol, Hoojie Makaselaaah." He sang his heart
out for an hour and some change. We were dancing up a storm and throwing
back double cognacs all night. When Fela got the bill, which included drinks for
about seventy-five people, he said to the owner, "I don't have this kind of
money, but I tell you what, I'll come and do a couple of nights here for you for
free." The owner agreed. He couldn't stop laughing. Fela couldn't either.

Back at the Mainland Hotel the next morning, I woke up early and realized
that I had run out of toothpaste, so I went into the marketplace next to the
hotel to find some. It was a long, rectangular structure with a corrugated iron
roof and large wooden beams holding it up. The earthen floor was swept spot-
lessly clean, and hundreds of stalls crowded neatly next to each other, display-
ing all manner of traditional herbs hanging from nails. The cabinets were lined

with thousands of bottles filled with dark mixtures of tonics with bark and roots floating at the bottom. The pungent smell of leaves, branches, and barks smoking on top of braziers filled the air. Many elderly men and women, their skin pulled very tightly against their skulls, stared at me with glazed, bloodshot eyes from their chairs and benches, where they sat looking past me into space. They seemed slightly hypnotized. From some of the shelves hung animal bones and human and animal skulls. I had just asked one of the attendants near the entrance if she could tell me where I could get some toothpaste, when I realized this was not a grocery store. Chills ran through my body, and goosebumps were breaking out on my skin. A cold feeling hit the back of my neck. I ran out of there with my hair standing on end, my teeth chattering. I was shaking like a leaf.

After breakfast we took a taxi to Fela's house. I told him about the mysterious market. He stood up. "Hugh!" he screamed. "Nobody has ever walked into that place alone and lived to tell about it. That is the supermarket where all the witch doctors, diviners, and traditional healers shop. It is the city's main juju and voodoo supply store. You are one lucky motherfucker to be standing here in front of me."

At the Gondola, we had met the managing director of Decca Records in Nigeria. Excited to meet me, he invited us over to dinner the following evening. That evening we left Fela's compound in a convoy of ten minibuses. The girls were carrying Fela's records and singing in the minibuses while hanging head and shoulders out of the vehicles' windows, banging on the side panels. In Frank Karefa-Smart's Mercedes, following the convoy, we were shaking our heads in utter bafflement. When we arrived, our host was startled to see close to one hundred people. Fela's girls burst into the huge living room, started to move furniture from the middle of the room, put on some of Fela's records, and began dancing frantically. It was the beginning of a roaring party. The poor guy's wife was crimson as the girls pulled her to the dance floor and gyrated sensually all around her ass, urging the woman to imitate them. The couple was mesmerized as we emptied their bar. Fela used the most vulgar language he could come up with in conversation with the man's wife. Our host was dumbfounded. We never got to eat. We just danced all night with the girls and drank ourselves silly. Our host and his wife had no choice but to join us.

I sat in with Fela's band at the Shrine, a shed with open sides and a corrugated fiberglass roof. The venue could accommodate up to a thousand people on the dance floor. There were seats near the stage on both sides and in the front. In the rear of the long hall were more terraced bleacher seats. Fela's band comprised two alto saxes, two tenor saxes, a baritone sax, three trumpets, four guitars, a bass guitar, four rhythm jembe hand-drum percussionists, one conga and bongo master drummer, a regular trap drummer, and two male percussionists who marched back and forth in front of the band playing a cowbell and wooden blocks called claves, acting as a metronome for the whole ensemble. Ten or more girls sang unisons with and background responses to Fela's guttural but beautiful melodic chants, scatting, and riffs.

Fela stood in front of the band, his keyboard on one side of his vocal microphone, his tenor saxophone on a stand next to its own microphone. Fela started every song with a long keyboard introduction while his "electric dancers" shimmied and shook their asses feverishly in front of the band on their own stands and all around him. When he broke into the vocal verse after rousing, jazzy passages by the saxes and trumpets with thumping drum, conga, and guitar cross-rhythms, the crowd would go crazy, screaming, "Felaaaa!! Chief Priest!! Black President!! *Fela I Yoo!!*" Then came his long saxophone solo, more vocal calls and responses, breaks, stops, conga flourishes, loud orchestral riffs, stops, rhythm grooves only, and shouts from the crowd. Then he would call me to the front to solo. Slowly the rhythm guitar would join Fela's keyboard behind me with the bass and tenor guitar relentlessly repeating the same licks they had commenced with, holding down the groove like a mighty herd of cool elephants, along with the percussionists. As I continued with my solo, the saxes, then the trumpets, would gently join the accompaniment, taking me to a climax in the song where the female vocalists were riffing in the upper register and I felt like I was sitting on a fat cloud of music with my eyes tightly shut. The experience was incredible. I did not want to stop soloing. When the roar of the band, the percussion, Fela's keyboard, and the girls' voices came to a sudden stop, leaving only the two male dancer-percussionists marching back and forth, tapping on the claves and the cowbell, with the bass and the tenor guitar, it felt as if I just had been pulled off at the height of very passionate lovemaking, just before orgasm. The anticlimax was painful as the crowd yelled joyfully, *"Ayeye! Ayeye! Na wow wo!"* applauding wildly while Fela smiled happily at me. What must have been easily twenty minutes, felt like thirty seconds. The textures were too beautiful. I just couldn't wait for the next solo. The band would sometimes play one song for three hours without stopping. Afro-beat's hypnotic vocals, Fela's quasi-rapping pidgin-English singing, percolating guitars, and haunting percussion counterpoint, all wrapped up in a burning, molten groove, was an intoxicating diet of

Dr. Tshidi Ndamse, holding our daughter, Motlalepula Masekela, with my nephew Mabusha looking on at our Congo Beach home in Monrovia, Liberia, in 1978. *Photo courtesy of the author.*

Selema Masekela, my oldest son, with his mother, Jessie La Pierre, in our Beverly Hills apartment in 1972. *Photo courtesy of the author.*

Selema, my sister Barbara, and I pose with Polina at Barbara's house in New York in the summer of 1978, shortly before Polina passed away. *Photo by John Pinderhughes.*

In 1978 at the Park West in Chicago, Herb Alpert and I play songs from our album, *Herb Alpert & Hugh Masekela*. *Photo courtesy of the author.*

Jabu, my third wife, and I at our wedding on August 14, 1981, at St. John the Divine Church in New York City. *Photo courtesy of the author.*

Blowing from Lesotho's mountain tops during a 1980 visit to the mountain kingdom for a Christmas Day concert with Miriam Makeba.
Photo by Raymond Cajuste.

My father, whom I had not seen for twenty years, joined me at the event.
Photo courtesy of the author.

In London in 1983, Father Huddleston presents me with a bust of Nelson Mandela after the concert for Mandela's 65th birthday.
Photo courtesy of the author.

Talking backstage with Harry Belafonte and vibraphonist Roy Ayers at SOB's in Greenwich Village after a performance with Kalahari in 1984. *Photo courtesy of the author.*

Sharing a joke with Kwame Toure (Stokely Carmichael) in 1991. Kwame, who married Miriam Makeba in 1968, died in Guinea in 1998. *Photo by Hakim Mutlaq.*

Playing my horn for the kids in the street where I grew up in Alexandra Township (1995). *Photo by D. Michael Cheers.*

Barbara and I at my father's funeral in 1996. I blew my horn for him as his coffin was lowered into the ground. *Photo by Alf Kumalo.*

I love this photo of my father in one of his thoughtful moments. *Photo courtesy of the author.*

My daughter, Motlalepula, bids me farewell after I gave her away to Monde Twala at their wedding in 2002. *Photo courtesy of the author.*

With Selema at the party following the Carnegie Hall performance on my sixty-fourth birthday, April 4, 2003 (above). *Photo courtesy of the author.*

Paul Simon also helped me celebrate my sixty-fourth birthday at the concert in Carnegie Hall (right). *Photo by Stephanie Berger.*

Elinam and I visited with Madiba, the "grand old man" of my country, who has the biggest, most loving heart in the world. *Photo by Kofi Asante (Nana Bediatuo).*

At our farm, one hundred kilometers west of Johannesburg, with Elinam and our two sons, Adam and Patrick. *Photo courtesy of the author.*

food for the ears and feet, a magical sound. With his band still playing, Fela would walk offstage, go across the street to change clothes, eat, or frolic, but they would just keep on playing. On his return he would pick up from where he left off and repeat the routine over again. I rarely enjoyed playing music as I did with Fela's band. They were tighter than a flea's pussy, meaner than a broke-dick dog.

I had enjoyed playing so much that when Fela introduced me as "this na JJC, na JJD," and the people applauded while roaring with laughter, I kept saying, "Thank you! Thank you!" It was only later that one of the girls whom I had met through Chuchu Horton, my banker friend in Liberia, was surprised that I had been so thankful. She was also a banker from a very upper-crust Sierra Leonean background, and held Fela in great contempt for his attitude toward women. "Hugh, 'JJC' and 'JJD' mean 'Johnny just come, Johnny just drop.' Johnny come lately. How could you let him make such fun of you in front of all those people?" She was truly upset, and I never saw her again. I knew Fela was having some innocent fun at my expense. When I asked him about the introduction, Fela said, "Hugh, I don't care how hip you are. When you get to a new place, you are a square until you pick up the slang and the local groove. That's a fact, my friend. Don't take it so seriously. How else are you going to learn our ways?" Fela was right.

One morning, Fela, Stewart, Fela's manager J.K., and I were smoking some serious spliffs in my hotel room. "Fela," I started, "I'm tired of having to write music down for the guys I've been playing with in the States and taking hours to explain the feel and the groove. I know that musicians in this part of the world all play mostly by ear, like you and me. I know that they will understand the grooves easily because of our similar beginnings in the way we were taught music. I would love to put together a good rhythm section of bass, drums, keyboards, guitars, and percussion to play with. I think you might help lead me in the right direction."

Fela said, "Hugh, I know exactly what you're looking for. Next week we embark on a West African tour, starting in Ghana. We leave here on Wednesday. Why don't you fly to Ghana and meet us in Accra? Check into the Intercontinental Hotel near the airport, and we will hook up with you from there. There is a fine band that is going to open for us. I think you will love them. If you don't, maybe we will have better luck in the next country after that." We agreed.

When we got to Accra, Ghana, Fela met us at the airport with a Lebanese dude by the name of Faisal Helwani. After checking into the Intercontinental Hotel, we went to Fela's evening show. The outdoor venue was packed to the rafters by the time the opening band, Hedzoleh Soundz, took the stage. They were dressed in traditional, stylized kente cloth and batakari outfits, with fancy boots also made out of kente. Lipuma played the pennywhistle and small hand drums, Morton played the tenor hand drums, and Okyerema Asante played about a dozen master drums mounted on wooden stands next to a conga drum. He was beating the hell out of them with two hoe-shaped sticks with hammer-like tips. He wore a Viking-style hat of animal horns. Salas played bass drum, high hat, and snare. He had all kinds of gourds of different sizes in place of tom-toms. Stanley Todd played the bass guitar, Jagger Nii Botchway, the guitar. They sang traditional chants with a modern highlife flair. They blew all kinds of whistles, and beat the shit out of the drums and all kinds of cowbells and percussion toys, creating a joyful mélange of the medieval and the contempo-rary. Their sense of fashion, a cross between 1970s disco haute couture and eth-nic Ghanaian royal garb, had a happy and humorous look to it. Their music, too, had a comedic flair—joyful, intense, and wild, sometimes very soft and then suddenly loud again. They blew us all away. Fela and Faisal, the band man-ager, came and sat next to me. Faisal asked, "What do you think, Hugh?"

Mesmerized, I replied, "I would love to play with this band."

"It's settled, then. I *thought* you would love this group," Fela said, then turned to Faisal. "I'm leaving Hugh in your hands."

Fela left the next day for the next stop on his tour, while Stewart and I stayed and met with Faisal at his Napoleon Club/bar/residence in the suburb of Osu. It was decided that I would spend the month of August in Ghana working with the band. Stewart would leave for Los Angeles and then return to Ghana the first week of September. We would then all go back to Lagos to record.

By the second week of rehearsals, I was conversant with Hedzoleh Soundz's repertoire, and was performing with them nightly at the Napoleon Club. I began to teach them some South African songs at rehearsals and began singing in Twi, Fanti, Ga, Ewe, and Hausa, the five Ghanaian languages they used. It was a joyful baptismal process. Even with the tight schedule, I still found time to make new friends among Accra's music lovers and hang out with some of the South African community in Accra. Stokely passed through Accra in tran-sit to Uganda, and passed on my mail from Guinea. Among the many letters was one from Jabu. She said that if I wanted to cultivate our relationship fur-ther, she would welcome it and I should call when I returned to New York. It made me feel good that she felt that way about me.

At the beginning of September, Stewart returned to Ghana and we flew down to Lagos. The band drove down with Faisal. Fela had arranged recording time at EMI Studios in the Apapa neighborhood of Lagos. Because we had jelled so well as a unit in Ghana, our recording sessions were smooth. Stewart engineered the recording, and after three days we had completed the project. We spent our nights at Fela's African Shrine, where I had a chance to sit in with his incredible band once again. Eventually we bade farewell to Hedzolah Soundz, who returned to Accra. Stewart and I then caught a flight for Monrovia. President "Speedy" Tolbert and his delegation were among the passengers on the Lagos-to-Liberia leg. It was a jovial flight until we ran into bad weather over Liberia. Rejecting advice to divert our course and land in Abidjan, Ivory Coast, the president instead ordered the pilots to continue to Liberia, saying, "We are in God's hands. He will see us through if He so deems." No one was more outraged than Milton Greaves, the president's personal secretary and one of my closest Monrovian drinking buddies, who had sent the note to "Speedy" suggesting that we divert to Abidjan. Sitting in the same row with Stewart and me, where we had been happily throwing down triple whiskies, his light-skinned complexion had changed to the same crimson as Stewart's. I must have been blue in the face from the fear of death. We were all shit-scared and pissed off at the president, especially the non-Liberian passengers, who felt that Tolbert did not have any rights over their lives. We were all fastened very tightly to our seats as the plane rollercoastered up and down with lightning bolts flaring all around us. After nine gut-wrenching, turbulent attempts to land in the electrical storm, we landed safely at Roberts Field airport on the tenth try. Some of the passengers wiped tears of terror and joy from their eyes. We were all so relieved that we even forgot how pissed off we had been with President Tolbert, who disembarked to a brass-band fanfare, a hero's welcome, and a throng of government officials, army and police officers, who applauded him for more than ten minutes while he smiled as he waved a white handkerchief high above his head. Stewart and I cursed him under our breath.

Stewart returned to the States with the completed mixes of the music we had recorded with Hedzoleh Soundz in Lagos, to see if Herb Alpert was still interested.

At the beginning of December, I went back from Liberia to Ghana after Stewart called to say Herb Alpert had offered some ideas to enhance the product, but Stewart was not keen on Herb's suggestions. Instead he had made a deal for Chisa to release the album with Bob Krasnow's Blue Thumb Records.

We tightened our sound by performing nightly at the Napoleon, and then boarded a plane for Washington, D.C., on December 31, for a three-month America tour. The album was called *Hugh Masekela Introducing Hedzoleh Soundz,* and the key songs on it were the catchy "Rekpete," an old fisherman highlife folk song, which is a sing-along all over West Africa, and "Languta," an old Shangaan/Tsonga folk melody from the northern part of South Africa about the dangers of going from the rural areas to seek a life in the big city of Johannesburg where you were likely to get defrauded, mugged, burgled, or conned out of everything you have. The rest of the songs were old Ghanaian folk favorites that I learned from the band. It was hell trying to sing in the languages, which were new to me, but in the end I got it all right, and it was a pure joy to play with this band. The percussionists were so powerful that I never had to think about the rhythm and time; I just sailed over the grooves with my horn. It was music heaven.

On January 3, 1974, Blue Thumb Records, in association with the Embassy of Ghana, launched our album at the Sheraton Hotel in Washington, D.C. Stewart flew in from Los Angeles with Bob Krasnow and Gary Stromberg, who would become our public relations man for many years to come. My sister Barbara, who was still an English professor at Rutgers University, came for the launch. We opened to a sold-out reception at The Cellar Door in Georgetown. The crowds were knocked out by the group. No African group had ever come to the States with such a genuinely traditional repertoire, mixed with guitar and trumpet solos and flavored with jazz, rhythm and blues, and rock and roll. The singing ensembles were laced with atonal harmonies and chord progressions straight out of rural Ghana. The textures of our music were so new to the Western ear that we attracted many musicians, anthropologists, and critics who did not know just how to describe what we were doing. They were truly fascinated.

Both in Washington and New York, Ghanaian diplomats and other people from Ghana attended the shows, invited us to their homes for dinner, and gave wonderful receptions for us where many other diplomatic personnel from other countries were present. Bob Krasnow and Blue Thumb Records really laid out lavish receptions for us where champagne, whisky, and cognac flowed freely, not to mention the coke we blew behind closed doors. None of the band did coke except Faisal and bassist/guitarist Stanley Todd, whom Stewart and I adopted as a kid brother. Stanley had real movie-star looks, and the women in the audiences screamed every time he soloed or was introduced. He was the heartthrob of the group.

We had asked the percussionists in the band to let us hold most of their money in safekeeping until the end of the tour, but they refused. On our first New York night they left their Broadway hotel with pockets filled with money to solicit women. That same night all five of them were robbed of more than ten thousand dollars when the hookers they were with fleeced them after spiking their drinks.

Faisal Helwani, the band's manger, and his sidekick-cum-bodyguard Roger "Al Capone" came on tour with us. We were expecting them to return to Ghana following the shows in New York, but they made plans to stay for the whole three months of the tour. We explained that we could not afford the extra expenses, as we were playing mostly clubs and the group had not yet built a name for itself. We eventually persuaded Faisal to send Al Capone back, but Faisal refused to go anywhere without his group. We had heated arguments with Faisal about his refusal to leave. He accused us of trying to steal Hedzoleh Soundz from under his nose and insisted that if he left, they would leave too. There was a very unpleasant atmosphere between us and the stubborn manager, whom the group detested with a passion anyway, something for which he blamed Stewart and me, accusing us of poisoning their minds against him. We finally relented and took Faisal everywhere with us, deciding to drop the acrimony and enjoy his company. He was actually an extremely funny person. We did about eight concerts where we opened for the Pointer Sisters. All the performances along the East Coast were sold out, and the audiences' reception was really enthusiastic. We played the Fillmore in San Francisco, where the flower children and rock fans gave us a tumultuous reception. The Bay Area audiences turned out to be the most receptive of our entire tour.

Our performance at L.A.'s Troubadour Club was attended by many of our old friends, including David Crosby and Stephen Stills, Peter Fonda, Dennis Hopper, the Crusaders, Stevie Wonder, Minnie Ripperton, and Alan Pariser. Los Angeles musicians, movie stars, and sports celebrities like Wilt Chamberlain, Kareem Abdul Jabbar, and O.J. Simpson all turned up to catch Hedzoleh Soundz. It was a star-studded night and a fabulous reception, but unfortunately it was our last performance of the tour. It was over for now.

In Los Angeles, Stewart and I moved into a mansion out in Brentwood, next to Pacific Palisades. Faisal was our houseguest while the rest of the group stayed in a hotel. When it was time for the band to return to Ghana, they refused to go. Faisal had literally owned the lives of most of the band members back home. They depended on him to put food on their tables. Fearing his

close friendship with the country's president, they thought he might just retal-
iate for the disrespect they had subjected him to during the entire tour. They
suspected that he might influence the military head of state, General Kutu
Acheampong, to punish them with imprisonment. The only people Faisal did
not have such a hold on back home were percussionist/master drummer
Okeyerema Asante, who came from the Ashanti Royal House of Koforidua,
guitarist Nii Jagger Botchway, another royal member of Accra's Ga aristocracy,
and Stanley Todd, a fairly well-off mulatto musician who was also one of
Faisal's close friends. Faisal tried to reason with the band, but they told him to
kiss their asses. He blamed us for spoiling them. We tried to explain that in the
United States nobody had personal ownership of another human being. When
he returned to Ghana, Faisal called a press conference, saying I had stolen his
band and that he would never allow me in the country again without making
sure I was imprisoned.

In the spring of 1974, I went into the studio with Hedzoleh Soundz to do a second album, on which we were joined by two members of the Crusaders, Joe
Sample on the piano and Stix Hooper on drums. It turned out beautifully and
contained the songs "Stimela," "In the Marketplace," "African Secret Society,"
and "Been Such a Long Time Gone," all of which have since become classics
and audience favorites. Gary Stromberg, our publicist, named the album *I Am
Not Afraid*. Our album became popular within the industry, but did not gener-
ate many sales. Blue Thumb had promised to support the band for the three-
month tour and no longer. The tour was over, and Stewart and I could not
sustain the band without gigs. We suggested that they return to Ghana and
then come back to the States when the album began generating radio play and
sales, which would not happen for at least three months. They refused. They
were staying in America, and had no intention of going back to be harassed by
Faisal. The guys took their instruments and, with the help of some friends
from Ghana, applied for asylum in the states. They also had the Musician's
Union Local 47 of Los Angeles sue us for $47,000 on some kind of bullshit
technicality. We paid the money. It was the last we heard from most of the
Hedzoleh Soundz guys.

Stanley Todd stayed with Stewart and me, but the rest took off. What had
begun as a wonderful pilgrimage back to Africa had very unfortunately ended
up in a very embarrassing shambles. Being back in the States with a group that
was so unique and greatly admired was like sweet revenge after I had left the

country with my tail between my legs. But with the breakup of the group because of factors beyond my control, I was feeling very stupid. The positive outcome of my pilgrimage was that I learned a great deal about Liberia, Guinea, Ghana, Nigeria, and Zaire in the three years I had been away from America. I had learned the French language, the Liberian slang, and the pidgin English of Nigeria and Ghana, as well as the customs and culture of the countries and a tremendous amount about their different styles of music. I came to understand the history and politics of the region, but most of all, I had made a whole lot of new friends, poor, rich, powerful, talented, spiritual, humble, learned, enterprising, and extremely beautiful, an education I could have never picked up at a school or in a book. So I was not discouraged. I was armed with new knowledge. I had crazy but good friends and had established a new foothold in the music industry. As an artist, I was once again commanding some respect, both in the industry and in my own heart.

15

ONE DAY AT THE BLUE THUMB RECORDS OFFICE, Stewart picked up a copy of the *New York Times* and saw an article about an upcoming heavyweight championship fight between Muhammad Ali and George Foreman. Hyped as the "Rumble in the Jungle" by new boxing promoter Don King, it was to take place in Zaire later in the year. King, who had served time in a Cleveland prison for having caused a death in a street fight, was a close friend of a man named Lloyd Price, and had roped him into the Zaire event to handle the entertainment aspects of the "Rumble in the Jungle." Lloyd Price had had major hit records in the early 1960s with "Stagger Lee" and "Personality," which had shot him to the pinnacle of rhythm and blues success. King felt he was just the right man for the job after having known him since the beginning of his entertainment career. When I was hanging out with Johnny Nash and Danny Sims in the mid-1960s, I had met Lloyd Price on many occasions, and over the years we had come to know each other quite well.

On our way out of the Blue Thumb office, all Stewart wanted to talk about was the Rumble in the Jungle as he, Krasnow, and I headed for Dan Tana's restaurant next to the Troubador Club on Santa Monica Boulevard, at the edge of Beverly Hills; it was our favorite watering hole. At our regular booth deep inside the restaurant, Stewart kept talking about the Rumble. "This is a great chance to have a festival of the greatest artists from America, Africa, and the host country, man. The film that could be made of the festival and Ali and Foreman preparing for the fight would be fantastic. The whole thing could be called 'Three Days of Music and Fighting' [a reference to the Woodstock Festival of 1969], and we should see if Lloyd Price would be interested in our helping him to put such an event together. Our advantage is that you lived in Zaire, Hugh, you know the top musicians there, like Franco and Rochereau, who'd put it together, and Lloyd is your friend, man. He'll listen to you. You should track him down and give him a call."

At first I wasn't too keen on the idea. I was still reeling from the breakup of Hedzoleh Soundz. Stanley and I had been talking a lot about getting Asante and Jagger to go with us to Washington, D.C., where the three of them knew some good musicians from Ghana and Nigeria. We were planning to hook up with some of them and put a group together so that we could go out on the road and promote the new album we had just made. Stanley's drummer brother, Frankie, was also in D.C.

I was rather surprised that Krasnow was impressed with Stewart's idea and actually thought it was worth following through. The next morning I called Lloyd from Krasnow's office and proposed our idea to him. He loved it. He said he was in a meeting then with Don King and Hank Schwartz, the owner of the broadcast rights and King's partner. He put King on the telephone. "Hugh Masekela, I have followed your career for a long time and I think that you are an essential brother. You have helped to inspire many of us to look in the direction of the Motherland to retrace our origins and to reconnect with our roots. I have no doubt that you would be a strategic participant in our effort to put together a festival to go along with the greatest fight of the century. As black brothers, armed with our different expertise in our chosen fields, we would capture the attention and the imagination of the entire world with our joint initiative. Billions of people will be watching this historical event. Let us join hands, my brother, and shake up the world. Any good friend of Lloyd's is a friend of mine. You are welcome to join this great initiative in the history of the world. Now tell me, my brother, your idea is going to need financing. What kind of backing do you have available to make our vision become a reality?"

I said, "Don, I'm sitting here with the president of Blue Thumb Records, who is very enthusiastic about this project." Don broke into a happy chuckle, "I love talking to presidents. Put him on the phone."

The following evening, Krasnow, Stewart, and I took the red-eye flight to New York, where we had set up a meeting with King, Schwartz, and Price. "You get the money to put on this festival and do a film of it. You give me ten percent of your budget and the profits, and you got yourself a deal," Don King told us. We all shook hands and asked them for two weeks and we would come back to them with the money. At that point Krasnow said to us that that was as far as he could go with the project. He had gotten us in the door. Now he had to go back to Los Angeles and run his record company.

Alan Pariser, from the Detroit family that owned the Solo Cups fortune, had put his trust-fund money into several enterprises that yielded very good returns on his investments. Pariser was fascinated with the Zaire project and formed a company with Stewart and me called the Ace Company.

In Liberia, I had been talking to Steve Tolbert, the president's brother, who had been named minister of finance because of his outstanding business background and international reputation. As far as we knew, he had made his money legitimately, beginning in the rubber business and then branching out. Some people thought his fortunes might have been ill-gotten, but then we came from the record business, one of the most exploitative and corrupt businesses in the world. We were about to get into bed with people from the highest ranks in the boxing industry, another business that was not too famous for honesty and fair play. As we looked around us, we saw very few businesses that were angelic. And not being angels ourselves, we did not care too much where the money came from—as long as it wasn't connected to apartheid. We would have taken it from the devil if we could find his dirty ass. We just wanted to be part of the Rumble in the Jungle. We knew it was going to be a huge task, and that we'd have to deal with major egos. This we were very much prepared for. What we did not anticipate was what a fucking nightmare it would finally turn out to be.

Steve Tolbert's portfolio included a plethora of interests ranging from shipping, fishing, banking, and food packing to international real estate. He was also interested in starting a recording company. He loved the idea of the festival, and suggested that Stewart and I fly to Liberia to discuss the project in detail. Tolbert's Liberian lawyer Steve Dunbar, his British business manager Ian Bradshaw, and a couple of secretaries were present at the meeting. After a few hours he decided he indeed loved the idea. "How much will it cost me?" he asked. "Two million dollars," we told him. Everything was agreed. Ace, Alan Pariser, Stewart, and I would be the production company. Bradshaw would fly to New York to do the final negotiations with King, Schwartz, and Price. When everything was signed, we could begin operations and put the music festival together.

The negotiations with Don King, Hank Schwartz, and Lloyd Price were very lengthy, but Steve Dunbar and Ian Bradshaw were tough with the fight promoter's team. By the time we finished haggling over the numerous little details, King was not so warm anymore toward Stewart and me. He had gotten the ten percent he demanded, but when King is not in total control, he has a tendency to become unnecessarily acrimonious and picky. After two weeks of negotiations that often went late into the night, a deal was finally sealed. We shook hands with King's team, and in the St. Regis Hotel's bar, we raised our whisky glasses and drank a toast to a successful collaboration. Bradshaw, Dunbar, Stewart, and I flew down to the Bahamas, where one of Tolbert's offshore companies was registered. We signed the final papers with his bankers so that money would be released to our company for funding, filming, and recording the festival. We popped a few bottles of Dom Pernignon with the bankers and went to bed laughing and backslapping. We had pulled it off.

Alan Pariser joined us in New York, and we went into business. We took some office space in the same building that King and Schwartz were working out of, and hired two secretaries and a runner. Alan, Stewart, and I moved into three suites at the Wyndham Hotel, four blocks up from our offices and directly across 58th Street from the Plaza Hotel. We worked from morning until past midnight on this festival. It was exciting, but very hard work. The festival began to take on an aura of glamour that was attracting more interest than the fight itself. Don King insisted that he be present at all the interviews with the media, where he could always be counted on to hog the microphone. "This is going to be the greatest show on earth. This festival will be greater than anything that was seen at the Monterey or Woodstock festivals. It's going to be the mother of all festivals, and yes indeed, it's gonna take place in the Motherland as a prelude to the fight of the century. I have placed the production in the able hands of Lloyd Price, Stewart Levine, and Hugh Masekela, and they are putting together the world's greatest artists. This is a spectacle, an extravaganza, a blockbuster that should not be missed by anybody. Billions throughout the world via satellite will see it. Yes sir, Don King put it all together with His Excellency the president of Zaire, the honorable Mobuto Sese Seko. Yes sir, Don King, a little black boy from Cleveland, putting together the greatest spectacle on earth, make no mistake about it!"

Among the artists who committed to the show was the elder statesman of Africa's Paris-based musicians, Manu Dibango of "Soul Makossa" fame, a vocal-instrumental Afro-beat rap hit that went to number one on the charts at

the beginning of the 1970s. "Makossa" was a major dance-floor craze. We had
the Fania All-Stars, which featured the cream of Latino-Salsa musicians such as
flutist Johnny Pacheco, percussionist Ray Barretto, keyboardist Larry Harlow,
Celia Cruz, the queen of salsa vocal artistry, trombonist Willie Colon, and
vocal master Cheo Feliciano. We booked more than thirty other acts, including Bill Withers, the Spinners, Sister Sledge, Miriam Makeba, the Pointer
Sisters, B.B. King, Etta James, and the Crusaders.

We traveled to Los Angeles and tried to get Stevie Wonder. I'd first met
Stevie in 1966 at the Queens Road house I lived in with Susie and Stewart. He
had come over with Martha and the Vandellas, with whom he had become
tight when he was a kid and Martha worked as a secretary at Motown. I had
just recorded Stevie's "Loving You Has Made My Life Sweeter Than Ever,"
which was a big hit for the Four Tops. He was curious about me, and arranged
a meeting. Stevie sang us song after song at my baby grand piano, and later on
regaled us with funny stories and engaged in spirited boxing matches with all
three Vandellas. He amazed us by blocking all their punches. We took to each
other very quickly, and he was keen to learn the Xhosa language of clicks. It
really fascinated him. The following year I opened for him at Lincoln Center.
Over the years, Stevie and I would become fairly good acquaintances.

We traveled to try to get him on the Zaire bill, but it turned into a hand-in-
hat opera because his two most recent albums, *Talking Book* and the double
album that followed, *Songs in the Key of Life,* had been such blockbusters. He
was now surrounded by a large entourage outside of his brother Calvin, who
always guided him around and who was on very good terms with me. The
stumbling block was Vogoda, Stevie's manager, who had one of the nastiest
dispositions I have ever encountered. Sarcastic, cynical, and dismissive, he
wouldn't let us begin talking to Stevie, who kept us at bay by playing us tape
after tape of his countless beautiful compositions. Stewart and I became very
frustrated. Vogoda just wouldn't laugh, regardless of how funny the situation
was. We followed Stevie to his house in Beverly Hills, his offices in Hollywood,
and his studio in the Wilshire neighborhood. He just kept encouraging me to
"come over and let's talk about it some more," but nothing came of it. But I
still loved Stevie.

He invited me to a party one night where Richard Pryor was also a guest,
and they talked so much funny shit we just could not stop laughing. I'd first
met Richard Pryor during my engagements at the Village Gate when he was
appearing across the street at the Whiskey à Go Go. At the time he was still

doing hilarious takeoffs on nursery stories like "Rumpelstiltskin" and "Rapunzel." We would run across Thompson Street to catch each other's performances, forming a mutual admiration society of sorts. Offstage, Richard was very shy and quiet around people he didn't know. He moved to Los Angeles around the same time I did, and turned out to be an old friend of our pianist Charlie Smalls. He was a regular at our Whisky à Go Go gigs and just cutting his teeth on the L.A. scene. Now, six years later, Richard and Stevie had changed considerably and I could hardly remember how they used to be.

After a week of giving us the runaround, Stevie and his manager promised to get back to us. We never heard from them. That week we also tried to get Barry White, who was at the highest point in his career. Barry was on the eve of a major American and European tour. He couldn't make it to the Rumble concert, but he was a real gentleman about it. Still, we flew back to New York empty-handed. Lloyd, Stewart, and I had several meetings with Cecil Franklin, Aretha's brother, to try to arrange for Aretha to play the festival. He also led us on—he did a lot of blow with Stewart and me, but ultimately Aretha would not be coming to Zaire. There were never any real reasons given, nor was money ever the problem. Lloyd and I went to see Gamble and Huff about trying to get the O'Jays on board. They were cooperative and even got Harold Levert to meet with us. He expressed interest, but in the end his enthusiasm fizzled into thin air.

James Brown was very keen to go to Zaire, a country he'd visited before. But he spun out dozens of unexpected demands and conditions. His manager, Mr. Bobbit, was an old friend of Lloyd Price and an extremely amicable negotiator. But his deep respect for, and fear of, James Brown always came through when we met with him. "Well, the King insists that he be the first to board the plane with his principal band members, and he must also be the first to disembark at Kinshasa airport after the plane lands in Zaire. The King wants to have the majority of the seats in the first-class cabin of the aircraft for himself and the principal members of his group. Furthermore, Mr. Brown wants a Mercedes-Benz limousine to be made available to him on a twenty-four-hour basis. He has to have an audience with President Mobutu, and he demands a luxury suite in the hotel, with adjoining rooms for his valet and master of ceremonies. Finally, Mr. Brown's entourage will be continuing on to Gabon after his Kinshasa performance. Because of this, the King insists that his equipment for his Gabon performance be accommodated on the plane that will carry us to Zaire. Mr. Brown also requests that he be paid one hundred thousand dollars for the Rumble in the Jungle performance." James Brown was at the peak of his career, and we needed him badly because in Africa he was the most popular American performer. Although we thought some of the demands rather unreasonable, we agreed to all of the terms.

Through Ray Lofaro, we hooked up with filmmaker Leon Gast, who agreed to direct the movie of the project. Leon selected twelve film crews, mostly black, to cover the happenings. All the print media were fascinated with the project, and we had journalists bombarding our offices around the clock. Quincy Troupe was assigned by *Rolling Stone* to come down with us. Hunter S. Thompson would come on board later for the same magazine.

With the contracted lineup of entertainers beginning to attract more media coverage than the fight itself, Don King began to draw much closer to our office operation, and took us out for drinks every evening, making sure that we reported every new development to him. He picked up all the food and drink bills and literally began to tell us how the entire festival production should be handled. Miles Davis was very keen to be in the festival, but I was the only one who favored his inclusion; everyone else gave him the thumbs-down. I hadn't seen Miles in almost seven years. He had sent his manager's personal assistant to talk to me. She was very determined, and came around to the office at the end of almost every day. She told me that Miles was very disappointed that he could not come along. I was so overloaded with work that I hardly found any time to go and explain the situation to him personally. However, Miles was going through his most avant-garde, ultramodern, impressionistic era, and the general consensus was that his type of music at the time would have been totally out of context with the festival's R&B and mainstream jazz, ethnic, and urban-African theme.

A few months earlier I had worked for a week with La Belle at the Apollo Theater on a Curtis Mayfield show. The ladies wanted to be part of the festival. I thought it was a fine idea, but was overruled by Lloyd Price and company. Patti La Belle never seems to have forgiven me for passing on them at the time.

Don King's partner Hank Schwartz invited Stewart and me to fly to Zaire to check out Kinshasa's infrastructure, interact with those Zaireans we would be working with, and examine the accommodations for the thousands of people we were expecting to come. Stewart and I passed through Monrovia to give Steve Tolbert a report on his investment. He was pleased with the progress. This festival was to be his entrée into the entertainment business.

Our Air Afrique flight from Liberia to Zaire resembled a freight train that makes frequent stops. We boarded about nine in the morning and stopped in Banjul, Gambia; Dakar, Senegal; Freetown, Sierra Leone; Accra, Ghana; Lome, Togo; Cotonou, Benin; Lagos, Nigeria; Douala, Cameroon; Libreville, Gabon; and finally Kinshasa. Each stop was for an hour, and all passengers had to disembark. Stewart and I drank cognac and beer at every airport bar. We finally arrived at our hotel around 2:00 a.m. After showering and changing clothes, Stewart and I hit the Un, Deux, Troix Club in Matonge. Feeling no pain, we grabbed a trumpet and saxophone from two of the band members and jammed with the TP OK Jazz Orchestra until near dawn.

Through Hank Schwartz we connected with a dapper young official named Lunkunku, who took us to all the available hotels, the stadium, the government transportation authorities, and the ministry of culture. We planned to have music, dance, and drum ensembles performing in the streets every day during the month of September leading up to the fight. These troupes would be strategically placed throughout the city, beginning at the airport and at the hotels. In Kinshasa, I also ran into Nga Machema, my South African guerrilla-fighter friend, who was recovering from a shrapnel wound incurred during one of his military missions. He was going to be in Kinshasa for the rest of the year, so we set him up as our head of security, another logistics problem solved. We returned to New York in possession of all the important details we would need to make the festival a success.

The months I spent in New York leading up to the fight gave Jabu and me time to rekindle our romance. She worked as a librarian at the *New York Times,* which was not far from my hotel. Sometimes we had major disagreements and she would take off in a huff. We wouldn't see each other for a few days, and then I would call to apologize. I could be careless with her sometimes, and she could be moody and temperamental. Things could be rocky, but I was happy to be with her again.

Being across the street from the Plaza Hotel, we would run into some of Alan Pariser's big-time friends who would be staying there from time to time, like Eric Clapton, Ringo Starr, and some of the Rolling Stones. Alan also had a large circle of friends in the music world whom he met when they first came to Los Angeles to play and needed to score something for the head. Later they not only became close friends, but would also depend on him for business decisions in connection with property and car purchases or financial investments and legal representation. Pariser was an expert in these matters. One evening

Mick Jagger, Ron Wood, and Carol Cole, one of Nat King Cole's daughters, came to visit Alan while we were getting high in his suite. Jagger was keen to meet Don King, this new giant of boxing. Alan called King's suite. Lloyd answered the phone. He said we should all come up and have a drink with them, because they were having fun with some babes. When Lloyd opened the door to Don's suite, we were shocked to see Lloyd and Don in their birthday suits. There were at least four very well endowed, nude black amazons in there with them, lounging on armchairs and couches. We were shocked at first, but our hosts seemed very laid back and relaxed. We declined the drinks we were offered and kept standing while Don's party were all sitting cross-legged. Jagger came down hard on Don King, telling him how disgusted he was to find some-one of his stature receiving guests he didn't even know in a state of undress, surrounded by sleaze, and that King should be ashamed of himself. King hit back, recalling some of the scandals he had read in the press about Jagger. Jagger said the tabloids made shit up, but this was disgustingly real, and people like King didn't have a leg to stand on when condemning musicians while they were carrying on in that manner. While the debate was going on, Carol Cole pulled me out of there and we ended up in my suite. I never found out how the argument ended.

Six weeks before the festival, Alan Pariser and I flew to Kinshasa to begin preparations for the onslaught of artists. We practically took over the Intercontinental Hotel. Lunkunku helped us prepare to accommodate the needs of the hordes of artists and technicians who were due to arrive soon. Nga had secured troops from the Zairean army as security. Last-minute reno-vations were being made on the stadium and many portions of the city. The whole place was abuzz with excitement. Chip Beresford Monck, who had once been Miriam's tour manager and had since become a top lighting, sound, and stage technician for mammoth rock tours, arrived with his crews to begin preparations for the events. Leon Gast also sent half of his film crews for reconnaissance and preproduction. Lloyd Price's assistants Rudy Lucas and Nate Adams arrived two weeks before the festival. It had been agreed between Steve Tolbert's Festival Productions representatives Steve Dunbar and Ian Bradshaw, Don King and Lloyd Price's office, and our company Ace, that a ten-dollar charge to see the stadium performance would help toward recouping Tolbert's investment. However, people in Kinshasa were hardly buying any tickets. President Mobutu told King and Schwartz that ordinary Zaireans could not afford ten dollars. Not even one dollar.

Another plan was that Stewart and our New York office staff would assist in logistics coordination. We wanted him to color-label the artists' luggage according to their assigned hotel. That way, when they disembarked we could escort them to their assigned vehicles and on to their hotels. It was chaos from the beginning. James Brown arrived late to the airport in New York with tons of his equipment because he was scheduled to continue onto Gabon after the festival. The plane was overloaded, so the pilot asked all passengers to sit in economy class. Brown refused, protesting, "I am the King," much to the discomfort of the other passengers. During a stopover in Madrid, Bill Withers apparently purchased a large dagger and put it to Brown's throat, forcing him to sit in economy. When the plane landed, Brown insisted on being the first to deplane, again citing his kingship. With all the difficult conditions he had presented to us, plus the overweight equipment and the trouble he had caused his fellow passengers, I was totally disgusted with his demands at this point. However, all we could do was watch patiently as he walked slowly onto the top of the stairs that had been rolled up to the aircraft for the disembarkation. With pageant winners Miss Ali and Miss Foreman on each arm, he smiled triumphantly and waved at the large, screaming crowd lining the airport building's observation deck, then slowly walked down the stairway. Nga, Rudy, Nate, Alan, and I watched with amazement as "the King" acted like a true brat. Exhausted as we were, we could not help but laugh. We had placed five different groups of performers on the tarmac to welcome the arriving group. Voodoo drummers and dancers, a traditional choir, a group of forest pygmies, a woman's traditional healers' ensemble, and Stukas, the leading Kwassa-Kwassa dance band, were all strutting and stomping their stuff. By now all 320 passengers were exhausted, and most of them were high. When the doors of the plane opened, they couldn't wait for James Brown to finish doing his "King" thing. They spilled onto the tarmac like mad people. Pacheco, the music director of the Fania All-Stars, rushed toward the Stukas band, pulled out his flute, and started jamming. Mayhem followed, and everyone was dancing. All we could do—Nga, his soldiers, our office personnel, the guides, the bus and car drivers—was to just look on in despair as our elaborate plans went up in smoke. It took us all day and night to sort out who would stay where and then sort out the luggage and the artists' equipment cases.

Once everyone was settled in, the mood was electric. The whole city was reverberating with music. Crowds followed Muhammad Ali and George Foreman wherever they went. For all the marijuana smokers, Nga had arranged for coconut shells to be filled with pot and placed in all the relevant rooms with rolling papers beside them. Many people had brought their own blow. We also had a considerable amount of cocaine stashed away for some of our staff that were users. Every morning after breakfast Ali's corner man, Bundini Brown, and one of his sparring partners knocked on my door to hit on me for some blow. "Come on, Hughie, give up the fucking blow." In general, most people were pleasantly bent out of shape most of the time.

The artists had a whole week free before the festival, and they spent it mostly on guided tours we had arranged for them to go around Kinshasa taking in the sights like the food and arts markets. With their Polaroid cameras they were able to barter for arts and crafts with the instant photographs, with which the Zaireans were truly fascinated. They loved to pose. The nightlife in Kinshasa was like manna from heaven for the artists, and they went club-hopping until dawn, dancing their asses off and making good friends with the local citizens, who were naturally hospitable but had also been exhorted by President Mobutu to welcome the guests with extra enthusiasm. The hotels were all five-star, and the performers were having the times of their lives, with the production company footing the entire bill. I was sitting at poolside one day having lunch with my co-workers when Don King joined us and began to accuse me of being an Uncle Tom.

"I am really disappointed in you, Hugh Masekela," he said. "You should be running this whole show, and instead you're letting that white boy Levine order you around."

Don was frustrated, mainly because Foreman was injured and the fight was postponed for more than a month. The festival had now taken center stage with the media. But I didn't like him taking it out on me. I went off on him. "In the first place, you have been doing all the fucking ordering around and always interfering with everything we are trying to do here. I don't know what the fuck you're talking about, Don, but don't you talk like that to me here in Africa, man. This is not fucking Cleveland! I will have you fucking wasted, man!" I was with Nga, who got even more infuriated with Don's attitude. It took two days for me to regain my cool. I never spoke to Don King again, and he kept away from me.

Steve Tolbert, who had flown down in his private jet, was infuriated with everybody, and King put all the blame on me. Steve was upset over the decision to make the concerts free to the public, because now he would have to wait till the movie from the event and the festival recordings were released before he could recoup his investment. The concerts themselves were a joyful spectacle. The local groups were given priority to perform by the Zaire big shots, and many of the visiting artists' performance times were reduced. The Cameroon jazz saxophonist Manu Dibango and rhythm-and-blues queen Etta James did not even get to perform. All three concerts started at seven in the evening and went on until around four in the morning. The fact that my colleagues and I had enough supplies to stay high helped us to keep up with all the mayhem and over-the-top demands. Tempers were on the edge all around. B.B. King would not talk to me when I came to ask him to stand by for his performance. He just sat there and stared at me, pissed off for having been made to wait so long. When he finally went onstage, our staring competition and my begging him to come on had lasted over twenty minutes while the capacity crowd waited patiently.

At check-out time, so many people had been charging drinks and food to their rooms that the incidental costs totaled about $190,000. The day after the last concert, Ian Bradshaw, Steve Tolbert's business manager, flipped out and had Alan, Stewart, and me placed under house arrest in the hotel by Mobutu's people. Nga managed to get Alan out of there and onto the plane with the rest of the departing musicians. All the film was confiscated and sent to Mobutu's office. Miriam Makeba helped us get it released by convincing the president that the film and tapes were better off if they were sent back for processing, editing, and mixing so that they could generate funds to pay off the outstanding debts. If the film and tapes remained in the president's vault, then everybody would be the loser. The president, who had great respect for Miriam, gave in to her request. A few days later, Nga and I saw Stewart off. Ian Bradshaw had left the country in a huff, cussing us out, but nobody was interested in listening to his shit. Life had to go on. We felt bad about Tolbert's financial setback, but we were certain it would be repaid through the release of the film, music videos, and recordings. Big Black, whom we had brought along as a spiritual drummer for the music festival, remained behind in Ali's camp. Ali wanted to train to his drum rhythms.

All in all, the experience had been extremely educational—I certainly learned a lot about working under acute pressure and unreasonable demands. Working with government personnel, the military, boxing promoters, recording crews, film crews, thousands of artists, more than 200,000 music fans, print and broadcast media, hotel staff, stage crews, construction crews, and travel agents had demanded a great deal of calm, presence of mind, teamwork, and temper control, which was very difficult at times. I had made great friends with many Zaireans, especially musicians and government officials. For a change, I had been too preoccupied with work to frolic with the beautiful women, even though I did have my fair share under the circumstances.

I totally lost touch with Steve Tolbert, who lost his life the following year when his plane crashed in Liberia on one of his many business trips. Our relationship with Don King worsened. When we returned to America, he demanded an additional ten percent from us for the film and recording rights, but we told him to kiss our asses. When we got back to New York, we were hit with a court injunction from King on all the film and recordings we had done in Zaire. Leon Gast waited until the statute of limitations expired and then got producer David Sonnenberg to raise some capital for its completion. Twenty years after the event, *When We Were Kings*, Gast's film, won an Oscar for best feature documentary. What is funnier than everything, though, is how Leon Gast and Lloyd Price forgot that the money for the project came from Steve Tolbert because of *our* initiative and hustle. They claimed all the credit and never gave us any. Most sickening of all was Don King's arrogance and how he sabotaged everything of ours once we wouldn't let him have his way with us. Perhaps he was still steaming from the embarrassment Jagger had laid on him in New York. I have never seen the film and have not had any desire to do so.

The experience armed us to tackle any big project, and earned us a great deal of respect in the entertainment industry—although we came out of the project with no material wealth, we had managed to put together one of history's most memorable music spectacles.

16

WHEN STEWART AND I left Los Angeles to set up office operations in New York for the Zaire festival, we had just moved into a gigantic mansion on an estate in Brentwood, one of north Los Angeles's most luxurious suburbs. With Hedzoleh Soundz having disbanded, Stanley Todd, the group's leader and bassist, had been talking up some Ghanaian and Nigerian musicians he knew in D.C. that we could use to replace the deserters. Stanley was anxious to go there and start organizing them.

When we returned from Zaire, Stanley had moved to Washington, D.C., and begun rehearsing with the musicians there, along with Hedzoleh percussionist Asante and guitarist Jagger. Stanley had now switched to guitar, and Yaw Opoku was playing the bass. Rounding out the outfit was percussionist Guy Warren and Stanley's drummer brother Frankie Todd, both from Ghana, and Nigerians Adelaja Gboyega on keyboards and saxophonist/composer Julius Ekemode.

After closing up shop on the Rumble concert, I spent some time in New York with my sister Barbara. During this visit, I saw trumpeter Donald Byrd at Carnegie Hall. Byrd, a fellow Manhattan School of Music alumnus, was performing with his group from Howard University, the Blackbyrds, on a bill with the great poet-musician and singer Gil Scott Heron. Donald introduced me to producer/promoter/manager Bob Young of Charisma Productions, which had offices in the nation's capital. When I got to D.C., I stayed with Bob Young for a while and he helped set up rehearsal arrangements for our newly formed group; later I moved out to my own place next to Stanley and Frankie Todd in

Alexandria, Virginia. We gave our group the name OJAH, Nigerian slang for "very close friend," because we wanted to put the memory of Hedzoleh Soundz behind us and also avoid more accusations of theft from Faisal Helwani.

OJAH was a more African-urban-oriented unit, and like Hedzoleh, we all sang. *I Am Not Afraid,* which I recorded in 1974 with Hedzoleh and on which we were joined by the Crusaders' Joe Sample on piano and Stix Hooper on drums, was instrumental in shifting our style more toward a heavy mix of jazz, highlife, mbhaqanga, Congolese rhumba, and rhythm and blues. On it, we did the very first versions of "Stimela," the song I'd composed in Woodstock before heading off to Africa. "The Marketplace" was about meeting a beautiful young lady at her stall in Kinshasa's public marketplace and the wonderful romance that follows. It begins as a typical Congolese rhumba, and then shifts into a fast Soukous–Kwassa-Kwassa dance rhythm, the kind made popular by Franco and Rochereau's bands back when I first went to Zaire. "African Secret Society" was a lilting rhythm and bluesish rhumba about young girls who went to initiation schools in Liberia when I lived there. On graduating, they were paraded through the streets, their bodies painted with different colored ochre clay, layers of beads around their waists and necks and loincloths cut out of animal skin. On "Night in Tunisia," Dizzy Gillespie's classic jazz composition from the early 1950s, we did a fiery drum and percussion "mambo" style with avant-garde harmonics based on the contemporary jazz styles of Cecil Taylor and Ornette Coleman. It had a dark, eerie jungle voodoo feel to it. Joe Sample really enjoyed setting atonal, dissonant chord structures into the texture of the song. It felt very much like "ethnic Africa meets Harlem jazz on a dark, misty night in old New Orleans."

We had never played the songs from this album at concerts. We started to rehearse them with OJAH for our upcoming shows. The group was also preparing new songs like "Excuse Me Baby Please," a spirited, up-tempo, township mbhaqanga, brassy dance groove with horns screaming in the upper register, riffing guitars, a bouncing bass line, and flowing electric keyboards, with the percussion and drums laying down heavy rhythm, pumping on the second and fourth beats. It was a happy dance instrumental with a foot-tapping, thumping, stomping, hammering thud repeating over and over.

Another instrumental, "A Person Is a Sometime Thing," was a medium-tempo, heavy R&B groove with a happy unison horn melody reminiscent of the 1950s–1960s Horace Silver Quintets. Julius Ekemode and I played solos on all the instrumentals. "Ashiko," written by Ekemode, was a very catchy, repetitive, Yoruba-lyric, Afro-beat groove with jazzy horn and keyboard riffs, dancing congas, and African jembes. Ekemode sang the lead vocals, and the ensemble singing chants were a cross between Osibisa and Fela's vocals. "In the Jungle," an African highlife, rhythm-and-bluesy, medium-tempo vocal with me singing lead and the band answering "In the Jungle" on the chorus, was a funny parody about Tarzan beginning to lose control of his powers deep in the African bush, and the modern African citizen forcing him to go back where he came from. "Mama" was another Afro-beat dance groove with a very heavy Fela influence and stinging horn riffs. Bob Young got us a few local gigs in clubs around the Washington and Baltimore areas. Oscar Cohen, at Associated Booking Corporation, lined us up on a tour that would take us through Boston, New York, Philadelphia, and Atlanta to Pittsburgh, Detroit, Chicago, Albuquerque, Phoenix, Denver, and Boulder, then to Seattle, Portland, San Francisco, and finally Los Angeles.

In Los Angeles, Stewart informed me that Bob Krasnow had terminated our contract with Blue Thumb Records because we had taken too long to go on the road in support of the *I Am Not Afraid* album. But Stewart had just completed a successful negotiation with Neil Bogart, who had left Buddah Records to form his own Casablanca record label, to which he had already signed Parliament Funkadelic, led by George Clinton and Bootsy Collins, and the rock group KISS. Right away, OJAH went in the studio with Stewart producing once again. We recorded all the new songs we had been playing on the road; the session went fast because we had dug so heavily into them over the six months we had been rehearsing and performing. The band members were outstanding musicians, each one really excelling on his instrument. They were also very good singers, and we really sounded great together. The audiences loved the band, the women were especially infatuated with Stanley, Adelaja, Yaw, Guy, and Ekemode, who were all very good looking and athletically built. The women were always screaming their names from the audience and went crazy when I introduced them individually on the last song of every show. The album, *The Boy's Doin' It*, became quite popular.

When Stewart and I first went to Lagos, Fela had taken us to a performance of young singer/composer/pianist Johnny Haastrup, whose quartet played an Afro-beat style that was heavily influenced by highlife, jazz, R&B, and Yoruba folk music. He had the most beautiful voice and a great personality. We encouraged him to come to America and try to break into the music industry there because we were convinced that he would make it. Johnny came to California without the rest of his group and stayed with friends in Los Angeles and San Francisco. Alone, he was not able to project his unique style, nor was he able to find musicians from his country who could do his style of music justice. He returned to Nigeria and Ghana only to return to L.A. two months later with the assurance that there was a major demand for our music in those countries. He had already lined up venues, and if we gave him the word, he would hurry back to West Africa and begin promotion for the concerts. This news excited the band members, except for Ekemode.

With the exception of Yaw Opoku and Ekemode, the rest of our band was heavy into cocaine, marijuana, and booze. Our master drummer/percussionist, Asante, was not into coke but loved smoke and the band's favorite liquor, Jack Daniel's. We drank beer like mineral water. The band lived for music, women, and getting high. Given our three vices, it escaped our minds that Johnny's idea was not such a great plan after all. Neil Bogart found it hard to understand why we were so keen to travel to Africa, at a time when his company was trying to promote our album in the States. But nothing could be done to change our minds. We were going to Nigeria and Ghana, and that was final. In our euphoria, we justified our trip by insisting that the majority of the band had not been back home in many years and needed the pilgrimage as a much-needed morale booster. We argued that we would come back strengthened and energized. "But you are good enough as you are. Why not go after a year of touring? Then you will really have established yourself," both Stewart and Neil observed. We were adamant. We just had to go.

The second week of July, 1975, we arrived in Accra and checked into the Tesano Gardens Hotel amid major mudslinging by Faisal Helwani, who had been giving interviews in the press and on radio stations, denigrating and vilifying my name with charges that I stole Hedzoleh Soundz from him in the United States. Nothing materialized from Faisal's past threats, and we ended up spending a lot of time at his Napoleon Club residence, where he entertained us lavishly during the duration of our stay in Ghana. We also found that cocaine had made its way into West Africa and was readily available at extremely low prices. Although our concerts flopped, we had a hell of a good time in Accra. I was only happy that Neil Bogart and Stewart Levine were not there to witness the futility of the first leg of our trip—much against their advice.

On July 24, we left Accra for Lagos. Our plane was the last one allowed to land in the country. A military coup had just taken place in which another soldier, Murtallah Mahomed, replaced Yakubu Gowon, who had been the head of Nigeria's military government. Our instruments were impounded along with our other equipment, and we were sent into the city to fend for ourselves. It was clear that no tour was going to take place while the country was in a state of emergency. To kill time, the band hung out a lot at Fela's home and his African Shrine club. Fela had just come up with a concoction called "Felagoro," which was a freshly squeezed marijuana paste extracted from the choicest flowers of the weed and bottled; one teaspoon completely blew you away, and you had to wash it down with freshly squeezed orange juice because it was very thick in texture, extremely bitter-tasting, and powerful. Fela warned us that one teaspoon was enough, but Stanley Todd vowed that he could take two teaspoons and nothing would happen to him. We were walking out of Fela's yard, when Stanley keeled forward and blacked out, landing face-first on the ground.

When the coup ended with the death of Murtallah and the ascension of Olusegun Obasanjo, the state of emergency was lifted and an army colonel friend of mine helped us retrieve our equipment. We never got to perform during the six-week state of emergency resulting from the coup. Broke and very embarrassed, I sent the band back to America, where we were scheduled to go on tour in a months' time, and cabled Stewart to wire money to me in Monrovia in care of my friend Chuchu Horton at the Bank of Liberia. Ekemode was very upset with me, especially for having agreed to embark on this trip after warning me of its futility back in L.A. He also reminded me of how much Neil Bogart had opposed it. However, the band wrote it off as bad luck and looked forward to the next tour in the States.

I returned to Washington, D.C., at the beginning of October to rejoin the band. We rehearsed in the nation's capital and after a couple of weeks we hit the road again, beginning on the East Coast. We went back to Pittsburgh, Detroit, and finally Chicago, where we played the entire month of December at the Jazz Workshop on the North Side and Purve's Place in South Chicago. At the beginning of 1976 we moved into a new studio belonging to singer/composer Curtis Mayfield. Stewart joined us there to begin production on a new album. In between touring, we completed the album, *Colonial Man*, at New York's Midtown Studios. It was full of satirical sociopolitical songs about colonization. "Vasco da Gama" was a cha-cha salsa condemning the Portuguese explorer for his expeditions to the Far East, during which he stopped at the South African coastal bays for fresh water and supplies. "Vasco da Gama, he was no friend of mine," the hook line went. "Cecil Rhodes" was a similar putdown, in this case of the British entrepreneur who exploited the rich mineral deposits of South Africa, Zambia, and Zimbabwe. "A Song for Brazil" was a samba-salsa in praise of the music of that country, which grew out of the slave community that was forcibly removed from Africa to the state of Bahía by Portuguese traders. This was the general flavor of the whole record. Neil Bogart gave us some trouble over the album's theme, because he was in the business of producing hit records, not political protests. He was deeply disappointed, and told Stewart and me that the record would not sell because the Casablanca sales staff would not know how to market it. Furthermore, only students of history would know what the fuck I was singing about. All in all, it was a major downer. In the spring of 1976, Neil Bogart made a last-ditch effort to help us come up with a hit record by spending time with us in the studio and exhorting us to think of popular subjects, catchy phrases, and commercial grooves—but to no avail. We weren't focused enough to understand what Bogart was trying to do. This was our loss because Neil, who had been very enthusiastic about OJAH, slowly recoiled from us and very soon had nothing to say about us, to us, or for us. The album was well reviewed and some of those songs have become classics in my repertoire, but at the time it just seemed like another opportunity lost.

Miriam Makeba was about to embark on a West African tour of Senegal, Togo, Benin, Liberia, and Gambia, and asked us to join her. She felt that it would be very significant to showcase South African music there. She had already invited Letta Mbulu, who had agreed to do it. This was the beginning of another ridiculous event in this period—I kept taking one step forward and two back.

Back in Los Angeles, when I told Alan Pariser about the tour, he said, "Hughie, I've always wanted to bring a planeload of gold bullion out of Ghana. They also have some of the world's best grass out there. If you can put it together on that side, I will supply the aircraft and the finance. Why don't you check it out and get back to me?" It sounded very attractive because I was quite broke—I was eating pretty heavily into my Casablanca money with all my personal travels and expensive lifestyle. When I laid out Alan Pariser's plan to Nga, he thought it was risky, but with the facilities Alan was making available and the connections we could hook up in Ghana, we might just pull it off. Miriam's West African tour was the perfect foil for Alan Pariser's adventurous idea, and I resolved to go through with it.

Another golden opportunity was laid at my feet by my cousin Peter Vundla, who had recently graduated from Columbia Business School and had returned home to South Africa, where he climbed to the very top advertising executive levels. His wife's family were highly successful entrepreneurs in Swaziland, where, together with him, they had planned a mega-festival in that country to take place right after Miriam's tour, in early October. My band was to be one of the top featured acts at that festival. Although Neil Bogart was disenchanted with the direction of our latest album, he had nevertheless primed his staff to try to promote it. Bogart had hoped that at least this time we would tour the States to back up Casablanca's marketing efforts. When he learned of my band's plan to go to Africa again shortly after the album's release, he was absolutely flabbergasted. I tried to convince him that we needed to market ourselves in Africa because it was our home, but Neil just looked at me in utter amazement. I was determined to do this tour with Miriam. Makeba was a goddess on that continent. Touring with her in Africa seemed to promise glory there, especially because in America I had more or less become a statistic. "Grazing in the Grass" seemed more and more like a last hurrah that would never be repeated again. Only Ekemode and Yaw Opoku sided with Bogart. The rest of the band members were very excited about returning to West Africa, even though our last visit there had been disastrous. They felt that with Miriam headlining, the sky was the limit. Bob Young joined the tour as OJAH's manager.

On the day I arrived, I was sitting with Miriam on Sister Gertie's wrap-around porch, planning the program for our concert tour the day after our arrival in Liberia, when two members of Monrovia's large South African exile community, Tshidi and Skhumbuzo Ndamse, her husband, walked in. Her face was bruised in several places. She also had both eyes blackened. He had apparently beaten the shit out of her. I was shocked and infuriated because my parents had been at Kilnerton Training Institute with her mother. When I had mentioned her among the South Africans who were living in Monrovia, my mother had written back asking that I look out for her and the two Nyembezi brothers, because their parents were very good friends of hers and my father. I subsequently managed to speak to Tshidi alone and asked her if she wanted to continue to live with Skhumbuzo. She replied that she wanted a divorce, but lacked the means to engage a lawyer to represent her. I offered my assistance, and engaged Steve Dunbar, who had been Steve Tolbert's lawyer for the Zaire festival, to represent her in filing for a divorce from her husband.

One day soon after our arrival in Monrovia, Nga invited Bob and me over for lunch at his house. After the meal, Nga pulled out a half-liter bottle with a skull-and-crossbones label. He asked me if this might be the same stuff we had been snorting in Zaire during the music festival. He had gotten the powder from his second wife, Hilda, who was a doctor in Kinshasa. Bob, a licensed pharmacist, opened the bottle and sniffed some, then sampled the powder on his tongue. "Hughie, this is pure, unadulterated, pharmaceutical cocaine. If you gonna do some blow, you cannot snort anything finer than this flaky shit. It's simply the best." We couldn't stop laughing. We hugged Nga and thanked him for turning us on.

Nga said, "You crazy people spend so much money putting this stupid powder up your noses. Because you are friends, and I had access to what I thought was pure cocaine, I asked Hilda to get me some so I could save my stupid friend from spending his money foolishly. I hope you enjoy yourself with this bottle. Me, I have no time for such funny things. I will just stick to my beer and brandy. Snort and be merry, gentlemen. Cheers. I drink this beer to you." We toasted with cognac, jumped into Nga's Volkswagen Beetle, and sped off to a restaurant-bar just outside of town for drinks and further sampling of the coke, which we kept in a matchbox. The flaky stuff was amazing because it did not dissolve into liquid in spite of the very dense humidity. It remained in its powder form. Stanley Todd and the other guys were excited over this windfall.

After two sold-out shows in Monrovia, we went to perform in Togo, where our concert was sold out, but we were bumped off our flight back to Liberia the next day. Eyadema, the president, held a grudge toward Miriam because she had been a close friend of the former president, Olympio, whose assassination he had engineered. He harbored even deeper resentment for Sekou Toure, who was his prime critic. Since Miriam, Philemon, and I were traveling on Guinean passports, it gave the Togolese officials immense pleasure to frustrate us in this way. We finally flew out of Lome airport in Togo two days later, and headed back to Monrovia, where the band was the toast of the town. We were just living on naps, hardly sleeping. This madness truly amused Chuchu and all our friends in Monrovia, because even though they were famous for their own craziness, they had never seen a crazier bunch of nuts.

Our next stop was Dakar, Senegal, where, at the very last minute, Miriam was forbidden to travel because of an age-old enmity between Sekou Toure and Senegalese President Leopold Senghor, whom Sekou considered a puppet of France. We played two sold-out concerts at the Serrano theater and another grand concert at the stadium, along with Xalam Deux, the pioneers of mbalax music, which has since been popularized universally by the Senegalese vocalist Youssou Ndour.

Miriam rejoined us in Benin, where the concerts were again a success. On the morning of our departure for Liberia, President Kerekou summoned Miriam and me and the concert promoter, Dagortey, to his office. Kerekou was notorious at the time for being a tyrannical, murderous, despotic autocrat. We were terrified. He came into the room where we had been waiting, sat down, and starred coldly at us for almost an hour without uttering a word. Finally he spoke in deep French: "I am angry and I find it difficult to speak. I cannot begin to fathom how two revered comrades of the African struggle for liberation can come to our beloved revolutionary republic and not be presented to me. That they can perform in this country without the participation, blessings, and presence of government members at their spectacles is a source of shame to me. I have been received in Guinea by my beloved brother, Comrade Sekou Toure, with so much love, pomp, and fanfare. How then am I supposed to explain to my comrade brother the absence of an official reception for these two revolutionary soldiers? Dagortey, you have shamed me beyond redemption with this contemptuous action. Were it not for the love of these two honorable comrades, I should have you sequestered and duly meted out the punishment you deserve for the treasonable act you have committed. I called you here, my beloved comrades, Makeba and Masekela, to apologize to you for this embarrassment our country has been subjected to, and belatedly welcome you to our land. As for Dagortey, he should give thanks to you for his life. Go forth into the world and continue your valuable work for our beloved continent. Please return soon so that we may afford you the due and truly respectful reception you deserve. *Au revoir! Prêt pour la Révolution!*"

Kerekou rose, turned around, and left the room with a pronounced military gait and the angriest expression on his hard face. We breathed a collective sigh of relief. A few hours later Philemon, Miriam, and I were on the plane headed back to Liberia for a show at the stadium. The audience reaction was overwhelming. They just couldn't get enough of Miriam Makeba and OJAH.

Altogether the tour worked out great for OJAH. After the last show in Monrovia, we were scheduled for the festival that my cousin Peter Vundla had contracted us for in Swaziland, but the event was aborted because the South African government was preventing the majority of the audience, which would be coming from that country, to leave for Swaziland. Neither our airplane tickets nor the money that was supposed to be sent to Chuchu at the Bank of Liberia ever materialized. This made a very big hole in our pockets.

Ekemode, Guy Warren, Yaw, and Adelaja decided to return to the States. They were finally disenchanted with OJAH, and told me so in no uncertain terms, especially Yaw and Ekemode, who had been vehemently opposed to the tour from the very beginning. The $60,000 Swaziland payday, which had been an additional justification for the trip, had flown out the window; I was not in too much of an enviable position now because even some members of this great band, which a few months ago had a very promising future, were now jumping ship.

Just before the West African tour, we had completed an album called *Melody Maker* in Washington, D.C. Stewart had flown in from Los Angeles to produce the album, and every evening after we left the studio, Stewart, Bob, and I would go to Stewart's hotel or Bob's apartment and consume loads of cocaine, marijuana, and tequila. It would be the last album Stewart produced for me. He had reached the end of his tether with our crazy friendship and was slowly trying to change his life and put more focused effort into sobriety. Chuck Kaye, our music publisher, who himself was a reformed nut, had told Stewart to "stop wasting your time with these crazy motherfuckers," referring to people like myself, Alan Pariser, and most of Stewart's other acquaintances.

It was now time for me to deliver my last album for Casablanca Records before my contract with the company expired. I decided to make it in Kumasi, Ghana, where Stanley and Frankie Todd told me there was a very good studio. Stanley, Frankie, Jagger, and Okyerema went ahead to set up recording schedules while I stayed in Liberia and slowly began a relationship with Tshidi, who was now divorced. Bob Young returned to Washington for a short spell to pack his bags because he was now determined to settle in Africa. He loved it. Nga and I began to prepare the groundwork for the gold-and-grass airlift with Alan Pariser. We spoke with him over the phone a few times, then he sent over an associate partner for the deal, Ron Scoggins, who was an old friend of Stewart's and mine. Ron, Nga, and I went to Ghana to make connections with Al Hajji, the grass farmer up in Kumasi, and an architect in Accra who had very strong ties with people high up in the gold mining community of Ghana. He gave us an ounce of raw gold as a sample for Ron to go and check out with Alan back in Los Angeles. It proved to be of high purity, and Ron came back for more preparations. Back in Monrovia, Nga and I had arranged for the Gulfstream jet to have landing rights before proceeding on to Kumasi, where our architect friend had arranged a landing permit.

· · ·

One day, back in Accra, I was visiting Geraldo Pino, the Sierra Leonean band-leader of the Heartbeats, a popular West African group, in his room at the Ringway Hotel, when the owner and manager, Mama Akufo-Addo, burst in and started having a lighthearted debate with Pino. It was a jovial and humorous argument in which he finally threatened her, "I will turn loose Hugh Masekela on you if you don't stop bothering me." "This little harmless thing?" she said, eyeing me nonchalantly. "You must be joking." Before Mama knew what had hit her, I playfully pulled her down onto the bed I was sitting on, jumped on top of her, and began to kiss her all over the neck and face until she was begging me for mercy. Stunned and breathing heavily from my aggressive flirtation, Mama got up and, in her clipped Oxford English, jokingly expressed her outrage at my roguish behavior. Pino laughed, "I told you not to mess with me." Pino and I were in stitches.

Mama must have gotten my number from Pino, because around five the next morning, she burst through my open door at the Tesano Gardens and did exactly what I had done to her the night before. But Mama wasn't playing. We attacked each other for the next two hours. Still dripping with perspiration, Mama dressed quickly. She complained, "Masekela, a person of your stature has no business staying in a dive such as this. I want you to pack your belongings and come stay at the Ringway with me." Soon Mama and I were inseparable. She had been educated in England, but her mother was a royal princess of one of the Akwapem ruling dynasties, and her father, Edward Akufo-Addo, was Ghana's president following Kwame Nkrumah. Mama only objected to my heavy drinking and drugging. My vices aside, a few months later she and I, along with her five-year-old daughter, Khaddy, moved into a beautiful home in Kokomlemle, and for several years Mama and I had a tumultuous relationship. Under different circumstances, perhaps we could have jelled and built something special. But I was in no shape emotionally or spiritually to put down roots in a serious relationship. Any time the phrase "Hugh, I need you" was spoken or implied by any woman, I retreated to my debauchery.

Okyerema Asante introduced Stanley Todd and me to a young business tycoon named Jojo Fosu. He was interested in collaborating with us on music-related projects and promotions. We decided to start a record company, and the first artist we signed was Miatta Fahbulleh. Miatta had great potential. She was strikingly beautiful and had a lovely, sultry voice. Through Sierra Leonean percussionist Francis Fuster, who had worked with Miatta before, we were able to put together Baranta, a band he played with in Lagos. We also managed to get studio time at the EMI complex in the Lagos suburb of Apapa with Fela's assistance. In Lagos, Fela took us out nightly to meet and hear other musicians. He particularly enjoyed taking me to hear King Sunny Ade and Colonel Ebenezer Obeyi, two of the country's wealthiest musicians. The joy for me, however, was being in Fela's company and sharing thoughts with him. We would talk for hours, sometimes until dawn, about the corrupt administrations in different countries all over Africa whose peoples were suffering from the tyranny of their power-hungry dictators.

Fela was also having major clashes with the current military government led by Olusegun Obasanjo. His songs that castigated the corruption of the administration were extremely popular with the young and the poor, and led to his periodic imprisonment and to abuse from police and soldiers against him and his followers, but his humor and stunning brilliance, his musical genius and his biting sense of absurdity, transcended all these obstacles.

"Hugh, this Obasanjo's people are no different from those who harassed me during Gowon's regime. Gowon started this confrontation against me with the army because I sang about the corruption of this country's establishment. I think that what really pissed him off more than anything is when I bought a small donkey and named him Gowon. The people used to come and stand outside my yard to watch me ride Gowon from my house to the African Shrine Club. They used to laugh their asses off every time I said, 'C'mon, Gowon, walk faster,' while sitting on the donkey's back. Word about this daily spectacle got to him, and that is when my troubles started."

I asked him about the present administration. Fela laughed. "These Obasanjo boys hate me even more because he was a couple of classes behind me in my father's school, and I don't let him forget it. He is out to kill me, this one, but I won't stop singing about his government's sick corruption." The military regime hated him for this and put fire under his ass whenever it could, which was almost always.

"What about the other artists?" I asked. "Doesn't Sunny Ade or Ebenezer Obeyi say anything about government corruption?"

"Hugh, those people are friends of the big shots. All their songs sing praises of rich men, chiefs, and individuals who are in power. The people they sing about dress in their most expensive lace *boubous* and go out dancing in those nightclubs to hear their names being immortalized. When they enter the venues, these musicians begin to sing about what wonderfully miraculous people they are. Then these fucking big shots, who have come with suitcases full of money, gradually throw it all onstage, competing against each other to see who will fork out the most cash. Colonel Ebenezer Obeyi makes a hundred times more money than you and me combined, just from deifying these big-shot monkeys. He never has to travel outside Lagos. They all come to his club to hear their names being lifted up to the status of gods. Ebenezer makes millions right there in his garden club. That is why he didn't know you when I introduced you to him. He doesn't listen to other people's records. His whole life is dedicated to learning the names of big shots, their families, and the heroic deeds he makes up for them. They lap it up and flock to his club. Why the fuck should he care about you and me? Colonel Ebenezer Obeyi? What an African phenomenon! This is life's cruel irony, my friend."

Fela loved paradoxes like this one. These two world-class musicians, who were almost totally unknown outside Nigeria, fascinated him.

We soon returned to Ghana with Miatta's new album completed, and I went back to Liberia with her. By now our romantic relationship was practically over with. In Monrovia, I hung out even more with Tshidi. In September 1976, Asante, Jagger, Stanley, Frankie, and I went up to Kumasi and began to record our last album for Casablanca. Miriam Makeba joined us in Kumasi, and we simultaneously recorded an album for her, which would be called *Country Girl*. It had covers of old South African township songs such as "Mbube," the lion-hunt song written in the 1920s by Solomon Linda. In the 1950s and 1960s it had become a folk-music hit after being performed by the Weavers under the title "Wimoweh." Millions of records were sold in numerous versions but Solomon Linda died a pauper. In South Africa's music history, this song represents the worst example of artist exploitation. "Country Girl," a rhumba shuffle I co-wrote with Stanley Todd, had a bridge heavily influenced by the Mandingo-griot style of Salif Keita, which is extremely popular folk music in Senegal, Gambia, Sierra Leone, Guinea, and Mali. "The African Convention" was a rhythm-and-blues-cum-mbhaqanga dance shuffle with lyrics way ahead of their time, about the African Union initiative that is just now starting to captivate the continent's politicians. The cover of the Harari-Beaters' "Inhlupeko Iphelile" (The End of Poverty), which became one of the anthems of township youth during the 1976 student uprisings, was one of the album's highlights. We could not complete *Country Girl* in Ghana, and opted to do the rest of it in New York with some of the cast of *Ipi Tombi*, a box-office smash South African revue that was showing to turn-away crowds on Broadway. OJAH's album was called *You Told Your Mama Not to Worry,* and it included "Soweto Blues," which I wrote as a tribute to the students who refused to accept Afrikaans as the language of school instruction in all subjects. It had a bluesy verse sung in English, and the bridge went into a Xhosa protest shout admonishing the adults for not joining in when the children were throwing stones at military tanks as they were being mowed down by machine-gun fire. It has remained a popular item in Miriam's repertoire.

During our recording sessions in Kumasi, Nga was concentrating on how we would acquire the gold bullion we were supposed to airlift out of Ghana. He was spending almost all of his time with our architect friend who was to facilitate the gold operation. From time to time, Nga would fly or drive up to Kumasi to give me progress reports.

Oscar Cohen at Associated Booking Corporation got word back to me in Ghana through Stewart Levine that he had lined up a major tour for OJAH. Back in the States, we rehearsed for a whole week in Washington, D.C., with all of the original members of OJAH. It was a wonderful reunion. After the tour, Stanley and I went into the Antisia Studios in New York, which were owned by Harry Belafonte alumni, percussionist Ralph McDonald, composer/vocalist Bill Eaton, and composer/bassist Bill Salter, who had played in Miriam's accompanying trio for more than ten years. The Antisia gang collaborated very closely with Bill Withers and Grover Washington Jr., and wrote hit songs like "Just the Two of Us," with Bill Withers and "Where Is the Love" for Roberta Flack and Donny Hathaway. They helped to engineer and conduct the overdub sessions we had to do with members of the *Ipi Tombi* cast while I worked with Stanley and the singers inside the recording room. Miriam wanted the tapes sent to her in Paris, where she planned to complete the recordings, but Stanley and I requested that she arrange for a payment of $10,000 to us for the work we did on the record, and to cover some of the studio fees we had paid back in Kumasi. She thought this was very unreasonable, and has never forgiven me for it. However, Ralph McDonald and his partners understood our position because they were record producers themselves. They did not release the tapes until Miriam's French record company, Sonodisc, paid the money and Antisia's own studio fees.

Following the recording sessions, Stanley and I went back to West Africa, first stopping in Liberia. I spent most of my time there with Tshidi, although I hung out with Nga, Bob, and Stanley every night while Tshidi concentrated on her studies for her final year at the University of Liberia's medical school.

Generously dipping into Nga's bottomless bottle of pharmaceutical cocaine, we prowled all over Monrovia's dance clubs, restaurants, garden discos, and after-hours joints, dancing, dining, drinking, debauching, and generally raising hell. One night after Stanley Todd had returned to Ghana, I was out clubbing and bar-hopping with Nga and Bobby Young. We ended up in Krutown, across the bridge from downtown Monrovia. This was the industrial part of the harbor city, where the drinking spots drew dock workers, fishermen, and sailors. Most of the clientele did not care too much for foreigners. Nga dared us to enter a bar that was a stronghold for Kru fishermen who were very resentful of President Tolbert's coddling of exiles from southern African countries. They especially hated South Africans with a passion. I was very reluctant to go, but Nga was insistent. "Look here, Masekela, this is a free country and we can drink anywhere we want." Before I could object any further, Nga had pulled me in by the hand up to the bar, where he was ordering drinks from the barman. "Give us three bottles of cold Heineken and a bottle of Courvoisier VSOP, no ice." All of a sudden the jukebox was turned off and the place was quieter than a graveyard.

While we were enjoying our drinks, some of the fishermen came to stand directly behind us. The burliest one, with rippling muscles and a body-fitting T-shirt, roared in a booming voice, "I'm tired of these fucking South African bitches coming into our country and taking all our women while Tolbert treats them like little babies and gives them anything they want. Meanwhile, we poor people's children are going hungry. I want to break these motherfucking bitches' heads into little pieces." I was terrified. I looked to see how far we were from the door so I could run out of there. I whispered to Nga that we should just pay our bill and get out of the place, but he ignored me. Instead he turned around to address the speaker. "Are you the leader of all these people?" Nga inquired coolly, a fresh cognac in one hand, a beer bottle in the other. "What if I am?" the man rumbled. Before he could continue, Nga, a guerrilla commander who was trained to kill faster than lightning, had put down his drink on the bar counter. He reached out to the man's ears, about a foot above his own head, pulled the man's face down to his, bit off the fisherman's nose, and spit it on the floor. He wiped his mouth with his jacket sleeve and pushed the bleeding man away from him. Nga turned around and picked up his drinks while the packed bar was emptying fast. All the fishermen were scrambling out of there except for one old man in the far corner of the joint who pointed angrily at Nga and shouted, "How can you bite the man's nose? How you expect him to breathe?" The bartender rushed to the bleeding fisherman's aid with a towel to try to stop the flow of blood. The man's nose was lying in a congealed clot on the sawdust-covered floor. Nga nonetheless stayed cool. "Bob, Masekela, let's finish our drinks."

About six policemen entered the bar. "Where the man who bite the man's nose?" one of them asked as two of the cops escorted the bleeding fisherman to an ambulance outside. They had picked up the fisherman's nose and wrapped it in a napkin. "Let's go, my friends," the cop said, and Nga and I were hauled off to a police van outside that was already filled with drunks. Bob was not arrested and went back to to tell Chuchu about the incident. At the police station popularly known as the "Junction Cage," we were herded into a large coop with barbed-wire fencing that was already overflowing with at least two hundred other prisoners. One of the policemen knew us as good friends of Chuchu Horton, who lived next to the "Junction Cage." He telephoned Chuchu, who came with Bob and arranged for our release, persuading the station commander to drop the charges against us. We never heard from the fisherman with the bitten-off nose, but word was that it had been reattached to his face and the bar incident had won South African exiles some respect.

The gold-and-grass airlift plan was finally in place. Alan Pariser landed in Monrovia in a private Gulfstream jet along with Ron Scoggins and a scientist from Switzerland who had secured a gold buyer in his country and two pilots from Los Angeles. The gold and grass had been pre-sold in Switzerland, where Nga, the scientist, Ron, Alan, and I would share the profits. The pilots had already been paid off in advance. Monrovia's chief of police, an African-American ex-army officer who had become a very close friend and drinking buddy over the years, had arranged the landing permit for us at Sinkor Airport. Sinkor was a suburb of Monrovia, about three miles from town. The architect in Ghana who had secured the gold and the marijuana farmer Al Hajji were the other two partners. They had secured landing rights at a private airfield outside Kumasi. Alan showed us the weapons we would be packing when we picked up the booty and flew it to Europe. Mine was a giant, nickel-plated .357 Magnum. Suddenly I began to realize that I was not cut out for this kind of caper. "Listen, Alan, I have gotten us this far. I ain't packing any pistol, neither am I going on the plane with you guys. You all take it from here on out. You can give me what you consider my fair share for connecting you to everybody. I can't go on with the rest of this plan."

Nga, Alan, Ron, and the scientist were disappointed in me because they felt that I was central to the plan's success. I disagreed. The possibility of a gunfight sent a shudder through my body. I wished them good luck and returned to Sister Gertie's Congotown mansion, bringing an end to a caper that could either have earned me a fortune or gotten me killed. I preferred to be a coward with still relatively clean hands. Bob Young was really pissed off with me for not telling him about the heist. "You should have told me about the fucking scheme. I could have taken your part and we could have pulled it off, man. Instead, you preferred to work with those fucking white boys without me, and the whole shit fell apart. That's what you get for keeping a secret from your best friend, motherfucker. I would have known how to do that shit right, man."

Bob was probably right, because over the years since then, he has mounted very successful business projects all over Africa in legitimate export and import initiatives. Today, he heads what is probably one of Africa's most efficient road-marking companies, doing business in more than twenty countries on the continent, and is the recipient of several prestigious international awards in that field. If he could pull that off, he probably could've figured out a simple gold-and-grass smuggling scheme!

Shortly after the gold-and-grass debacle, I got word from Casablanca Records that they'd booked us on a tour with George Clinton's Parliament Funkadelic and Bootsy Collins, with OJAH as the opening act. The two groups traveled in a convoy of four buses and a few limousines. A bevy of beautiful groupies followed the buses in their cars. We hardly slept from snorting cocaine around the clock with this musical entourage. Just before our fifth concert, we were hit with the bad news that OJAH was not making it with the audiences and Jeffrey Osborne and LTD would replace us. Neil Bogart had been less than impressed with the recording material we'd delivered to Casablanca. Nonetheless, he felt that touring with Bootsy and Clinton would introduce us to a new audience and perhaps boost my chances of getting my recording contract renewed. Being dropped from the tour signaled the end of my Casablanca chapter. This would also be the last tour I did with Stanley Todd and the West African Band. Many of us had been together since the summer of 1973, when Fela introduced me to Hedzoleh Soundz. We had come to the end of the line, and it was heartbreaking to say good-bye.

Before returning to Liberia, I spent some time with Stewart Levine in Los Angeles. He was now living with Quincy Jones's oldest daughter, Jolie, and her son Donovan. Jolie and Stewart had been having an on-and-off relationship for some time, and had finally decided to tie the knot.

One evening the telephone rang. Stewart was on the other line and asked me to answer the call. It was Herb Alpert, in the studio with Letta Mbulu, whose album he was producing with Caiphus Semenya. He was calling Stewart for advice because of his experience with South African music. Herb was surprised to hear my voice, and suggested that we get together and explore the possibilities of doing something together before I headed back to Liberia. Caiphus, Stewart, and I met with Herb the following day.

When I returned to Liberia in September 1977, I arrived to find that Tshidi was five months pregnant. She had moved in with a friend from Zimbabwe named Netsai, whose brother was a lecturer at the University of Liberia. They had a beautiful home, and I moved in with them. With Nga's assistance, we found a luxurious two-story beachfront mansion with a tennis court facing the Atlantic Ocean. I rented it right away, and before I went back to Los Angeles to begin recording with Herb Alpert, Tshidi, Mabusha, and I moved into the beach house, which I had already partly furnished. I opened an account with Chuchu Horton at the Bank of Liberia, and left Tshidi with funds to complete furnishing the house. From Los Angeles I sent her more money so that she could buy a car, because the house was far away from public transportation. The recording with Herb was a joyful experience, with Caiphus and Stewart producing. We did an old Zimbabwean classic dance hit from the 1940s, "Skokiaan," which had once been a smash hit for Louis Armstrong; "Ring Bell," first recorded by Miriam Makeba on her *Phatha-Phatha* album; "Lobo" by Brazil's Edu Lobo; a Caiphus Semenya ballad; and six other favorites of Herb's. The album came out quite strong, and we planned a tour in the spring of 1978. Two weeks later I was asked by Philemon and Miriam in Paris to come and help them complete her album *Country Girl,* which we had started in Kumasi, Ghana.

I arrived in Paris to an acrimonious Miriam complaining about how Stanley and I had ripped her off when we had requested that she pay us $10,000 for producing her album in Ghana and for part of the studio expenses in Kumasi. Throughout the entire week that I spent working with her, Philly, and a couple of Paris-based African musicians, Miriam only spoke to me about completing the album, which songs to attend to, how the record company was in a hurry to release the album, and how much of her time and money had been wasted. And she kept reminding me that the deadline was in a week. No hotel accommodations had been arranged for me, so I slept on the floor in Philly's hotel room. We were picked up early in the morning and driven to the studio, ordered to do what was expected, then taken back to the hotel after the sessions, which often lasted beyond midnight. It was a very unpleasant week, but one that showed me that Miriam had developed a love-hate disposition toward me after all this time. She was nice when she needed me and mean when she was avenging the string of wrongs she felt I had done her. There were a few occasions over the years after the Paris recordings when she would suddenly lay into me in public and remind me of all the things she'd done for me and how I'd treated her ungratefully in return. I don't think she ever forgave me for walking out on our marriage.

At Charles de Gaulle Airport, I had just finished checking in when I saw a beautiful, jet-black teenage girl of about eighteen sitting on one of the benches crying her heart out. I walked up to her and asked what was troubling her. She told me she was on her way to Accra on vacation from school in Los Angeles. She had been let out of the airport by mistake, and the immigration officials were refusing to let her back inside the terminal gate area. A new shift of immigration officers had come on duty since then, and they were claiming that she had entered the country illegally. I was feeling no pain at the time, since I'd been celebrating the completion of Miriam's album and was looking forward to sleeping in a bed again. In my street French, I let the immigration officers know that if the young lady was not immediately put into my custody, an international incident was going to be unavoidable.

French officials are immune to insults as long as they are expressed in their language. They soon released Elinam into my custody, and I checked her in on the same flight that I would be taking. I bought her some perfume and we had a bite in the airport café and flew to Accra sitting next to each other.

Elinam's parents, Mark and Diamond Cofie, who had been worried about their daughter's no-show, were relieved when we arrived in Accra. Stanley Todd had come to the airport to fetch me, and all of us ended up at Elinam's house for a festive meal. We left the Cofie household laden with drinks and food—all in appreciation for my having looked after their daughter.

After a week in Accra with Mama, I was off to Liberia, where Tshidi would soon give birth to our baby. Aside from providing financially for Tshidi's comfort, my behavior was clearly far from what might be expected of a father-to-be. But Pula was born on the first evening of the 1978 rainy season, on the 20th of January. When it rains in Liberia, it comes with a violent introduction of thunder, winds, and lightning that makes one wonder if the world is coming to an end. Motlalepula, her maternal grandmother's name, means "the one who comes with the rain." I pretty much stayed around the house for the first three months, taking care of my beautiful daughter while her mother went to work.

When March rolled around, I had to head back to Los Angeles for rehearsals with Herb Alpert before our national tour. Larry Willis picked the band, mostly old friends of ours from New York: Buddy Williams on drums; "Boyzie" Williams on bass; Larry on piano; Arthur Adams on guitar; Manolo Badrena on percussion; and Jonas Gwangwa on trombone. We rehearsed for a couple of weeks and hit the road beginning in San Francisco. We played medium-sized clubs all over the country. I was completely crazy on this tour, drinking, smoking, and partying like a pirate. That Herb Alpert was able to stomach my insane behavior without coming down on me still boggles my mind, but he was enjoying the camaraderie of the great musicians we were playing with. More than that, he was able to talk a lot of jazz shop with all of us. For a long time Herb had been perceived as a multimillionaire who played mariachi-flavored pop Muzak and knew very little about other contemporary music. On the contrary, not only was he responsible for guiding A&M Records to become one of the world's top music companies, but he was able to bring to the label unknown artists who became major icons in the industry: the Carpenters, Paul Williams, the Brothers Johnson, Sergio Mendes, Joan Armatrading, Quincy Jones, and the Tijuana Brass. But people who considered themselves jazz purists liked to attack him. One night Herb and I went to catch a Joe Williams performance at the Century Plaza Hotel near Beverly Hills. Between sets, Joe came over to our table and started to put Herb down by claiming that he "wasn't really happening." I was more embarrassed for Joe than for Herb, because I thought he was being picky, petty, and perhaps a tad jealous. Herb was actually an avid scholar of jazz, with one of the richest libraries of the genre, a very keen student with a sincere desire to excel in it. This tour gave him a chance to spread his wings and stretch out.

Herb was traveling with his wife, Lani, and their three-year-old daughter and suggested I have Tshidi and Pula join me on tour. But I was too crazy even to entertain such a thought—I was at my most pathetic. At the end of the tour, Herb felt that we should go for a second album. I first went to Liberia to spend some time with Tshidi and Pula. When I returned to Los Angeles toward the end of the summer, I was thirty-nine years old and had three children, but was not much of a father to any of them. I knew I needed to change my lifestyle. Deep down in my soul, I wanted to. I was beginning to realize that I was making a great many bad decisions at a time when I had a golden opportunity to do many wonderful things.

17

Y 1968 ROLLERCOASTER RIDE with Chris Calloway came to haunt my judgment badly from then on—only I didn't realize how addictive, impulsive, selfish, and totally insensitive I had become about the feelings of those who had my welfare at heart. I had slowly changed into a greedy, ugly bastard, probably out of a deep bitterness instilled by the failure of our partnership, something I had sincerely hoped would finally translate into a very blissful life. That totally the opposite had happened left me so subconsciously wounded that I could not find beauty in anything whatsoever. To anesthetize that pain, all that really mattered to me was the procurement of as much good cocaine, pussy, alcohol, and smoke as I could possibly consume, only to wake up wherever I had gone down and to start all over again.

When Herb Alpert suggested we bring back Caiphus and Stewart to produce our next album, I replied glibly, "No, we can do it ourselves." I was so high I wasn't even listening to what I was saying. In fact, I was on my way to score some cocaine and then meet with one or another of the women I was seeing at the time. I believe Herb Alpert was optimistic about my possibly changing my life as time went by, thinking that I would finally realize the opportunity he had opened up for our potential as a duo. Herb was not only overly accommodating, but also unreasonably generous, trying his utmost to see that Jonas and I were always comfortable. We were living in giant chalets at the Chateau Marmont, and had a twenty-four-hour limousine service and an unlimited expense account—we were truly living the life. I was just taking, giving nothing in return. We finally got around to producing the album. After spending about six weeks in the studio, *Main Event,* a simulated live-performance recording, could best be described as a damp squid.

In the spring of 1978, Barbara said to me, "Hugh, we haven't seen our mother in a couple of decades. You are really in a good position to bring her now. Send her a ticket and let her come and see us. It will be the greatest thing you could do for your mother, boy." That July we brought our mother to Los Angeles. I also sent for Selema from New York. I hadn't seen Polina in eighteen years. It was the most wonderful reunion. The four of us stayed in the Chateau Marmont's largest luxury bungalow, with four bedrooms. I arranged for a car to take my mother, Barbara, and Selema sightseeing all over Los Angeles County and on Sundays to drive my mother to the local Catholic church to worship. She was overjoyed to be with her children after such a long time, and we could not have enough of her wonderful cooking.

While I was in the studio recording *Main Event,* Barbara learned about our sisters Elaine and Sybil, Grandma Johanna, my father, and the rest of our family from spending long hours talking to our mother. At night she would bring me up to date when I returned from the studio. I did manage to spend the weekends and mornings with Selema and Polina, even taking them to Disneyland one day. I had never been to any of the favorite tourist stops in America in the eighteen years I had been there.

All of my friends and many of my girlfriends—Stewart and Jolie, Zakes Mokae, Lionel Ngakane, Calvin Lockhart, Barbara Alston, Celeste Peters, Azizi Johari, Vertamae Grosvenor, Larry Willis, Jonas, Carrie White, and Caiphus and Letta—all came by to meet Polina. My mother's cooking had some of them coming by almost every day until she had to ask me one day, "My child, don't some of your friends have homes?"

I taught Selema to swim at the Chateau Marmont's gigantic pool, and he became so obsessed that at six in the morning he'd be standing at my bedside dressed in his swimsuit and goggles, saying, "Dad, let's go to the swims." Today he is a surfing champion and a water and winter sports commentator for ESPN.

Herb Alpert invited my mother and me to lunch at his home, and took a beautiful photo of the two of us, which he sent to me years later. I treasure it dearly.

Polina was shocked at the wrinkly old ladies wearing hot pants all over Los

Angeles. "My children, how can you live among these naked grandmothers? This is a very bad omen and a source of bad luck. It is no wonder that so many unfortunate incidents took place in your lives. This is absolutely shameful." She also told us how difficult it had been to hold down her job as head of the African Child Welfare in Johannesburg during the 1976 student uprisings. Given the cruel disposition of the apartheid machinery toward dissidents, keeping a balance between initiating welfare care and not treading on the toes of the white administrative heads she was working under had been very stressful.

My mother and father were also under obvious pressure from the apartheid government's intelligence police, because Barbara was a leading member of the African National Congress hierarchy and very active with other colleagues in pressuring U.S. and European businesses to disinvest in South Africa, lobbying against the South African government at the United Nations, participating in demonstrations, and delivering strategic talks at forums in solidarity with our liberation struggle. She persuaded many influential Americans to support the battle being waged by oppressed South Africans. My records had long been banned by the South African broadcasting media, and my condemnation of the South African government in print and broadcast interviews did not help to endear me to the apartheid regime. They hated my protest songs.

My parents first knew Winnie Mandela when she worked on her final social work study under my mother's guidance at Entokozweni Family Welfare Center in Alexandra Township. Later on, when her husband was imprisoned at Robben Island, my father kept in close touch with her, and visited her regularly at her place of banishment in Brandfort. This infuriated the overlords of apartheid.

Since 1958, Winnie had been harassed, banned, and detained (often in solitary confinement) on numerous charges that ranged from demonstrating against the issuing of passes for women, promoting the ANC, attending political gatherings, and promoting communism. She was first banned for two years and restricted to Johannesburg. As a result, she lost her job with the Child Welfare Society. A banned person was prohibited from associating with other banned persons and from having more than one person at a time in her place of residence. In 1977, a month before the first anniversary of the Soweto uprisings, Winnie was arrested at her home in Soweto for violating the anti-terrorism act, and was banished to Brandfort, an impoverished little township in the middle of the Orange Free State. The homes of both my mother and father were often raided. Drawers and closets in every room were trashed, ransacked, and destroyed as agents of the intelligence department searched for evidence pertaining to treasonable activities. "Where is your bloody daughter?" the agents would scream as they violently destroyed part of the house. "Where is that fucking son of yours, Hugh?" My mother told us about these raids while Selema, Barbara, and I listened in shocked amazement. My sisters Sybil and Elaine, my nieces and nephews, my grandma and my father, also related these stories to us when they visited us in Lesotho, Botswana, and Zimbabwe during our years in exile in the 1980s, and more so when we returned home in 1990.

This visit to the United States could not have come at a better time for my mother. That she was allowed to leave the country was in itself a miracle. For Polina, it was "God's gift" to be able to reunite with her oldest children after almost two decades. Her life had been difficult: raising Sybil and Elaine alone; caring for my grandmother Johanna; witnessing the destruction of my younger sisters' marriages to alcoholic, abusive siblings and its negative effects on her grandchildren; and enduring the lingering pain of her divorce from my father. Even though the joy of being with Barbara and me resuscitated her soul and spirit, the trials and tribulations of South Africa had carved wrinkles in Polina's psyche. The weary lines etched along my mother's face revealed years of silent tears and heartache.

After a memorable month in Los Angeles, Barbara, my mother, and Selema returned to New York. I joined them in New York two weeks later, when the recording with Herb was completed. As in Los Angeles, my mother met many of our friends and colleagues. We took her to all the city's tourist attractions. After a tearful farewell from Barbara, Polina came with me to my seaside home in Liberia, where she spent time with Tshidi and me. She coddled little Pula and sang her the lullabies she had probably sung for my sisters and me when we were babies. My mother especially bonded with Mabusha, whom she had been endlessly asking about in Los Angeles and New York City. She found it hard to fathom why he was not with us. Sister Gertie and Polina hit it off like they had always known each other. Sister Gertie took her to have lunch with President Tolbert who wanted to meet her. They apparently spoke for hours. My mother was very touched and inspired by the fact that she had dined with an African president, something that was utterly impossible in her own country. When my mother left for South Africa at the beginning of September, she was a different person, fulfilled, overjoyed, and feeling blessed to have seen her children again, and politically more radical from having been with Barbara and me and all of our friends. Although she was apprehensive about returning to racist South Africa, her heart was truly at rest from the satisfaction of finding both of us in good health—but she was curious about the funny smell coming from my bedroom from time to time. "What are you children burning in there?" she would ask. If my heavy drinking disturbed her, she did not mention it, but deep down it must have hurt her terribly because most of her family had died from alcohol-related illnesses, and the bestial cruelty of the merciless apartheid regime. Many of those overlords, lawmakers, and police were themselves pathetic alcoholics and drug addicts. It was a sad day to say good-bye to my mother at Roberts Field in Monrovia.

On arrival back in South Africa, Polina was met by mournful relatives who told her that Kenneth, her favorite brother-in-law, whom she had helped to raise from his late teens until his marriage to Aunt Bellie, had been brutally murdered the previous month behind his store in Kwa-Thema, Springs. His remains had to be literally scraped off the ground. Our family had not wanted to convey the sad news to us while my mother was visiting; they didn't want to spoil her vacation. She was shattered. Uncle Kenneth had been like an older brother to Barbara and me. Barbara called me from New York to tell me the sad news. She had received a long letter from my mother. Barbara also told me that Kenneth had written her a letter that she had received shortly after we departed for Liberia, in which he said he was looking forward to a trip he was planning to America to visit us.

I went to Ghana and spent two weeks with Mama Akuff-Addo. A few days after my return, Chuchu called me. He said he needed to see me urgently at his office at the Bank of Liberia. I drove over there with my nephew Mabusha. Chuchu had a blank expression on his face. He told me to sit down and remain calm. He handed me a telegram. It was from my father. "Your mother lost her life in a motor accident a few days ago. We'll be burying her over the weekend. Be strong. Love, Papa."

I sat there stunned as Chuchu searched for something to say. "Hugh, isn't it strange that when my mother died, you brought me the bad news? Now I have to do the same for you."

I left the car parked outside the bank and walked aimlessly around downtown Monrovia with Mabusha at my side, holding the telegram in his hand. After walking for a little while, I would say, "Let me see that thing again." I read the telegram, shook my head in disbelief, and began walking again. I did this several times until Mabusha finally suggested, "Uncle Hugh, why don't we go back home?"

It was only then that I realized just how stunned I really was. "Yeah, let's walk back to the car," I said. Back at the house on the beach, I called Jessie, Selema's mother. She and Barbara had a close friendship. "Jessie, please get over to Barbara's with some of her friends and tell her about our mother. I know you're the best person for her to be with at this time."

That evening Barbara called. She was calm, and begged me, "Hugh, don't hold it all in, and try not to act so strong. Cry. Please cry and let it out." To this day, I have never been able to cry for my mother. The fact that Barbara and I could not fly home to bury our mother really hardened my emotional reaction to her demise. My hatred for the apartheid government reverberated through my body. I swore to myself that I would not rest until it was brought down. I would do all that I could do to assist those elements that were engaged in bringing about its eventual elimination. However, this did not lead me toward thinking about changing my life. Instead, I was embittered into escalating my drinking, drugging, and womanizing. My mother's demise radicalized my political activism even more. I never believed the official explanation given about the car accident. Sunday, the day before the "accident," Sybil, Elaine, and their children had celebrated my mother's return. The next morning she drove her normal route to work. While crossing a railroad track, her car stalled and a train hit it. I'll go to my grave believing the South African government was involved in my mother's death.

I sent Pula and Tshidi to South Africa to represent Barbara and me at my mother's funeral. The Home Affairs Minister of Liberia insisted that an escort from his department accompany them, because my daughter and I were Liberian citizens and the apartheid government couldn't be trusted. Two weeks later my father telephoned and told me that Tshidi and her three siblings had missed the funeral. The escort returned shortly after my father's call and said that Tshidi had abandoned him at Jan Smuts International Airport. They had come to my mother's house three days after the burial—dead drunk. Baby Pula was the only sober one.

When Tshidi returned to Monrovia with Pula, after being away for about a month, things fell apart between us. We engaged in bitter arguments about my infidelity and her negligence in burying my mother, which led Mabusha to move back to Philly's house. Little Pula, who was now only about ten months old, was this beautiful, happy baby who was always smiling and hardly ever cried. Her little life had been so blissful and full of joy until now. I wondered if deep down in her infant heart she could make any sense at all of all that was happening around her.

Shattered, angry, and ashamed, I returned to New York with only my trumpet and a few clothes in a small bag. Tshidi did not stay long in the house, but moved with Pula to a small flat in town.

I took over a furnished apartment on 107th Street and Broadway that belonged to a friend of Quincy Troupe's who had moved out to L.A. All I had was my clothing, a keyboard, a stereo, and my trumpet. When I was working with Herb Alpert, I used to drop in at Mikell's, a club at 97th Street and Columbus Avenue. At one time the proprietors, Pat and Mike Mikell, had asked me to play the club for a few days. I'd put together a group with the bistro's resident pianist Don Blackman, drummer Omar Hakim, bassist Richard Allen, and saxophonist René McLean. It had been a quickly assembled group of musicians who needed only one day's rehearsal to learn songs like "Grazing in the Grass"; "The Healing Song," from my *Ooga Booga* album; "The Marketplace," which I had recorded with Hedzoleh Soundz, Stix Hooper, and Joe Sample; and a few other compositions by Blackman, McLean, and Hakim. We played in the style of the massively successful group with whom I'd recorded "Grazing in the Grass"—a jazz quintet with a major flavor of township mbhaqanga and rhythm and blues. Hearing that I was back from Africa and living in New York, Mike Mikell asked me to play his club again. With South African bassist Victor Ntoni, young drummer Poogie Bell, Don Blackman, and René McLean, we began to play Mikell's almost every other weekend to packed houses.

Apart from the fact that Mikell's was one of New York's most reputable jazz clubs, my own reputation as a musician appeared to have been resurrected. The audiences loved what we were doing, and returned regularly every weekend, bringing along new recruits. Oscar Cohen at ABC Booking also sent us out on the road on the East Coast and in the Midwest and Canada. I was making a considerable return to the music scene, and it was helping me to revive my self-esteem and get over my mother's sudden passing.

Hotep Galeta, who was now living in New York, joined our group as an additional keyboardist. We began to attract many other musicians who would come and sit in almost every night. Many of them were young disciples of Don Blackman. Bassist Marcus Miller, guitarists Bobby Brown and Jeffrey Eubanks, and even fifteen-year-old pianist Bernard Johnson, were all so young that Mike Mikell was terribly nervous, thinking the police would come in one day and take his license away because he allowed minors to perform in his establishment. We soon replaced bassist Victor Ntoni with young Victor Bailey, who came to sit in with us at a club we were playing in Boston while he was studying at the Berklee College of Music. "You need me, man, Hugh," he said to me. He was right. The group became stronger after Victor joined us. Bassist Alex Blake and his younger brother, also an outstanding bass player, both did stints in our group. Stevie Wonder also came in to jam with us a few times. Happily, he was back down to earth, and nothing like the way he'd been when we were trying to contract him for the Zaire festival. He sang popular R&B standards by his Motown colleagues and other composers and artists whose work he loved, and we would blow with him. Stevie was an outstanding jazz accompanist. Sometimes he would whip out his beloved harmonica and throw down, bringing the house to its feet. The cast of *Ipi Tombi* would come by after their show on Broadway and join us on songs such as "Stimela," "Bajabula Bonke," and other traditional songs like "Mbube" that I had learned from Miriam and Bongi. The joint was always jumping when we played Mikell's.

Quincy Troupe was a regular at Mikell's, always bringing his artist, poet, and writer friends like Ishmael Reed, Terri McMillan, Toni Cade Bambara, Toni Morrison, Sonia Sanchez, Felipe Luciano, Ntozake Shange, Amiri Baraka, and Nikki Giovanni. It was a thrill to be once again part of this small but influential community—the folks who finally drove the racially prejudiced literary world to open its doors to nonwhite writing talent. The great James Baldwin always came to our shows at Mikell's when he was in town. He spent a lot of time at the club because his brother David was the head barman there.

I was spending a lot of time with Quincy, who got us a great number of university gigs through several of his friends who headed African Studies departments where he regularly did poetry readings and talks on literature. Quincy was living with Margaret Porter, a fine lady from Mississippi who was a colleague of Jabu's at the *New York Times*. This led to a reunion with Jabu, who lived across Columbus Avenue from Mikell's, at Park West Village. She too became a regular at the club.

In the spring of 1980, Vertamae Grosvenor invited me to a birthday picnic in Central Park. At the party was Jackie Battle, whom I'd first met in 1966 at Johnny Nash's apartment, where she was living with Danny Sims. We had always been attracted to each other over the years, and in the early 1970s, long after she and Danny parted, I had invited her to spend the weekend with me at Ray Lofaro's Fire Island summer estate. I was unattached at the time I went to Verta's birthday bash, because Jabu and I just couldn't seem to get it back together. She eventually moved in with Eugene, her on-and-off boyfriend from Bermuda.

Jackie and I hit it off so well at the picnic that over the next few weeks we were practically living together. My old friend Frank Karefa-Smart, with whom we'd spent some very enjoyable times with Fela in Lagos, was also a regular at Mikell's when he was not pursuing his diamond business in Nigeria, Sierra Leone, and Niger. He was married to James Baldwin's sister, and often came to New York to bond with his children and liaise with his business associate, the great diamond magnate Maurice Templesman. Because of mounting business commitments in Sierra Leone, Frank was looking to sublet his luxurious Riverdale apartment in upper New York City. When he asked me to help find him a prospective tenant, I offered to take over the place.

It was at the end of the summer when I got a call from Blowie Moloi, one of South Africa's most successful African businessmen. He was one of the country's top township concert promoters in the 1950s when we were just starting out in the music business with the Huddleston Jazz Band, in which his younger brother Prince played the alto saxophone. In New York on business, Blowie said, "Hugh, you and Miriam have now been gone from home for over twenty years, and even though most people have been buying your records, they would love to see you perform in person. I know you cannot come to South Africa, but we could organize three stadium concerts in Swaziland, Botswana, and Lesotho. Why don't you come down and do it for the home folks? They would come out in multitudes to see you. What do you think?"

"I would love to do that, Bra Blowie, but we have to ask Miriam." By sheer coincidence she was in New York at the time. I called Miriam at her Southgate Towers suite, across from Madison Square Garden, and she was very keen to speak to Blowie. Miriam was extremely enthusiastic about Blowie's proposal, and left all the negotiations to me since she was leaving for Guinea the very next day.

I asked Quincy Troupe to represent us in the negotiations with Blowie. The two of them took to each other right away. A deal was sealed, and we informed Miriam, now back in Guinea, about the itinerary for December. She would bring her musicians from Conakry, and I would bring my Mikell's band. On December 18, 1980, Miriam, Thembi, and I left for Swaziland via Kenya on Pan Am Airways. The rest of the musicians and singers would be leaving the following day on South African Airways to Johannesburg and then take a connecting flight to Lesotho. When we arrived in Swaziland, Blowie had very bad news for us. Bowing to pressure from the South African government, both the Swaziland and Botswana administrations had canceled our concert on the pretense of a cholera outbreak. Lesotho, on the contrary, had refused to cave in, and kept our concert as scheduled for Christmas Day, 1980. For Blowie, the cancellations spelled financial disaster. We flew to Lesotho in a twelve-seater Lesotho Airways plane. Besides incredible air turbulence, reports that the South African government had brought down aircraft flying over its airspace and arrested the antiapartheid passengers made the two-hour flight seem like a lifetime. Miriam was praying, just as I was, that the Afrikaners in power there would not order the pilot to land as we flew over the city of Bloemfontein, one of South Africa's most racist communities. But we made it to Maseru, Lesotho's capital city, in one piece and were greeted at the airport by a full contingent of the southern African press corps. Word quickly spread that Miriam and I were in the region and the concert was to go ahead as planned.

Miriam and I were assigned bodyguards from the top ranks of the Lesotho police, but Miriam felt very uneasy because of the possible presence of South African government hit men in our midst. Miriam stayed at the home of Monsieur Jabbie, a powerful Guinean businessman she knew from Conakry. Only when Alf Kumalo requested a photo shoot did Miriam leave Jabbie's house. The only other times she came out were for the pre-concert sound check and the performance.

I was taken to the home of Maggie and Mpho Motloung, who, although younger, had been very close friends of my father and my late mother. Maggie and Mpho had been blessed with great business success in Lesotho, and enjoyed a life of unfathomable wealth. At their luxurious hilltop home, they had a large suite for me, and proceeded to spoil me like a long-lost child. My father and stepmother, Abigail, and my stepbrother Lesetja arrived the day after we landed in Maseru. A few days before the concert, my younger sisters, Elaine and Sybil, also arrived with their seven children. Unlike my father's new family, who came to stay at Maggie and Mpho's house, Blowie had arranged accommodations for my sisters near my cousin Kay, my uncle Bigvai's third-born daughter, who was married to the head of the Lesotho postal service. It was only a few minutes' drive from where I was staying.

My grandmother Johanna also arrived with several of my great-aunts from

Witbank, Natal, and Ennerdale. Her entourage occupied the guesthouse next to Elaine and Sybil's. Hundreds of people I had grown up with and old school-mates invaded Maseru, anxious to reconnect with Miriam and me. I had trouble recognizing most of them after I'd spent so many years abroad. I had not seen my father, sisters, and grandmother in twenty years. There was obviously a great deal of history to catch up with, and that meant I would have to spend more time separately with my grandmother, my dad, and my two sisters.

Out of traditional respect for age, my first obligation was to sit down with my grandma and give her a full account of my life's activities since I last waved good-bye to her in May of 1960. I gave her an intensely edited version of my twenty years abroad, and although she was hip to the fact that I was leaving out all the juice and sleaze she had been informed about, unlike in our Witbank days, she was not persuaded to lay into me with a belt or a switch from the apricot tree in the backyard, or with painful pinches deep inside my armpits. Instead, Johanna and her traveling companions stared joyfully into my face as I spoke, smiling in pure amazement at the tales I was unfolding, hardly asking any questions. When I came to the end of my story, all Johanna said was, "My child, you have seen the world and escaped many dangers. Your mother and I prayed for you and Barbara every single day that God gave us. I am really happy that you are looking so well and God was kind enough to let me see you before I died. Let us be truly grateful that your mother was fortunate to see you and your sister before she left this world." Johanna then said a long prayer in which she thanked God profusely for all the blessings our family had been so fortunate to receive. After the prayer, she never mentioned my mother's name again. Instead she brought me up to date with what had happened to the Witbank people, almost all of whom had since passed away: Uncle Putu, Uncle Nico, her sister Ouma Sussie, her brother Jacobus and his wife Polintjie and their son, Uncle Warra, their daughters Sibi and Dolly, Gigigi's sisters; her cousin Ouma Tolman; Boy Miga, who was uncle Kalu's nemesis; Kalu's lover; Tilly Miga and Mrs. Miga; her customers George, Molly, Oom Jack, Uncle Bassie, Oupa Legwale, and on and on. They were all gone, and her misfortune appeared to be long life. She had not changed too much, although she was more bent over, her fingers bent out of shape from arthritis, and she used a walking stick. She had to be helped when climbing or descending stairs. Apart from that, she was her old self, talkative, humorous, and as stubborn as ever. She argued endlessly with Elaine and Sybil, disputing just about everything they said.

My two younger sisters were quite the opposite of Johanna. Although happy to be with me again, they were very bitter that Barbara and I had been away from them so long. "You and Barbara just abandoned us and left us to rot in this godforsaken South Africa. You could have sent for us, but all you thought about was yourselves." We were drinking together, which seemed odd because the last time we had been together, they were seven and thirteen years old. They both appeared older than Barbara and me. The violent fights they had endured with their sibling Britton husbands were etched all over their faces. Sybil and Elaine had lost most of their front teeth. When I had last seen them in 1960, they were rosy-cheeked, with cherubic, angelically beautiful faces. This sight of them was tearing me apart deep inside. It broke my heart to see them in this light. Visions of our joyful years in Witbank and in Alexandra Township as a happy family came flooding back to me, but even with these thoughts, I could not cry for what we had lost. I stayed high from cognac and smoke, my hatred for the apartheid regime hardening me. My mother's exit from our lives shortly after her visit to America only increased my venom toward the racists. It is a deep bitterness that has stayed with me ever since, one that makes it absolutely impossible for me to consider reconciliation.

Sybil and Elaine never once mentioned that they were glad to see me, nor did they inquire after my well-being. They just dwelt on their misfortunes and how most of those were directly caused by my abandoning them. They described my mother's funeral in detail, and how devastated my father was by her death. He apparently wept like a little baby and had to be supported by several people at the graveside to keep him from falling down and passing out from hysterical crying. They sobbed and cried painfully while relating all this to me. Although their sad state and their stories were breaking my heart, I just could not shed a tear. My anger was too strong, completely overshadowing any sadness I felt. My father was very relaxed now. He seemed to have gotten over the loss of Polina. He kept assuring me that she'd had a premonition that she was about to leave this world and had repeatedly told him that her heart was at ease because she had seen Barbara and me; she would be able to die in peace. I found this piece of news amazing because she never indicated these feelings to us before she was about to return to South Africa.

I spent a great deal of time shuttling between my grandmother's bungalow, Elaine and Sybil's, my cousin Kay's house, and Maggie and Mpho's mansion. My stepbrother Lesetja went everywhere with me during the day, asking endless questions about America. My cousin Billy, Uncle Kenneth's son, had also come with his wife, Lorna, who told me that we had gone to nursery school together in Payneville, Springs. Billy was in great shape and appeared to be quite successful, holding a top job at IBM in Johannesburg. He related the story of his father's murder in sordid detail. His mother, Aunt Bellie, his brother Boro, and all his other siblings had resolved to drop charges against his killers, who were said to be mindlessly roaming the streets of Kwa-Thema Township, apparently having lost their sanity. Many of my childhood friends came to Lesotho with their families. I could recognize only a few of them. The ravages of apartheid had aged most of them into looking like my father's generation; the effects of heavy drinking were vividly imprinted on their blotchy, toothless faces. There were, however, those who were still in good shape, having taken care of themselves—successful doctors, lawyers, and entrepreneurs. I spent some wonderful times with them at the Holiday Inn and Lancer's Inn, talking about the old days and drinking into the early mornings. There was hardly any time for the reckless womanizing I had anticipated. I now actually wished I had brought Jackie along with me.

It was especially frustrating to look into South Africa from Maseru's high elevation and have to absorb the pain of not being able to cross the border to go home. Alf Kumalo took a striking photo of Miriam and me looking over the border. It appeared on the front page of the *Star*, graphically depicting our painful presence so close to the country of our birth, which we dared not enter.

By Christmas Day, my grandmother's ninetieth birthday, close to 100,000 people had invaded Lesotho to attend our concert, which also included other top South African groups, like Lesotho's outstanding Uhuru, led by Tsepo Tshola and Frank Leepa. The audience was made up of all colors of people, cars were lined up for miles across the border where their owners had parked them and walked into Lesotho on foot to see us perform. There was a carnival atmosphere in Maseru. There was no hotel space; people walked the streets in a spirit of revelry.

Miriam and I both put on performances, which lasted over two hours each, singing and playing all the South African songs that had been made famous through our recordings. The audience clapped, screamed, and sang along frenziedly while they danced up a storm to "Phata, Phata," "The Click Song," "Grazing in the Grass," "The Marketplace," "Ashiko," "Thanayi," "Umqhokozo," "Amampondo," "Part of a Whole," and dozens of other songs we played for them. The entire celebrations tore a gaping whole in the insulation the apartheid overlords had tried to build for the protection of their racial superiority.

Throughout the night following the concert, some slept on the sidewalks, in doorways of storefronts, and in the parks. The country ran out of all commodities. Lesotho's army deployed military transports to fetch supplies from South Africa's neighboring cities. Miriam's and my performances reverberated right across the Drakensberg Mountains and valleys into the most venerated corners of South Africa's white-supremacy citadels.

I deeply admired the government of Lesotho for having refused to be intimidated by the South African government into canceling the festival. Pascal Ngakane, the country's chief health officer, who was an expatriate South African, had proved beyond doubt that cholera could not develop in the mountains of Lesotho, where stagnant water was almost unheard of and the climate was too cold for the bacterium to thrive. This theory left the apartheid regime's argument totally without any foundation. The outrageously huge attendance and success of the concert left them absolutely without a comment.

Not being able to observe the South African government's reaction in person, I imagined that the screaming headlines must have left the regime's big shots in a furious state, especially because Lesotho had a very large political exile community from South Africa, and the country's prime minister, Leabua Jonathan, had already infuriated the racists by allowing the Chinese and Russians to open embassies in the Mountain Kingdom, as Lesotho is popularly known to tourists. I thought that the festival had been a major coup. I was seriously considering settling down in Maseru.

René McLean and I stayed behind after the concert and embarked on an initiative to build a recording studio with the help of Mpho Motloung's financial muscle and the Lesotho Development Corporation, headed by Sam Montsi. René McLean met Roma University English professor Thandiwe January and the two fell madly in love. I continued to stay with Mpho and Maggie after my South African family went home. It was sad to say good-bye—our time together had been too brief after two decades away. Shortly after their departure, my dad's youngest sister, Aunt Clara, called from Natal, and Mpho invited her to come and visit. I hadn't seen her since 1956, when the family had spent the winter holidays at her home in Durban. She stayed for a week and regaled us with outrageously funny stories about her youth with her siblings and parents in Randjiesfontein, which is now known as Midrand, one of

Johannesburg's most upscale neighborhoods, from which Africans were forcibly removed in the very early 1900s. Aunt Clara was a bundle of joy. This was the last time I saw her, because she died in an automobile accident in Melmoth, Natal, a year before my return to South Africa. The deaths seemed to be piling up.

Before René and I left Lesotho, after staying in the country almost three months, I got a call from George Phahle, my childhood friend from Alexandra Township. He was in Botswana. He insisted that I come and see him before I headed back to the States. I promised Maggie and Mpho that I would do thorough research into what we would need to build our recording studio. When we arrived in Botswana, George and I were thrilled to see each other after a whole twenty-five years. George planned a welcome party for that evening, to which he had invited a major cross-section of Gaborone's prominent citizenry. At the party, George played only South African township mbhaqanga music, pointing out to me that he had no time for jazz, pop, or rhythm and blues; the only music allowed in his house had to be township grooves, of which he had the most amazing collection, ranging from Zakes Nkosi and Ntemi Piliso to Ladysmith Black Mambazo, the Dark City Sisters, and Mahlathini and the Mahotella Queens. When this music was on, it was difficult to get George off the dance floor. His wife, Lindi, shared his passion, and the party lasted into the early hours of the next morning.

George had left South Africa for exile in 1977 when the apartheid administration was gunning for him after he had allegedly been involved in a bombing attack on the Carlton Center in downtown Johannesburg. He was running a successful transport company. Jonas Gwangwa was also now living in Botswana, married to Violet, his childhood sweetheart. Jonas was director of the African National Congress's cultural group, Amandla. In Gaborone, there was quite a large presence of South African exiles, the majority of whom were liberation cadres who had been fleeing that country since the 1976 student uprisings. Many of that group were ANC, and George, Lindi, Jonas Gwangwa, and Wally Serote held vital leadership roles. They had formed the MEDU Cultural Trust, which was planning a cultural and resistance festival in July 1982. George also introduced René and me to a local group called Mother. After a few rehearsals with the band, in which Jonas joined us, we played a benefit concert for former first lady Ruth Khama's children's charity. The show, which was staged at the University of Botswana, was a sellout. Afterward, George suggested I stay in Botswana to teach music, cultivate a band, and build a studio, instead of in Lesotho, which he noted was landlocked and could become a trap should the South African government decide to attack. René returned to his love, Thandiwe, in Lesotho.

An intended weekend stay stretched into a month as relatives and childhood friends kept coming across the border to see me. I was having the time of my life with George and Lindi. Wally Serote gave me an invitation to deliver to pianist Abdullah Ibrahim for the cultural resistance festival. When I left Botswana, I promised to come back for the festival the following year. Back in Lesotho, Thembi Mtshali told me of how she would be stopping in Nigeria on her way back to New York, and I should join her because she was a big star there after having taken the country by storm when she toured with *Ipi Tombi*.

When we arrived in Lagos, the crowds went crazy over Thembi, screaming "Queen! Queen!" until we drove up to Bobby Benson's hotel, where the place was surrounded by more frenzied fans. I hadn't realized what a heavy impact *Ipi Tombi* had had on the audiences who got to see it all over the world. I never attended the show because all the solidarity groups such as the antiapartheid movement and the African National Congress had blacklisted it under the cultural boycott, which discouraged people from attending shows that came out of South Africa and patronizing artists who had performed in that country. In New York City there had been pickets outside the Broadway theater where it was showing, but every performance was sold out. My friend Rudy Lucas apologized to me: "Hughie, you know I love you, my brother, but I just had to go and feed my eyes on those South African thunder thighs, and I gotta say one thing for your country, boy. It is definitely the undisputed home of the big ass. Don't get me wrong, though, I really loved the music and you know I support the cultural boycott with all my heart. However, I have to confess that I've been to see the show five times already." Then he laughed like a little schoolboy who didn't give a shit if he was caught with his hand in the cookie jar. Although the picketing forced *Ipi Tombi* to close down on Broadway, it played in Las Vegas for several years. Rudy wasn't the only friend of mine who snuck in to see the show.

A couple of days later I took a plane to Liberia, hoping to see my daughter Pula, who was now three years old. The country had been through a bloody coup, in which Major Samuel K. Doe, who had been a presidential guard, took over as president after he and his comrade Kwingpah led a massacre of president Tolbert and most of his cabinet and friends, including acquaintances of mine. To a certain extent I was taking a chance by going to Liberia; the men now in power were not likely to be very civil to a friend of the old regime.

Sister Gertie's description of how Tolbert and his friends were mowed down after being marched down to the beach in Mamba Point, next to the city center, was bloodcurdling to say the least.

I found Pula playing alone near a rubbish dump across from where Tshidi was renting a flat. The little girl was beautiful, calm, and friendly. She clung to me like chewing gum to the sole of a shoe. Tshidi had completed her medical studies and was now working as a doctor at Monrovia's John F. Kennedy Hospital, where she was making a very decent living. I regretted the way things had gone down between us, but Tshidi had changed her life for the better, and she still practices medicine in South Africa, where her talents as a doctor command great respect.

That weekend Pula, Philemon Hou, his wife, Georgia, and my nephew Mabusha, who was now fifteen and really tall, went to a picnic out on Zuma Beach. The seaside picnic spot was full of revelers who had forgotten about the recent coup and were barbecuing and dancing to the loud music of a local DJ. Pula and I swam in the lagoon with scores of other folks, and she wouldn't let me out of her sight, clinging to me for dear life in the water.

After dinner at Philemon's house, I went to Eddie Dunn's nightclub, where I had spent many wonderful nights with friends who were now dead as a result of the coup. Many others had fled the country. Except for the midnight curfew, there was no real evidence of tension around the city, although soldiers were at many roadblocks, on patrol through the streets and at the bars all over Monrovia. Eddie told me not to worry about the curfew, and said that I was safe inside his establishment. Sitting next to me was a lieutenant who smiled at me and said, "Hughie, you don't remember me, but you took a few girls away from me when I was a presidential guard, but those days are gone, bubba!" I froze, thinking the shit was about to hit the fan. "Anyway," he continued, "you were always okay with us soldier boys, Masekela. You bought me beer many times, man, and were always friendly to a fellow. You even gave me twenty dollars whenever Speedy had you come over to the palace. I always carried your trumpet for you. You take your time, man, and when you're good and ready, I will personally take you to the Ducor Hotel. Eddie, tell this man he's in good hands with me." I was so relieved that I didn't even notice how much I was perspiring in spite of the serious air conditioning.

The next morning I wanted to revisit some of my favorite haunts and see if some of the old regulars were still around. I drove to El Meson, an old favorite bar where Nga, Bob Young, and I had shared many wonderful breakfasts together followed by our first double cognacs of the day with an ice-cold beer chaser. We used to love this spot, where we regularly conducted early-morning business meetings. Sitting in my customary corner in an old wicker lounge chair, I was on my third double cognac when the waiter brought my breakfast. As I dug in to the food, the place went quiet. A uniformed group of generals walked in, and were escorted to the corner in the far end of the lounge. Shortly afterwards, my waiter came over to me and said, "General Kwingpah sent me to bring you to his table, sir." I obediently abandoned my meal.

"Sit down, Hugh," the soldier said without looking at me. "Welcome back home. It's good to see you in Monrovia. I just want you to know that you were always okay with us, my man. I will tell President Doe I saw you. You must come to the palace and greet him. If you need anything, just give me a call. This boy here," he said, pointing to the soldier sitting next to him, "will give you my telephone number. Again, welcome and enjoy your stay." With that, he waved me away I felt very uncomfortable.

I paid my food and drinks bill and went straight to the Pan Am ticket office to book a seat on that evening's flight to New York. From there, I went to get an exit permit at the immigration offices, where the soldier in charge made me aware that things had changed in Liberia. "Hughie, I can't give you an exit permit just like that. You got to give up something, my man." I gave him a hundred-dollar bill, drove to the hotel, and started packing.

I spent the rest of the day at Sister Gertie's house with Pula, Philly, Mabusha, and Georgia. That evening Philly drove me to the airport. I was relieved when the plane took off, even though I didn't know what New York had in store for me. Through most of the flight, the innermost fear haunting me was what might happen to my little daughter and my nephew Mabusha. My life was in shambles; my career was in limbo. After being away from New York for three months, I didn't have a band to speak of. I was actually returning to start again from scratch.

18

WHEN I GOT TO NEW YORK, Pat and Mike Mikell encouraged me to get a band together so I could come in and start playing their club again. René McLean had telephoned saxophonist Fred Foss to stand in for him. The rest of the band members from the Lesotho festival reunited with me, and we were soon back together at Mikell's, with Hotep Galeta rejoining us on second keyboards. We got some bookings outside New York, and it wasn't long before I was back on my feet again.

René married his lover Thandiwe in Lesotho, and they planned for her to move in with him in New York as soon as she could make arrangements. René returned to the States after a couple of months to prepare for his bride's arrival, and rejoined our band. Quincy's wife, Margaret, told me that Jabu was about to marry her old boyfriend Eugene. This news made me very unhappy. "Leave her alone, Hughie. You're not going to make her life a nightmare again," Margaret warned me, but I begged her for Jabu's number, and right away we began seeing each other again. I did not even have the decency to call the woman I had been living with before I left for Africa. I had completely forgotten about Jackie Battle, and dropped her unceremoniously. Something was definitely wrong with my head, and I didn't know it.

Blinded by jealousy, I could not stand the thought of Jabu marrying anybody but me. I was certain that we were made for each other. I proposed marriage to Jabu, and she readily accepted. I was warmly welcomed into her family by her mother, Beatty, who literally adopted me as her own son. Mama Beatty made it a rule that every Friday evening we must come to her place at

5th Avenue and 107th Street for family dinner. I absolutely loved this experience, which previously I had only seen in the movies. The Friday evenings
were special; I always made sure to bring beautiful flowers for my future
mother-in-law. Barbara and I arranged for Mabusha to return from Liberia.

I moved out of my Riverdale apartment and in with Jabu at 400 Central Park
West at 100th Street. Although unhappy to lose me as a tenant, Frank Karefa-
Smart was very thrilled for me. Jabu and I got along extremely well, unlike
before, when we used to have sudden arguments whose sources we could
hardly retrace. We were madly in love, and I began to make a major change in
my previously insane lifestyle. Every morning I would walk Jabu to the bus
stop on the corner of 100th Street and wave good-bye to her as she went to her
job downtown. Then I would run through Central Park for a full hour and do
another hour of stretches and exercises before returning home to eat breakfast, practice the trumpet, and then go down to the 63rd Street YMCA for a
swim, steam, and sauna, followed by an occasional massage. Jabu also put us
on a serious diet, and after six weeks we looked like fashion models.

Following African custom, I asked my sister Barbara, my cousin Collins
Ramusi, who was teaching in Chicago, my cousin Gaby Magomola, who was
the "golden boy" at Citicorp, and my cousin the actor, playwright, and theater
director Selaelo Maredi, to ask Jabu's family for her hand in marriage.

That August we were married at the Cathedral of St. John the Divine. We
had an afternoon reception at the Village Gate, where my band played. Collins
recited the Batlokwa praises of our clan. Jabu's father, Mphiwa, reciprocated
with some awesome Zulu praises. That evening we moved the wedding gala
and get-down party to Mama Beatty's apartment complex community hall,
where a DJ played South African township dance hits. There was a wide variety of African home cooking and every kind of drink imaginable, including
traditional sorghum beer. South African wedding songs were sung as we
marched in rhythm around the block. People were hanging out their windows
in the summer heat at a total loss as to what we were all about. Some of the
more curious were screaming, "Hey, what's going on down there?" We yelled
back, "It's a South African township wedding."

"Right on," someone shouted. "I love it! It's fucking beautiful, man. I wanna
get married like dat."

We danced furiously back at the party, with everybody else trying to out-
dance us. But Jabu is one of the meanest dancers ever to step onto the dance
floor. Jabu and I left the revelers shortly after midnight and shared a taxi with

Remi Kabaka, our band percussionist from Nigeria, who is very difficult to shut up. High out of our skulls from the all-day-and-night drinking, smoking, and snorting, Remi and I couldn't stop running our mouths, and when we got to Remi's house on the same street as ours, he invited us upstairs, where we thought we would just have one drink. However, Remi and I continued our yapping, snorting, drinking, and smoking. Jabu, who had taken only a couple of glasses of champagne and was nowhere near as whacked as we were, finally exploded. She had had enough. She stormed out of Remi's apartment, slamming the door behind her. I ran after her, apologizing, but it was too late. I had ruined our wedding night and she was furious. At our flat, she quickly changed clothes and stormed out, slamming the door in my face. I stood there dumbfounded and speechless. Less than an hour later she returned. We made peace, but Jabu looked me straight in the eye and said in a sullen voice, "We are doomed."

I replied, "Don't say that."

She repeated coldly, "We are doomed."

When Barbara moved to Zambia to join Oliver Tambo's ANC office staff in that country, it happened very suddenly and she asked for Mabusha to come and stay with us. Right away, Mabusha and Jabu did not get along, so I asked Jane and Mburumba Kerina to take him in, and he was extremely happy there with their children Kakuna, Kambandi, and Mandume, who were already quite grown up. Kakuna was now working at *Essence* magazine, Kambandi was an architect, and Mandume a doctor. I thought that this would be a major inspiration for Mabusha, and it was. He had really been through the mill. Born when Miriam and I lived in New Jersey, he'd spent his infancy on the Lower East Side with Barbara in her friend's apartment. Barbara had taken him to Zambia, where she attended the university in Lusaka. Miriam had come and scooped him up when he was two years old, and taken him on the road all over Europe and America. I'd taken him from Miriam when he was three years old, and he'd gone to California with me, where he lived through my mad period with Chris Calloway and the great drug bust. He'd lived with Big Black's family until he moved in with Jessie and me. He'd then gone to Athens, Ohio, with Barbara, then to New York, from where I'd taken him to Guinea and Liberia. He'd come back from Monrovia a few days before I married Jabu. He was now fifteen years old and had lived in more places than most nomadic adults do in a whole lifetime. Still, Mabusha passed his high school finals with flying colors. Don Will, Jabu's brother-in-law, who was married to her sister Ntathu, arranged an inter-

view for him at Pennsylvania's Haverford College, where he was due to start in
September of 1983.

A few times when the situation between Jabu and me got volatile, I would
ask Mama Beatty to intercede, but the lull wouldn't last for too long. By June of
1982, Jabu and I were hardly speaking. A few times I would go up to Stewart
and Jolie's upstate farm in Oliverea, or to my cousin Gaby Magomola and his
wife Nana's Roosevelt Island home on New York's East River, just so the two of
us could get a break from our madness. Finally, when the time came for me to
go down to Botswana for the Cultural Resistance Festival, I left without saying
good-bye to Jabu. I just packed my suitcases and took off while she was at work.

When I arrived in Gaborone, rehearsals for the festival were already on the
wing. Many actors, writers, poets, activists, and musicians from South Africa
and other parts of Africa had rolled into town for the workshops, seminars,
readings, and performances. The great saxophonists King Force Silgee, Barney
Rachabane, Duke Makasi, and Mike Makhalemele, the trumpeter Dennis
Mpale, and the keyboard genius Tony Cedras were all in town. Along with
Jonas Gwangwa, we began rehearsals. Dorothy Masuka prepared all of her
wonderful compositions of the 1950s, which were the era's mega-hits, with
most of us accompanying her. The crowds went wild! Dorothy sang
"Nontsokolo," "Kutheni Zulu," "Khawuleza," "MaGumede," "Imali Yani,"
and "Khanyange." It was a mbhaqanga feast. When we played Abdullah
Ibrahim's "Mannenberg," everybody screamed with delight. People came
from as far away as Holland, Germany, the United Kingdom, West Africa,
Scandinavia, the Soviet Union, Japan, and China. They danced like it was the
end of the world, many of them weeping with joy. It was an unforgettable
week. We were sure that Abdullah would join us on the last night, but he
requested that we all leave the stage. He then played an hour's concert of solo
piano. We were mesmerized by his genius performance, but surprised that he
refused to play with us. The audience went crazy over him.

The band Mother had recently added John Selolwane, an outstanding guitarist and vocalist who drove the crowds wild with his solo work. The band
served as the main rhythm section for the entire festival, and afterwards I went
on to play with Mother all around Gaborone and Botswana's eastern towns
and villages. We renamed our band Kalahari, after the famous Botswana
desert. We quickly became one of the hottest bands in southern Africa. We
toured and played six-hour shows. The Botswana people simply love to dance,

and at the end of the night, usually just before four, they would complain that it was still too early to go home.

During all this time, I was living with George and Lindi in their four-room Broadhurst home. Housing was an extremely scarce commodity in Gaborone. However, at the beginning of 1983, George helped me find an affordable four-room house in Gaborone's Section 12, about a mile and a half from his place and a fifteen-minute walk to the city's business district. With the help of Seemisho Motuba, our band manager and driver, and a neighbor, Tsepo Koka, we painted and fixed the disheveled dwelling over a two-week period. Our childhood friend Julius Mdluli, who visited us regularly from Johannesburg and had helped to set George up in his transportation business, brought me a used stereo set, a fridge, and some old cooking utensils. I furnished the house sparsely with the bare essentials, like beds made by a carpenter friend, a kitchen table and chairs, cutlery and crockery, and curtains that Violet, Jonas's wife, sewed for me. In my heart and mind, I was through with Jabu and preparing for divorce proceedings, but many people, including George and Lindi, my father, Violet, Jonas, and Jabu's South African cousins, were pressuring me to make up with her. I finally gave in and invited Jabu to come back. She made a major sacrifice by resigning from her highly lucrative job at the *New York Times* to come and live with me when I was basically quite poor and in the process of building a new life in a place that was foreign to me. In the beginning it was very difficult. Not owning a car, we had to walk to the city center when taxis were unavailable from the main road at the end of our street, then hire one when we returned from shopping. We had to take taxis if we wished to visit anywhere else. As the weeks went by and I played more shows with Kalahari, we were able to properly furnish the house and buy a small Datsun 1400 pickup. Soon we had living room and guest room furniture, a stereo, television, new kitchen fittings, and a garden that was producing beautiful flowers.

My father came to visit us from time to time and arranged a ceremony at his home in Sharpeville to introduce Jabu to our clan. My aunt Ackila, the wife of my father's brother Bigvai, was another regular visitor. Her daughter Maphiri, who was a political exile in Tanzania, always came to our house to be with her dear mother. The great thing about Gaborone was the four-hour drive to Johannesburg. Friends and relatives visited regularly. It was also a gateway to the rest of Africa, which enabled our friends and relatives who were in exile in Angola, Zimbabwe, Zambia, and Tanzania to visit. Barbara came once from

Lusaka when our grandmother Johanna was also visiting. It was a great reunion, but Barbara warned George and me: "You people must be vigilant. The Boers will come and try to kill all of you South Africans one day." We didn't take her words lightly.

Jabu's sister Mpozi and her husband, Fana, had decided to send their three-year-old daughter Deliwe to his parents in Soweto while working on being more stable financially. When Jabu visited her, however, she came back distraught because the environment where she was staying was so rough. We decided to adopt Deliwe temporarily until her parents were ready to take her back. Deliwe was a pure delight, a joy to have with us, and a wonderful addition to our home. She became a major catalyst to our happiness. We enrolled her in the YMCA nursery school a short walk from our house, and in a few weeks we made great new friends who were parents of her classmates. Around this time, without any particular incident or influence, I found myself losing interest in alcohol. I just stopped drinking, and it felt absolutely wonderful. I was now quite settled in Botswana, and my marriage had become very well stabilized except for the occasional flare-up. I am convinced that we owed this stability to the fact that I stopped drinking.

In May 1983, Malombo jazz group founder Julian Bahula, who was now a budding concert promoter in London, called me with an invitation to perform at the first Mandela birthday concert. It was to be at London's Alexandra Palace, presented in conjunction with the ANC office in that country. In London I rehearsed with a group of South African musicians led by saxophonist Dudu Pukwana. It was also a joy to see Bishop Trevor Huddleston after twenty-three years. Unfortunately we spent very little time together because the Anti-Apartheid Movement and the South African Defense and Aid Organization, both of which he headed, were directly responsible for this first celebration of Mandela. He was a very busy man. It was also the affirmation of ANC president Oliver Tambo's campaign to promote Nelson Mandela internationally as the central symbol in South Africa's liberation struggle, and further raised the awareness of the world concerning the outrageous barbarism of the apartheid regime.

My performance at the concert and the entire proceedings of that week were reported negatively in the South African press. My recordings were already banned on the government-owned South African Broadcasting Corporation. My participation on the seventeenth of July, the day before Mandela's sixty-fifth birthday, only helped to exacerbate the regime's hatred of me.

South African–born producer Clive Calder, who was just establishing Jive/Zomba Records, attended the concert and expressed his interest in signing me to his label. He decided that it would perhaps be smart to bring a mobile studio to Botswana and bring the South African musicians I needed to Gaborone. He was highly enthusiastic about the idea, and wanted to bring Stewart Levine on as producer.

Around this time, I received word from Miriam that Philemon Hou, who composed "Grazing in the Grass," had died of kidney disease in Liberia, which devastated me. I wondered if he had not been afforded the care he required because of shortages of equipment, medicine, and personnel since the regime of Samuel Doe had resulted in a major exodus of the professional community from Liberia. I thought about our wonderful days at the Queens Road house in Los Angeles. I was crushed that one more South African had died in lonely exile, far away from his extended family.

One day in Gaborone, Tsepo Tshola, from Lesotho's Uhuru band, showed up at my front door with his suitcases. Very surprised, I greeted him with a welcoming embrace and asked, "Are you guys playing in town this weekend?" Tsepo replied with a big smile on his beaming face, "I have come to you, Bra Hugh." Kalahari was sizzling. Tsepo Tshola had left Uhuru and was now singing with our band. We toured extensively throughout Botswana when we were not playing gigs at the Woodpecker Inn on Friday nights, the "500" Club on Saturday nights, and poolside at the Oasis Hotel on Sunday afternoons. Then we were invited to play in Maseru, Lesotho, during the Christmas and New Year holidays.

In 1982 the South African Defense Force death squads had raided Maseru and massacred forty-two people, mostly exiled ANC members and their families. They were murdered under the guise of destroying terrorist strongholds of guerrillas that allegedly raided South Africa from time to time. South Africa's death squads were in the habit of raiding Zimbabwe, Swaziland, Namibia, Lesotho, and Zambia, where Barbara was now working in Oliver Tambo's office in Lusaka. South Africa supported RENAMO in Mozambique and UNITA in Angola and the Ian Smith regime in Rhodesia, as well as Kamuzu Banda in Malawi, all of whom were against the "left-wing devils" in the region. The raids caused major destabilization in the entire region neighboring South Africa. Lesotho, which had been a major tourist attraction, had been quickly impoverished. Botswana had not yet suffered the same nightmare. Tsepo explained to me that Maseru had been transformed into a cultural and recreational desert. He felt that instead of rotting there, he should come and join Kalahari. "Besides," he said in his joyously boisterous fashion, "you guys need a lead singer."

The people of Botswana fell in love with Tsepo. Out of the blue, Valentine Pringle, whom I had met through Harry Belafonte in 1962 with guitarist Bruce Langhorne and spent such memorable "party times" with at my 82nd Street apartment, invited me and Kalahari to come and play a few shows at Maseru's Lancer's Inn over the 1983 year-end holidays. He was managing the establishment and was in the middle of negotiations to purchase the place.

Mpho Motloung had died along with his parents in a car accident a few months after I last saw him. When I arrived in Lesotho, by air from Botswana, the first thing I did was to visit his widow, Maggie, and their daughter Millie at their mansion, which, although as majestic as ever, was now missing the bright spark of his electric personality, his loud laughter and ever-smiling face. Maseru felt like a ghost town. Gone was the sparkling, lively chatter of its citizens. Gloom pervaded the air. Absent were the tourists and the festive character for which this beautiful mountain kingdom was famous.

Our audiences at the Lancer's Inn during the festive season were minuscule compared to the 100,000 people who had filled the stadium when we performed there on Christmas Day in 1980. We also did a show in Mafeteng, an hour's drive from Maseru. Jabu and Deliwe had arrived a few days earlier, and the three of us were staying with her cousin in Morija, a town halfway between Maseru and Mafeteng. After the Mafeteng gig, I ran into an old friend who invited me to his home for drinks. A few hours later I was driving to Morija when a car approached from the opposite direction with its bright beams on. I flashed my headlights and before I knew it, the car had made a U-turn and started to chase my vehicle with its siren blaring. I pulled over and two soldiers with AK-47s jumped out and stuck their weapons in my neck from both sides of my car. One jumped into the front passenger seat and the other behind me. With their weapons still pressed to my neck, they ordered me to follow the car they had been riding in. We ended up in the police station, where all my valuables and my belt and shoes were taken. I was thrown into a dank, smelly cell with a bucket half-full of shit and piss with green flies hovering around it. The cell next to mine housed two teenaged girls who told me they had been falsely arrested for prostitution. I was terrified.

I had not been officially booked, and the soldiers who had arrested me began to ram my ribs with the buts of their weapons. One of them kept punching my forehead with his long, dirty nails till he pierced the flesh and blood started dripping down my nose and onto my shirt. He promised to put a bullet through my head at dawn. The soldiers accused me of being an underground member of the Lesotho Liberation Front, a militant faction that was attempting to overthrow the Leabua Jonathan regime. Jonathan had founded the Basutoland National Party, which worked for separate independence from Great Britain rather than becoming a part of the Union of South Africa. He became prime minister in 1965 under a constitution that preceded Basutoland's independence as Lesotho in 1966. He lost the national election in 1970, suspended the constitution, ruled by decree, and exiled the opposition. South Africa blockaded Lesotho when Jonathan provided sanctuary to ANC guerrillas.

Before dawn, the three soldiers returned and tried to get me to sign a confession. They refused to accept that I was in Lesotho for concert performances, and pretended not to know who I really was. At around six that morning I heard the voices of my friend with whom I had been drinking the night before, and that of my wife, her cousin, and her cousin's husband. The policeman who had just come on duty could not find my name in the charge book, and Jabu was repeatedly crying, "Are you sure there is no Hugh Masekela here?"

I screamed through the bars of my cell, "I'm here! I'm here!"

Jabu started crying loudly, calling out, "Hughie! Where are you?"

"I'm here!" I screamed. "Don't leave me here. They want to kill me. I'm here! I'm here!" My friend telephoned his uncle, who was the chief of Mafeteng's police. He soon arrived, very angry to be awakened so early in the morning, cussed out the police on duty, and ordered them to release me immediately. He then called the head of the Lesotho army, who came to meet us near the prison. The general apologized profusely and gave his assurance that my money and valuables with which the soldiers had absconded would be returned to me. He begged my forgiveness and asked me not to speak to the press about the incident. I got a call from the prime minister's office the following day with more apologies and the same request to keep the matter a secret. A few days later Jabu, Deliwe, Tsepo, John Selolwane, and I flew out of Lesotho in a private plane because Botswana Airways had just discontinued flights to Maseru. The six-seat airplane flight was like a horrible nightmare. Amazingly, little Deliwe slept throughout the entire two hours of violent turbulence. However, it felt wonderful to be out of Lesotho. My new record company had chartered the airplane because we were due to begin recording at the new mobile studio, which was parked next to the guesthouse whose lounge we would use as the recording room. This facility was part of the Woodpecker Inn, where Kalahari performed on Friday nights. Julia Helfer, the Ghanaian proprietor of the Woodpecker, who was also my attorney, was a naturalized Botswanan citizen. She was extremely accommodating in agreeing to lease us one of her guesthouses for use as a recording studio.

Stewart Levine arrived in Gaborone shortly after the engineer sent down from England by Clive Calder had spent a week wiring and setting up the equipment at the Woodpecker. After a false start, with some of the musicians in Kalahari not being able to record as well as they played live, Stewart decided that we should invite some members of the Soul Brothers, South Africa's premier mbhaqanga band, to play on the recording. Bassist Zakes Mchunu, keyboard and organ wizard Moses Ngwenya, and drummer Bongani made all the difference. Veterans of more than twenty hit albums, their experience propelled us forward at a very fast pace. From England came programmer and Fairlight keyboard genius Peter Harris and the Nigerian percussionist Gasper Lawal.

In the blistering heat of Botswana's midsummer, bare-chested, sun-baked, and dripping with perspiration, we finished the rhythm tracks in one week and bade farewell to our Soul Brothers colleagues. We recorded an old composition of Tsepo Tshola's called "Pula Ea Na" (It's Raining), a happy song exhorting the villagers to prepare to plow, the herd boys to rein up the fieldwork bulls, the women to plant the seeds, and the children to come out from under the trees where lightning usually strikes, because the rain is coming down. "Motlalepula" was a sung poem for my little daughter, Pula, who was now living in Mafikeng, South Africa, where her mother, Tshidi, was practicing medicine after recently returning from Liberia. *"Motlalepula is the irrigator, the owner of the waters; her home is in the clouds. She has turned her back on us. But she will send back the water if we go down on our knees and supplicate our ancestors to send her back to us so she can bring back the water to Africa."*

At this time, Botswana was in its first year of a menacing drought that was bringing even the reptiles and the strangest-looking insects out from under the ground. At the Woodpecker Inn, which was on the banks of the Notwane River, every manner of nearby bush animal was migrating to the waterside. Giant lizards, all kinds of snakes, birds, bucks, and rodent were running to cool themselves down by the riverside. The inn manager's pedigreed Alsatian was gobbled up by a hungry python, and one music-loving baby cobra actually perched itself up right against one of the studio windows on the outside and swayed from side to side to the rhythm of "Don't Go Lose It, Baby," a fast-paced disco track with a Fela-like Afro-beat rhythm and happy lyrics, "Everybody out here loves a winner, don't go lose it, baby." I did some rapping on this track at Stewart's urging. "Everybody's rappin' in America, Hughie, let's try some," he said. We co-wrote the lyrics to this song and the rap went, *"A winner ain't a loser and a loser ain't a winner. Let me tell you that's the name of the game, when you lose you booze and when you booze you lose and then you wonder why you lose your shoes. I met a girl one day. She was on her way, to make a movie down in L.A. She said, 'I'll never lose!' I said, 'You'll never win.' I bet you never ever heard her name. Well, every winner's name is in the Hall of Fame, and you're a winner when you beat the game; you're a winner when you beat the game."* This song went to the number-two spot in the American dance charts behind Prince's "When Doves Cry," helping me to bring the Kalahari band to Europe and America. We also did a disco medley to "Skokiaan," "Grazing in the Grass," "Mbube," and a few other South African township favorites. After Stewart and I completed the recordings in London, the rest of Kalahari came to join me on a UK tour before we went on to the States. By the end of the summer of 1984, we had toured the East Coast and the Midwestern states to much acclaim.

Before we left London, I went to see a brilliant two-man play at the Criterion Theatre in the West End, called *Woza Albert*. Mbongeni Ngema and Percy Mtwa started their show with a riveting version of "Stimela," the now-famous coal-train song I had written ten years earlier. After the show I went backstage to meet the actors, and complimented them on their brilliant arrangement of "Stimela." Mbongeni took credit for the arrangement and told me that he was a musician. I had always wanted to do a musical, and asked him if he would be interested in collaborating on one in the future. We exchanged addresses and telephone numbers and promised to keep in touch.

Clive Calder and the rest of the Jive Records staff were very happy with the results of the *Technobush* album we had just recorded. Clive suggested that we go back to the Botswana studio for a second album. Stewart and I had begun an initiative for a music school in Botswana during the *Technobush* recording. We received enthusiastic support from the American embassy and the Botswana Music Society, and from European and American expatriate development organizations around the country. With their concerted efforts and several fund-raising concerts by Kalahari, we were able to lease a small build-ing and buy instruments. Members of the Music Society volunteered their teaching skills, and before long the ministry of education assisted us in launch-ing the Botswana International School of Music. Khabi Mngoma, founder of the music department at the University of Zululand, was a friend of my mother from their Jan Hofmeyer school days in the early 1940s. He guided us on how to run the school—a priceless gift to us, because he was a furiously busy man in South Africa. Nevertheless, he contributed his valuable time to get us off the ground without demanding a cent for his guidance.

Toward the end of September, Bishop Trevor Huddleston came to visit Botswana and stayed at the home of Archbishop Makhudu, a few minutes' walking distance from my house. Jabu and I went to have lunch with them, and Huddleston was so impressed with the Botswana International School of Music initiative that he suggested we should do a fund-raiser for the institution when I was next in London. He promised that he would give a speech on that occasion. Although Huddleston was beginning to get bent over from age, he still maintained his awe-inspiring air of dignity and was even more eloquent than ever. He told us about his wonderful experience as archbishop of Tanzania, Zanzibar, and the Indian Ocean Islands. After that, he was made archbishop of Stepney, in the rough East End of London, where he started the Human League, another music group that became world famous. He was very proud of them. Huddleston was now in retirement and stationed at St. James Church on Piccadilly in Central London.

Since 1984, many car-bomb assassinations had been targeted at exiled polit-ical activists in Europe and in the countries neighboring South Africa. After collecting the mail, Dulcie September, who headed the ANC's Paris office, was opening the door to her office on March 29, 1988, when an assassin believed to be working for the South African hit squads shot her five times. It was written in her obituary that forty-five-year-old Dulcie, a soft-spoken, dedicated worker, had never handled anything more deadly than a pen or a typewriter. The ANC's London office in Camden Town had also been bombed. Many libera-tion activists in Windhoek, Dar es Salaam, Harare, Gaborone, Maseru, Mbabane, and Luanda, and in Lusaka, Zambia, had been murdered by the apartheid regime's death squad assassins. The South African government deployed death squads wherever it felt individuals should be eliminated.

Robben Island was overcrowded ever since the 1976 student uprisings. The exodus from South Africa of people who were eager to receive military train-ing abroad was at an all-time high. Friends and family who visited exiles such as George and Lindi Phahle and those of us considered to be antiapartheid activists were harassed and summoned to John Vorster Square police head-quarters once they returned to South Africa for interrogation. Julius Mduli, who called us a few times a week on the telephone and visited us regularly, was constantly hounded by the South African police, but he always told them that he was not about to turn his back on his friends because the government authorities objected to his visits. The police constantly terrorized our parents, siblings, close relations, and friends, and their homes were regularly ransacked by the South African Gestapo. People who were not imprisoned but deemed dangerous were placed under house arrest or banished. Winnie Mandela, Albertina Sisulu, and the families of the Robben Island prisoners were terror-ized daily. The atmosphere was very tense. We were all living in fear.

At the beginning of 1985 I was still living a sober and clean life, much to the surprise of all those who knew me. I was still smoking marijuana, but I would not touch any alcohol. Around March, Kalahari and I began to work on *Waiting for the Rain,* our follow-up album to *Technobush.* We added on cele-brated singers Mara Louw and Anneline Malebo from South Africa, and Sonti Mndebele, who had toured Europe and America with Kalahari and was visiting Botswana. I also fetched keyboardist/saxophonist/guitarist/composer/musi-cal genius Bheki Mseleku from Harare in Zimbabwe. They were all featured as guest artists on the recording. Barney Rachabane and Bheki played great sax-ophone on some of the tracks, including "Tonight, Tonight, Tonight," an R&B love duet between Tsepo Tshola and Anneline Malebo set in a medium tempo with heavy mbhaqanga harmonies and guitar/piano riffs. The solos by Barney and me turned out to be some mean jazz statements. The fast-tempo "Politician" was a heavy indictment of African leaders who overstayed their welcome on the gravy train, with brilliant solos by Bheki on piano and tenor sax, Barney on alto sax, and me trying to keep up with them. "Zulu Wedding" was a traditional Soul Brothers–style vocal mbhaqanga, and we did a happy cover version of Fela's Afro-beat "Lady," which was probably his first major hit. The highlight of the album was a Brazilian ballad called "The Joke of Life." A video of the song was filmed in which I played my flugelhorn to a dancing Neneh Cherry, several years before she started her own singing, rapping career, which turned her into an international star. Clive at Jive Records was very happy with the album. Being an American soul-music worshiper, he was especially partial to "Tonight, Tonight, Tonight." The album was released to a fairly enthusiastic reception, and a European-American tour was scheduled for June of 1985.

Life in Botswana started to be very risky for antiapartheid activists. Most South African exiles in the region had to spend many nights with their families away from their homes for fear of being murdered in their sleep. We were scared of starting our cars in the mornings because so many of our friends had been killed by bombs rigged to explode when they turned on the ignition. We had devised ways of starting our cars with long strings from a safe distance, lest we detonate booby traps. Despite the nerve-racking atmosphere, we all tried to lead normal lives. Just before my birthday on April 4, Nelson Mandela had a birthday card smuggled out of Pollsmoor Prison where he had since been transferred from Robben Island. Mandela learned of all my activities from his wife, Winnie, whom my father regularly visited in Brandfort, her place of banishment. During these visits, which were monitored by the South African police, he would bring her up to date on Barbara's and my activities. Winnie would then pass the news on to Mandela during visits to him. In the card, he requested me to pass on his fondest greetings to Jabu, whose father had been his schoolmate at Fort Hare University, and to little Deliwe, too. He encouraged me to keep up the efforts with the mobile recording studio and the school of music. It was overwhelming to receive such encouragement from a person who had been in prison for more than twenty years and was selflessly encouraging the efforts of people who were free outside, cheering them on in their endeavors to elevate the continent's music and its youth. I was so moved by his gracious and generous gesture that I immediately went to sit at the piano and started singing, *"Bring back Nelson Mandela / Bring him back home to Soweto / I want to see him walking down the streets of South Africa / I want to see him walking hand in hand with Winnie Mandela."*

Jabu came from the bedroom and stood listening behind me. "When did you write this song, Hughie? I never heard it before." I turned around to face her with tears in my eyes. "I didn't write it, Jabs, Mandela just sent it to me."

Just before Easter 1985, I went to Harare, Zimbabwe, to view a house I was intending to buy. Jabu and I had decided to move to Zimbabwe because the environment in Botswana was becoming intolerably dangerous. On my way back to Gaborone, I was arrested at the Harare airport for possession of eighteen grams of marijuana. I was jailed overnight and arraigned in court two days after my host and dear friend Job Kadengu bailed me out. I had to pay a fifty-dollar fine in court on Easter Monday and was declared persona non grata in that country. It was an extremely embarrassing episode because I had been scheduled to play two performances that weekend with Kalahari in Botswana. My father was visiting us, along with Aunt Ackila and her daughter Maphiri, who had come from Tanzania for the Easter holidays. Newspapers all over southern Africa had front-page coverage of my drug bust. I arrived home Tuesday with my tail between my legs.

Early in the evening of June 14, I had just finished a sound check at the Blue Note Club, where we were preparing a farewell performance before leaving for England on June 17. On my way home, I stopped by George and Lindi's house. They had recently installed burglar bars on their doors and windows following a break-in.

Jabu and I put Deliwe to bed early, listened to some music and watched television, and went to bed shortly after midnight. At around three in the morning a mighty explosion and the roar of machine-gun fire awakened us. A bomb had just destroyed a house near ours. Anyone inside the dwelling, I figured, was surely dead. A public-address system came on, with a heavy, guttural Afrikaans accent commanding, "Stay in your houses. Don't come out. We know who we are looking for. I repeat, stay in your houses. Don't move. We know who we are looking for."

Jabu and I lay motionless, fearing we were the death squads' next target. I immediately thought of George and Lindi as we heard other explosions in the far distance. I wondered if they were still alive. The voice from the loudspeaker grew faint. We checked on Deliwe. She was in dreamland. Mrs. Koka, our South African neighbor in the corner house up the street, called us on the telephone and asked in a shaking voice, "Are you still there? Everybody is running to the police station. We are going. Shouldn't you?" I said, "Ma Koka, just stay put."

Jabu and I lay stunned until around five-thirty that morning, when we got a call from Nkopeng Matlou, a friend who worked for the Botswana Broadcasting Corporation. "Bra Hugh, Bra George and Ous Lindi are dead. We were just escorted to their home by some members of the Botswana Defense Force. Twelve other people have been killed. I'm so sorry, Bra Hugh." Although I wasn't surprised by the news, I was still stunned. I got out of the bed and stood in the middle of our bedroom. I just stared into space. Jabu tried to console me, but I wept uncontrollably for what seemed like an eternity.

I called Louis Molamu, George's closest friend in Botswana, and John Selolwane around six. They were both in shock. By seven, they were at my house. I pulled out a bottle of XO Courvoisier from my bar and we began to drink. By nine, when we drove over to George's house, we were on our third bottle. We were numbed by the trauma, not the booze. We said very little. George had been unable to get out of the house with Lindi and their two brothers because the windows had all been burglar-proofed. The assassins had been informed that three people lived in the house, the third being Livi Phahle, George's younger brother. Lindi's brother was visiting for the weekend from Soweto. Livi, a pianist, was thrown to the floor and George put his piano over him so that he could be concealed. George then threw himself over his wife to protect her as he was being mowed down by machine-gun fire. The bullets pierced her body as well. Her brother hid in a closet, but the assassins shot him through the door when they heard him stirring inside. Having killed their quota, the assassins left with Livi still hiding under the piano. We learned later that the assassins had entered Botswana two weeks earlier, and had checked into the Oasis Hotel in the guise of hunters who were en route to one of the country's animal safari parks. During that period they had done a thorough reconnaissance of their intended targets with the assistance of collaborating exiles, called Askaris, pretending to be political activists. The media reported the murder squads had abducted them. The truth was, they were going back home, their mission accomplished. They had lived among us and gained our trust, yet during all those years these Judases were laying the ground for this ultimate attack. We were shocked to learn who they were after they were gone.

The following evening Kalahari performed a farewell concert at the Blue Note Club in Gaborone's Mogoditshane suburb. The next day we left for London. I was shattered that I wouldn't even be present at the burial of my dear friends, George and Lindi Phahle, who had been an inspiration for me to come and live in Botswana. I had lived in their house for almost a year before I found my own place, with their help. When I was weeping for them, after just receiving the news of their brutal murder, Jabu put my head against her bosom and said, "I'm really sorry about your friends, Hughie." That was the first time she had expressed any warm words for them. She had previously accused them of introducing me to many women with whom I had affairs before her arrival in Botswana.

I sent for Jabu and Deliwe to come and join me in London, where I was staying at the home of my niece, Sisai Mpuchane, and her husband, Sam, who was Botswana's ambassador to the United Kingdom. When they arrived, I told Jabu we could no longer live in Botswana. The murders had left me disillusioned.

The government had informed the South African exile community, especially the activists, that they could no longer guarantee our safety because the South African death squads were unpredictable. A United Nations repatriation program was put into place, and most of the South African exile population was transplanted to many countries around the world that offered to take them in and provide educational opportunities.

Khabi Mngoma had organized a workshop in celebration of the first anniversary of the Botswana International School of Music. As one of the founders, I felt obligated to attend, and I needed to sell some of our belongings and arrange shipment of the rest to London. Once I returned in August, it took only a few days to settle our affairs. George's brother Levi repatriated to New York, and today teaches music in Manhattan. The workshop was a success. Eventually the music school was absorbed by the Ministry of Culture and renamed the National Cultural Center. Clive Calder had requested that I find a business manager to represent me, because he was finding it a little awkward to deal with me directly. I asked Dennis Armstead, and he jumped at the opportunity. Clive Calder arranged for the sale of the mobile studio to EMI Records in South Africa. It was a sad ending to a great but short period in Botswana.

When I boarded my flight back to England, I knew that I would probably never return to Botswana. I was forced into a second exile. I still mourn George and Lindi, and I find it hard to forgive the perpetrators of this heinous act. Nothing galls me more than the millions of white people who are always trying to tell us to forget the past while they enjoy the fruits of the sacrifices made by people like George and Lindi. I will never forget that only a few thousand whites helped contribute to South Africa's freedom. The other millions bask in the sunshine of our losses and protection and live off those privileges that were made possible for them by apartheid. They never form their lips to express any gratitude for the good life they enjoy today, still at the expense of the impoverished masses. Damn them!

19

J ABU TOOK DELIWE to New York to be reunited with her parents. I
hated to see her go. Johny Stirling, my European music publisher and fellow trumpeter, with whom I had become very good friends, arranged
some advance money from Warner Brothers Music to help me settle in
England. With assistance from Francis Fuster, who was now our percussionist
and had acquired several properties since immigrating to England, we moved
Kalahari into one of his homes in the suburb of Manor House. Mbongeni and
I finally found time to work on our idea for a theatrical musical. He came to
visit me for a fortnight, during which time we developed the idea for *Sarafina*.
Mbongeni took some unreleased Kalahari recordings we had done at the
Botswana mobile studio back with him to South Africa; one of those songs
was "Sarafina," around which the musical was built. He put together a group
of youths with singer/composer Tu Nokwe, and began to workshop the musical in Durban. *Sarafina* was a dramatization of the political coming of age of
a high school girl and her schoolmates. They are at the forefront of the student
protests in the bloody confrontation with government troops during the 1976
uprisings in Soweto.

With the Kalahari band, we got a booking agent through Johny Stirling and
began to get steady work around the United Kingdom and Europe. Johny and
Stewart were not comfortable with Clive Calder's trying to influence me into
concentrating more on rhythm and blues. They advised me against that direction, and I eventually terminated my contract with Jive Records. Johny Stirling
was able to secure a deal for me with Warner Brothers Records, and we began
recording our first album for the company.

The standout song on our Warner Brothers album *Tomorrow* was the Mandela song that came to me when I received his birthday card. "Bring Him Back Home" went on to become a regular anthem during his travels after his release from prison, and remains the finale in all of my performances outside South Africa, where the audiences jump up to dance in joyous celebration as soon as the song begins; it is a testimony to the man's popularity abroad. Ironically, the song doesn't cause the same amount of excitement at home, probably because of differing political allegiances.

In the spring of 1986, Dennis Armstead ran into Paul Simon in London. He had just returned from recording his *Graceland* album in South Africa—by the end of that year, the album had sold millions. Dennis arranged a meeting for us at Paul's Savoy Hotel suite. Paul and I hadn't seen each other since the Monterey Pop Festival in 1967. We discussed the possibility of a tour with South African artists. I suggested he bring the basic rhythm section from his album, Ray Phiri on guitar, bassist Bakithi Khumalo, and drummer Isaac Mtshali, along with Ladysmith Black Mambazo, and select the rest of the musicians from my band and from among other South African musicians living in England and the States. I also urged him to invite Miriam Makeba on the tour with her three South African backup singers.

In the summer of 1986, Caiphus Semenya approached me to participate as a band member in a theatrical production he was putting together based on the idea of how it would be in South Africa when Nelson Mandela was released from prison. The rehearsals and premiere would take place in Harare. Since I was persona non grata in Zimbabwe, Caiphus had to arrange for special permission for me to enter the country. I flew down to Harare in November and joined the huge cast of South Africans. The show featured Letta Mbulu and Dorothy Masuka, among others. In the orchestra were saxophonists Barney Rachabane and Duke Makasi, with whom I had worked very extensively when I first came to Botswana. Tony Cedras was the keyboard player. After a month's rehearsals, we opened at Harare's Playhouse Theatre to a week of overwhelmingly enthusiastic audiences. Barbara was down from Lusaka to represent the African National Congress, which had helped to raise funds for the production. At this time she was heading the organization's cultural department. The highlight of my Zimbabwe visit was that we were able to arrange for my father to come over from South Africa. He stayed at my friend Job Kadengu's home. It was a great reunion for him and Barbara. They had not seen each other in twenty-four years. We had a glorious time with my father, showing him off to everyone and posing for photographs together. It was amazing just how many people knew him from what their parents had told them about the times they worked as migrant laborers at City Deep Gold Mines and how Thomas Masekela helped them in one circumstance or the other. This was very heartwarming. Thomas and Job Kadengu became the greatest of friends.

At the end of December I returned to London and was pleasantly surprised to find that guitarist John Selolwane, saxophonist Barney Rachabane, pianist Tony Cedras, percussionists Francis Fuster and Okyerema Asante from Hedzoleh Soundz and OJAH, were all in the Graceland band. Miriam Makeba began rehearsals during a very difficult time in her life. Apart from having gone through a divorce from Stokely Carmichael (who had changed his name to Kwame Toure), her only child, Bongi, who I had helped raise, had recently lost her life during childbirth in Guinea. As I thought about all the wonderful times we had spent together, singing her grandmother's songs, riding in the bus to Downtown Community School, braiding her hair, and learning her beautiful song compositions, so many sweet memories of her flashed through my mind. It pains me to think of her early death. For Miriam, it was one of her life's most heartbreaking tragedies. But Miriam was the pillar of strength she's always been. She held herself together admirably, and demonstrated her resilience by giving the rehearsals her all and singing more beautifully than I'd ever heard her sing before. She was pulling the performances from the very depths of her soul when she belted out "Soweto Blues," a requiem for the lives that were lost by so many young people during the 1976 uprisings, and "Patha, Patha," which always got the house on its feet, whooping, dancing, and singing along. Miriam Makeba is a performer's performer when she hits her stride.

We rehearsed for six weeks in London at the beginning of 1987. Excited by the upcoming *Graceland* tour, Warner Brothers, to whom Paul Simon was also signed, figured that if we could get "Bring Him Back Home" on the British top-ten charts, we would be able to break into the U.S. markets with a high entry onto that country's charts. The American record industry took a lot of its cues from what was popular in England during this period. We were scheduled to appear on the *Tube* music show on BBC television, a very influential program that catapulted many new releases to the top. The record company's public relations people called my manager, Dennis Armstead, who was vacationing in the Caribbean with his fiancée. They wanted to discuss the arrangements with him, but claim he abruptly told them, "My artist does not do television." Warner Brothers dropped all plans to promote *Tomorrow.* I confronted Dennis.

He denied making the comment. The damage had been done. Warner dropped me from their label. I bade farewell to Dennis Armstead as my manager. It was a very bad end to a potentially great relationship. I have not spoken to him since and probably never will.

The *Graceland* revue opened in Germany, and for the next nine months we toured the world, playing to sold-out audiences all over Europe and the United States. Most of these people were totally ignorant of the atrocities of apartheid, and this show not only gave them the awareness, but inspired them enough to begin questioning their country's association with the South African regime and demanding that all ties with that country be terminated. Furthermore, it helped to escalate the number of antiapartheid songs being recorded by the international music community in every corner of the world. After *Graceland*, it became the rule rather than the exception for every recording artist to have at least one Mandela or antiapartheid song on his or her album, without any coercion. However, pockets of activists picketed in front of many of the venues we played in the U.S.A. and the United Kingdom, claiming that the entire *Graceland* entourage had sold out on the principle of the cultural boycott against South Africa because Paul Simon had made a recording in that country. The cultural boycott, as we knew it, had always focused on opposing international artists performing in South Africa, but nothing had ever been said about someone who went there to record with the country's artists. Malcolm McLaren had a huge hit with "Double Dutch," which he had recorded the previous year in Johannesburg to nary a peep by the activist community.

The English antiapartheid movement had even gone to the extent of banning South African artists from performing in the United Kingdom, with the hope of extending it to the rest of the world. This I found absolutely absurd. The international media jumped into the fray and began to editorialize vehemently against *Graceland*. Many press conferences took place, and interviews where we had very unpleasant exchanges with journalists. I had no doubt that our shows helped to raise the awareness of millions of people who had never heard of apartheid. The simple fact is that the concerts directed attention to South Africa's oppressed millions and to the wide array of world-class talent that it was unable to promote because of the isolation, resulting from the hideous system of apartheid.

I had furious exchanges with white South African journalists, who were the most accusatory about the tour; meanwhile, they lived privileged lives back home at the expense of the oppressed millions whose interests they claimed to be protecting. Sadly, one of my bitterest arguments was with Bishop Trevor Huddleston. He believed that artists from abroad should not perform in South Africa, nor should South African artists perform abroad. "Father," I argued, "these artists are not able to get the recognition they deserve back home. By performing overseas they get a chance to enhance their careers and reach larger and more diverse audiences. If they are prevented from performing abroad, you are subjecting them to further oppression and poverty back home. If that makes political sense to you and your colleagues who believe in this kind of policy, then all of you should honestly ask yourselves if some of your initiatives are justifiable."

Huddleston only replied, "Well, creature, we can't make any exceptions. We must stick to our principles."

Fortunately, our difference of opinion did not destroy our long-established friendship.

The irony, however, is that four years later, when Paul Simon did some concerts in South Africa and Nelson Mandela hosted a reception for him, many of the people who had headed the picket lines against the *Graceland* show were the very ones who were now escorting Paul to the podium where Mandela was awaiting him with open arms. In the process, these "bodyguards" were rudely pushing us out of the way.

At the end of the tour, Mbongeni arrived in New York with the cast of *Sarafina* after a long and successful run at Johannesburg's famed Market Theatre. We began six weeks of rehearsals and previews, during which time Mbongeni and I spent many nights in the bar of the Mayfair Hotel on Central Park West, where we were staying with the cast. We would guzzle down triple cognacs with beer chasers till the bar closed at four in the morning. Despite our nightly ritual, and after numerous revisions, the musical opened to rave reviews at Lincoln Center's Mitzi Newhouse Theater. We were sold out through the summer of 1988, and owing to popular demand, we moved to the Cort Theatre at Broadway and 48th Street. By now the musical was the talk of the town. Steve Backer, who had overseen the *Sarafina* soundtrack cast album recording, listened to some recordings I had done on my own with Morris Goldberg on saxophone, Bakithi Khumalo on bass, Tony Cedras on keyboards, Damon Duewhite on drums, John Selolwane on guitar, and Francis Fuster on percussion. Named *Uptownship*, the album's highlight was a cover of the Kenny Gamble–Leon Huff composition "If You Don't Know Me By Now," with Morris Goldberg and me playing the original vocal melody to Branice McKenzie's improvised countermelody sung with breathtaking soul. The video for this song helped catapult the album into the top of the jazz charts in the states. "Uptownship," the title song, was a lilting mbhaqanga groove based on the feel of the famous "Skokiaan" that I had done with Herb Alpert ten years earlier. On the background vocals, we featured singers from the cast of *Sarafina*.

Uptownship is a very popular album to this day. *Sarafina's* run on Broadway over two and a half years brought out a wonderful mixed audience of school kids, religious groups, tourists, and a very large African-American representation. The crowds laughed and cried and stood up to dance in the aisles when the young actors sang the finale of "Freedom Is Coming, Tomorrow." The show went on to tour the United States for two years before the cast returned home. By the time the youngest members, who had arrived in New York at age sixteen, finally returned to South Africa in 1992, many of them were over twenty-one. Having taken high school tutorial courses during the run of the show in America, several of the cast members had graduated with high marks and went on to pursue higher education on their return home. Several of the more frugal and business-minded cast members had managed to save substantial amounts of money, enough to buy or build fine homes for their families. Almost the entire cast of *Sarafina* came from extremely poor households. A second company of the show opened in Vienna, Austria, two years after the Lincoln Center debut, and went on to tour Europe very successfully until 1991. A film starring Whoopi Goldberg, Miriam Makeba, and Leleti Khumalo, who had originated the title role of Sarafina, was released around 1993 to favorable reviews internationally. Unlike the stage version, the film was not a box-office smash but was still a success.

During the Broadway run of *Sarafina*, Jabu and I terminated our London residence and she returned to New York, where we acquired a very beautiful little town house up the street from City College on Manhattan's famed Sugar Hill. We also purchased a small farm with a new house outside Margaretville in upstate New York's Catskill Mountains. I loved it up there and began to spend a great deal of time composing and writing on the farm. The downside was that I had to break up Kalahari, because I couldn't afford to bring them to America.

Guitarist John Selolwane stayed on in London and continued to work with Paul Simon from time to time. Rhythm guitarist Banjo Mosele registered at

Goldsmith College of Music to further his studies. He eventually formed a group called Bushmen Don't Surf. Bassist Aubrey Oaki married a Russian musician and disappeared into London's punk community. Tsepo Tshola recruited his old partner Frank Leepa to London and they formed Sankomota, a group that would later become extremely successful back in South Africa. Pianist Bheki Mseleku began to carve out a niche for himself as an international jazz icon. Francis Fuster continued to play with me in the new band I put together with Tony Cedras on keyboards, Morris Goldberg on sax, Damon Duewhite on drums, and Chulo on bass, who was soon replaced by Bakithi Khumalo and Lawrence Matshiza on guitar.

Life was good, except my cocaine, booze, and womanizing had kicked in again. Jabu and I discussed the possibility of my going for substance abuse recovery because I was in the habit of disappearing from time to time, only to return after a few days from a booze, sex, and cocaine binge. But somehow she would always manage to accept my lies after having worried hysterically about my whereabouts, sometimes going to the extent of reporting my disappearance to the police. I believe that had I gone into a sanitarium for rehabilitation, Jabu and I would have had a very successful life together and probably resolved her resentment against most members of my family. I am convinced that one of the reasons this did not happen was that we drank together a lot, and she did not hold her drink too well. Her guilt about her own love for drinking made it difficult for her to insist that I do something about my addiction. In hindsight, my selfishness, greed, and self-indulgence were the reasons we were not able to salvage what was potentially a wonderful relationship.

Sarafina was nominated for five Tony awards, but we did not win any, and despite its box office success, offstage the musical had its problems. The cast was thrown out of the Mayfair Hotel because of their riotous behavior. They played their new stereo sets at peak volume with their doors open and their televisions turned up loud while they visited one another's rooms late at night and raced up and down the corridors and emergency exits, banging on doors, talking and laughing aloud, screaming on the telephone when calling home, and generally partying all night. These were young kids, fresh from South Africa's troubled townships. Maintaining any kind of discipline was almost impossible. They were discovering a new world that most of them found wild and exciting. The cast was moved to the Hotel Esplanade on West End Avenue. The mayhem continued.

We had always warned the kids never to go into Central Park at night. One

Monday evening, Duma Ndlovu, who was now a resident in New York after having graduated from Hunter College, had a party at his Harlem residence for the cast. He was helping with public relations matters for the show. This was a night off, and after the party, five of the girls decided to walk through the park from 100th Street. They were chased for about thirty blocks by would-be muggers and came running into the hotel lobby with their shoes in their hands, dripping with sweat and terror-stricken. Another time I had to stop a fight between two girls as the curtain was about to go up. They were fighting over a boy who was two-timing them. We sent two boys home for coming to the show drunk and unable to perform. One girl became pregnant by one of the boys, and we had to send them home. The problems were endless. Many of the cast members' telephone bills were astronomical because they called home every day and often asked the people on the other end to hold on while they checked on their pots on the kitchen stove or went to fetch someone else from another room to come and talk on the telephone. The damage control Mali, the company manager, and I had to apply was nerve-racking. Mbongeni was constantly shuttling between the two companies and the two of us literally had to babysit the New York cast. The European one was, by contrast, extremely well-behaved.

In 1989 I rejoined Paul Simon for a second *Graceland* tour that took us to France, Spain, Australia, Scandinavia, Germany, Russia, and many parts of the United States we had not touched before. The U.S. portion of the tour was dedicated to raising funds for the poor in each city, for child education in South Africa, and for a mobile soup kitchen, which Paul Simon still continues up to this day. At Madison Square Garden, Paul Simon handed over a check for more than a quarter of a million dollars to South Africa's great antiapartheid activist cleric, Reverend Alan Boesak, who had been sent to accept it on his behalf by Archbishop Desmond Tutu. Boesak gave a rousing speech on receiving the check, prompting the entire twenty thousand-plus audience to give him a standing ovation. My nephew Mabusha was one of the road managers on the original tour. Paul invited Selema on the second leg. He came to like him a lot and thought that he had a very positive influence on his own son, Harper Simon.

We found Russia to be surprisingly racist. In Moscow we stayed at the Hotel Rossiya, right next to the Kremlin. One afternoon, Francis Fuster, Bakithi Khumalo, and I planned to visit Patrice Lumumba University, which Nikita

Khrushchev's regime had established for the education of African students. When we told the taxi driver where we wished to go, he said, "Oh, you want to go to ze zoo, hey!" I replied, "No, we want to go to Patrice Lumumba University."

"Yes, the driver repeated, "Zat is ze zoo!" A scuffle ensued as we disembarked from the cab and confronted the driver over the insult. His fellow drivers sided with him. We eventually found a friendly driver who explained to us that many Russians called the institution "the zoo" because they considered Africans to be from the jungle. At the school, where we visited my niece Zanele Ngakane, students told us that some of the male African students had been murdered because they were dating Russian girls. The maid in the hotel refused to clean my suite, claiming that she could never work for a black man. Miriam and Paul's CD players, CDs, and clothing were stolen from their VIP suites. On departure, some of the porters at the airport refused to carry our bags and equipment, and the airport staff treated us like shit. For the first time during my thirty years in exile, I preferred to be in apartheid South Africa than in racist Russia. It was the worst bigotry I had ever encountered.

On Sunday, February 11, 1990, Jabu and I were sitting in our upstairs bedroom in our Harlem town house watching television with baited breath when Nelson Mandela walked out of Victor Verster Prison outside Cape Town. With tear-filled eyes we watched the gray-haired legend strut his stuff next to his wife, Winnie, their fists almost touching the sky. The parade in downtown Cape Town was sardine-can tight, people jammed shoulder-to-shoulder waiting to hear Mandela's first public words in twenty-seven years. The crowd roared when he saluted them. The old man asked us to forgive but not to forget, to embrace our ex-oppressors, to reconcile, and to refrain from burning the country down. For some of us it was hard to digest what he was asking. He told us that his release and that of his colleagues was our victory. South Africa would never be the same. It was a new dawn. Some skeptics like me were perplexed, but our love for Mandela and his colleagues was persuasive enough to prevent any hotheaded, emotional, destructive activity. We have lived not to regret it.

Two months later Barbara and Miriam called me and said they were in Johannesburg. I thought they were joking. Barbara said, "Hugh, go to the South African embassy and have them give you a visa in your Ghana passport. Come home, boy!"

I was pleasantly dumbfounded. I soon got a call from Nelson Mandela. He was in Tokyo. "Hugh," he said, "I want you to please speak to your grandmother and father on my behalf. Sincerely apologize to them for the fact they will not be seeing very much of Barbara in the next four years. I cannot function without her assistance, and our schedule is going to be extremely hectic to say the least. I am appealing to you, as the head of your family, to do this for me." Barbara headed a staff of five women in Mandela's office charged with managing his life during this transitional period. As chief of staff, she also traveled with him. In the months following his release, Mandela toured the world to a tumultuous universal reception such as no statesman in history had ever seen.

That September, after thirty years, I returned to the land of my birth. After I landed and disembarked, it took forty-five minutes for the immigration officer in charge of returning exiles to clear me through customs. She had gone on her morning tea break. During my wait, I became afraid that perhaps something sinister was afoot. Outside, my father, sisters, distant relatives, old friends, and reporters were all waiting for me to emerge. When I came out, a chorus of roars and ululations pierced the air.

Mbongeni Ngema had arranged for a welcoming party at the home of his friend Sol Pienaar, a wealthy French Afrikaner heir who was very close to the ANC leadership. It was a very strange time in South Africa. There was a great deal of manipulated political conflict in the country, which had obviously arisen from major dissatisfaction with the prospect of change by members of the white right wing, Afrikaner racist groups, and the homeland governing establishments of the artificially self-ruling autonomous regions of Venda, Bophuthatswana, Ciskei, and Kwa-Zulu, headed by Mangosuthu Buthelezi, Lucas Mangope, Gabriel Ramushwana, and Oupa Gqozo. There were frequent incursions by Inkatha Freedom Party warriors into areas purported to be ANC strongholds, where the killings of many innocent people were carried out. Snipers were scattered around many townships. Death squads attacked commuter trains and riddled the coaches with machine-gun fire, often leaving many Africans dead.

Feeling that it was not safe for me to stay at my father's house because of the ongoing clashes between ANC cadres and Inkatha Freedom Party warriors, snipers of mysterious identity, and other dangerous elements, Julius Mdluli and Barbara arranged for me to stay at Jiji Mbere's home in Westcliff, one of Johannesburg's luxurious suburbs. My father and stepmother were very disappointed because they had hoped that I would stay with them. But they understood. Julius chauffeured me where I needed to go and helped reorient me to the country of my birth. We went to see many childhood friends and relatives, especially in Soweto and Alexandra townships.

It was both wonderful and increasingly sad to be back home. The population had quadrupled. The townships were overpopulated. The air was filled with violence and fear. Black militants were murdering whites. White racists were murdering Africans. Political gangs were at each other's throats. Hundreds of people were dying daily during these conflicts as the unbanned political groups hunkered down in negotiations with the government of F. W. De Klerk to discuss the future of South Africa. It was a tense and unpredictable time. The disenfranchised in most of the townships and rural areas lived in abject poverty compared with the opulent white wealth that surrounded them. Poor white folks presented a strange irony in the face of so much privilege. They harbored deep hatred for Africans, and were easily manipulated by their racist leaders. Another group that hated Africans was the white immigrant Portuguese community, which had been forced to abandon their ill-gotten comforts in Angola and Mozambique when the new democratic dispensations were put into place there. The former Rhodesian right-wing community that had fled Zimbabwe for the same reasons was similarly hate-filled. What must have pleased these two types to no end was the ongoing government-manipulated black-on-black violence that was unfolding before their eyes every day. It was enough for them to justify their age-old belief that Africans were incapable of governing anything.

Nevertheless, it was wonderful to be reunited with my sisters, my father's family, and my grandmother Johanna, who would be turning one hundred years old on Christmas Day. I went to visit her in Ennerdale Township, where she lived with Sybil, Elaine, and their eight children. My younger sisters were very affectionate this time, and an absolute pleasure to be with. After three weeks I returned to New York, and to juggling my hectic touring schedule and my responsibilities to the *Sarafina* cast. Although Jabu and I were living well, something was not going right with our marriage. She hadn't worked in seven years and appeared resistant to my suggestion that she find employment. She'd leave the house almost every morning to go shopping and to hang out with her friend Janet Carter. Jabu had impeccable taste in everything. We went to the best restaurants and enjoyed good theater, movies, and concerts. We lived well, but our problems were just as great. I was still snorting cocaine like a vacuum cleaner, drinking the best cognac and red wines as though my life depended on them, and smoking ganja like a reggae dance-hall dealer. Jabu did not mind the smoke and booze, but was not happy about my cocaine use, especially because it was responsible for my disappearances for several days at a time. We would go for days without speaking to each other.

In February 1991, I kicked off my official return to South Africa with a tour that coincided with the national launch of National Sorghum Breweries, an African-managed company. Called Sekunjalo, the tour included my band plus the country's two top groups, Bayete and Sankomoto, along with backup singers (Palesa) and dancers (Baobab). The idea was to start the tour in the northern part of the country, in Pietersburg, the capital city of my ancestral region. After an initial false start, we decided to bring in the accomplished promoter Irfaan Gillan. For the next two months, with Irfaan at the helm, we performed to sellout crowds in Johannesburg, Mafikeng, Durban, Grahamstown, East London, and Cape Town. I have to admit that part of the early problems resulted from my imposing my perspective on how to promote the tour. Having been away from South Africa for three decades, I should have left the details to the experts. But my boozing and drugging, coupled with the adulation I was receiving, let my egomania get the best of me.

John Cartwright, my former Manhattan School of Music classmate who had played bass for Harry Belafonte, was our tour manager. He brought with him Phil Mosley as stage manager and my son, Selema, as assistant stage manager. We had a security company composed of sixty guards, a cast of forty, a film crew, and a stage crew with scores of set-builders. A convoy of trucks, buses, and cars carried us up and down the land. Brewery executives followed us around the country in jets. Hundreds of fans drove from city to city to see the show. Sekunjalo was dynamite, and when it finally connected, it took the country by storm.

Jabu had accompanied me to South Africa, but from the onset of the tour we disagreed on most issues. She'd take off to Durban to see her folks, or to visit friends. Shortly after the tour, Jabu returned to New York. I followed at the end of August. The band regrouped and we began a late-summer tour of the United States.

Whenever we were in Los Angeles, we would go to Richie Druz's studio, where we had started work on a new RCA album he was producing for me.

Richie and I were overindulging, to say the least, which contributed very little to the progress of the album or its quality. Steve Backer was not at all impressed with the final results, an album we titled *Beatin' Aroun de Bush,* and he refused to pay more than $40,000 for the master of the album. We'd been expecting more. Richie flipped out. He put an ad in the *Hollywood Reporter* claiming that I owed him $35,000. He also initiated a lawsuit against me. This was a wakeup call that I was heading for rock bottom, but I did not heed the alarm. The court ordered a lien against all my earnings as well as Jabu's income (she was now working for the New York Public Library).

The *Sarafina* income began to dwindle as audiences who had filled theaters in Europe and America reached a saturation point. My relationship with Jabu reached its lowest point with me spending more and more time alone at our upstate New York farm. After one of my disappearing acts, I decided to visit the *Sarafina* cast in Washington, D.C. I called Jabu and told her that I would not be returning in the near future. A few days later she sent a message informing me that her mother had passed away. I frantically rushed back to New York, only to be told that my mother-in-law was neither dead nor ill, but in good health. Jabu said she had concocted the story to get me back to New York. I warned her that her antics would translate into bad luck. After some time, Jabu's mother suffered a fatal heart attack. It was a devastating loss for all of us. I was heading back into dark times.

20

INSTEAD OF EMBRACING THE TURN MY LIFE HAD TAKEN—the success of *Sarafina* and the *Graceland* tour, the moments of happiness I had eked out with Jabu and Deliwe in Botswana, and, most of all, the progress toward liberation in South Africa—I sank deeper into my addiction. And rather than stay and sort out the mess I'd made with my finances and marriage, I returned to South Africa.

Miriam had been asked to participate in a Children for Africa fund-raising festival in Lagos, Nigeria, and I was asked to be the music director. Ladysmith Black Mambazo, Bayete, the cast of *Sarafina,* and Yvonne Chaka Chaka, a brilliant South African singer, known throughout the continent as the Princess of Africa, were also part of the South African delegation. Knowing the uncertainties of African projects, I made sure that the monies for Bayete, with whom I was performing, and me, were paid in advance. This turned out to be a good move, because chaos and confusion would mar the festival. When we arrived, our delegation, which numbered two hundred, was given the red-carpet treatment complete with lavish hotel accommodations and carte blanche to sign for meals and drinks.

The three-day festival began on a Friday night. Kool and the Gang, Rita Marley, Nina Simone, and other American groups appeared along with some leading local acts. Some acts played longer than they were supposed to, and groups that weren't even on the bill suddenly appeared and performed at the insistence of their patrons, who were usually rich, powerful chiefs and politicians. We never went onstage. The same mayhem happened the remaining two nights. Miriam and Yvonne Chaka Chaka left the stadium on the final night of the festival in disgust while the rest of us finally performed on the Monday morning at five to a handful of people. Our organizers were unable to facilitate our departure, so for ten days we were all stranded at the hotel. With relentless efforts by Yvonne and Miriam, who lobbied government heads, our departure was eventually finalized. On the day we ultimately departed, several government officials came to see us off. They apologized for any inconveniences and handed Miriam 100,000 pounds to settle outstanding accounts with the artists.

When we returned to South Africa, the local newspapers had well documented the festival's mishaps. They headlined our travails, reported that Miriam was the reason our party was stranded, and wrote that she had pocketed the money the Nigerian government had given her. I immediately called a press conference in which I expressed my disgust at their shoddy reporting and set the record straight. Nelson Mandela called me a few days later and thanked me for coming to Miriam's defense. I told him I was just telling the truth.

By the end of 1991, I had moved into an apartment in the Johannesburg suburb of Berea. My relationship with Jabu had deteriorated so much that I felt much more content living in Johannesburg than in New York. I was working very hard to convince her that it would probably bring harmony into our lives if we moved back to South Africa, which I was absolutely passionate about. I had waited thirty-one years to be able to return home, but she couldn't understand why it was not possible for me to live in both America and South Africa. It could have been that having been able to come home every year on her vacation, she didn't ache to live in South Africa as I did. Barbara and I found ourselves trying to solve many of our family problems—which included my fetching Pula when her mother ran into some problems—that were created during our years in exile, while trying to settle down in South Africa and relearn the country from scratch. So much had changed, so many friends and relatives had died or settled elsewhere. If I had idealized a return to South Africa at all during my exile, my actual return was a sobering—if not depressing—experience. The political turmoil and violence further discouraged Jabu from coming back home for good. Furthermore, I had already once caused her to leave a job at the *New York Times* to come and join me in Botswana. Asking her to leave her job at the New York Public Library to start a new life once more was too much for her, especially because we had also spent four years in London, where she could not obtain permission to work either. The Richie

Druz lawsuit, which had imposed a lien on our earnings, made it even more unattractive for me to contemplate returning to live in America.

My cousin Billy had enrolled Pula in a progressive high school on the northern outskirts of Johannesburg called Phuthing. Thirteen years old, shy, and turning very beautiful, she was a boarder during the week, but allowed to come home on weekends. I finally got to really know Pula. She was sweet and so undemanding that I had to persuade her to accept clothing and pocket money. "Really, I'll be all right," she would say in her quiet, deep voice. I went to visit my aging father and stepmother as often as I could. I was forging a whole new life for myself back home.

The bitterness generated by the poisonous effects of apartheid was deeply implanted in the psyches of Elaine and Sybil, exacerbated by the loss of our mother thirteen years earlier. Polina had been the anchor of this family. Her violent death had left a void in all our lives that was impossible to fill. Our visits were spiced with arguments, but even though the moments of peace and quiet were few, I was happy to have them back in my life.

I was planning to form a South African group, but in the interim I was doing a lot of performances with Bayete. Together with the great group Sakhile, we were the first Africans to play Sun City's previously blacklisted Super Bowl, breaking all attendance records. In 1992 I formed my first South African group, with seventeen-year-old Moses Molelekwa on piano, Lulu Gontsana on drums, McCoy Mrubata on saxophone, and Bakithi Khumalo on bass. We opened at Kippie's, a popular local and tourist music haven in the Market Theater complex. For the next two years this group changed personnel from time to time, with Vivian Majola on sax and Vusi Khumalo on drums, later Khaya Mahlangu on sax, Mandla Zikalala on bass, and Themba Mkhize on piano. Sadly, in 2001 Moses committed suicide after his wife also died mysteriously on the same night. Bakithi married and settled in New York, where he freelances and often performs with Paul Simon's band. Themba has become a world-renowned pianist with two great CDs to his credit and countless awards. McCoy has also carved out a stellar career for himself, as have the others. Khaya is an outstanding performer and a great arranger, and assists me in producing artists for our label, Chissa Records.

I was struggling to get into the mainstream of the South African music industry, and I didn't even have a recording deal. Jabu called me frequently, ranting and raving over the phone that Richie Druz's lien, which had now been extended to her, was taking all her pay. She eventually had to sell all of our belongings from our Harlem town house and our country home and move into her late mother's apartment with her sister Busi. It didn't make me happy, but there was little I could do about it. Business was very slow.

The new year of 1993 dawned with a lot of promise for South Africa. A government of national unity had been agreed upon, and the country's first democratic elections were set for April 1994. Sadly, the violence continued. A year before the elections, Chris Hani, one of the ANC's top commanders, leader of the Communist Party, and a deeply loved son of the soil, was gunned down by a right-wing Polish immigrant racist named Janusz Walusz and his partner Clive Derby-Lewis. Both are now serving life prison terms. In the spring of 1994, Miriam went on tour in the United States, and I joined her. On April 27 we voted for the first time at the United Nations, where facilities had been set up for South Africans living abroad, together with the members of our group. We missed the excitement and fever taking place back home, but watched the events on television. It was a great day. We watched with pride as Nelson Mandela did his celebratory "Madiba jive" at the ANC's headquarters on the night he was elected the new president of the Republic of South Africa. During the same tour, my group recorded a live album at Blues Alley in Washington, D.C. Titled *Hope,* it remains my biggest-selling album of the last three decades. We took this tour to Europe, where we also enjoyed tremendous success.

At 104, my grandmother became very ill from a badly infected knee, which began to poison her system. Barbara and I spent many of her last days with her, during which she passed on to us old family heirlooms, photographs, and stories. Barbara spent her very last seconds with her. They were singing songs she had taught my sister during happier days back in Witbank. We had lost the woman who had raised and nurtured so many of us, and in whose house Barbara and I were born and Elaine was raised. She had lived a full life, and in spite of her bullying ways and her domineering character, we were happy for Johanna because she had outlived her entire clan and family. She always scolded God in her prayers for letting her live such a long and lonely life. All her great-grandchildren cried with a deep sadness over the loss of their great-grandmother. Although she had terrorized their little lives, she had also made them laugh a lot. Because she was one of Ennerdale's first residents, almost the entire township lined the streets as her cortege drove by. Many people came from Witbank, and all my friends and those of my sisters came to help us say farewell to Johanna Mthise ka Mahlangu, Mabena, Mganu-ganu wa Maghobhoria. We buried her in Ennerdale's new cemetery.

Barbara was appointed South Africa's ambassador to France, and at the beginning of 1995 she took off for Paris. She asked me to move into her house on the next street from my apartment, which I subleased to three of Elaine's oldest children, Miles, Candice, and Lyle.

In early 1995, Jabu and I actually reconciled. By this time I had been able to pay off my debt to Richie Druz after Johny Stirling helped me renew my publishing deal with Warner Brothers Music and secure a large advance. The lien was removed. Jabu came to visit South Africa, and we spent a great deal of time with her relatives in Durban and other parts of Natal, but in the end we weren't able to reconcile, and two years later we divorced.

Later that year I was appointed deputy director of the Performing Arts Council, with executive offices in Pretoria's State Theatre. I had to be at work every morning at eight. I was provided with the penthouse apartment atop the State Theatre, a brand-new Mercedes-Benz sedan, and a full bar for entertaining guests. The entire staff of 750 was headed by the director and me, and I had every possible perk. I would have a couple of tots of brandy before going down to my office. Part of my portfolio was to help in the transformation of the arts in South Africa. At first I was excited over my new job and very enthusiastic to make things happen. I soon discovered that my energies were futile.

The most frustrating thing was that all the wonderful ideas I had hoped to turn into reality got bogged down at middle-management level and never really got approved in time at cabinet level. The best example was the 1996 Freedom Day celebration. The Minister of Arts and Culture, Dr. Ben Ngubane, came to my office and told me, "Hugh, we have been charged by parliament to produce next year's celebrations, and we have to come up with a concept. How do you feel about it?"

"That's wonderful," I said, very excited. "Let's produce a one-day festival where all the ethnic groups of South Africa show off their music and dance cultures. We'll start off with a parade down Pretoria's Church Street, and then they can use different parts of the parks to show off their stuff. The rest of the day will be a mammoth concert outside the State Theatre, featuring all the greatest artists from every segment of our nation's society."

"Great," said Ngubane, "let's put together a proposal and a budget." In one week we had these together, and submitted them to the minister's office. It was September 1995. We proceeded to put venues, artists, and service providers in place. By October my department was ready to go. Then the waiting began. The process went from the deputy director general to the director general of arts and culture to the deputy minister and then the minister's office. From there it went to parliament. By the end of February 1996, I had long forgotten about this initiative, when the director general burst into my office and said, "Cabinet has finally approved. Let's go."

In South Africa, as part of the reconciliation process, the old apartheid civil service was kept intact, which helped in some ways to prevent widespread disruptions and bloodshed—but also crippled the new regime. A great portion of the white civil service workers, the country's middle management, would deliberately slow down the transformation of the government's services to discredit the new government, thereby providing evidence that Africans were not capable of governing the country. This pervaded every government department.

By the time the director general gave me what he considered wonderful news, the majority of the leading artists had taken alternative engagements because they had grown weary of awaiting confirmation from us. What followed was a nightmare. We had to renegotiate with all of those artists and get them to cancel their confirmed engagements, so most of them had to be paid double or more of our original offers because they had to pay cancellation fees to their would-be promoters. Our budget ended up double its original amount.

Before this episode, I liaised with the maintenance department. Most of them were Africans, and their complaint was that their working conditions were horrendous. No one cared about their welfare, and I was the very first director ever to visit the basement and address their concerns. After promising to improve their lot and be an advocate for most of their crucial demands, I personally paid the theater's cafeteria for a catered lunch for the entire maintenance staff. That evening I was told that ninety percent of them had been victims of food poisoning. They had been fed old meat and contracted botulism. I was furious, and raised hell. I also found out that the downstairs toilets for the staff had a special locked toilet for the whites. That toilet was out of bounds for African workers. When I raised it with the State Theatre's executive director, he said to me, "Hugh, things have to change gradually, you know. No place is going to be perfect overnight."

That was when I realized that even though things had changed drastically on the surface, and South Africa appeared to be a wonderful miracle in the eyes of the rest of the world, we were a long way from freedom and justice. It was going to take many generations for the majority of whites to accept reality, and for transformation to trickle down to the poor, unskilled, formerly oppressed millions. When the end of my one-year contract approached, I didn't even bother to attempt to apply for an extension. It seemed absolutely pointless. I didn't want to waste my time fighting the old establishment from the inside.

Nonetheless, during my short tenure I helped bring in African performers such as Rebecca Malope, Brenda Fassie, Bayete, and Don Laka, all of whom were never allowed to showcase their talents there during the apartheid years. With the help of stellar promoter Peter Tladi, we were able to bring an African character to the State Theatre, which had previously been a white preserve. My office helped organize the 1996 independence celebrations. In spite of slow-moving bureaucracy and a lot of red tape, we were able to stage a festival featuring just about all of South Africa's leading artists. A cultural potpourri of traditional groups representing all ethnic groups marched and danced through Pretoria's streets and parks. There were stage plays and state banquets hosted by Nelson Mandela and Vice-President Thabo Mbeki.

Early in 1995, with initiatives by the foreign affairs departments of France and our newly democratic country, Barbara organized a South African exposition in Paris, which included a large musical company that I was part of. On my return to South Africa, I found that my father's health had deteriorated so much that he had to be hospitalized. He was released after a week, but had to remain in bed at his home in Sharpeville, where he had a relapse. I brought him and my stepmother to stay in my house so that he could have access to better medical attention. Pascal Ngakane, who had been chief medical officer of Lesotho, was now heading Johannesburg Hospital. I had him come and examine my father, and he told me afterward that it was all over. Thomas Masekela maintained his wonderful sense of humor right to the very end. He said to me, "Boy, do you mind if I linger around for the next two weeks?"

"Papa," I replied, "I want you to get better and get your health back."

"No, boy, it's all over. I'm crumbling. There's no chance. However, let me tell you I have never had so much attention in my entire life." Then he laughed his crazy, infectious laugh.

After a week, Pascal transferred him to Johannesburg Hospital. The last time I saw him, he said to me, "Make sure you bury me quickly. You may be famous, but I'm very well known and if you wait too long, you will not be able to afford my funeral because of the crowds." Then he laughed from deep down inside.

On April 27, he passed away. Barbara came from Paris to see him off and visited with him in the hospital before his last breath. People came from all over southern Africa to bid farewell to Tom. The speakers told us about a very generous, hard-working, dedicated, and funny community worker, who was admired and loved by all. At the funeral my cousin Ramapolo Ramokgopa, who is the premier praise-singer of our clan, came down from Pietersburg at my request and recited Thomas Selema's praises from the time his coffin was taken from the house to church, and from the church to Sharpeville's gigantic reception hall, which was filled to the rafters. There I played an old folk holler on my flugelhorn for the old man in between speeches. At the graveside, as the crowds were leaving, I played again while Ramapolo was reciting. Our duet was a memorable send-off for a great soldier of South Africa's poor masses and elite alike. For many days after his burial, which was attended by thousands of mourners, people called to scold me for not letting them know in time about my father's passing. They called from as far away as Zimbabwe, Zambia, Lesotho, Botswana, Mozambique, Malawi, Europe, and America, and all over South Africa. Thomas was right. The street his house was on and the surrounding blocks were all impassable from the congestion of cars, which were parked side by side, delivering the thousands who had come to say good-bye to him. If we had waited another three days, Sharpeville would have been inaccessible.

Sony Records opened for business in South Africa and attempted to change the playing field by appointing an African manager of business affairs, Lazzie Serobe, and hiring Lindelani Mkhize as head of the artist and repertoire department. This was history in the making. Lindelani and Lazzie signed me as one of their first artists on the label. At the time I was midway into recording an album with the talented Cedric Samson as producer. This was during the period when I was seriously mixing business with pleasure. We stayed ripped during the making of *Notes of Life,* and I was doing it in my spare time, away from my job at the State Theatre and concert engagements. Although the results were good, *Notes of Life* did not prove to be a successful album, in spite of Sony's relentless efforts at promoting and marketing it. Eight years later, I doubt very much if it has reached gold status in South Africa. A dear friend of mine, South African filmmaker Jo Menell, who has lived abroad in England, then America, since the mid-1950s, had just completed a documentary called *Mandela* and asked me to do the soundtrack music for most of it. Unable to oblige him because of the little time I had available, I introduced him to Cedric, who did a magnificent job and had me play on the main songs of the soundtrack. *Mandela* was expected to win an Oscar for best documentary and best soundtrack. Relations between Cedric and me had soured considerably after he demanded that my name be removed as co-composer of some of the music. At the Oscars, *Mandela* was edged out by *When We Were Kings,* the documentary about the 1974 Rumble in the Jungle festival, for which

Stewart and I had chosen director Leon Gast and raised the money for the music and film crews from Steve Tolbert in Liberia. It was a cruel paradox that Leon had patiently outwaited the statute of limitations and gone on to score a big hit with a film that Don King had put a court injunction on after Stewart and I refused to succumb to his demands for an additional ten percent for the rights to film it, more than twenty years earlier. I have never seen either film, though Leon and I have remained friends.

Later that year, with recommendations from Komlah Amoaku and Korkor Amartefio, the directors of the National Theater, the Arts Critics and Reviewers Association of Ghana voted to award me the Music Star of Africa prize. When I arrived at the Tulip Hotel in Accra, there was a message from Elinam Cofie, the girl I had found crying at the Paris Airport in 1977. She had left a message with her phone number and a request to call her. I had last seen Elinam in 1988 at Shelley's Manne Hole, in Hollywood, where I was appearing with some of the members from the *Graceland* band. At that time she was living with her sister Yealla, after her divorce from a four-year marriage that had produced two beautiful sons. She gave me her phone number and asked me to call her, saying, "I suppose you won't be so interested in me anymore because I'm old and divorced now. Anyway, call me and let's get together for a drink or a meal. Promise?" I never did call that time—I was probably too high or drunk to remember.

This time I invited Elinam to lunch at the Tulip Hotel's poolside, and she agreed to bring her two boys with her to meet me. We had a wonderful afternoon. Her two sons brought their swimsuits and Elinam watched the three of us frolicking in the water from the poolside. Patrick and Adam were eight and ten years old. Although I saw Elinam every day during my week-long stay, I didn't think she might be interested in me because she only demonstrated friendship, nothing more. I was invited back to Ghana in December for the annual children's festival, Kiddafest, where I performed with the famous Winneba Youth Choir. My old friends Francis Fuster and Okyerema Asante were both living in Ghana and helped me put a great band together for the performance. Again I saw a lot of Elinam. We became even closer and spent a lot of time together.

The problem was I was still drinking, snorting, and smoking heavily. I was very reluctant to start anything with her because she was such a good and beautiful person and I knew I was absolutely bad for her—she had a good soul that I was afraid of damaging. "When are you going to invite me to South Africa? What are you afraid of?" she kept asking, but I kept putting her off. I began to sleep only every other night, partying with several different women, snorting up ounces of cocaine, drinking cognac like a buccaneer, and smoking pound after pound of marijuana. I had finally come back home and was—after a million women—given another chance at love, but I was once again self-destructing. I didn't know what to do.

My sister Elaine together with my nieces and nephews had helped me a great deal to raise Pula, who was not a shy little girl anymore. Confident, talkative, and funny, she had developed a loud, deep voice and a boisterous laugh. Having graduated from Phuthing, Pula was now attending Damelin College in Central Johannesburg to help raise her grades for university entrance. Pula moved in with me and Mama Johannah Mathibela, who had been my part-time housekeeper at my apartment. Although Pula had her own room in the house, she was obviously getting disturbed by all the commotion going on because of my partying. Later, Ryan, Sybil's oldest teenage son, also came to stay with me and I began spending more of my nights at the homes of the women I partied with. I'd come home in the mornings or late afternoons to wash, change clothes, and eat a little, but I tried to keep my debauchery far away from my nephew and my daughter. Pula and I had become friends, and although she was not saying it, I knew that both she and Mama Johannah were becoming troubled by my reckless behavior.

As time went on, Pula and I started drifting apart. She had been leaving the house every morning to go to school—or so I thought. One day I went to Damelin College to pay her overdue school fees, but the principal told me that the school owed me money because Pula hadn't been to school in months. Mama Johannah was a spiritual leader of the Zion Christian Church, yet she tolerated my madness. She knew all the women and some of the dealers who frequented 49 Honey Street, but she kept my secrets. She prayed a lot for me, laughed sadly at my follies, and tried her best to hide what was happening around our home from unsuspecting neighbors, visitors, and my relatives. However, she was expressing some of her concerns to Barbara, who obviously realized that the house was not as she had left it when she departed for Paris, even though we spruced up the place before her arrivals.

By 1997 I was really drowning. Since my return to South Africa, I had been invited to theater openings and award nights, premiers, weddings, and funerals, which I had either missed or arrived late for, or had gone to the wrong place because I was either scoring, waiting for my dealer, or recovering from the night before. I'd often wake up with strangers in my house or in my bed. On many occasions I had to come up with excuses and even blatant lies for postponing appointments or not showing up for rehearsals. I cannot recall how many times I drove women home in the morning, in peak traffic or stormy weather, high as a kite, hoping that no one would recognize me. Many people would roll down their car windows and yell, "Bra Hugh, where are you going this time of the morning?" Embarrassed, all I could do was muster a half-baked smile and explain that I was on my way to an early business meeting, rushing to the airport, or returning from an all-night recording session to drop off the background vocal singers who were half-asleep in my car. Having given Mama Johannah the day off, I would be back in bed by nine with a mind full of air-tight excuses. I would then cancel meetings and appointments. Most people would believe me and understand, but the musicians I was playing with were getting tired of my lies.

Stewart, Chuck, and Johny Stirling had all been through substance-abuse therapy and were now clean for over ten years. They attempted to persuade me to do likewise, but I was totally deaf to their pleas. They were urging me to accept assistance from the Musician's Assistance Program (MAP) based in Los Angeles, which was prepared to lend me money to enter rehabilitation at a center in England that Johny Stirling was recommending, but I was in another world. They called Barbara in Paris to voice their concerns about my condition and state of mind. I wasn't listening. I thought I could quit on my own, and just like so many other addicts, I was reluctant to admit that I had finally hit rock bottom. Johny Stirling had sent me a registered letter from London in which he pleaded with me to lay everything down and submit to rehabilitation before it was too late.

In July, Barbara took me on a two-week vacation to Mauritius with her young son, named Selema like my own son. She urged me to submit to treatment, and I finally agreed. We called Johny from our Indian Ocean villa, and he began arrangements for me to be admitted to Clouds House, a facility for drug and alcohol abuse recovery and therapy. Stewart and Chuck coordinated with the Musician's Assistance Program office in Los Angeles to guarantee Clouds House that my expenses would be taken care of by MAP.

I returned to Johannesburg at the beginning of August to fulfill concert and club engagements. Barbara, Stewart, and Johny had hoped I would go straight to England from Mauritius, but I had some debts to clear up and wanted to wait until my divorce from Jabu was final.

Sensing, perhaps, that I had changed my mind, Barbara wrote me a scathing letter, in which she said, "I don't know you anymore. You have deprived me of your friendship. You have stolen my brother. You were my first friend and only brother. I will have nothing to do with you anymore." I was ashamed and shattered. At the beginning of September I received a tearful phone call from Stewart, begging me to drop everything and get to England for treatment. He also canceled me out of his life.

I felt like shit, but sank even lower.

Sony Records was very upset at this time because I had been missing many radio, television, newspaper, and magazine interviews that were crucial to the sales of my new album, *Black to the Future*. Following the dismal sales generated from my previous album, *Notes of Life,* Sony had high hopes for this project. It had already sold more than four times as many units as *Notes of Life,* and they wanted it to go through the roof. My lack of cooperation had them considering dropping me. Don Laka, my producer, was ecstatic over the sales of *Black to the Future,* and just itching to go into the studio with me for a follow-up album.

I had recently taken a business trip to Ghana, and was very excited about the possibility of hooking up with Elinam. However, when I arrived in Accra, our mutual friend Edward Akufo-Addo, who arranged accommodations and business appointments for me, informed me that she was visiting her sister Yealla in Los Angeles. I was disappointed. I left a letter for her with Edward, in which I asked her to consider spending the rest of her life with me.

On my return to Johannesburg, I jumped back into my life of debauchery with even more gusto, for hours on end and days into nights, frustrated, lonely, unhappy, and directionless. My nightclub, Hugh Masekela's J&B Joint, closed down after my partners and investors realized that I was a very bad risk and they were losing a lot of money.

On December 4, 1997, my lawyer, Mncedisi Ndlovu, accompanied me to the Johannesburg Supreme Court, where I signed my final divorce decree documents before a judge. A dark cloud lifted, and so did what seemed like a very heavy weight off my drug- and alcohol-weary shoulders. I called Johny Stirling to tell him that I would be arriving in London on December 16, ready to enter Clouds House. He was absolutely elated, even though his voice betrayed a bit of disbelief, which was understandable, given my history. Mabusha had recently returned from the United States to settle permanently in South Africa. He was living with me, now thirty-two years old and working as my band manager. Pula, who had disappeared for a few months and was secretly living with Monde Twala, her future husband, had also come back to live with us. My nephew Ryan was now living in a Catholic boardinghouse in Springs, and going to a technical college there.

I had one more gig before I left: December 13 at Moretele Park in Pretoria's Mamelodi Township. There must have been close to twenty thousand people at the Moretele Park Festival on that Sunday. Sibongile Khumalo, who was my broadcasting partner on a Sunday radio show and one of South Africa's top jazz and opera divas, was also performing. After our radio show that morning, our last one together, I told Sibongile that I would be leaving for substance-abuse recovery in England. She was so happy for me that she jumped up and down for joy, shrieking with joy and relief. It started raining like hell just as Sibongile finished her performance. The twenty thousand people who had waited for me all day didn't care. The rain seemed like liquid sunshine to these folks, the culmination of a whole day of listening to some of South Africa's greatest artists. I closed the show by wishing everyone a joyous festive season, and exited stage left as the rain kept pouring down.

That night I had one last crazy fling with coke, booze, smoke, and sex. Early the next afternoon I telephoned Mama Johannah and asked her to start packing my suitcase. I could sense over the telephone that she was quietly shedding tears of joy. Later that afternoon, Peter Tladi and Mabusha drove me to Johannesburg International Airport. I called Johny Stirling from the departure lounge and told him I was on my way to London. Johny could not stop repeating on the phone, "You have made me the happiest person in the world, Hughie. God bless you, my dear friend." Dawn Zain, my friend from way back during the *King Kong* days and one of the investors in the defunct Hugh Masekela's J&B Joint, pulled together her frequent-flyer miles and gave me a round-trip business class ticket.

I was exhausted when I boarded the airplane. I had dinner and passed out until the flight attendant woke me up to the announcement that we were landing at Heathrow Airport. I took the express train to Paddington Station and a taxi to the Covent Gardens flat of my childhood friend Sanza Loate. Sanza was now singing with the Manhattan Brothers, who had been living in London since *King Kong* closed on the West End in 1962. That night they were to perform at the South African embassy as part of the entertainment that would precede the premiere of a documentary about the vocal quartet. I was also featured in an interview in the film. After spending a very enjoyable day with Sanza and his wife Joy-Njabula, we repaired to the embassy for the premiere with many other South African friends. A party followed and later moved to Sanza's house. That afternoon, Johny had taken me to the Clouds House processing center in London's Chelsea suburb for the brief formalities of screening and filling in forms. When he dropped me back at Sanza's, Johny Stirling said, "Enjoy your last drink tonight, Hughie. Make sure you have a good blast, because tomorrow you begin a new life and a future full of miracles." I did just that. I had my last bottle of cognac that night.

The next morning, Johny picked me up in his Land Cruiser for the three-hour, winding, hilly drive to Shaftesbury. We had a hilarious time, laughing about my past and telling outrageous jokes all the way to Clouds House.

When we arrived at noon on December 18, 1997, I gaped at this 150-year-old, three-story English manor, some two thousand feet above sea level, spread over several wooded acres. They told me the estate had been used as the governmental residence for Winston Churchill during World War II. That I had recorded thirty-seven albums, sold more than five million of them, and squandered millions of dollars didn't mean a thing. All the residents were equals. We were all addicts trying to get well. After registering, seeing the doctor, and settling into my five-man dorm, I sat on my small bed and reflected with a relieved smile about my forty years of sex, drugs, and alcohol addiction. It was a cold, rainy winter day, and looking out of the dormitory windows, I began to count the forming snowflakes and estimated the money I had spent on drugs, parties, lawsuits, legal fees, tax penalties, divorces, and women. With the canceled engagements and royalty losses from a string of terminated recording contracts, luxury airplane junkets, hotel suite and telephone charges, expensive cars and abandoned houses around the world, the money squandered easily amounted to at least $50 million.

After my orientation, I was given my first house chores as the assistant kitchen cleaner, waiter, and chief dishwasher for the thirty residents. Our dormitory was warm on this cold English night. I glanced out the window at the full moon that illuminated the frost gathered outside our bedroom window. I was assigned to a room with four other men. No privacy. No queen-size bed, but a single bunk with a not-so-soft mattress. No curvaceous beauties sleeping peacefully at my side, just the occasional moans, groans, and farts of my roommates. I felt like I was starting over.

Some of the patients were going through very painful recoveries, especially those who were in their first day or two coming down from heroin or heavy drinking. They were going through cold sweats, shivers, convulsive shakes, fevers, vomiting, and nightmares. Some were desperate to leave the sanitarium immediately and return to their lives of addiction. A few such people left every week. The night nurses were kept very busy. There were endless trips to the bathroom from every dorm.

When I arrived at Clouds House, unlike many patients, I didn't need to go through detox. By the third day of treatment I knew I was going to be well forever. After a week I called Mabusha and told him to go through the house and get rid of whatever drugs he found. We had daily writing assignments, which we had to submit at the end of the evening, and the mornings began with a short reflective prayer, meditation, breakfast, then group therapy sessions that involved intense and helpful truth-seeking exchanges but were sometimes very confrontational, with the entire group scolding you if they felt that you were lying, secretive, isolating, or in denial. Everybody broke down in tears at one time or another. We had to write our life stories, critique each other, and have regular one-on-one sessions with our individual counselors. On Saturday mornings the entire group of inmates sat in a large circle in the main lounge, and each one spoke about how the week had gone. More crying. More confrontations. All these sessions forced me to share my demons and look where the debris lay, deep inside my soul. We were allowed to call out or accept incoming calls after a week in the joint. Trips to the town of Shaftesbury were arranged for Saturday afternoons, when a bus would pick us up and bring us back in time for supper. The same buses would take us out one night a week to the town of Salisbury for Alcoholics Anonymous and Cocaine Anonymous sessions with the local addicts, at a community center. On Thursdays we were taken to the local health club for a swim. Daily walks through the village were allowed for groups of four. Permission for these had to be obtained from the administrative offices, where everyone was required to sign for an exit permit of no more than one hour. There were no free moments; one exercise or the other occupied every single minute. By lights-out at eleven, we were totally exhausted. I lay in bed at night and thanked my ancestors for being at Clouds House, before fading into a deep, tranquil sleep. We were allowed to play our instruments over the weekends, and when I played my trumpet at the end of my first week, it was the first time I had played it sober since I was sixteen years old. I had so much power in my lungs. It felt awesome, effortless. Exercising really helped. I would do stretches every morning and walk around the sprawling grounds or through the village in the afternoons, sometimes twice a day. In that freezing weather, I could feel my body moving toward a healthier state. A few weeks before my departure, I wrote in my journal: *I know the rest of the journey is not going to be easy, but painful. But I have hope that when I face the outside world after I leave Clouds, I will be ready to say to myself, I have found Hugh.*

21

DURING MY MEDITATION TIME, I wrote letters to just about everyone I could think of whom I had offended over the years. I hadn't written a letter in twenty-five years. I asked for their forgiveness. In my
deep, private thoughts and in accordance with my upbringing, I released my spirit.
I prayed to my ancestors to intercede on my behalf and beseech the Creator to
help me be restored to sanity and health in order for me to lead a better life.

Having come seven thousand miles, I often contemplated and got lost in
thinking about Witbank, Johanna Bowers, my first years on this earth, Springs,
my first piano lesson, Alexandra, the township carnival weekends, St. Peter's,
Huddleston, the Huddleston band, the Merry Makers, African Jazz & Variety,
King Kong, the Jazz Epistles, America, West Africa, Botswana, Zaire, my late
friends, my family, my wives, and many women. I had come a long way and
was very lucky to be alive. By the end of my stay at Clouds House, I had been
house head for two weeks, and at my departure, everybody came out of the
building to bid me a hearty good-bye.

I was released on January 29, 1998. During my stay, I had called Stewart, Johny,
Peter Tladi, Dawn Zain, Sibongile, and my sister Barbara quite regularly,
thanking all of them for helping me make the best decision of my life. Barbara
insisted that I come to Paris and spend two weeks with her before going back
to South Africa.

One day I was on my way to an Alcoholics Anonymous meeting when my
cousin Mfundi Vundla came by. Mfundi has the top television show in South

Africa, a soap opera called *Generations*. I told him that I wanted to form a foundation in South Africa to promote substance-abuse awareness and recovery. He said he would help. True to his word, the Musicians and Artists Assistance Program of South Africa (MAAPSA) has assisted scores of artists and other individuals toward recovery. The organization holds all its board meetings at Morula Pictures, Mfundi's business offices. In existence now for four years, it has assisted more than fifty South African artists and others in their quest to kick their addictions.

When I returned to South Africa, Peter Tladi arranged a reception for me at Miriam Makeba's home. I made a thank-you speech in which I apologized for my past misdeeds and went public about my addiction and recovery. I was glad to see my many friends. A few months later I was visiting Peter and Jean Davidson at their farm in Tarlton, a rural hamlet about sixty-five miles west of Johannesburg. I had roomed with Peter shortly after my divorce from Miriam, and we'd spent wonderful years together. When I'd hit with "Grazing in the Grass," I invited him to come out to Los Angeles, where he unintentionally became our tour manager. Peter told me about a fifty-four-acre farm that was for sale about a half-mile from his place. The minute I saw it, I fell in love with it. He helped me make a deal with the sellers, and I purchased the property.

With my life turned around, I felt that I might now be good enough to live with Elinam without reverting to my old, crazy ways. At first she was curt with me because I hadn't called or kept in touch as I promised. I was returning from an American tour in July of 1998 when Barbara invited Mabusha and me to visit her in Paris. From her residence, I called Elinam in Ghana and said, "When can you come and visit me in South Africa?" She was shocked because she had not heard from me since I wrote her the note I had Edward Akufo-Addo pass on to her, in which I asked her to spend the rest of her life with me.

"I am really angry with you for disappearing like that. What happened to you, anyway?" she asked.

"I came to Ghana and you were not there, so I thought you had canceled me out of your thoughts," I replied.

"Well, when I didn't hear from you, I figured you had lost interest in me. Anyway, I can't remain angry with you too long. Where are you?"

I told her about my rehabilitation and explained that in my former state of mind, "I would have been bad for you, but now I know that we could be very happy together if you will still have me. When can you come?" I asked anxiously.

"As soon as you can write me a visa request to your embassy here," she said.

I was so happy I wrote the visa request right away and instructed my travel agency in Johannesburg to send her a ticket. A couple of weeks after my return to South Africa, Elinam arrived. After she'd washed and changed into fresh clothes and Mama Johannah prepared breakfast for us, I drove Elinam to the Tarlton farmhouse. I had not begun to furnish the house, and the only person living in the worker's quarters was Alfred Hlatshwayo, the groundskeeper who had stayed on after the old owners left. He welcomed us heartily. The only thing I had in the house were the samples Barbara's curtain maker had given me to look through. Before we entered the house, I asked Elinam, "What do you think of this place?"

"It's beautiful," she said, not sure what the hell was going on.

"Well," I said, "I just bought this place. I was hoping that you might like it. If you come and live with me, this will be our home."

We spent the rest of the morning in the empty house. We lay down on the bedroom carpet and began choosing curtains for the many windows and planning how the place should be furnished, then walked all around the farm grounds and spoke to the eight cows we had inherited with the property. Everybody fell in love with Elinam. Mama Johannah and Pula couldn't stop marveling over her.

I was not letting Elinam go out of my life.

AIDS has become South Africa's most dreaded plague since smallpox, tuberculosis, and polio took the lives of millions of rural and township dwellers during the 1950s, when my father was a health inspector and spent almost every waking hour of his life inoculating people. There has been no preventive administrative strategy to deal with AIDS. On the contrary, almost a decade has gone by while an internal debate has raged about the causes of AIDS, with the president and the minister of health, Dr. Manto Tshabalala-Msimang, claiming that the disease was not caused by HIV but by poverty, malnutrition, and so on. On the other side, international and domestic AIDS relief organizations have been urging the roll-out of antiretroviral drugs. The country's populace, meanwhile, has gone through a long period of denial, during which time millions of people have died from the pandemic. Relatives have actually shunned, rejected, or even evicted family members who turned out to have full-blown AIDS. Many artists and political and business leaders and ordinary people have gone to their graves denying that they suffered from the disease and calling it everything but AIDS, while their relatives, their government, and their employers colluded with them right up until they were lowered into their graves and thereafter. Those spouses who were infected suffered quietly and awaited their own deaths without admitting the truth. It is a dismal era of head-in-the sand, turn-a-blind-eye folly.

My sister Sybil concealed her HIV-positive status from us for four years, eventually hiding from us after abandoning a lucrative position at Sun City as a head chef. It was only after Barbara and I sought her out and coaxed the truth out of her that she surfaced. By then she had developed full-blown AIDS. For the next year she attended group sessions, moved to a shelter, and eventually entered a hospice not far from my house on Honey Street. We ensured that she received the best medical treatment that was available, and tried our best to keep her spirits up. The staff at the hospice and the numerous doctors we had caring for her were very supportive and extremely forthcoming in their efforts to help her and us to cope calmly and honestly with the situation. It was too late. Mama Johannah and I visited her every day, and so did Elaine. I had Mama Johannah take her food at lunchtime and dinner. Johannah was truly a pillar of strength for us during this difficult period. It was daunting for Barbara, who was calling the doctors and me regularly from Paris, trying to keep abreast of the situation. I took Elinam to meet Sybil. They bonded as though they had known each other for years. Elinam cried. I cried. Sybil tried her best to console us. It was one of the saddest moments in my life. Elinam returned to Ghana, and on September 18, Sybil died, ten days before her forty-fifth birthday. I blew my trumpet at her graveside.

Five years later, I mentioned Sybil's misfortune in a newspaper feature interview about AIDS. Most of my maternal relatives came down on me like a ton of bricks. How could I shame the family like that? What about her children? The newspaper had sensationalized my interview tabloid-style. MY SISTER WAS KILLED BY AIDS, read the front page of the City Press, the nation's largest weekend paper. When the furor finally died down, many AIDS organizations and people who had been through the same misfortune in their families commended me for going public. I thought that under the circumstances it had been the sensible thing to do. I was unaware that almost all my young nephews and nieces had been told that Sybil had died of pneumonia. Happily, the government has changed its stance on AIDS and is now rolling out antiretroviral drugs, having finally decided to confront the pandemic head-on. Unfortunately, one of Sybil's daughters has turned out to be HIV positive, too.

On the upside, we have entered a new era when many prominent people are talking about their HIV status, and the public's attitude toward the ailment is moving away from denial. We are supporting my niece in her dilemma and being as helpful as we can to ensure that she receives proper care. We hope a cure will soon be found for the dreaded monster.

In 1998 my old friend Bishop Trevor Huddleston passed away after a long illness. He had excitedly returned to South Africa in 1996 to settle, but was immediately disgusted with what he observed to be the blatantly racist continuation of apartheid in the attitudes of most white people. Aside from the fact that the old civil service was still in place, the social system had hardly been dented, he said, and the new administration refused to give him an audience. He was being snubbed. Huddleston was not happy about the reconciliation process; he thought that the perpetrators of past apartheid atrocities should be prosecuted and imprisoned. He went back to England reluctantly but utterly disgusted. I spent time with him while he was in South Africa. I was invited to Westminster Abbey in London for a national memorial service in his honor. There I blew my trumpet for him from the pulpit, just as I had for my sister Sybil, my father, my cousin Collins Ramusi, my niece Bontle Modise, and my childhood friend Aggrey Mbere. I never got a chance to blow the trumpet for my mother at her funeral. However, it was the first thing I did when I visited her grave in Ennerdale, a few days after I landed back in South Africa following an absence of thirty years.

At the beginning of 1999, I brought Elinam and her sons, Adam and Patrick, to South Africa. On February 10 we were married in a civil ceremony witnessed by Peter and Jean Davidson. I enrolled the boys in St. Peter's, my alma mater (which is now called St. Martin's). At the end of 2002, Adam graduated from St. Martin's and is now attending Santa Monica College in Los Angeles, living with his aunt Yealla and about to enroll at the University of Southern California as a film major. Patrick graduated from St. Martin's at the end of 2003, and intends on following the same course. They'll be able to hang out with Selema, who shares a house in West Los Angeles with Stewart Levine's composer/producer son, Sunny Levine. Yeah, life does repeat itself sometimes. It warms my heart to know that they will not raise as much hell as Stewart and I did when we were their age. These are neither jazz hippies nor flower children. They are seriously focused young explorers who already know what they want, with no time for the madness we swam in. When we tell them about our youth, they look at us as if to say, "What a couple of nuts you were." I also wonder if I will ever meet my Swedish daughter. I certainly hope that happens one day.

• • •

Elinam and I live quietly on our farm, which we named "Polinam," after my mother and Elinam. When I'm not in the recording studio or on tour I spend a lot of time with her going to movies, the theater, and concerts, or visiting with friends and relatives, especially Barbara, whom we will miss very much after she leaves for Washington, D.C., to take up her new post as South Africa's ambassador to the United States. We often take long walks together in the morning. I'm up before six, writing, composing, or answering correspondence from business associates and concert offers. I've been working on this manuscript for thirty years, the last nine years full-time. I've also completed a novel. There's another musical on the horizon, as well as a television series and movie scripts in various stages of development. Pula works with me at our company, the Chissa Group, which specializes in recording, film, artist management, events, theater productions, and my bookings. Irfaan Gillan, who promoted my first South African tour, Sekunjalo, is our managing director. My son Selema is a television commentator for NBA games on ESPN. He's thirty-two. We speak often and try to hook up when I'm in the United States.

At Chissa we are making records that people seem to enjoy. Tsepo Tshola, Busi Mhlongo, and I are the first three artists on the label, distributed by Sony. My current band is tight! We play about two hundred gigs a year around the world. John Selolwane is still with me on guitar. Arthur Tshabalala is on piano, Mandla Zikalala is on bass, Ezbie Moilwa is on keyboards, and Dumisani Hlela is on drums. Francis Fuster plays percussion with us on most European and U.S. tours.

Pula got married on November 16, 2002, to a wonderful young man, Monde Twala. The ceremony, executive produced by Mabusha, was held at a wedding village. Some three hundred friends and family members attended the ceremony. All my closest relatives who could come were at the wedding, and so were many of my old friends. I missed my grandparents, mother and father, sister, aunts and uncles, and those friends who had passed on. As I walked Pula down the aisle, I thought how lucky I was to be alive after such a crazy life. When I stood to address the gathering as the father of the bride, I looked into the audience and there was Sam Mosikili, who had made Sekunjalo possible. He was sitting next to my dear friends Julius Mdluli, Jiji Mbere, and Ntinyane Matabane. At the next table were my cousin Peter Vundla and his wife. Mfundi Vundla could not attend, but his wife, Karen, was there. My attorney, David Dison, and his wife, Rinkie, were there. Elaine was surrounded by her children and Sybil's children. Barbara was seated with my cousins Billy and Mokgadi, surrounded by many of her new in-laws, Pula's cousins, sister, and brother, and her mother, Dr. Tshidi Kgware. Adam and Patrick were sitting with Monde's mother and her other son and nephews. Pula's girlfriends from Phuthing High School were all there. They were now stunning grown women with their own homes and big jobs. My daughter was beaming as she waved to me from the bridal table. When Pula's new husband spoke, my son-in-law recited two beautiful poems he had written for his bride. Monde made us cry, just as he had done when he couldn't hold back tears after the priest asked him to repeat his vows. While driving back to the farm, our two boys were laughing in the backseat while I held Elinam's hand and watched the deep green South African landscape blurring past the window.

Many of the people I grew up with have left this world. In the early nineties, Ray Lofaro was diagnosed with terminal cancer, and the very last day I spent with him at his loft apartment in the SoHo area of Manhattan he was bald from chemotherapy. "What are the chances?" I asked. "It's a very long shot, Dukie," Ray replied. We were not laughing. I never saw him again. A memorial service for Ray was held at the Cathedral of St. John the Divine. Together with Morris Goldberg, Tony Cedras, Damon Duewhite, Bakithi Khumalo, Lawrence Matshiza, and Francis Fuster, we played some of his favorite songs at the request of his brother Gene. May his soul rest in peace.

Alan Pariser succumbed to throat cancer at the end of 2001. I spent time with him in Los Angeles. His voice was gone and he could only communicate through a voice-amplifying machine, or in writing. But his spirits were high. I think about those two people a lot, and never fail to remember them when I do my meditations. I miss them a lot, along with all the others who touched my life intensely: saxophonist Al Abreu; Philemon Hou; my stepdaughter Sibongile Makeba; Godfrey Mochochoko, who died in our dorm at St. Peter's in my first year at boarding school; Bishop Trevor Huddleston; Dizzy Gillespie; Miles Davis; Jimi Hendrix and his companion; Devon, my elementary school buddy; Mohale Mpiti; Kippe Moeketsi; Johny Gertze; Dudu Pukwana; Todd Matshikiza; Elijah Nkwanyana; Gwigwi Mrwebi; Patience Gcwabe; Monty Berman; Lindi and George Phahle; Fela Kuti; Hopane; Mamoshaba; Polina; Thomas; Bigvai; Clara; Mpho Motloung; Kenneth and Mokonye Masekela; Collins Ramusi; Rhodes Gxoyiya; Washa; Johanna Bowers; Sybil; George Molotlegi; Uncle Putu; and Stanley Todd. May their souls rest in peace. My deepest and sincerest gratitude goes out to them and the many others who helped me to make a life out of my compulsive nature and all my crazy notions. I am truly lucky to be around. Let the music play.

Recommended Reading List

Abrahams, Peter. *The Coyaba Chronicles: Reflections on the Black Experience in the 20th Century.* Cape Town: David Philip Publishers, 2000.

Achebe, Chinua. *Home and Exile.* New York: Oxford University Press, 2000.

Adjaye, Joseph K., and Adrianne R. Andrews, eds. *Language, Rhythm, and Sound: Black Popular Cultures into the Twenty-First Century.* Pittsburgh: University of Pittsburgh Press, 1997.

Angelou, Maya. *All God's Children Need Traveling Shoes.* New York: Random House, 1986.

———. *The Heart of a Woman.* New York: Random House, 1981.

Armstrong, Louis. *Satchmo: My Life in New Orleans.* London: Windmill Press, 1955.

Azikiwe, Nnamdi. *My Odyssey.* New York: Praeger, 1970.

Bailey, Jim, and Adam Seftel. *Shebeens Take a Bow!!! A Celebration of South Africa's Shebeen Lifestyle.* Johannesburg: Bailey's African History Archives, 1994.

Baker, Chet. *The Lost Memoir: As Though I Had Wings.* New York: St. Martin's Press, 1997.

Belton, Ralph. *Remembering Bix: A Memoir of the Jazz Age.* New York: DeCapo Press, 1974.

Bergreen, Laurence. *Louis Armstrong: An Extravagant Life.* New York: Broadway Books, 1997.

Bernstein Hilda. *The Rift: The Exile Experience of South Africans.* London: Random House, 1994.

Bhabha, K. Homi. *The Location of Culture.* London and New York: Routledge, 1994.

Bojut, Michel. *Louis Armstrong.* New York: Rizzoli International Publications, 1998.

Brink, Elsabe. *1899, The Long March Home: A Little Known Incident in the Anglo-Boer War.* Cape Town: Kwela Books, 1999.

Brothers, Thomas, ed. *Louis Armstrong, in His Own Words—Selected Writings.* New York: Oxford University Press, 1999.

Bryant, Margot. *As We Were, South Africa 1939–1941.* Johannesburg: Keartland Publishers, 1974.

Carmichael, Stokely, and Charles Hamilton. *Black Power: The Politics of Liberation.* New York: Vintage Books, 1967.

———. *Stokely Speaks.* New York: Vintage Books, 1971.

Carr, Ian. *Jazz: The Essential Companion to Artists and Albums.* London: The Rough Guide, 2000.

———. *Miles Davis: A Critical Biography.* New York: Random House, 1982.

Carson, Clayborne, ed. *The Autobiography of Martin Luther King, Jr.* New York: Warner Books, 1998.

Collins, Lewis John. *African Pop Roots: The Inside Rhythms of Africa.* London: W. Foulsham, 1985.

Cooke, Mervyn. *Jazz.* London: Thames & Hudson, Ltd., 1998.

Cooper, Brenda, and Andrew Steyn. *Transgressing Boundaries: New Directions in the Study Culture in Africa.* Athens: University of Ohio Press, 1996.

Crapo, Richley H. *Cultural Anthropology: Understanding Ourselves & Others, 3rd Edition.* Guilford, Conn.: The Duskin Publishing Group, Inc., 1993.

Cromwell, Adelaide Hill, and Martin Kilson, eds. *Apropos of Africa: Sentiments of Negro American Leaders on Africa from the 1800s to the 1950s.* London: Cass, 1969.

Davenport, Rodney, and Christopher Saunders. *South Africa: A Modern History.* New York: St. Martin's Press, 2000.

Davis, Miles, and Quincy Troupe. *Miles: The Autobiography.* New York: Simon & Schuster, 1989.

Denniston, Robin. *Trevor Huddleston: A Life.* London: Macmillan, 1999.

Diop, Cheikh Anta. *Great African Thinkers, Volume 1.* New Brunswick, N.J.: Transaction Books, 1989.

Esedebe, P. Olisanwuche. *Pan-Africanism: The Idea and the Movement, 1776–1963.* Washington, D.C.: Howard University Press, 1982.

Floyd, Samuel A. *The Power of Black Music: Interpreting Its History from Africa to the United States.* New York: Oxford University Press, 1995.

Fordham, John. *Jazz: The Essential Companion for Every Jazz Enthusiast.* London: Dorling Kindersley, 1993.

Garrow, David J. *Bearing the Cross: Martin Luther King Jr. and the Southern Christian Leadership Conference.* New York: First Vintage Press, 1988.

Gates, Henry Louis, Jr. *Harlem On My Mind, Black America, 1900–1968.* New York: The New Press, 1995.

Gates, Henry Louis, Jr., Nellie Y. McKay, William L. Andrews, Houston A. Baker, Jr., and Barbara T. Christian, eds. *The Norton Anthology of African American Literature,* New York: W.W. Norton, 1997.

Gatheru, Mugo. *Child of Two Worlds.* London: Heinemann, 1964.

Geen, M.S. *The Making of South Africa.* Cape Town: Maskew Miller Ltd., 1958.

Gershoni, Yekutiel. *Africans on African-Americans: The Creation and Uses of an African-American Myth.* New York: New York University Press, 1997.

Gibbs, Henry. *Twilight in South Africa.* London: Jarrolds Publishers, 1950.

Golden, Marita. *Migrations of the Heart.* Garden City, N.Y.: Anchor/Doubleday, 1983.

Gordimer, Nadine. *Living in Hope and History: Notes from Our Century.* Cape Town: David Philip Publishers, 2000.

Graham, Ronnie. *The World of African Music.* London: Pluto Press, 1992.

Haley, Alex. *The Autobiography of Malcolm X.* New York: Ballantine Books, 1965.

Harris, Eddy L. *Native Stranger: A Black Man's Journey into the Heart of Africa.* New York: Vintage, 1992.

Harris, Joseph E. *Africans and Their History.* New York: Penguin Books, 1972.

———, ed. *Global Dimensions of the African Diaspora.* Washington, D.C.: Howard University Press, 1982.

Hickey, Dennis, and Kenneth C. Wylie. *An Enchanting Darkness: The American Vision of Africa in the Twentieth Century.* East Lansing: Michigan State University Press, 1993.

Huddleston, Trevor. *Naught for Your Comfort.* London: Collins, 1956.

James, Joy. *Transcending the Talented Tenth. Black Leaders and American Intellectuals.* New York: Routledge, 1997.

Johnson, Charles, and Patricia Smith, eds. *Africans in America: America's Journey Through Slavery.* San Diego, New York, London: Harcourt Brace & Company, 1998.

Kebede, Ashenafi. *Roots of Black Music: The Vocal, Instrumental, and Dance Heritage of Africa and Black America.* New Jersey: Africa World Press, 1982.

Keiler, Allan. *Marian Anderson: A Singer's Journey.* New York: Scribner, 2000.

Larkin, Colin, ed. *The Virgin Encyclopedia of Jazz.* London: Virgin Books, 1999.

Lees, Gene. *Waiting for Dizzy.* London: Oxford University Press, 1992.

Levett, Ann, Amanda Kottler, Erica Burnam, and Ian Parker, eds. *Culture, Power & Difference: Discourse Analysis in South Africa.* Cape Town: University of Cape Town Press, 1997.

Lewis, David Levering, ed. *The Portable Harlem Renaissance Reader.* New York: Penguin Books, 1994.

Magubane, Bernard. *The Making of a Racist State—British Imperialism and the Union of South Africa, 1875–1910.* New Jersey: Africa World Press, 1996.

———. *The Political Economy of Race and Class in South Africa.* New York: Monthly Review Press, 1979.

———. *The Ties That Bind, African American Consciousness of Africa.* New Jersey: Africa World Press, Inc., 1987.

Makeba, Miriam. *My Story.* New York: Penguin Books, 1987.

Mandela, Nelson. *Long Walk to Freedom: The Autobiography of Nelson Mandela.* New York: Holt, Rinehart & Winston, 2000.

Marx, Anthony W. *Making Race and Nation—A Comparison of the United States, South Africa, and Brazil.* United Kingdom: Cambridge University Press, 1998.

Matshikiza, Todd, and John Matshikiza. *With the Lid Off: South African Insights from Home and Abroad 1959–2000.* Johannesburg: M&G Books, 2000.

McRae, Barry. *Dizzy Gillespie: His Life and Times.* New York: Universe Books, 1988.

Mingus, Charles. *Beneath the Underdog.* New York: Alfred A. Knopf, Inc., 1971.

Mingus, Sue Graham. *Tonight at Noon: A Love Story.* New York: Pantheon Books, 2002.

Moleah, Alfred. *South Africa: Colonialism, Apartheid, and African Dispossession.* Delaware: Disa Press, 1993.

Moleffe, Z.B. and Mike Mzileni. *A Common Hunger to Sing: A Tribute to South Africa's Black Women of Song, 1950 to 1990.* Cape Town: Kwela Books, 1997.

Muller, C.F.J., ed. *Five Hundred Years: A History of South Africa.* Pretoria and Cape Town: Academica, 1969.

Platzky, Laurine and Cheryl Walker. *The Surplus People: Forced Removals in South Africa.* Johannesburg: Raven Press, 1985.

Reed, Ishmael. *The Reed Reader.* New York: Basic Books, 2000.

Robinson, Randall. *Defending the Spirit: A Black Life in America.* New York: Dutton, 1998.

Santoro, Gene. *Myself When I Am Real: The Life and Times of Charles Mingus.* New York: Oxford University Press, 2000.

Schadeberg, Jurgen. *The Fifties People of South Africa.* Johannesburg: Bailey's African Photo Archives, 1987.

———. *The Finest Photos from the Old Drum.* Johannesburg: Bailey's African Photo Archives, 1987.

———. *Images from the Black '50s*. Johannesburg: Nedbank, 1994.

Segal, Ronald. *The Black Diaspora*. New York: Farrar, Straus and Giroux, 1995.

Shipton, Alyn. *Groovin' High: The Life of Dizzy Gillespie*. New York: Oxford University Press, 1999.

———. *A New History of Jazz*. New York: Continuum Publishing Group, 2001.

Simpkins, Cuthbert Ormond. *Coltrane: A Biography*. Baltimore: Black Classic, 1975.

Skinner, Elliott P. *African Americans and U.S. Policy Toward Africa 1850–1924*. Washington, D.C.: Howard University Press, 1992.

Smuts, J.C. *Jan Christian Smuts*. Cape Town: Heinemann & Cassell, 1952.

Sparks, Allister. *The Mind of South Africa—The Story of the Rise and Fall of Apartheid*. New York: Alfred A. Knopf, 1990.

Steinhorn, Leonard, and Barbara Diggs-Brown. *By the Color of Our Skin: The Illusion of Integration and the Reality of Race*. New York: Dutton Books, 1999.

Stevens, Ethlebert J.C. *White and Black: An Inquiry into South Africa's Greatest Problem*. Cape Town: Darter Bros. and Co., 1914.

Thomas, Anthony. *Rhodes: The Race for Africa*. Johannesburg: Jonathan Ball Publishers, 1996.

Troupe, Quincy. *Miles and Me*. Berkeley: University of California Press, 2000.

Walters, Ronald W. *Pan Africanism in the Diaspora: An Analysis of Modern Afrocentric Political Movements*. Detroit: Wayne State University Press, 1993.

Wamba, Philippe. *Kinship: A Family's Journey in Africa and America*. New York: Plume, 1999.

Ward, Brian. *Just My Soul Responding: Rhythm and Blues, Black Consciousness, and Race Relations*. Berkeley and Los Angeles: University of California Press, 1998.

Weinstein, Norman. *A Night in Tunisia: Imaginings of Africa in Jazz*. Metuchen, N.J.: Scarecrow, 1992.

Weisbord, Robert G. *Ebony Kinship: Africa, Africans, and the Afro-American*. Westport, Conn.: Greenwood, 1973.

Wicker, Tom. *Tragic Failure: Racial Integration in America*. New York: William Morrow and Company, Inc., 1996.

Acknowledgments

Hugh Masekela: My sincerest gratitude, love, and admiration goes to my sister Barbara Masekela; my wife, Elinam Cofie-Masekela; my sisters Elaine and Sybil and their children; my cousins Billy Masekela and Mokgadi Masekela Tlakula; my dearest friends Stewart Levine, Johny Stirling, Chuck Kaye, Jessie La Pierre Gonzales, and Tshidi Kgware. My guiding lights and mentors Miriam Makeba and Harry Belafonte; Bishop Trevor Huddleston, who got me my first trumpet; my first piano teacher, Madevu; Uncle Sauda and Mr. Cecil Collins, who taught me how to play the trumpet; my classmates and teachers at St. Michael's Primary School, St. Peter's Secondary School, and Manhattan School of Music; and childhood playmates in Witbank, Springs, and Alexandra townships. Thanks to Myrtle and Monty Berman and trumpeters Elijah Nkwanyana and Banzi Bangane from the Merry Makers orchestra in Springs, who started me out playing at concerts and dances in that band's third trumpet chair. Thanks also to Jonas Gwangwa, Moon Masemola, Chips Molopyane, George Makhene, Monty Mahobe, Zakes Mokae, Solly Kgoleng, and all the members of the Huddleston Jazz Band. To Victor Ndlazilwane, Ntemi Piliso, Zakes Nkosi, Skip Phahlane, Mackay Davashe, Sol Klaaste, Kippie Moeketsi, Todd Matshikiza, Boycie Gwele, Vandi Leballo, Joey Maxims, John "Fingers" Dlamini, Harold Jephta, Gwigwi Mrwebi, Stanley "Spike" Glasser, Abdullah Ibrahim, Johnny Gertze, Makhaya Ntshoko, Dolly Rathebe, Ben "Satch" Masinga, Morris Goldberg, George Kussel, Nathan Mdledle, Joe Mogotsi, Rufus Khoza, Dorothy Masuka, Peter Ntsane, Bob Lesia, Thandie Klaasens, Ray Mokalane, Louisa Emmanuel, Alfred Herbert, Alan Harris, Pumpy Naidoo, Jackie Marks, Tessa Kahn, Selwyn Kahn, Chris McGregor, Dudu Pukwana, Mike Miller, Jack Katz, Goolam Lombard, Ian Bernhardt, Peggy Phango, Mary Rabotapi, Johannah Radebe, and Mike "Mazurkie" Phahlane who taught me all about friendship, music, and loyalty.

To my bosom soulmates Shunna Pillay, Pat Bannister, Charlie Smalls, Rhodes Gxoyiya, and Nga Manelisi Ndibongo. Also to Ronnie Valjean, Mary Vonie, Susan Belink, Sharon Johnson, Ruth Nkonyeni, Vera Pitso, Duku Napo, Thelma Oliver, Barbara Alston, Dawn Levy, Pearl Reynolds, Joan Treisman, Mama Akuffo Addo, Jabu Mbatha, Chris Calloway, Abbey Lincoln, Miatta Fanbulleh, Thembi Mtshali, Thembi Nyandeni, Ndo Nyembezi, and Ladyfair Mngadi, for whom I was an absolute nightmare and who gave me all their love and support and many sadnesses.

To Jane and Mburumba Kerina and their children Kakuna, Mandume, and Kambandi; Larry Willis; Astley Fennel; Lorraine and Dizzy Gillespie; Franco; Albert Geduldig; Danny Sims; Rudy Lucas; Janet Dubois; Johnny Nash; Adam Wade; Miles Davis; Louis Armstrong; Art D. Lugoff; Terry and John Mehegan; Carla Pinza; Jean Johnson; Priscilla and Bob Bollard; Bruce Langhorne; Millard Thomas; Edith Marzani; Mrs. Miller; Alan Pariser; Howie Folta; Elmer Valentine; Mario; Alvinia; Betty Mabry; Herb Alpert; Paul Simon; Hotep Galeta; Ned Tannen; René McLean; Don Blackman; Pat and Mike Mikell; Clive Calder; Bob Krasnow; Russ Regan; Al Brown; Devon Wilson; Jimi Hendrix; Sly Stone; Quincy Jones; Manu Dibango; Bob and Shirley Young; Joe Glaser; Oscar Cohen; Susan Cederwall; Nomkondelo Christina Makeba; Sid Kaiser; Peter Fonda; Mim Scala; David Crosby; Al Abreu; Les McAnn; Big Black and Ginger Ray and family; Carrie White; Richard Alcala; Letta Mbulu and Caiphus Semenya; and Yvonne Chaka-Chaka and Tiny Mhinga, who have always been family to me.

For my dearest friends Lindi and George Phahle, who were assassinated by the apartheid death squads in Botswana; Job Kadengu, who gave Zimbabwe to me; Fela Kuti, who gave me Nigeria and West Africa; and Stanley Todd, my little brother, whose love and friendship I will always cherish, may they all rest in peace. Thanks to all the members of the Hedzoleh Soundz and Kalahari who reintroduced me to Africa.

To my brother Quincy Troupe and his wife, Margaret; Mama Beatty Mbatha and all her daughters; Maggie and Mpho Motloung; Ntombi and Lepetu Setshwaelo; Tshenolo Modise; Gale Gaborone; Sisai and Sam Mpuchane; the Ramusi and Mokgokong families; Mbongeni Ngema; Peter and Mfundi Vundla; Aggrey and Jiji Mbere; Ray Lofaro; Ntinyane and Sebiletso Matabane; Caroline and Julius Mdluli; Tshipa Mothibatsela; Moss Tau; Arthur Habedi; Lazarus Serobe; Lindelani Mkhize; Themba Mkhize; Matwetwe Ntombini; Sipho Mabuse; Tsepo Tshola; Jabu Khanyile; Busi Mhlongo; Vusi Mahlasela; Angelique Kidjo; Sanza and Joy Loate; Esther and David Goodyear; Irene and

Edward Akufo Addo; Nana Akufo Addo; Komlah Amoaku and Korkor Amartefio; Isaac Thapedi; Prudence and Gerry Inzerillo; Venashree and Anant Singh; Chuchu Horton; Steve Horton; Pat Dambe; Philemon Hou; Gertylue Brewer; Willie Kgositsile; Zenzi and Lumumba Lee; Sam Mhangwani; Jane and Peter Tladi; Rosie Katz; Sibongile Khumalo; and Khabi Mngoma, Letitia Montalvo, Olara and Ami Otunnu, and Jean and Peter Davidson, all of whom are my very close family.

To my mothers-in-law Diamond Cofie and Matilda Dzamposu; my brothers-in-law Mark, Ben, and Wellie Cofie; my sisters-in-law Yealla, Gifty, Mercy, Mawusi, and Obi Cofie; and all my dear friends in Ghana.

To my present-day music colleagues John Selolwane, Fana Zulu, Khaya Mahlangu, Ezbie Moilwa, Tom Nkabinde, Arthur Tshabalala, Dumisani Hlela, Mandla Zikalala, Blondie Makhene, Don Laka, Oscar Mdlongwa, Francis Fuster, Irfaan Gillan, Pula Twala, Fiona Domingo, Jimmy Dludlu, Themba Mokwena, and Johnny Hassan, a very heartfelt thanks.

Most of all my deepest love to my children Patrick, Pula, Adam, Mabusha, Selema Mabena, Selema Makgothi, Sunny, Sophie, Sibongile Makeba, Monde Twala, and my daughter in Sweden, whom I have never met.

Thank you Marie Brown, Michael Cheers, and Chris Jackson for making this book possible. Thanks to Autshumato, Robert Sobukwe, Nqika, Hintsa, Monomotapa, Makana, Adam Kok, Moshoeshoe, Shaka, Biko, Cetshewayo, Bambaatha, Oliver Tambo, Walter Sisulu, Nelson Mandela, and all their comrades. To Khama, Ramokgopa, Lilian Ngoyi, Winnie Madikizela Mandela, Ida Mtwana, Carole and Buddy Arnold, and the staff of Clouds. I am particularly grateful to all those I might have overlooked on this list but without whom I could never have gotten where I am today. Finally, thank you, South Africa!

D. Michael Cheers: Thanks to Dr. Robert J. Cummings, professor and chair, Department of African Studies at Howard University, for guiding me through this arduous process. Thanks frat! Also much appreciation to professors Sulayman Nyang, Luis Serapaio, Robert R. Edgar, Wilfred David, and Mbye Cham. Professor Doris E. Saunders (Ret.), Jackson State University, you have been a friend and mentor for almost three decades; *Jet* magazine's Robert E. Johnson, who taught me how photojournalism can impact community, and the importance of "arguing the case for black folks"—Hamba Khale!; and also thanks to Gordon Parks, Moneta Sleet Jr., Morris Henderson, Robert P. Knight, Doris E. Barnhart, Albert Johnson, Vivian Mahathey, Gretchen Ronnow, Howard Emerson, the staff at the Moorland-Spingarn Research

Center at Howard University, and the J. William Fulbright Foreign Scholarship Board for awarding me the Fulbright Scholarship that led to my first interview in 1995 with Hugh Masekela.

Hugh Masekela—thanks for allowing me to travel with you on this remarkable musical journey. Marie Brown, the doyenne of literary agents, I'm humbled and deeply gratified by our belief in this project. To the many South African musicians and singers I interviewed, thanks for sharing your "Bra Hugh" stories with me. A special thanks to Caiphus Semenya and his wife, Letta Mbulu. Your insights into those crazy episodes in America in the 1960s were valuable morsels. Mabusha Masekela, you are a walking history book of world music. Matse Keshupilwe, thanks for believing in this idea and for helping me get this project off the ground. Ambassador Miriam Makeba, "Mama Africa," just being in your presence is a precious experience. Trevor Huddleston, thanks for a wonderful afternoon filled with reflections on Bra Hugh—Hamba Khale! Chris Calloway, thanks for opening up to me and sharing your thoughts and memories. And thanks to the numerous friends and associates of Bra Hugh for sharing your reflections.

To all the archivists, translators (especially Tshidi Bookholane), graduate teaching assistants (Manda Banda and Cara Polinski), and photo researcher (Jacqui Masiza), thanks for your assistance. Bra Alf Kumalo, one of South Africa's finest photographers, thanks for sharing your images with this project. Chris Jackson, my editor at the Crown Publishing Group, you are a special brother! Genoveva Llosa, Chris's assistant, much thanks! Stuart Bullion, chair of the Department of Journalism at the University of Mississippi and a longtime Hugh Masekela fan, thanks for helping me get *Still Grazing* across the finish line. To Burnis Morris, my mentor at the University of Mississippi, Penny Rice and Amelia Rodgers, two superb information technology specialists, and to all my current and former students, my sincerest gratitude for your kindness and patience.

Finally, this work is dedicated to my children, my nephews, and to my extended family.

Index

living arrangements, 195, 207, 222, 233, 250
music written by, 195–96, 333
on tour, 173, 177
Hubbard, Freddie, 142, 237–38
Huddleston, Fr. Trevor:
  activism of, 39, 56, 62, 69, 87, 114, 332, 348
  and band, 63–64, 65, 73
  as Bishop, 332, 338
  death of, 376, 378
  in England, 81, 86–87
  and Hugh's request for a scholarship, 81, 86, 93,
    98–99, 104, 114–15, 119, 133
  and St. Peter's, 46, 54, 56, 60, 61, 62, 67
Huddleston Jazz Band, 63–66, 70, 71, 72–75, 82, 86,
  88, 132, 157, 317
Huff, Leon, 348
Hughes, Langston, 137–38
Ibraham, Abdullah, 94, 101–3, 124, 125, 324, 330
Ink Spots, 10
Ito, Yoshiko, 131

Jackson, Jesse, 236
Jackson, Mahalia, 79, 104, 166
Jackson Five, 232
Jagger, Mick, 284
James, Etta, 128, 280, 287
James, Harry, 59
January, Thandiwe, 322, 324, 327
Jazz Crusaders, 231–32
Jazz Epistles, 102–5, 108, 125
Jazz Maniacs, 3–4, 9, 63, 70, 73
Jefferson Airplane, 181, 186, 188
Jenkins, Henry, 142, 164–65, 181, 184
Jive/Zomba Records, 333, 337, 339, 344
Jobim, Antonio Carlos, 189, 240
Johnson, Bernard, 203, 315
Johnson, Jean, 123, 127, 136, 147, 149, 178–79
Johnson, Lannie, 234
Johnson, Sharon, 131
Jones, Elvin, 125, 126
Jones, Quincy, 142, 154, 172, 236, 308
Jones, Tom, 181
Joplin, Janis, 181, 191
Jordan, Louis, 9, 22, 32, 57, 78, 177
Juba (street fighter), 31–33
Kabaka, Remi, 329
Kadengu, Job, 340, 345–46
Kalahari (band), 330, 333, 334, 336–39, 341, 342,
  344, 349
Kaloate, Knox, 63, 64
Karefa-Smart, Frank, 266, 267, 317, 328
Kaunda, Kenneth, 160, 194
Keita, Salif, 250, 256, 301
Kelly, Paula, 153
Kelly, Wynton, 118, 142
Kerina, Mburumba, and family, 122, 129, 135–37,
  142, 144, 145, 171, 329
Kgositsile, Willie, 155, 164, 243–44
Khama, Ruth, 323
Khanyile, Dalton, 70
Khoza, Betty, 194
Khrushchev, Nikita, 127, 351–52

Khumalo, Bakithi, 340, 345, 348, 351, 359, 378
Khumalo, Sibongile, 369
Khumalo, Vusi, 359
Kieviet, Linda, 64, 71
Killens, John, 136
King, B. B., 123, 190, 280, 287
King, Don, 276–79, 282, 284–86, 288, 365
King Kong (jazz opera), 94, 97, 98, 99–100, 118, 151,
  171, 195, 369
King, Martin Luther Jr., 81, 127, 133, 138, 197
Klaasen, Thandie, 10
Knecht, Peter, 225
Koka, Tsepo, 331
Koola Lobitos, 244–45
Kool and the Gang, 357
Korda, Zoltan, 71
Kouyate, Kemo, 250
Kouyate, Sekou, 250, 251–54, 258
Krasnow, Bob, 237, 246, 271–72, 276–78, 291
Kumalo, Alf, 109, 318, 321
Kuti, Fela Anikulapo, 244–45, 246, 254, 262–71, 291,
  293, 300–301, 305, 317, 339
Kwankwa, Dixie, 70

Ladysmith Black Mambazo, 323, 345, 357
Laka, Don, 363, 368
La Lupe, 128
Langhorne, Bruce, 153, 161, 195, 334
Langhorne, Gloria, 161
La Pierre, Jessie, 229–30, 231, 233, 235–36, 239, 314
Latino Variety Revue, 128
Lawal, Gasper, 336
Laws, Ronnie, 238
Leballo, Vandi, 70
Lee, Archie, 148
Lee, Canada, 71
Lee, Jimmy, 131, 153–54
Leepa, Frank, 321, 350
Lekhela, Woodrow, 47, 54, 58, 113–14
Levine, Stewart, 196, 310, 344
  and Ace Company, 278
  and African trips, 246, 262, 270, 271, 276–83, 285,
    287, 292, 293, 336
  and albums, 177, 189, 195, 271, 272, 294, 298,
    306, 309, 333, 336, 337
  and Chisa Records, 189–90, 191, 197, 262
  and Chris, 202, 203, 204–7, 210, 212–20
  drinking and drugging with, 154–55, 187, 188,
    193, 194, 197, 231–32, 233–34, 298
  and drug bust, 222, 223–25, 230
  and Hedzoleh Soundz, 270–71, 274
  living arrangements, 188, 233, 240, 273, 280, 289
  and music school, 337
  and OJAH, 302
  and Oo-Bwana, 174, 175, 177, 184, 185
  and rehab, 298, 367–68
  and "Rumble," 276–83, 285, 365
  son of, 376
  and Susan, 154, 174, 188, 193, 202, 217, 222, 224
Levy, Dawn, 101–2
Lincoln, Abbey, 125, 137, 238, 247
Linda, Solomon, 301

ABOUT THE COAUTHOR

D. Michael Cheers received his doctorate in African Studies from Howard University. He coedited *Songs of My People: African Americans: A Self-Portrait*. His next book, *Mission Accomplished: A Photographic Memoir of South African Photographer Alf Kumalo*, will be published by STE Publishers (Johannesburg) in 2005. Cheers currently teaches at the University of Mississippi in Oxford.